The Bee Gees

Also by David N. Meyer

Twenty Thousand Roads:
The Ballad of Gram Parsons and His Cosmic American Music

The 100 Best Films to Rent You've Never Heard Of

A Girl and a Gun: The Complete Guide to Film Noir on Video

The Bee Gees

the biography

David N. Meyer

Da Capo Press

A Member of the Perseus Books Group

Copyright © 2013 by David N. Meyer

Editorial production by *Marra*thon Production Services. www.marrathon.net

Design by Jane Raese
Set in 12-point Electra

Library of Congress Cataloging-in-Publication Data is available for this book.
ISBN 978-0-306-82025-0 (hardcover)
ISBN 978-0-306-82157-8 (e-book)

Published by Da Capo Press
A Member of the Perseus Books Group
www.dacapopress.com

Da Capo Press books are available at special discounts for bulk purchases in the
U.S. by corporations, institutions, and other organizations. For more information,
please contact the Special Markets Department at the Perseus Books Group,
2300 Chestnut Street, Suite 200, Philadelphia, PA 19103, or call (800) 810-4145,
ext. 5000, or e-mail special.markets@perseusbooks.com.

to and for
Jené LeBlanc
with love

Devin McGinley

Lester Bangs

contents

The essence of BeeGeeness, the reason why I love them so, is that they're so astonishingly unhip.

—Simon Frith,
"Confessions of a Bee Gees fan," *CREEM*

Disco will never be over. It will always live in our minds and hearts. Something that was this big and this important and this great will never die. For a few years and maybe many years it will be considered passé and ridiculous. It will be misrepresented and sneered at or worse, completely ig-nored. People will laugh at John Travolta, Olivia Newton-John, white polyester suits and platform shoes and going like this! (Shoots fist into the air diagonal to body.) Those who didn't understand will never understand. Disco was much more and much better than that. Disco was too great and too much fun to be gone forever. It's got to come back someday. I just hope it will be in our lifetimes.

—Josh Neff,
The Last Days of Disco
written and directed by Whit Stillman

The central difficulty in analyzing the Bee Gees' lyrics is that in order to understand them, you have to forget that the Bee Gees wrote them.

—Bruce Harris, "Please Read Me:
A Definitive Analysis of the Bee Gees' Lyrics," *Jazz & Pop*

introduction

Beyond the basic Bee Gees mystery of "who are these guys?" lies the more pervasive and enduring mystery of "why do we all so respond to their music?" When I started this book and began to tick off Bee Gees lyrics in my head, I was surprised at how many songs I remembered whole or in part. I was also surprised, given that I cannot carry a tune, at how many I could hum or sing. When I asked my music-obsessed friends—none of whom ever mentioned the Bee Gees—I learned that all of them could hum or sing multiple Bee Gees songs.

The Bee Gees are everywhere and in everyone's heads, and still—outside their legion of die-hard fans—don't get the respect they deserve. They are never held up as icons of anything we hold up pop stars as icons of: not of genius or sex appeal or style or innovation or imagination or transgression.

The most unfair and least accurate slander to hurl at the Bee Gees is "imitators." Over the decades, so many rock and cultural writers—most of whom should have known better—defaulted to that slander instead of listening with open ears. To name only the best-known examples of the Bee Gees' singularity, "Jive Talkin'" sounds like nothing else before or since. It's wholly original; revolutionary. "New York Mining Disaster 1941 (Have You Seen My

= 1 =

Wife, Mr. Jones?)" and "To Love Somebody," ditto. "Nights on Broadway" and "Stayin' Alive," like "Jive Talkin'," owe nothing to nobody. The early Bee Gees may evoke the Beatles or the Hollies. The middle Bee Gees may evoke Donovan. The later Bee Gees may evoke Stevie Wonder. But that's all they do, evoke.

In their early days, The Beatles and the Rolling Stones imitated or covered their influences. Both bands' early records feature covers of—or direct cops from—their idols. Few accused them of imitation, either because nobody knew the music of their influences (Irma Thomas's version, for example, of "Time Is on My Side" for the Stones or the Isley Brothers' "Twist and Shout" for the Beatles) or because by the time the Beatles and Stones imitated their influences, their influences had become part of the canon (Muddy Waters for the Stones, for example, or Little Richard for the Beatles). The Bee Gees came to rock and roll so late, and were so young when they hit big, that their main influences were still on the charts.

You might hear aspects of the Beatles or Herman's Hermits or the Band or Eddie Kendricks or MFSB in their music. But all Bee Gees songs, no matter how clearly an influence can be perceived, sound like the Bee Gees. And the Bee Gees, unlike every one of their peers, never covered anybody. Their records contain only originals. The Bee Gees belong to no broader musical movement and work in no genre save the one they invented.

Except disco.

The top-selling acts in pop music have sales totals so close, if you start rounding off to millions of units, that comparing their successes becomes absurd. The Beatles, Michael Jackson, Paul McCartney, Garth Brooks, Madonna and the Bee Gees: nobody has moved more product.

The Bee Gees never get their proper due, in part, because they always seemed odd—off, somehow—always awkward and clueless.

Never mind that nobody achieved remotely their level of success showcasing such misguided fashion sense, not even Garth Brooks. Never mind Bee Gees' bowl haircuts in the late 1960s and, really, never mind the windblown sateen disco jackets and crotch-grabbing glimmering trousers with two-foot flairs, because during disco, everybody dressed like that. Give the Bee Gees a fashion period and they always chose the worst possible options.

No matter how they tried, their innate yobbo insecurities— their enduring self-perception as penniless, twerpy, working-class outcasts—led them to make self-defeating, self-defining choices. In defense of what they knew to be true, like most twerpy outcasts, they developed an uncrackable arrogance, even when they dressed like their mother bought their clothes at the Dollar Store. Or, at the bespoke rock-and-roll version of the Dollar Store. Always trying too hard, the Bee Gees never got near hipness or cool.

There's so much they never got. Even when selling 25 million copies of one album, the Bee Gees always seemed on the outside looking in, noses to the glass, half disdainful, half dying for an invitation to the party. Their pre–*Saturday Night Fever* lyrical content suggested few other concerns—all those aching orchestral elegies to alienation, loss and heartache. Were they singing about unrequited love or their inability to connect in the world, or were they singing about dealing with one another? Robin said of their lyrical content: "I can't imagine why anyone would want to hear a song about my emotions." Viewed through that prism, it was only popcraft.

As family acts go, the Bee Gees are an anomaly. Given their longevity, universal popularity, sales figures and idiosyncratic sound, they're anomalies on pretty much every level. But most family acts—like most successful child stars—have at least one abusive parent. Most family acts never outgrow the abuser who controls them. And woe betide the offspring who demonstrates genius in the face of a mother's or father's mere talent. When an abusive parent sees the child moving beyond his or her control—from Mozart onward—violence is the default response.

The first and worst rock father that comes to mind is Murry Wilson, sire of three-fifths of the Beach Boys: fat, balding, oily hair, cheap suits, jaw-up posture, pushing himself forward like the worst bullying salesman. Murry the abuser, fond of popping out his glass eye at parties and shouting at his son in the studio. Murry shouting at his son Brian—the American Mozart—that Brian's version of a song didn't sound as good as Murry's version. Murry, beating Brian so badly and so often that Brian ended up deaf in one ear and mad as a Hatter. Brian eventually severed ties with Murry, but not until Murry had inflicted so much damage that his son could never be what he might have become with the blessing of paternal love. Or even the absence of paternal hate.

Such behavior was anathema to the loving Hugh Gibb, perhaps the most fortunate child-managing parent in the history of child-managing parents. Mr. Gibb had, prior to guiding his boys' early career, demonstrated that he was the absolute model of a guy who could fuck up a baked potato. Hugh never succeeded at anything. He had, however, played drums in dance bands, and he had an ear. His boys—the thirteen-year-old fraternal twins Maurice and Robin and seventeen-year-old Barry—barnstormed Australia, singing the songs Hugh insisted they sing: English music-hall ditties or standards that were already three generations out of date. Slowly the boys came to listen to—though they don't sound like they ever fully understood—the music their contemporaries were listening to and creating. Then things began to happen.

Ever the anomaly, Hugh never seems to have resented his boys' success. He never seems to have intruded in their lifestyle or tried to shape their music. It's as if the unlikeliest person to do so recognized the Gibb boys' genius, found his role and peace serving it, and stayed out of its way. How many parents could do that?

But, after the single luckiest act of his life, his only moment of unvarnished good fortune—sending his boys' acetates to Robert Stigwood—Hugh Gibb proved inert as a parent, passive and on-looking. The Bee Gees' true paternal figure became and remained their mentor and manager, Robert Stigwood. Stigwood evinced all the mythological paternal aspects of provider, arbiter, would-be destroyer and aspirational model. Decisive, relentless, impatient, ambitious, aesthetic, ruthless and grasping, Stigwood would sup-ply the fuel, the drive and the all-necessary object of resentment and inspiration that Hugh Gibb could never provide.

Despite Stigwood's power over them, the Gibbs were and re-main a closed shop, a family affair. Hugh and Barbara lived most of their lives with one son or the other. Their sons had enormous mansions, but still. The boys wanted their parents close and vice versa. Is that touching and inspiring, or perverse and unsettling? Are those ideas even mutually exclusive when applied to families?

Anyone who's been in a band—a band that made a living being a band—will tell you: being in a band is more complicated than family, more complicated than friendship, more complicated than brotherhood, more complicated than marriage.

Being in, say, a quartet is not like being in four marriages. It's like being in four to the power of four marriages. Every relationship intersects every other and every relationship within the band is af-fected by every relationship without. Band members—Fleetwood Mac, Blondie, Yo La Tengo and the Raveonettes aside—don't usu-ally expect sex from their band mates, and so bands lack the primal pressure valve and intimacy restorer that marriages rely upon. Band members—Richard and Linda Thompson aside—don't usually have children together, and so can't find in all the humbling as-pects of parenthood what all parents discover: a constant reminder of their total lack of hot-shittedness.

In working bands, work schedules, travel circumstances, and the likelihood of drug, alcohol and crappy food consumption raise the pressure. Add to that pressure that any successful band is either an absolute monarchy—the Ramones or the Rolling Stones—or an absolute democracy—R.E.M. or U2. There is no middle ground. All band power-paradigms devolve into one or the other or the band breaks up. Either somebody is in charge or everybody is in charge. Either someone is telling you what to do all the time while ignoring your suggestions, belittling your input and making more money, or you have to put up with everyone's stupid face and stupider opinions that you've seen and heard a million times already. How does any band survive?

The short answer is: by every band member resenting, if not loathing, every other band member and being resented, if not loathed, in return. Except for when two band members get along for a while and resent everybody else together. And by all the ancillary benefits that band life provides. What makes that resentment even more virulent is that every band member needs every other to do the one thing in life that grants each the most joy and self-satisfaction. That paradigm, too, is inescapable. Doubters need only listen to Mick Jagger's solo records. Or Keith's.

When asked—during the era of rumors of George Harrison quitting the band—if he ever considered joining the Beatles, Eric Clapton said: "They were like the most close-knit family. And so the cruelty and the viciousness could be unparalleled." And the Beatles weren't even related, let alone brothers. The Beatles all made viable, best-selling music on their own, even Ringo. Free of the group, George blossomed; John, in his way, blossomed. Paul stayed the same, but he made a pile doing so. Each learned they did not need the others to express themselves or please the marketplace. When the Gibb brothers tried separating, they learned the opposite.

The inescapable dynamics of band and family life make the Bee Gees even more anomalous, opaque, indecipherable and bizarre. They composed, played and toured together for forty years! With their parents right there on the bus, in the studio, waiting in the kitchen, minding the kids, loading the dishwasher all wrong, etc. If family dynamics are unbearable and band dynamics are unbearable, how did the Bee Gees bear it?

One way was by conspicuous consumption of almost anything that could be consumed—women, clothes, drugs, liquor, cars, boats, houses, etc. But compensatory overconsumption's a sadly normal feature of family life and one great allure of being in a band. That the Bee Gees' success allowed them to consume like King Farouk seems hardly worth mentioning. The wages of their various sins became all too apparent over the years.

Most family acts that endure for decades cite outside religious influences. Not the Bee Gees; they learned how to live with each other, however painfully. Also, they never trusted anyone outside the family, save Stigwood. Periodically, they didn't trust him, either. Until the various resentments became too deep, they took advice and support from one another. And for decades, the Gibb twins took orders from Barry.

Hands down, Barry won the Gibb genetic lottery.

From the earliest photographs of the boys performing together in their pathetic tuxedos in the dinner theaters of Australia, seventeen-year-old Barry looked indestructible. As the band got popular, then famous, then forgotten and then more famous than anyone in popular music before them, Barry became only more radiant. The Beta twins, Robin and Maurice, took second and third to Barry's incontrovertible Alpha. Andy, some years later, had the looks and energy to surpass the twins, but proved weaker on the inside. Andy had Barry's head hair and chest hair and teeth and inner glow. But Andy lacked a sufficiently bulletproof shell to live the famous Gibb life. That life ate him up. Barry gobbled it down and asked for more, never once saying either "please" or "sir." Now, Barry's the last man standing.

Barry evokes a centaur. His long glossy mane and glowing equine eyes, that Roman nose with its great horsey nostrils and those piano-key teeth shining above an endless jaw just waiting for a bit. He looks like a stallion, of course, which means he bestrides the planet as he pleases and as Keith Richard said: "has the right to piss in the street." In those outsized eyes burns the flame of shrewdness, remove, constant strategy and no small amount of hostility. Barry possesses the voice of an angel, and that isn't a devil on his shoulder. It's a chip, and fifty years of unimaginable success have neither reduced nor dislodged it. Barry's a centaur, and he's also always been Odysseus, a cunning, distanced man prepared for the journey, determined not merely to survive but to prevail, to cope with whatever and impose his will. Barry is not a guy to get lost in song, to give in to the frailer emotions. And so far, Barry's never been bested.

You might think that between the Beatles and McCartney's solo records, Sir Paul is the most successful, Alpha of the Alphas. But Paul never purpose-built #1s for others. Barry has written double-digit #1s for other artists, songs tailored to their sounds and personae that rang the bell worldwide. When he was only twenty-two, Barry wrote the greatest Otis Redding song Otis Redding never recorded, "To Love Somebody." And if Otis never recorded it—he died before he could—everyone else on the planet did. Barry's purpose-built #1s are hard to identify because he seldom copped to writing something for somebody else. He'd say: "Oh, I found an old song and it worked out for them." Only Odysseus pulls off such self-deprecating boasting.

Barry's Alpha-hood spawned some tough moments. Barry stopped letting Robin sing lead, even on Robin's own compositions. Robin absorbed a hard lesson in what it meant to be a Beta younger brother, one of many such lessons inflicted over the decades. Maurice had subsumed those same lessons long before. Maurice, who—until alcohol overtook him—could play any instrument he touched, routinely spent three-quarters of a set onstage without getting near a mike. Andy Gibb was handed a career based on singing songs that Barry had written or co-written and produced. The gig paid large, and made Andy an international heartthrob. But Andy couldn't live out the basic premise—that his career was Barry's Lite—and his overconsumption took a bad turn.

Throughout the years, no matter how successful or reviled, the Bee Gees remained, in so many ways, ridiculous. Their ridiculousness forces even those who love them to shrug and smile. Those who find the Bee Gees a contemptible plastic amalgam of cheesy pop and pernicious disco still admit, in whispers, to having deep emotions or meaningful memories built around one or two Bee Gees' tunes.

Everyone on the planet knows all or part of a Bee Gees song. No matter who you ask, no matter his or her level of hipness, musical sophistication, literacy, geographical location or familiarity with the English language; in Timbuktu or Mindanao, in Buenos Aires or Shanghai, in Kiev or Nairobi, in Bishkek, Kyrgyzstan, or Gainesville, Georgia, stop the first person you see who's older than fifteen and ask them to hum a Bee Gees song. Not to name one—to hum or sing. And they will, smiling guiltily. Then ask them the same thing about Garth Brooks . . .

With the Beatles or Madonna, that kind of global market penetration makes instinctive sense. It's easier, somehow, to acknowledge that their songs are in the ether.

The Bee Gees are the ether.

The Bee Gees made hits for forty years, they sold a quarter of a billion albums, everyone on earth knows their music and yet, they still seem like they don't really belong.

"lollipop"

he Bee Gees' origin story is straight out of Dickens: so difficult and so foreordained. They came out of nothing, worked their asses off and were incredibly lucky. But, like the show-biz cliché that they are, every time they got a lucky break, they had the will and talent to make the most of it. Their ambition never flagged. Among the most compelling conundrums of the Bee Gees' rise is, Where did they get their drive, their motivation, their determination to overcome every obstacle?

Most likely, they did not get it from their dad, Hugh Gibb. Hugh was a pretty good drummer. In all the universe, there are only two kinds of drummers. There are the bullying, atavistic, wildly talented, competitive madmen who will only play it their way and insist that you do, too. Avatars of the first kind are Ginger Baker of Cream, jazz great Elvin Jones and big-band psychotic Buddy Rich. That's the first kind of drummer. The second kind is everybody else. The second kind of drummer is best characterized by Ringo. When asked why he became a drummer, Ringo said the bass was "too hard." Hugh Gibb is the second kind of drummer.

Hugh had a dance band during World War II. As a musician, he was granted a deferment from military service. He met Barbara May Pass in 1941 at a gig in Manchester, England. Barbara sang occasionally. Some histories present her as a professional vocalist; that's an exaggeration. They dated for three years and married on May 27, 1944. As they emerged from the church, they passed through a column formed by Hugh's band members, their instruments held aloft in a gleaming V-shaped roof of unplayed music protecting the newlyweds. Seven months later, Barbara gave birth to their first child, Lesley, and shortly thereafter, the Gibbs moved to the Isle of Man—in the Irish, or Manx, Sea—between northern England and Northern Ireland. Hugh found a steady gig playing the tourist hotels on the Isle.

Barry Gibb was born on September 1, 1946. In the signature event of his early childhood, he spilled a cup of scalding tea on himself at eighteen months. Barry went into a coma and was ill for half a year. The accident and the illness seemed to slow his development. On December 22, 1949, Robin and Maurice, fraternal—not identical—twins, were born, in that order. Later in life, Maurice would assume the role of conciliatory middle brother and Robin the role of perpetually petulant younger brother.

Things turned tough for Hugh in 1954; the cream of his band split the isle for better work on the mainland. In 1955, Hugh lost his contract with the hotels and took odd jobs to pay the rent.

"As much as our mother doesn't like to hear about it today," Robin said, "we were flat broke. It was post-war Britain and people were finding their feet. I have memories of my father counting out pennies to see if we'd make it to the end of the week. It was almost Dickensian. But we weren't aware of finances. We were too busy having fun."[1] The family moved back to the mainland, to the grimy, industrial city of Manchester. Almost all English rock stars born in this era, whether in big cities or rural areas, stress how gray and desolate post-war England could be. Gas and sugar were rationed; unemployment was rampant. In a gray, harsh nation, few places were as gray and harsh as Manchester. It was one tough town.

The Gibb boys had little or no parental supervision. They ran rampant. All three were obsessed with fire, and proved to be urchin pyromaniacs. "We used to set fire to allotments and shops," Barry said.[2] "Barry and Robin used to set fire to shops and billboards and things," Maurice said.[3] While such behavior used to be regarded as pathological, current thinking suggests that the urge to light things up and burn them down is a natural aspect of childhood development. In other children, however, this urge is often subject to parental restraint. "We're more like friends than parents," Barbara Gibb later told an interviewer. "We're not pushy—we just get a kick out of being with the boys."[4]

In the Bee Gees' official autobiography, Barbara Gibb laughingly characterized young Robin as "a firebug." Robin would come home from school, grab matches from the kitchen and take off. Barry planned their fire expeditions; Robin usually caught the blame. "The police would come to the door all the time demanding that our parents 'get these boys off the streets,'" Barry said. "We were going to end up in Borstal (the fearsome English reform school/juvenile penitentiary) if our parents didn't take control. Mum and dad were trying to earn a living—I don't think they were aware of what we were doing."[5] In a town as hard as Manchester, the nine- and six-year-old brothers Gibb were already regarded as a threat to public order.

The boys started singing together under the loose guidance of their father. One of their first numbers was "Lollipop" by the Mudlarks, perhaps the most content-free hit of the doo-wop era. They soon moved on to originals. "When I was about ten, and Robin and Maurice about seven," Barry said, "we started writing songs. Now that's a bit young for writing songs and we certainly didn't write anything that was worth anything. We wrote one song called 'Turtle Dove' and another about a year after that called 'Let Me Love You.' We were little kids sitting at home thinking, 'Let's write songs.' We had natural three-part harmony . . . No one knew how we got it, least of all us, but we had it without understanding anything we were doing. There was something there that said, 'You guys are going to be on stage the rest of your lives.' There wasn't any question what we were going to do . . . we knew where we were going and what we wanted to do even as children."[6]

All future performers seem to say this; it's a trope of success. In the Gibbs' case it seems to be true. As boys they never pursued anything else—excepting fire—and poured all their energy into developing as singers and performing. The need to be seen, to be acknowledged by a crowd, came as naturally to them as harmony. "Even in those early years," Hugh Gibb said, "their whole lives revolved around waiting to be discovered. They'd stand on street corners singing 'Wake Up Little Susie' to passersby. They had to have an audience."[7]

On a fateful Christmas in 1955, Barry got a guitar; or maybe he got it for his birthday. As with so many foundation myths, the details are murky. "I got a guitar for my ninth birthday," Barry said. "The guy who lived across the road from us had just come back from Hawaii, so he taught me that tuning. 'That'll get you started,' he said, and I never changed from that tuning!"[8] Barry was probably taught an open tuning, in which the strings are tuned down to form a chord without fretting. This eases learning the basics of creating harmonious sounds on a guitar, but would confound anyone trying to play complex lines or learn detailed fretwork. This never posed a problem for Barry, who viewed his voice as his instrument and approached the guitar as a prop and songwriting tool. The unusual chord progressions that become natural in open tuning in some part explain the singular sound of their first hit, "New York Mining Disaster 1941 (Have You Seen My Wife, Mr. Jones?)."

Local kids would perform every week at a Manchester movie house, the Gaumont Theatre. They'd mime to a current hit record played on a scratchy phonograph backstage. "We used to watch them every week," Robin said. "We thought: 'Why can't we do something like that?' There were five of us, Maurice and Barry and myself, and our neighbors Paul Frost and Kenny Oricks. We called ourselves the Rattlesnakes." The Rattlesnakes decided to mime to the Everly Brothers' "Wake Up Little Susie." "The Saturday morning came, just before Christmas," Robin said. "We were going up the stairs of the Gaumont when Barry dropped the record! It smashed. We thought: 'What are we going to do?' Barry had his guitar, which he had taken along to help the miming, and he suggested that we really sing. So out we went and sang 'Lollipop' by the Mudlarks, and it went well . . . and that was how the Bee Gees began."[9]

As every great origin myth must, this tale features the perfect Jungian symbolic moment. Barry, the eldest, the Alpha, the most ambitious, the one with the guitar, bears the precious object—the record. But that precious object also contains falsity—under the spell of that falsity, the boys will deny their gifts and only pretend to sing. When Barry enters the temple—the Gaumont Theatre—in a moment of apostasy, he drops the sacred object; he smashes it to the floor. With that "accident," Barry frees himself and his brothers from imitation, from false performance, from false ceremony, from living a lie in front of the congregation. Barry, consciously or not, had no interest in going onstage and faking anything. By smashing the record, he allowed the brothers' true natures to be revealed. Smashing the record meant that the Gibbs expressed themselves in their own voices. Smashing the record gave their voices primacy. Smashing the record meant they were ready to own their abilities and own the ritual of performance.

"It was amazing," Barry said. "I started singing and trying to play, and suddenly I found the six-year-old twins with me doing three-part harmony. I fiddled with the guitar until I found my own chords. I still play that way."[10] The urchins were in business. They sang in theaters, talent shows and on street corners. Passersby would fling coins at them and they'd root around the Manchester gutters, scrabbling for every copper. "Our next date was at the Walley Range Odeon," Robin said. "Maurice and I added banjos. We did the Palentine Theatre as Wee Johnnie Hayes and the Bluecats—Barry was Johnnie Hayes. We got £5 a week for our act. This was in 1958 and we went on doing matinee performances for about two years."[11]

Their first adult gig came shortly after the Odeon. Hugh's band was playing the Russell Street Club. He snuck the boys through the backdoor and rushed them up onstage before anyone could stop them. The crowd loved the brothers.

The British had transported convicts and undesirables—mostly Irish—to Australia since the "First Fleet" established a penal colony there in 1788. Australia was built and maintained for decades on the slave labor of convicts administered by a series of corrupt gangs of soldiers and their administrative lackeys. A gold rush in the 1850s brought Englishmen to Oz of their own volition, and "transportation" began to wind down. But traditions die hard in the UK, and in the late 1950s, England began to encourage emigration. Australia needed families to rebuild the post-war economy. England, paralyzed by terrible unemployment, fearing labor unrest, sought to reduce the number of the unemployed not by hiring them, but by chucking them out of the country. The solution was simple: transport the unemployed and undesirable to Oz at state expense, and let them make the best of things when they disembarked.

The police came, as they often did, to the Gibbs' door in July of 1958. The boys were becoming worse delinquents; their public performances had not deterred their vandalism. The brothers were considered such a menace at ages twelve and nine that they were being thrown out of the toughest town in England and ordered overseas. It was that, or Borstal. An added inducement to the authorities for shipping out the Gibbs was Hugh's chronic unemployment, and his place on the dole. He was considered a drain on the Manchester economy. "The policemen had three words for my dad," Robin said. "'The 'Ten Pound Plan.' Our behaviour and dad's inability to find an income was the reason we left. Parents [paid] 10 pounds each and kids [traveled] free. We went by ocean — 12,000 miles over five weeks."[12]

The family arrived on September 1, Barry's twelfth birthday. Hugh took a miserable job as a salesman — traveling on the massive truck convoys known as "road trains" that served the consumer needs of boondock towns and isolated ranches in the outback. He would be gone for months at a time. When he returned, his gambling and living expenses had eaten most of his pay. The family was destitute. Within a year of landing, the boys were selling sodas at a racetrack, the Brisbane Speedway. As they sold, and when they weren't, they sang for tips and to draw customers. Once again, the crowd threw money at them and the boys scrabbled around gathering it up. "Not that we ever put any pressures on them," Hugh said. "Most kids want to be train drivers at one time or another, but singing was the only thing the boys ever wanted to do. We couldn't stop them. It's no secret. They kept us going for a long time."[13]

Bill Good, a local racer, heard the boys and had them sing over the racetrack loudspeakers during breaks. Bill Gates, a local disc jockey, heard the brothers at the track and recorded them for his radio show. "They had a unique sound even then," Gates said. "We bought them new guitars and made tapes for air play. This got them known, and jobs followed in hotels . . . . until the problem of their ages arose [with the Child Welfare office]. At early recording sessions the big problem was keeping the twins from wrecking the place. We'd spend a whole day mucking around trying to get them organized. Barry could knock out a song in five minutes. One time we had three songs ready to tape and wanted another. We asked Barry if he had a song written and he replied: 'No, but I'll write one now.'"[14]

Bill Gates and Bill Good created the name, the Bee Gees, from their own initials. Though stories vary over time and with who's doing the telling, it seems that the brothers Gibb's name or initials never figured in their professional moniker. Yet, they never changed it. They got famous Down Under as the Bee Gees, and the Bee Gees they remained.

The radio shows brought requests from local TV, and by 1960 the boys were regular visitors to the households of Brisbane. "My boys have got the show business bug," Barbara said. "I can't remember when the boys haven't been singing. On the boat coming to Australia they entertained the passengers all the way."[15] "Show business," Robin said, "is something you have to have in you when you're born."[16] From the start, the boys never saw themselves as rock and rollers or folkies or as belonging to any type of music or scene. They were performers, in show business, and their duty was to the audience, not themselves.

The brothers set up a pretend studio beneath their home to practice for their TV appearances. Maurice, aged ten, told the *Australian Women's Weekly*: "We have a different script every day, and we're always changing the floor plan and the sets around."[17] "We got on to television in Brisbane in 1960 with our own show, 'Cottie's Happy Hour,'" Robin said. "We got very big in Brisbane. The three of us played Surfer's Paradise at the Beachcomber Hotel for six weeks, three shows a night."[18]

Barry, age thirteen, told the *Weekly*, "I like to make up the tunes I sing. I get the words from romance magazines and stories my 16-year-old sister, Lesley, reads."[19] Barry was writing songs in a serious, professional way, looking for a hit. Robin joined him, and later, tried to take more than his share of the credit. "The first song we ever wrote was 'Let Me Love You.'" Robin said. "Our first song-writing success was 'Starlight of Love,' which was recorded by producer Col Joye and got to No. 1. We became an overnight success but our first hit didn't come until 1965, although the Bee Gees were always big TV-wise."[20]

As their fame increased, Bill Gates no longer wanted to deal with the logistics. Hugh was reluctant to take the reins, but Barbara insisted. She wanted any managerial money kept in the family and she wanted the boys to have paternal supervision. "Is it my job or is it going to be them?" Hugh told the Bee Gees' official biographer, David Leaf. "I felt their future's going to be stronger than mine, so, to be quite frank, they kept us. I gave up my work to drive them around. They were only kids; they had to have somebody. I never wanted to be their manager, but by force of circumstances I had to be."[21] "If he would've had his opportunity in his own life he would have been a big star," Barry said. "But he didn't, so it was through us that he was going to make it."[22] "We're an extension of father's frustration. He never quite made it, but he can live it with us."[23]

It's never easy for anyone when children start supporting parents. The "parentified child" is a recurring motif for every child performer. The kids have to take on aspects of adulthood they cannot perceive or understand, but they do understand that crucial roles are being reversed. Hugh would try to maintain control by making the boys sing and dress like little adults—like his modeling of proper showbiz. The boys would react to the discomfort of the situation by turning Barry into the surrogate father. Barry could write songs and play the guitar—he was the de facto breadwinner. The twins looked up to and followed Barry as if he were the parent. By turning a brother into a paternal figure, the twins only delayed their own development. This dynamic functioned for a good long while. But when it blew up, as it did during the recording of *Odessa* in 1969, there would be considerable collateral damage.

The boys played a lot of dives, and always for adult audiences. "The only way we could capitalize on our popularity as boys in

Australia was doing club work for an adult audience," Maurice said. "The rock 'n' roll touring circuit for kids hadn't completely happened yet."[24] "We used to hit clubs in Australia where I'd have to sneak them 'cause of their ages," Hugh said. "But even then they had a professional show. I've always enjoyed the touring more than the studio work."[25] "We worked places," Maurice said, "where the men were so drunk they couldn't stand up, so they would fight sitting down. Wonderful, innocent times they were."[26]

Referring to such a brutal memory as "wonderful" and "innocent" might be the essence of denial. Maybe the boys didn't know how tough their circumstances were, but no child likes to watch drunken adults beating one another. Any kid who lives through that while having to be "professional"—which means masking one's true feelings—can scarcely be called a youngster. Traveling and performing under those conditions taught the boys early, if it taught them nothing else, to depend only on one another. As is often the case for the parentified child, there is no actual childhood.

Hugh was a tough taskmaster; he evaded child labor laws and booked the boys for show after show. They had to perform his choreography, do the material he chose, dress just so and smile. Hugh seldom encouraged the boys and never told them whether their performances were objectively good or bad, improving or worsening. Hugh's only concern, and the only subject of his feedback, was whether the audience liked them. "My father never called me 'son,' or 'lad,'" Maurice said. "It was always 'Ya sung flat.'"[27]

They grew up as performers with no real sense of themselves. The person who knew their music best never told them if they were getting better, and perhaps he never knew. The Bee Gees would forever suffer from not being able to tell their best material from their worst. Sincerity and artistic expression were never their concerns. Making an audience like them was their only job. Proper timing, being charming, smiling, singing in tune and harmony, and dancing correctly were all that mattered. Hugh taught the boys early on to be artificial and he taught them well. In films of them at this time, singing old English music hall numbers like "My Father Was a Dustman," the boys' robotic movements and fixed facial expressions are heartbreaking. Barry, certainly old enough to know better, seems horribly sincere. The twins sing and move like soulless automatons.

As they got older and heard the music their contemporaries were listening to, they wanted to grow their hair. Hugh asked them, "Will you sing any better with longer hair?" (Robin later had a specific agreement with Bee Gees manager Robert Stigwood that his hair length was his own business.) It's hard not to feel compassion for Hugh. His music never made it. His other attempts at earning all failed. His children were his only shot, the only thing he might control, and control them he did. Hugh drove his boys hard, but he was never physical or emotionally abusive, which puts him well above the bar set for parents of child stars. His children never expressed regret.

"We had a great time," Maurice said. "Schooling was never any good for us. We grew up with adults, other artists, strippers, jugglers. I got laid when I was nine though I didn't enjoy it."[28] "When a kid wants to be a rock star he isn't thinking how much money he will make," Barry said. "He's thinking about being famous, and for us it was the idea of being famous, not the idea of making money. What came along was, 'Oh, you can make money out of this too.'"[29] The boys dressed like little adults—or monkeys—for their club gigs, in tuxedos with slicked-back hair. In some early TV appearances, they wear tuxes or dress like Theodore Cleaver. Barry looks so much older and sturdier than the twins, who seem tiny and underdeveloped. Barry's a teen heartthrob and the twins are two of the gooniest-looking kids on the planet. It's wrenching to see them working their act, being so impenetrable, and still so young and clueless.

In 1962, Colin Jacobson, better known as Col Joye, a popular Australian singer of the period, began recording and producing singles for the boys, who sang backed by the Joy Boys—Joye's studio band, comprised in part of Col's brothers. The Gibbs ascended through the snake pit of the Australian music business, which was isolated from the rest of the world, self-contained and competitive. As their earnings increased, the Gibb family moved to Sydney, and the brothers opened for Chubby Checker at Sydney Stadium. "We went to Sydney, which was like going to London," Robin said. "It was the biggest break we ever had."[30]

They dropped out of school at the minimum legal age to do so. The twins lied about their ages, claiming to be fourteen, and dropped out a year early. In October of 1963, Barry signed a composer's agreement with Belinda Records and started writing songs for other artists. He was seventeen. The Bee Gees kept recording their own songs, but could not get airplay. The Bee Gees signed an onerous agreement with Festival Records in 1963. While the boys recorded their own material for Festival, they also appeared without credit on the recordings of other Festival artists. Festival owned the rights to the Bee Gees' Australian music until 2005 and released and rereleased the same music constantly, much to the chagrin of the Bees Gees.[31]

"The first hit we had in Sydney was 'Wine and Women,'" Robin said. "But we had to buy out the record shops ourselves to give it a chance. We had the wrong image to sell a record, we were too young. It wasn't like today when any age is no barrier if the record is a hit. Then, you had to be sort of near enough to 18. We weren't even in our teens, although Barry was about creeping up there. So we assembled our fan club in Sydney Town Hall, about ten people." "We found out from the record company when radio stations check the stores to compile the charts," Barry said. "We got together £200, about $400, and sent our fan club into the most important city shops and department stores and had them buy our record. We told them to go into the record shops that the radio stations used as a guide. It was basic mathematics. How do you get on the charts? Answer: Sell records! How do the radio stations know what's selling? We figured the radio stations would call the biggest shops and the key department stores to see what was selling. So that's where we had our fan club do the buying." "We found out what day," Robin said, "TUE, which was the biggest Top-40 record station at that time in Sydney, made up their chart. It was done on Tuesday, printed on Tuesday night, and was in the stores on Wednesday. So we got together on Friday because we had to have a good sale on that weekend for them to pick up on Tuesday." "No one," Barry said, "was buying our record." "It went in on the Tuesday after that weekend," Robin said, "at #30 on the charts. They stepped up the airplay, the airplay got the people to buy the record, and that was it. I guess that was a cheat, but you always spend a bit of money on PR don't you?"[32]

The boys were unknowingly following the example of many great rock producers and promoters. Their business savvy—their understanding that music was nothing without promotion—was incredibly advanced for their age. As was their shamelessness and determination to succeed.

"We were hyper, paranoid, neurotic and wanting to make it," Barry said. "We followed that with three complete flops," Robin said. "The first, 'I Was a Lover, a Leader of Men,' won an award for the best composition of the year but it wasn't a hit." Shortly after "Lover/Leader" flopped, in October of 1965, the Bee Gees released their first LP, *The Bee Gee's* [sic] *Sing & Play 14 Barry Gibb Songs*. The album got decent reviews, but even then, the Bee Gees were accused of writing obscure and confusing lyrics; no one could tell what they meant.

The Gibbs met another producer, Ossie Byrne, who gave them unlimited time to work on some follow-up songs behind a local butcher's shop. "We met Bill Shepherd, who [later when he reunited with them in England] became our musical director, and Ossie Byrne, our producer. We were on the Spin label [which also belonged to Festival] and used to record until seven in the morning. 'Monday's Rain,' our first for him, was an absolute flop. Our next, 'Cherry Red' (1966) again, an absolute flop." "The producer of Spin records, Ossie Byrne," Barry said, "gave us a drummer and all the time we needed to experiment. Over six months we recorded an album which included the song 'Spicks and Specks.'"[33]

The Bee Gees knew they had exhausted the commercial possibilities of Australia. Barry, with good reason, feared the draft and compulsory military service, which might well have meant being sent to Vietnam. The Gibbs made plans to leave Oz for England.

On August 22, 1966, Barry married his girlfriend of two years, Maureen Bates. Barry was approaching twenty; Maureen, a year younger. She had assumed the title of Secretary of the Bee Gees Fan Club so she and Barry could be together as he toured and the family moved around. Maureen had been pressuring Barry to marry her. She knew if they were not married, she would be left behind and that the only way her parents would let her travel to England with Barry was as husband and wife.

The newlyweds were estranged almost from the start. Six months after the wedding, when the Gibbs readied to leave, Maureen was not invited to travel with her husband. She would stay in Australia, at least for a while, and follow on a later boat. It's questionable whether Barry gave Maureen much thought during his voyage. She, however, was reminded of him often. "Spicks and Specks" was getting airplay and moving up the Australian charts.

bee gees' 1st

$\mathcal{A}$s the Bee Gees worked their way upward in Australia, Robert Stigwood was doing the same in England.

Stigwood was born in Australia—Adelaide—to a lower–working class household. He escaped at twenty-one, in 1956, shipping out to England. After years of low-end jobs and running a home for delinquents, he opened a talent agency, offering actors for TV commercials. "We found a niche," said Stigwood's partner at the time, Stephen Komlosy. "There used to be 'advertising magazines' on British television, actors discussing products for fifteen minutes. Advertisers who couldn't afford to buy their own commercials would take time on the magazines. There were eight presenters and we had them all."[1] One of Stigwood's actors was a young heartthrob, Johnny Leyton. Leyton could sing, but every UK label rejected him. Stigwood took Leyton to Joe Meek.

Meek was a rarity. He could arrange, record and produce a record, an unusual set of skills to be found in one man in England at the time. He had a home studio, which was equally rare. Among Meek's trademarks was his "futuristic" sound featuring electronic bleeps and tons of reverb. He would later produce and release a huge hit, "Telstar," by the Tornadoes. Meek worked with Tom Jones, Petula Clark, Gene Vincent and hundreds of others. He's recognized as a pioneer of audio production for his overdubbing of multiple tracks using only two-track machines, and for his use of compression, which would figure heavily in—to name only one band—the early recordings of the Who. (The Who would later end up briefly on one of Stigwood's labels, a move that cost them dearly in the litigation that followed.) Meek was a pioneer in his business practices; in his day the major record labels in the UK ran a functional monopoly. If the majors did not sign someone, he or she would never be heard. Meek—and Stigwood—broke that monopoly. Meek would bring a completely finished song to the majors and sell only the record, not the rights to the performer. Meek was unstable and, at times, dangerous. He suffered from depression, and from the legal and social oppression that came with being gay in England when homosexuality was illegal, as it remained until 1967. Gay men were subject not only to harassment by the police, but also to blackmail from lovers and associates. In 1967, Meek suffered a breakdown, murdered his landlady and killed himself.

Stigwood brought Leyton to Meek as a potential teen idol. Leyton recorded "Johnny Remember Me," and Stigwood made sure Leyton sang it on the television series that had recently cast him. When the song hit #1, "Stigwood was in business, he claims, as Britain's first independent record producer."[2]

Stigwood established from the start the model he would follow in music, theater and movies. "We conceived the idea that in show business you can monopolize all areas of income by controlling and managing the artist," Komlosy said. "If you start with the star, you control when and where he appears; if you promote him yourself, you become the record company. If you publish his music, you get the publisher's cut. The idea was not to let anyone in from the outside."[3] Stigwood and Komlosy watched the Beatles' ascent with dismay; by writing their own songs, the Beatles rendered Stigwood's business model obsolete. The Beatles didn't need songwriters and they didn't need someone to tell them how to sound. The

Elvis-imitating pop of the "single, hip-swiveling artist was no longer what was wanted," Komlosy said. "It was all groups—and they really flooded in."[4]

Stigwood adapted, as he always would. After a few setbacks, he joined Beatles manager Brian Epstein's management and promotion company, NEMS. Stigwood was the booking agent for the Who when his big break arrived. Eric Clapton left John Mayall's Bluesbreakers—whom Stigwood managed—and Jack Bruce and Ginger Baker left the Graham Bond Organization—whom Stigwood managed. Clapton, Bruce and Baker formed Cream, Stigwood became Cream's manager and Cream blew up huge.

Brian Epstein was tired of managing the Beatles. He was an overwrought, fragile soul, and was burning out. With the Beatles no longer willing to tour, Epstein understood that managing them would be little more than office work—dealing with contracts and difficult personalities without any of the rock-and-roll fun. The Beatles had matured beyond Epstein's ideas; they weren't going to dress alike, they weren't going to appear in movies, their public pronouncements would be what they really thought, they were going to do drugs without pretending they weren't and they wanted to be left alone.

Brian Epstein saw in Stigwood a possible means of escape. "The first night they met at a party at Stigwood's, a plan was made to go to Paris together for what [Stigwood's financial backer and partner] Shaw called 'a dirty weekend.' In Paris, in a three-bedroom suite at the Lancaster Hotel, Brian told Stigwood he was planning to retire. He wanted to go to Spain and manage bullfighters." Hanging with bullfighters was Epstein's oft-stated fantasy retirement goal. "To Brian, Stigwood and Shaw seemed like the perfect choice to take over the daily operation of NEMS. Brian felt that Stigwood had the creative potential and that Shaw had a sharp financial mind. Most important to Brian, Stigwood was intelligent, amusing, and affected an elegance similar to his own."[5]

When Epstein told the Beatles he was considering selling his management company, NEMS, to Stigwood, they reacted strongly. McCartney in particular wanted nothing to do with Stigwood. It's not clear where his dislike originated, but it was formidable. "We told Brian," Paul McCartney said, "that if he sold us to Stigwood, we would only ever record out-of-tune versions of 'God Save the Queen' [for the remaining five years of our contract]."[6] Epstein backed off and in a complex transaction, Stigwood and his partner agreed to acquire 51 percent of NEMS after a twelve-month period of working together. The contract was signed in early January of 1967.

With that deal, unknowingly, Stigwood and the Bee Gees began to vector toward one another.

On January 3, 1967, the Gibb family embarked from Australia, bound for England, aboard the SS *Fairsky*. The boys, frustrated by a ceiling they could not break in Australia, were determined to go to England, even over Hugh and Barbara's protests. "It doesn't matter if you become the biggest thing in Australia," Maurice said. "Because the furthest away you're known is New Guinea and Tasmania."[7] When their parents saw that the boys would go without them, they decided that the family would return to their homeland together. Hugh and Barbara had little desire to leave Oz. Once again, the Gibb parental-child structure was overturned as the kids made adult decisions for the whole family. "They wanted to stay in Australia," Robin said, "but we said no."[8] "We came back to England because of them," Hugh said. "I had a good job, but it was me or them. One day they said they wanted to go home so I said: 'OK, off we go.'"[9]

"There was no choice," Robin continued. "The manager of our record company said, 'Look, you're out, get out! We don't want to make another record with you!' In those days, a record company had its top artists and its nobody artists. We were the nobody artists. The top artist would get all the time in the studio. The most recording time they gave us was an hour to make a two-sided record. Every time we released a record they said (spoken in a weary voice for emphasis), 'Here they go . . . trying again.' Those were our reviews! That was all our reviews consisted of: 'Another Bee Gees record. Phew!' That's what they'd write, an exasperated 'phew,' like why didn't the Bee Gees give up the ghost?"[10]

The Bee Gees reached a certain level, and the structure of the business in Australia meant they could go no higher. "Big artists would come to top the bill there," Barry said. "But we were young and sweet and killing their acts and doing great! We thought: if we can do this well—why not have a crack at Sydney? We went to Sydney and got a recording contract and made the first of 15 flop singles in a row. People would tap us on the head and say: 'Go play with your toys.' They thought we were kids who would never make it. We got into the Australian Top 10 with 'Wine and Women'; then 'I Was a Lover, a Leader of Men'; then 'Spicks and Specks.' It was No. 1 when we decided to leave Australia. But we went without one word of Press."[11]

"Spicks and Specks" wasn't #1 when they left, but it was rising. There was no press in part because the Gibbs did not want any. They'd seen groups abandon Oz for the big time, only to return less famous and more broke. The Bee Gees wanted to slip away. The Bee Gees' official autobiography, published in 1979, claims that Festival records tried to serve them with an injunction to prevent them from leaving the country. Later research makes that seem unlikely.

"In August 1966," Robin said, "we went into the studio desperate to get a hit before we left for England. We made 'Spicks and Specks,' but Spin didn't want to release it. They thought we were finished, a financial loss. It was released eventually and went to the top in four weeks. It had been in our minds for the past years to come to England. 'Spicks and Specks' gave us the money."[12] But not quite enough money for the entire family's passage. Hugh made a deal with the ship: the boys would perform nightly to cover his and their fare.

The Bee Gees sailed away as "Spicks and Specks" rose on the charts. "The memories I have of Australia," Barry said, "were that they were unfair to us right to the end. Even on the boat, we'd get reports from friends about 'Spicks and Specks.' The record became a hit while we were on the boat and the local papers had stories like: 'Bee Gees Abandon Australia.'"[13]

The boys thought they'd be singing for their supper the entire voyage. "We got on the boat," Maurice said, "and they didn't even know we were supposed to be there. If Dad hadn't gone to see the purser, we could've travelled for free and never worked. But we only did about six shows in six weeks." "The entertainment room was over the captain's cabin," Barry said, "which was good for us because he said, 'No, no, no. I don't want entertainment at certain times, because I've got to go to bed.' The captain called the purser in and told him he didn't care. So we did one show a week." Those shows were encouraging. The kids on board turned every performance into a celebration. "Puff, the Magic Dragon" was a particular crowd-pleaser.

"We worked our way over," Maurice said. "We had heard that the original Seekers [a folk group that hit with "I'll Never Find Another You" and "Georgy Girl"] had worked their way to England, too."[14]

"We stopped off in India, the Middle East, Cairo, the Pyramids," Barry said. "And the things we discovered in back street bazaars! You could buy bottles of Dexedrine, every kind of stimulant, no questions asked. We were on a ship, but we flew all the way."[15] "We were up all night writing," Robin said, "because we'd bought some Dexedrine in Aden. It was legal there. There was a war in Aden, and warships in the harbor. We went into a drugstore, and the owner said, 'There's a war on, and I'm getting out. Here, take what you want.'"[16]

"Spicks and Specks" became the top single in Oz more or less while the family was still on the *Fairsky*. It's a structurally complex song, built on weird chords. The chopping guitar, bouncy beat and layered voices evoke Herman's Hermits. In mid-bounce, though, the songs stops dead and Barry sings a—soon to be characteristic—solo lament with no instrumental backing. A Beatles-esque cornet takes the song out. "Spicks" is a sophisticated pop construction, a harbinger of the idiosyncratic lyrics, rhythms, pacing and embellishments that would become the Bee Gees' sound.

If the music of your puberty shapes your taste for the rest of your life, what about your scars from the same period? Their #1 caused little rejoicing among Barry, Maurice and Robin. They'd been treated shabbily, they knew it, and were in no mood to savor the irony. Their feeling toward Australia was good riddance and kiss my ass. They looked toward England feeling like battle-scarred veterans of the record label wars.

And like teenagers on Dexedrine.

The *Fairsky* docked in Southampton on February 6. The family stayed the night in a crap hotel in London. They reached out to Colin Petersen and he found them a cheap furnished flat. Colin was from Brisbane. When he was nine he starred in the Australian movie *Smiley*. He also had roles in *The Scamp* and *A Cry from the Streets*. Colin starting drumming at twelve, and joined the Australian band Steve and the Board. They moved to Sydney in 1965 and released their first single on Spin. He met the Bee Gees in Sydney, and moved to England shortly before they arrived in London.

"When we arrived in London," Barry said, "we had nothing. We were unknown. We had no recording contract and no work."[17]

"So we reach England," Robin said, "and what happens when we arrive? The first people we meet coming off the ship is another rock group who advised us to go back. They told us the Walker Brothers were fading and Eric Clapton was rising and they tried to convince us not to try to make it in England. That gave us the added incentive to give it a go. We had sent tapes ahead before we left Australia and had hopes that someone who heard them would contact us."[18]

Hugh's luck is worth pondering, as is Barry's. Hugh never caught a break on his own, yet the Bee Gees' luck in those early years was phenomenal. Hugh, in his determined but hardly dazzling way, attempted things that never work out for anyone, and yet, for his boys, they did. Before leaving Australia, Hugh had sent acetates of Bee Gees material, along with a painfully earnest letter, to several UK labels and management outfits.

Hugh's letter arrived at NEMS on December 3, 1966, and read in part:

> This is just a preliminary letter to advise you of the arrival in London of a young vocal group, who, having reached the top of their field in this country, are returning home to the UK to further their career. They are the "Bee Gees," who consist of three brothers, Barry Gibb, aged 19, and twins Robin and Maurice, aged 16. . . .
>
> Although still youngsters, the boys have had an enormous amount of experience in all facets of show business: TV, recording, pantomime, hotel and club work etc. Naturally, their records have been aimed at the teenage market and at the time of writing they have a hit record, "Spicks & Specks," which has just reached the number 3 position in every state in Australia. We quite realise that this does not mean very much overseas, but considering the enormous size of Australia, this is considered quite a fest here.

That Hugh cited "pantomime" and "hotel and club work," suggests that he had not the slightest idea of what the music business in England would be like.

Like every other manager of every other aspiring band on the planet, Hugh sent music to NEMS. The odds of anyone at NEMS sorting through their weekly pile of unsolicited material to uncover a diamond in the rough are incalculable. Yet, somebody did. Epstein handed the acetates off to Stigwood. He played them, and, being Stigwood, starting searching for the Bee Gees.

That is the canonical version, as told in the Bee Gees' authorized biography and elsewhere.

There's another, only slightly less romantic version, and it showcases every bit as much luck. It might also have the virtue of being true. In 1966, a representative of Barry's Australian publisher reached out to Ronald Rennie, the managing director of Polydor, UK—a small subsidiary of the enormous German record label. Rennie received recordings of "Spicks and Specks" and other tracks. Rennie wrote back to Festival as a preliminary to making a deal to release the Bee Gees music on Polydor in the UK. If the music sold well enough, Rennie would bring the band from Oz to tour.

But suddenly, here's Barry off the boat, making the rounds, with no idea that Festival had reached out to Polydor. Barry knocked on Rennie's door, introduced himself and gave Rennie another set of acetates. Rennie thought Barry had appeal, and called his buddy Robert Stigwood to suggest that Stigwood immediately sign the Bee Gees and manage them.

Stigwood knew where the boys were and how to reach Hugh because Rennie told him. Rennie knew that because Barry had left him a contact number. Showman that he was, Stigwood never spilled the beans.[19]

However it happened, Stigwood thought what he heard had promise. Since he wasn't going to manage the Beatles, Stigwood was searching for a vocal group he could guide and shape, one that might possibly outdo the Beatles. Stigwood never thought small. His ambitions were matched by Barry's.

"One night in 1967, I turned up at Robert Stigwood's place," Paul McCartney said. "He said, 'What do you think of this record?' And he played some young songwriters. It was a couple of their early songs. I liked them, and he said, 'Oh, great, 'cause I'm thinking of signing them.' And that was the start of them for me."[20]

"I loved their composing," Stigwood said. "I also loved their harmony singing. It was unique, a sound only brothers could make."[21]

Stigwood found out the Gibbs were heading to England. He knew the date of their arrival. One way or another, Stigwood got the phone number of the rental house they'd occupied for only two days. He called and kept calling. Hugh had never heard Stigwood's name; he only knew about Epstein. When he first called, the boys were out making the rounds.

"We trudged around Denmark Street," Maurice said, "and saw the manager of The Seekers, the manager of Cliff Richard, and they all told us we were wasting our time. We were staying in a semi-detached in Hendon wondering what to do when my mother said we'd had a call from Robert Stickweed. We had no idea who that was."[22] Stigwood asked them to come around. They met briefly and scheduled an audition.

"We did our nightclub act," Maurice said, "and he watched and listened and never smiled once. Then he said, 'Be at my office at six o'clock,' and we were and we signed contracts."[23] Within less than a month of getting off the boat, the boys signed five-year deals: recording contracts, publishing contracts and management contracts. They were Stigwood's and he was theirs. The five-year deals started out with £25 a week for each.[24] That was not bad money for 1967; five-year deals were unusual at the time. Stigwood was investing for the long term and wanted his investment locked up. The day they signed, Polydor, under a deal with Festival, released "Spicks and Specks" in the UK.[25]

Describing Stigwood at the time, Barry said: "He looked Edwardian, with sideburns and a velvet-lapel jacket, Oscar Wilde-ish, with grayer hair. We went into his office, next to The Palladium in Argyll Street, and he gave us 20 pounds each to buy clothes in Carnaby Street." Carnaby Street was the epicenter of Swinging London and the locus of all the groovy clothing stores.

Barry returned to the office wearing a black shroud, tights and carrying a sword. Eric Clapton was already in the NEMS elevator, dressed head to toe as a cowboy. As the elevator rose, the two eyed one another and neither said a word.[26]

Peter Brown, a personal assistant to Brian Epstein and the Beatles who went on to be president of RSO, chronicled the Fab Four and their scene in *The Love You Make: An Insider's Story of the Beatles*. "Brian hated the Bee Gees from the start," Brown wrote, "perhaps because they weren't his discovery. When Stigwood told Brian on the phone that he had bought 51 percent of the Bee Gees' publishing for NEMS for £1,000, Brian shouted, 'Well that's a thousand out the window!' Almost immediately the Bee Gees had a number-one hit single with their own composition, 'New York Mining Disaster 1941,' and Brian was even more annoyed."[27]

A thousand pounds for 51 percent of the Bee Gees' publishing proved to be one of the greatest bargains in music industry history, as later Bee Gee lawsuits against Stigwood attempted to prove. Paul Simon, when asked what he learned writing songs in the factory atmosphere of the Brill Building, said: "I learned to keep my publishing." The Bee Gees, like the Beatles and the Rolling Stones, would come to legal blows with their management over getting a fair share of what was owed them.

Stigwood set the Bee Gees up with Dick Ashby as their factotum, manager of the day-to-day and go-to guy when the Bee Gees wanted to communicate with the world or vice versa. Stigwood went off to America to find a US label for the band. Epstein wanted them to sign with Capitol, which handled the Beatles in the US. Capitol had famously screwed Epstein on the Beatles' US royalty deal. Epstein's continued loyalty to Capitol suggests—as do several Epstein contemporaries—that Epstein didn't understand how thoroughly he'd been hosed. Stigwood certainly did. Atlantic had signed Cream and Stigwood got along well with Atlantic's legendary president, Ahmet Ertegun. It took a while, but Atlantic signed the Bee Gees for £80,000, the largest contract given to a new group at the time.

The Bee Gees headed into Polydor studios in London in late April 1967. They brought in drummer Colin Petersen and Aussie guitarist Vince Melouney to round out their lineup. "I didn't even know they were in England until they phoned," Vince said. "I had known them in Australia. We worked in the same places and did session work together. Everybody knows everybody else in Australia. They said they would like me to play guitar on the session. That first time in the studio together we recorded 'New York Mining Disaster.' After that I joined the group."[28]

The band worked on material written since their last recordings made in Oz. They did not recycle older songs. Stigwood tells a story of a power failure at Polydor, and of the boys sitting on the stairs in the dark. Inspired by the claustrophobic feel, they wrote "Mining Disaster," he says, in ten minutes. "There was a power outage at this demo studio at Polydor at Stratford Place in London," Maurice said. "The lights had gone out. We walked outside the studio and into the hall, and there was this echo that came from the ground floor right up to where we were on the fourth floor. There was this whole atmosphere of being in a mine hole."

"We were sitting in the lounge, in the dark, and we got the first line," Barry said. "'In the event of something happening to me.' And we thought, 'Oh, that's a good line, people will know what we're talking about.'"[29]

The single was released on April 14, 1967. Stigwood bought a full-page ad, citing the band as "the most significant new musical talent of 1967."[30] "When people put out ads saying you're the most significant new talent of 1967," Robin said, "you've got to live up to it. So you do as much as you can to keep away from the basic chords and rhythms."[31] "The old concept of writing about love and romance as the basis of every pop song has changed," Barry told *Melody Maker*. "We still write romance songs, but most of our writing is about contemporary things, situations, people. The Beatles have started to write about subjects not connected with love. We do too. 'New York Mining Disaster' is about some people trapped in a mine.

"We can write a song about almost anything, to order. We write all the time. We finish four or five songs a week on average. We drive the producer and technicians mad. We have nothing worked out. We sit about and think up a subject, then write a song on the spot. We did the whole of our first LP like this. We may all have ideas beforehand, but we're never sure what the end product is going to be like until we're in the studio."[32] "It's really the only way we can work—spontaneously, off the cuff."[33]

"New York Mining Disaster 1941 (Have You Seen My Wife, Mr. Jones?)" introduced one of the band's many quirks: a preference for parentheses in their song titles. It would persist at least until 1979's "Spirits (Having Flown)." Most reviews gave the song respect—which it deserved, as it went to #14 on the US charts and #12 in the UK. But the first review raised the dreaded B-word. "The Aussie Bee Gees group are now in Britain—and very talented they are, too," *Melody Maker* proclaimed. "A story-in-song ballad that's folksy in some respects, and a bit like the Beatles in other ways. Fascinating harmonies, underlined by cello, and a lyric that keeps you glued to the speaker. I found it wholly gripping—congrats to the boys."[34]

Stigwood, Polydor and Atlantic were determined to promote the boys as the next Beatles. That meant telling everyone that the Bee Gees had a Beatles-like sound and a round of Stigwood-generated rumors that this or that apocryphal DJ mistook "Mining Disaster" for a new Beatles single. Right from the jump, the band had to endure Beatles comparisons. But "Mining Disaster" does not sound like the Beatles. The song is startling, original and just plain weird. It doesn't sound like anyone but the Bee Gees.

The Bee Gees could not read or write music. Sometimes they hummed approximations of the horn and string parts for Bill Shepherd, their composer-arranger. Sometimes, Shepherd composed Bee Gees horn and string arrangements himself. During this period, the Bee Gees took credit for a number of in-studio things they did not do, and it's not entirely clear who did what. Later in their career, the Gibbs—and especially Barry—would meticulously hum or whistle exactly the horn or string parts they wanted. It's likely that for "Mining Disaster," Shepherd originated the parts.

"Mining Disaster" is a good old-fashioned tragic saga, a throwback to English and Irish folk ditties and skiffle tragedies. The guitar strums a skiffle beat, the foundation of so much early UK pop, which the Beatles hadn't used unironically in some time. It's easy to picture Lonnie Donegan or Pete Seeger a decade earlier on a grainy black-and-white telly, strumming away with his head thrown back, shouting out "Mining Disaster" with unbearable folkie sincerity. But the song is odd, off in an ineffable way, like many of the Bee Gees' early hits. There's an air of otherness, something askew in its sincerity and solemnness. The arrangement, especially of the harmonies, is sophisticated far beyond the boys' years.

"They have been hailed as 'new Beatles,'" *Melody Maker* said. "And even compared to the Beatles sound-wise, though they refuse to agree that their music has any Beatle flavourings." "I think it's because we write songs and are with the same management, NEMS, that the comparisons have arisen," Barry said, disingenuously, as if that very management had not been flogging the com-

parison worldwide.[35] "There are no songs you could say were Beatles' songs, or tunes or words you could say were Beatles' words,"
Maurice said, unknowingly beginning a ten-year process of defending the band's originality. "Our harmonies are sometimes similar. But we can't sing any differently, we don't consciously try to
sound or not try to sound like anybody. All I can say is we try to be
ourselves."[36] "We made a demo once," Robin said, protesting too
much. "Just a rough recording, and we thought it sounded Beatle-
ish so we threw it away."[37]

On May 11, the boys made their first appearance on the iconic
British music TV show *Top of the Pops*. They shared the bill with
the Rolling Stones, the Move and the pop singer Lulu, Maurice's
future wife. Lulu performed her recent hit "The Boat I Row."
Lulu was tiny, with enormous, lovely eyes and a megawatt smile.
She had a perky, indefatigable Georgy Girl persona—down to
earth, working class, accessible—and a soaring voice. She was,
even then, a wise showbiz pro. Lulu and Maurice remember
checking one another out that day, but they did not speak. From
there, the band appeared on *Beat-Club*, the German equivalent
of *Top of the Pops*. In late May, the Bee Gees played live at Liverpool University, and in June at the Saville Theatre in London and
at concert venues around the country, including Manchester, the
city they once tried to burn down.

Shortly after their *Top of the Pops* appearance, Lulu got a call
from her friend Joanne Nuffield. "Maurice Gibb fancies you,"
Nuffield told her. Maurice was too shy to call Lulu himself. And
despite Nuffield's urgings, Lulu didn't call Maurice. They met by
chance in the south of France, when the Gibbs were staying at
Stigwood's house. A week later, Maurice called Lulu up in London, and took her to see Pink Floyd. They tried to have a romance, but Lulu's career was thriving. She was busier than
Maurice and ambivalent about him. They "often had to make do
with talking on the phone."[38]

Lulu, an unpretentious girl with a dispassionate eye for the pop business, sussed the Bee Gees' dynamic. "All the brothers seemed to vie for Stigwood's attention—Mo and Robin especially," she wrote in her autobiography, *I Don't Want to Fight.* "Barry was eighteen months older and more secure. He was the strongest creative force when it came to songwriting and singing. Robin had the most unique voice and Mo was the strongest musically, capable of picking up almost any instrument." Maurice's skills and adaptability meant the Bee Gees' five-piece lineup could produce the instrumentation they wanted without having to deal with outsiders.

By the summer of 1967, either despite or because of the Bee Gees' early success, Epstein regretted his "option agreement" with Stigwood and Shaw. "With every day he was growing increasingly more upset over what he saw as Stigwood's personal extravagance," Peter Brown wrote of Epstein. "NEMS executives had a charge at a local butcher where they were charging Sunday turkeys; articles of personal clothing were charged to the company account at Harrods; and when Stigwood took the Bee Gees to New York for a promotional trip, he rented a yacht for them to sail around Manhattan Island. Stigwood told Nat to charge the boat to his personal account, and Nat forwarded this information to Brian in London. 'What personal account?' Brian fumed. 'When the Bee Gees are as successful as the Beatles, then Robert can rent them a yacht around Manhattan.' Brian's personal hope was that Stigwood and Shaw would not be able to raise the £500,000 to close the option. There was some doubt they were going to be able to raise the money in the financial community, but Stigwood insisted there was no problem and that Brian should inform the Beatles of what was taking place."[39]

Stigwood's words only inflamed the situation: "We all believe that potentially the Bee Gees can develop to the point where they earn as much money in record sales as the Beatles. Their first six months' progress on an international basis has been fantastic."[40]

As a promotion for the July 14 release of their first United Kingdom LP, *Bee Gees' 1st*, NEMS released the Bee Gees' next single in June. The A-side was "To Love Somebody," and the B-side, "I Can't See Nobody." Barry wrote "To Love Somebody," at Stigwood's request, custom built for soul immortal Otis Redding. Barry had met Otis on a March trip to New York and admired him greatly.

If Barry Gibb never wrote another number—he shares songwriting credit with Robin, but it's Barry's song—"To Love Somebody" should be enough to cement his reputation as one of pop's most important songwriters, and perhaps the one with the most underappreciated range and breadth. Barry was not yet twenty-one. When asked to create a song for Otis Redding, a difficult and particular assignment, Barry sat down and wrote not only a classic, but the greatest Otis Redding song Otis Redding never recorded. For Otis fanatics, among the many tragic aspects of his death—in a plane crash on December 10, 1967, at the age of twenty-six—is that Otis never got to sing "To Love Somebody."

If you gathered the top songwriters of 1967, locked them in a room and told them to write a song for Otis, none of them—Sly Stone, Bob Dylan, Smokey Robinson, Carole King, Paul Simon, Booker T., Laura Nyro, Brian Wilson, Lennon and McCartney, Leonard Cohen, Holland-Dozier-Holland, Lou Reed, Randy Newman, Barry Gordy, Pete Townshend, Sonny Bono, Willy Dixon, Norman Whitfield or Neil Young—could have written a song as soulful, yearning, memorable and yet so attuned, for emotion and commerce, to Otis's voice, breathing, timing and performance style. Maybe Van Morrison could have, back then. But nobody else.

The proof that they couldn't is that they didn't. Only Barry Gibb could and only Barry Gibb did. That took extraordinary songwriting chops and studious attention to Otis's sound. Barry would later take a lot of grief, much of it deserved, for being a selfish megalomaniac. But at the time, he could really listen. And listening bespeaks compassion.

The song has, to say the least, endured. It's easier to list who hasn't covered it: soul great James Carr did; as did Tom Jones, Janis Joplin, Lulu, calypso deity the Mighty Sparrow, Nina Simone, Dusty Springfield, the Black Crowes, blues guitarist Little Milton, Gary Puckett and the Union Gap, Joe Cocker, Roberta Flack, Simply Red, and Michael Bolton, among an infinity of others. Gram Parsons sang the most harrowing version with the Flying Burrito Brothers; Parsons understood how much soul and pain Barry had written. Eric Burden, of all people, produced the most fantastical, rococo and peculiar cover with the Animals. Even Eric's distracting, overproduced arrangement is moving. Almost every arrangement moves the listener, including Michael Bolton's. The song is strong enough, deep enough, to overcome the limitations of second-rate singers and give first-rate singers raw material they dream about.

"To Love Somebody" fared poorly on the UK charts, reaching only #41. In the US it made #17, but after the success of "Mining Disaster," #17 felt like a disappointment. "Everyone told us what a great record they thought it was," Robin said. "Other groups all raved about it but for some reason people in Britain did not seem to like it."[41] "It's odd that other artists don't get hits with our songs," Barry told *Melody Maker*. "I believe it's because they don't put enough feeling into them. Too many artists do a song rather than act it. It's like an actor who plays a part instead of becoming that person."[42] Maurice interrupted to say that Lulu had done a good cover of "To Love Somebody,"[43] but that was probably his crush on her doing the talking.

"'To Love Somebody,'" Barry said, offering the first appearance of a lifelong readiness to disavow anything that wasn't a hit, "was a good record, but 'Massachusetts' [the upcoming single] is a commercial record."

"Love Somebody/Nobody" prefigured the slowly building—but not yet surfaced—divisive issue in the band: Who would sing lead? The B-side, "I Can't See Nobody," is Robin's commanding, Phil Spector–style lament. He sings with a tragic resonance that Barry never attempted. Robin connects to his inner pain; Barry doesn't seem to have any. Robin's lost-love songs carry true heartache. Barry's voice can be generic; no one sounds like Robin. "Nobody" has a kick-ass arrangement, a good hook and a memorable lead vocal. Why wasn't it the A-side of its own single? Pairing it with "Love Somebody" serves both songs poorly. "Nobody" ended up ignored. Was this an early sign of power struggles to come? Was Barry reluctant to have Robin singing lead on an A-side?

Bee Gees' 1st hit at #7 on the US *Billboard* charts and #8 in the UK. The psychedelic album cover presents all five members of the band as equal in stature in a line across—no separation is made between the Gibbs, Vince and Colin. Barry is, of course, in the middle. Below the photo is a brightly colored abstract illustration evoking flowers, or something. Bass player Klaus Voorman, who created the Beatles' *Revolver* cover and played on George Harrison's and John Lennon's solo projects, designed and executed the sleeve.

The album was recorded on four tracks at both Polydor and at IBC Studios, where Stigwood routinely sent his bands. It was released in the States on Atco, a division of Atlantic. As was usual at the time, both mono and stereo versions were available. Maurice played bass and anything with a keyboard: piano, mellotron, organ. Robin sang and contributed some piano.

Bee Gees' 1st shows that the Bee Gees had developed a unique sound, and were only waiting for a first-rate studio and arranger to explore it. They sing and play with palpable confidence. The stronger tracks—"Holiday," "Mining Disaster," "To Love Somebody" and "I Can't See Nobody"—showcase singular, instantly memorable melodies, unexpected chord changes and indivisible harmony: the essence of the Bee Gees sound. The lyrics of the more meaningful songs address yearning, an inability to connect, desperate loneliness and a desire to be seen: the lyrics of alienation, sung with an aching heart. Robin's vocals are especially affecting.

The pain of the singer, except on "I Can't See Nobody," is never stated directly; the Bee Gees' mode is misdirection. It's not exactly clear what Robin's singing about on "Holiday" or what the lyrics mean, but the sadness is inescapable.

On the weaker cuts, the influence of contemporaneous London bands intrudes. "In My Own Time," "Please Read Me" and "I Close My Eyes" evoke the Hollies; "Turn of the Century" and "Craise Finton Kirk Royal Academy" reflect the faddish nostalgia for Edwardian–Aubrey Beardsley motifs and English dance-hall sounds from bygone times. With "Craise," at last the band could be accused of copping Beatles-esque atmospherics, especially the music-hall irony and tinkling piano the Beatles adored. "Cucumber Castle" features too-busy horns and strings that sound right off the Beatles' studio charts.

The album is not exactly rock and roll; there are no 4/4 ravers. Rhythm never dominates; it's music of melody, and as white as can be—almost completely free of blues, R&B or soul influences. "To Love Somebody" is sung as a ballad, not a soul song. This is a record to be listened to or sung along with; it's not for dancing or making love.

"I Close My Eyes" ends with the corny, twee horn and keyboard embellishments that Barry always liked. But it's followed by the show-stopping, mournful, Righteous Brothers–style rave-up of Robin shouting out his broken heart on "I Can't See Nobody." The melodramatic arrangement; the quiet, almost spoken vocals that turn into full-volume anguish; the rich bed of strings and reverb-drenched drums sound more like Phil Spector songwriting and production than anything else the band ever did. The power and expressiveness of Robin's voice is a revelation. On all his lead vocals, he's unbearably sincere. Barry sounds more disconnected, almost emotion free. Robin sang lead on two tracks, Barry on four and Maurice, as per their custom, never took a solo vocal.

The less compelling cuts seem almost contentless—songwriting exercises, pure filler or pop indulgences instead of self-expression. The transition from "Cucumber Castle" to "To Love Somebody" is like moving between different planets. If they weren't side by side on the same record, it would be hard to believe the same band did them both.

By early July, the Bee Gees were back in IBC working on their second Polydor LP, to be entitled *Horizontal*. They took a break from recording for a quickie promotional tour of New York in July. On July 27, the band made their first appearance—along with the Doors—on Dick Clark's *American Bandstand* to sing "Mining Disaster." True to his philosophy, Stigwood did not waste an opportunity to cross-promote. The *Bandstand* appearance coincided with the American release of *Bee Gees' 1st*. Stigwood, demonstrating his belief in complete control, signed Colin and Vince to their own contracts with NEMS.

On August 9, a historic day for the Bee Gees, they recorded their next single, "Massachusetts." "We were sitting in our New York hotel doing send-ups of Tom Jones and Engelbert Humperdink," Maurice said. "We came up with this song and Robert came in and said: 'Record that.' We didn't really agree with him. We agreed to record it but we didn't think it had any hope of making the charts, so we recorded another song as well, just in case."[44]

"We worked out the basic melody in about five minutes when we were in New York. Robin and I began, then Barry started throwing in ideas. I'm not quite sure why we thought of Massachusetts in the first place because we weren't even sure how to spell it."[45]

On August 26, 1967, Brian Epstein died of what was called an accidental overdose of sleeping pills. The night before, Robin was visiting NEMS's receptionist-secretary, Molly Hullis. Since May, he and Molly had slowly been getting to know each other.

Robin saw Brian go into Stigwood's office. "He closed the door and there was a lot of shouting," Robin said. "When [Epstein] came out he was crying. I said, 'What's the matter?' He said, 'I can't talk.' And he went straight out." Stigwood emerged from his office and told Robin and Molly about the conversation. "Brian had pleaded with Robert to go to Sussex with him that weekend because he didn't want to be alone. The Beatles were in Bangor [India], with the Maharishi Mahesh Yogi. And Robert had said no."[46] Robin, Molly and Stigwood went to Monaco as they had planned. Epstein died that night.

"We had this terrible midnight cruise to Nice," Robin said, "so Robert could catch a plane back. He had nothing to do with Brian's death, but he felt tremendously guilty, because if he'd stayed that might not have happened."[47]

"At NEMS there was a wild scramble for power," Peter Brown wrote. "The old guard Liverpool contingent, which included me, among others, lined up against the newer partners like Stigwood and Shaw who had been brought into NEMS later. Stigwood and Shaw had one major problem: they had to convince the Beatles to stay with them. Stigwood hardly even knew the Beatles. The Beatles were shocked to learn that Brian had planned to sell NEMS. As far as the Beatles were concerned, Brian's option agreement with Stigwood didn't include them anyway. When they heard that Stigwood and Shaw were claiming otherwise, they met with Stigwood to set him straight."[48]

"Brian kept trying to tell us something before he died—but he never got round to it," George Harrison said. "He had a big party down at his house and we were supposed to go there and have a meeting before the party. Unfortunately it was in the 'Summer of Love' and everybody was wacko. We were in our psychedelic motor cars with our permed hair, and we were permanently stoned (Brian wasn't doing so bad himself, either)—so we never had the meeting.

"Later, we found out that he'd given Stigwood the option to acquire 51% of NEMS, which in effect meant management of The Beatles. So we had a meeting with Robert Stigwood and we said, 'Look, NEMS is built basically on The Beatles, so you can bugger off. We'll have 51%, and you can have 49%.' He backed off then, and formed his own company."[49] Stigwood and Shaw resigned from NEMS. NEMS released a statement in November.

"Following upon the death of Mr. Brian Epstein, various policies agreed between him and Mr. Robert Stigwood are not now practically possible," the statement read. "In these circumstances, it has been agreed by the board of NEMS Enterprises Ltd., on the most amicable basis that NEMS Enterprises Ltd., and the Robert Stigwood Organisation will go their separate ways. The Beatles' contract with us is due to expire shortly, and they have asked us to stress that it WILL be renewed. Furthermore they have said that in future they wish to take a more active part in the running of NEMS, of which they are share-holders."[50]

"It was simply that certain ideas and policies on which I was co-operating with the late Brian Epstein are now no longer practically possible," Stigwood told *Melody Maker*. "I also wish to expand my international plans, and I intend to develop television and theatrical interests."[51]

"Holiday" was released as a single in the US in September of 1967. Polydor decided to delay the UK release until the Bee Gees' next album. "Holiday" served as a placeholder, a way of keeping the Bee Gees in the public eye. It peaked in America at #16. In a strange piece of timing, "Massachusetts" was released not long after "Holiday." "Massachusetts" hit the UK charts on September 20.

"We were undecided amongst ourselves about 'Massachusetts.'" Maurice said. "We thought it might be a bit too country and western for the pop market. But it was picked as the best single from eight tracks by the staff at NEMS, so we released it."[52] When asked why the band liked "Massachusetts" more than "Mining Disaster," Barry said: "This is our first really big British hit. Wouldn't it be nice if we got to No. 1?"[53]

Also on September 20, while rehearsing for their appearance on *Top of the Pops* on the 21st, Barry met a seventeen-year-old *Top of the Pops* hostess, Lynda Gray, a former Miss Edinburgh. Lynda—often described as "a Bond girl"—was a tall, brunette bombshell who radiated warmth and kindness. Maurice had met his future wife on *Top of the Pops*; so did Barry. Barry was still married to Maureen, but barely.

For the next week, the Bee Gees raced around, playing live gigs, another German TV show and returning to IBC to cut more tracks for *Horizontal*. This would be their life for October, November and December: a one-night stand, a TV show, a couple sessions at IBC and back out for another one-night stand. Almost every other night, the Bee Gees performed live, on TV or in the studio.

By October 14, "Massachusetts" was the Bee Gees' first #1. It would go on to be #1 in the US and sell over 5 million copies, putting the Bee Gees on par with Elvis and the Beatles.

The Gibbs left Oz for London in January. By October they had released four singles. Three made the top 20 and one was on its way to quintuple platinum and #1 on both sides of the Atlantic. Here a Beatles comparison is finally apt. Like the Beatles, who spent years honing their craft in Hamburg shitholes, the Bee Gees were an overnight success after a decade of brutally hard work. There are few richer pleasures than being underappreciated in the sticks, daring to move to the big city and discovering that the major leagues recognize all your virtues that smaller minds were too small to perceive. The boys believed they had it coming, and sure enough, they got it. How many get to say that? If they became a little full of themselves for a while, who wouldn't?

"'Massachusetts,'" Robin said, "is not talking about people going back to Massachusetts. It represents all the people who want to go back to somewhere or something. It is all about people who want to escape." Robin was asked if "Massachusetts" represented the band's state of mind. "No, not now," he said. "It did. But we have already gone back to Massachusetts. When we were not recognised we were trying to escape—to recognition. That is something we have always wanted. We came to England searching for it and we found it."[54]

The Gibbs could now afford a Rolls-Royce. "We've wanted one for as long as we can remember," Maurice said. "Now we've got it. I don't care if it never moves out of the garage. We've got one . . . that's all that matters."[55] Maurice would apply that outlook to fancy cars his entire life; it's rumored he spent an aggregate of $100 million on automobiles. "We've only just realised something about our singles," Maurice told *Melody Maker.* "'New York Mining Disaster' had a place in the title. Then came 'To Love Somebody' which didn't do much. Now there is 'Massachusetts,' a place name again, getting to number one. We should be safe. Our next single is called 'World.'"[56]

When asked about their success, Barry said: "Firstly, I think we give the public melodies. And secondly we don't attempt to preach at anyone. There are so many groups which try to change the world. We are simply a pop group which writes all its own songs. We write songs about people and situations—we tell stories."[57] "We always try to put ourselves into our records," Robin said. "We've never tried to write anything that wasn't us. What we are doing is sort of writing down people's thoughts; nobody has ever thought of writing down things exactly the way people think."[58]

Now that they were #1, the Bee Gees got the full star treatment from the press. Barry was asked about the band's stage presentation and style. "We'd like to bring back some of the glamour that's gone out of pop. I think that the visual impression given by a group on stage is perhaps more important in some ways than the sound they are laying down. The glamour started to go out of pop when groups started wearing jeans and any old clothes on stage. Pop groups are there to entertain. We have to go on stage and project something that's entertaining visually and musically to earn our wages. It's not enough to go on stage and play the music. A lot of groups talk to each other, have private jokes on stage—that sort of thing. But once you start cutting the audience out, they'll cut you out, too. We spend a long time before a gig deciding what to wear on stage because we are concerned to give a good show for an audience who've paid and so that we can go back there again."[59]

Others disagreed. "Well, they're in their own little fantasy world," Keith Richards said. "You only have to read what they talk about in interviews . . . how many suits they've got and that kind of crap. It's all kid stuff, isn't it?"[60]

Barry, hardly past his twenty-first birthday, already sounded like a fifty-year-old record executive. He carefully parsed out pop, and did not fall prey to the conceit that the advent of rock and roll meant that all pop music was countercultural. He describes his work as entertainment, not self-expression. Barry avoided a precious trope of the day, that the artist and audience formed a commune, with the artist representing all present. Barry regards the audience as a separate beast, gazing at him hungrily, waiting to be fed. He didn't think it was "enough to go on stage and play the music." But that was the current vogue; rock bands were moving away from being consciously entertaining in favor of "authenticity." Barry was too vested in old-school showbiz for any of that nonsense. Who he was and what he did remained forever distinct.

At times, Robin and Maurice registered the unspoken psychic connection that only twins possess.

"When Robin was late for a press conference," Maurice said, "I said, 'There is something wrong. Something has happened to Robin.' And Barry said, 'What do you mean?' And then we found out. We watched the news, saw the train disaster and I went, 'Robin was on it!' We went to Hither Green Hospital and there was Robin—his [girlfriend Molly Hullis] was in having x-rays—sitting there going, 'I didn't think I was going to see you guys again.' He pulled six people out of a carriage and he said, 'I never knew I had that much strength.' He laid them on the lawn, and they were all dead. I knew he had been through a strenuous thing—my own arms were aching."[61]

Robin and Molly were on a packed Sunday night train on November 5, 1967, returning from Molly's parents' house near Hastings to London Charing Cross. At the Hither Green maintenance station, the train derailed; eleven of twelve coaches went off the tracks and four landed on their sides. Forty people died and another seventy-eight were injured. It was an epoch-making accident in England, one remembered with horror for generations. A broken rail at a track joint was later found to be the cause. "We were approaching Lewisham at about 90 mph (the train was actually going about 60 mph) when I heard a clattering," Robin told the *Daily Mail*, "as though a stone was being thrown at us. What I didn't realise was the engine had become uncoupled. Then the carriage rolled over and big stretches of railway line came crashing in straight past my face."[62]

Molly and Robin clung to each other as their coach tumbled over and over until it came to rest a thousand yards from the tracks. "When the train stopped there was a hissing sound, then the gut-wrenching screams. They pulled 24 people from the second class carriage with railway lines through their bodies. Some were unconscious, some had no legs. I was lifting badly injured people about three times my weight out of the compartments."[63]

Robin later claimed that "Massachusetts" had saved their lives, because it enabled him to buy first-class tickets. Most of the dead rode the second-class cars, which lacked a central corridor to absorb the shock of the coaches' rolling. Robin heroically pulled the living from the wrecked cars and helped move the dead. "People had to be amputated on the railway line and I was talking to them as they were being injected. All I wanted to do was escape. It was like *Dante's Inferno*. At the time you can't feel fear or anger, you can only deal with one emotion at a time. Survival took over, eating up my energy. I was covered in blood, had glass in my eyes and mouth. But when I got to the hospital, it was like a scene from World War One. I felt so guilty being there I jumped in a car and went home. Later I got delayed shock, didn't sleep for a long, long time afterwards."

Neither he nor Molly was hurt. Both credit the incident with bringing them closer together, and making their marriage a certainty.

"For ages, I didn't talk about the crash," Robin said. "Then I went through a guilt trip of feeling people were hurt, so why wasn't I? I've travelled in trains since but I don't like it, always keep listening for a change in the sounds. For a while I felt fragile and vulnerable; everything seemed paper-thin."[64]

Robin wrote "Really and Sincerely" the day after the Hither Green crash and recorded it the day after that. Over a mournful accordion, Robin sings from the perspective of what seems to be the recently dead or recently rejected. It's a melancholy cry from the heart, and a perfect example of how all the Bee Gees—but Robin foremost—transferred real experiences into lyrics of vague or opaque meaning, but of great emotional power. The song never cites the crash, or fear or its effects on Robin. "It doesn't mention anything about the train crash," Robin said, "but it does reflect the

mood I was in." Robin's mood, if the song is any judge, was ele-
giac; it sounds like his hymn for the dead of the crash.

Barry, talking about Robin, and fears of traveling, said, "We
cannot sleep in planes. Robin is as nervous as a kitten. I know that
you can say there is more chance of a crash on the roads, but it
can happen in the air, too. Or on a train like Robin in the Hither
Green tragedy. He could well have been killed."[65]

On November 17, the band switched on the Christmas lights
on Carnaby Street. On November 19, the Bee Gees mounted what
would become their prototypical stage show for the coming years.
"We're all excited about the Saville show," Barry said. "It's really
going to be something that people have never seen before." "We're
having a thirty-piece orchestra," Maurice said. "And a hundred ex-
tras to enact scenes from mythological and historical events."[66]
The show featured "World," their next single, and the first from
their upcoming LP.

Back in October, England's Home Office told Vince and
Colin that, as Australians, their visa time in England was up and
they had to go home. "It's no use getting dragged about it," Colin
said. "We never discuss it among ourselves. There's no point.
We'd sooner wait and see what happens. It's unfair though. We
are making money for Britain and as a child I made three films
here on which I paid tax. But now I can't live here. If we weren't
in the public eye, no one would have noticed how long we
stayed."[67] November 30 was their deadline. "This has been as far
as the Prime Minister," Stigwood said, "and Home Office still
says they must leave the country for six months on November 30.
At the moment our legal representatives are presenting the Home
Office with evidence of the group's foreign currency earning
power—Atlantic Records are furnishing them with their royalty
earnings to date. It seems ridiculous to force them to leave when
they are bringing so much money into the country."[68]

The Bee Gees planned to use temporary replacements. "The

problem will not be finding good musicians," Colin said, "but finding two guys who will harmonize personally within the group." "Six months' holiday," Maurice said. "Lucky swine!"[69] During the publicity over this dispute, Maurice took his driving test. The tester said, "You're one of the Bee Gees, aren't you—the ones getting deported?" Maurice said: "I was about to say this applied to only two of the members, when this bloke says: 'Then why the hell are you taking your test?' That got me. My blood really boiled, and I thought, 'Right, mate.' I gave it to him at 80. We were going along like there was no tomorrow. When we got out, he said, 'Mr. Gibb, I'm happy to say you've failed.'"[70]

Stigwood and the Bee Gees fan club staged a series of rallies and publicity stunts in support of Colin and Vince. Fans blocked the entrances to government buildings and rained abuse on officials. Stigwood kept up the pressure by proving to the Home Office how much tax revenue the Bee Gees were producing and how much would be lost if they took a six-month hiatus. Stigwood's cross-promotional strategy of low-end public pressure and high-end private negotiation proved successful. The Home Office amnestied Vince and Colin and gave them unlimited-time work permits.

"World," the lead-in single for *Horizontal*, was released in mid-November. It's generic psychedelia, a *Magical Mystery Tour* rip, with a ringing, sad piano and wavering organ/mellotron that evokes a Theramin. The drums, though playing forward, are produced to mimic the backward-Ringo on various Beatle tracks. Barry whisper-sings of his memories and aspirations. The big revelation is that "the world is round." For a band trying to avoid being compared to the Beatles, "World" was not the best career move. The *New Musical Express* liked it, though: "It seems a little early for the Bee Gees to release another single, but that won't prevent it from being another big 'un. It's another hauntingly simple tune like 'Massachusetts' and registers as quickly—maybe because it immediately reminds you of something else. And it's encased in a gorgeous backing of shimmering strings. But this time, between each of the stanzas, there's a contrasting instrumental passage of twangs and other raucous sounds. The combined effect is quite stunning! It's melodic, delightfully harmonized and incredibly well produced. I can't get the tune out of my mind!"[71]

It's hard to say what the reviewer was actually listening to, because "World" could not be less like "Massachusetts." It has no hook, no singable chorus, no air of evocation. The lyrics suggest Barry reaching for profundity and not quite grasping it. "I think 'World' is certainly a deeper number than 'Massachusetts,'" Barry said. "'World' means a lot and I don't think that many people have caught on to all the implications of the song yet. We were making the point that we thought people were taking flower power far too seriously. No matter which way you look at things, flower power doesn't change it.

"Somewhere in the world, every day, people are fighting— somewhere every day it rains!" Barry said, paraphrasing the lyric. "There were only a minority of people in the midst of the whole flower thing who really loved their neighbors. That's why it's died out—because there is still a majority of people who are fighting all over the world. Let's face it; few people were true to the origins of flower power, nobody really thought about it. Anyway, why do you need LSD if you're truly peaceful and love everybody? Why do you need it to make creative music? You don't if you're using your imagination properly. And not if you have faith in what you're doing. 'To Love Somebody' flopped—but we didn't start flapping about it—we went on and we came up with 'Massachusetts.' We knew 'To Love Somebody' was a good record—so it wasn't as though we lost faith in ourselves. And then we did 'World'—you know you've got to keep going. We're halfway through our third album at the moment and we've still got about another dozen songs to do. We're writing more songs in the studio all the time. We hope to be able to continue doing what we're doing now and being successful. If we drop, it won't stop us trying and trying."[72]

"World" stayed on the charts for sixteen weeks, topping out at #9.

The day after Christmas, the Bee Gees appeared on *Top of the Pops* once more, and closed out the year by returning to Germany's *Beat-Club.* Barry and Robin were knackered. Constant performing, traveling, recording, writing and the wages of fame—celebrated company, sleepless nights, various indulgences, fans and press everywhere—had taken their toll. In the world of music, "nervous exhaustion" is usually a euphemism for "too drugged out or drunk to work." For once, this was not the case. One measure of the stress they were under is that Barry admitted he felt worn out. Robin was a sensitive creature at the best of times. Barry was an iron man. If Barry needed a lie-down, then their lives were stressful.

They flew to Australia for a break and to visit Stigwood's family, but quickly turned around and left. "We should have gone on from Sydney to Melbourne, but the pressure was too great and we decided to fly back to Britain," Barry said. Stigwood had arranged for press and fans to show up everywhere, and the boys couldn't take it. "We didn't know, but our manager Robert Stigwood only booked us as far as Istanbul. He wanted us to rest there for a day. As it happened, we couldn't have gone any further anyway. We went to hospital from the airport for a check-up, and they let us go to a hotel. We stayed in the hotel for a couple of days resting and then flew to London."[73]

Horizontal came out on January 1.

"We did a lot of the production on this album ourselves," Barry said. "Far more so than on the first album. There are a lot of numbers on the first album that we wouldn't do now, so I suppose the second album is a progression. We try to progress naturally without going out of our way to do ridiculous things for the sake of different sounds."[74] "On the new album, there is more of the group and less orchestrated things than on our first album." Robin said. "There's none of that seven hundred piece business—just a mere string quartet, occasionally." "It's the same kind of things as we've been doing all along." Barry insisted. "We've not changed that much since the first album! We'll still keep on doing the same type of music—and we hope eventually it'll be recognized here—but it's not lots of word messages, not like Dylan or somebody like that. People find it more fun to live in fantasy." "I mean look at most people," Robin said. "They wake up in the morning and they say, 'Today I'm going to face the world,' and by the afternoon they're ready to commit suicide! They hate reality." Maurice, who seemed to be rooting hard against reality, said, "If you're not in reality, then you don't have to face your trivialities."[75]

The reality was that critics were unimpressed with the record. Robin's description is an exercise in denial of reality—the album is drenched in strings, to its detriment. "To comprehend the Bee Gees is to comprehend much that is banal, without grace, and trite," wrote Jim Miller in *Rolling Stone*, overstating the case but encapsulating US critical opinion. "Hell-bent on sounding pretty, defiantly reactionary and out no doubt for the bread [money] and popular air-play, the Bee Gees have their game down very well."[76]

Critics often painted the Bee Gees as false and mercenary even though their early albums were desperately earnest. The boys wanted to write hits, but so did everybody else with a record deal. The press party line became that the Bee Gees somehow operated on a lower level of authenticity than other bands with their sales. It's the single most unfair aspect of how critics viewed them, and that view has unfairly endured. It shows, too, how little attention their strongest critics paid to their music; not to their clothes or image or haircuts or presentation, but to their music.

Horizontal set patterns that would endure: a Bee Gees album will have at least three great pop songs—a couple of hits and at least one sadly overlooked gem—and the rest will be filler. Some of the filler will be ornate and strained, some overly simple. The hits will have hooks; the filler meanders. "Lemons Never Forget," "Day Time Girl" and "Earnest of Being George" are Beatles-esque, with a heavy drum sound and quavery vocals. "George," as close to rocking as the Bee Gees ever got, is a mélange of "Hey Bulldog" and "Eleanor Rigby," with fantastic, backward-Ringo-like, heavily treated drums. "Massachusetts," "Really and Sincerely" and "And the Sun Will Shine" leap out from the rest. "Really" is a Robin opus: tortured, beautifully realized and stunning. "Massachusetts," like "Words," is pure pop, beautifully arranged, unforgettable and free of decoration. Robin's "And the Sun Will Shine" furthers a recurring pattern. Every Bee Gees record will showcase one of Robin's over-the-top orchestral confessionals of pure crazy emotion, a commitment to anguish and sincerity that only an eighteen-year-old genius could produce. Otherwise, the songs with hooks are irresistible; the songs without are hard to sit through. *Horizontal* went to #12 on the US charts and #16 in the UK.

As the saying goes, you get twenty-five years to make your first album, and a year to make your second. In the Bee Gees case it was barely twenty—for Barry—and a little less than six months. To create even two great tracks on a second major-label album is a worthy accomplishment. "I've been listening to our album, and listening to other albums to compare it," Vince said. "I find that on most albums three, maybe four, tracks are good and the rest are pretty well rubbish. There are only about two tracks on our album I don't like." Here, Vince demonstrates prudent denial of his own reality. "You try to give people quality all the time and you benefit from it in the long run. If people like you and go out and buy your singles, you should not put out rubbish on an LP."[77]

But fourteen songs are a lot, and a few, of necessity, must be rubbish.

In the buildup to the release of the "Words" single, Barry said: "We were not striving for originality, but for melody. I think pop people have been ignoring melody."[78] "We always keep the public in mind when we do a record," Maurice said. "We'll never progress from melody. Nobody knows what commerciality is, if people can whistle a melody and keep it going through their minds, that's enough."[79]

"Words," a straight-up romantic ballad, sincere with a little frosting of cornball,[80] came out on January 26. In the UK it hit #8, but in the US made only #15. The band regarded "Words" as a near failure. "I thought it would have been a bigger hit than it is, because it is very commercial, as commercial as 'Massachusetts,' and basically it is on the same lines," Vince said. "I thought it would have been a No. 1." "We set our own trends," Robin said. "We avoid influences. We never look for ideas. You look for ideas and you become unoriginal. You leave your mind open."[81] "We don't like anything to do with trends," Vince echoed.

It's a tough stance, insisting that they ignored trends, when to listeners and critics, the effect of their influence was obvious. "The Bee Gees are to the Beatles as Cliff Richards was to Elvis Presley," writes Miller, wrong-headedly dismissing their originality. He argues that the Bees Gees' music represents a "virtuoso codification of British group conventions."[82] He means that the Bee Gees do a great job of synthesizing the conventions of British pop: strings, Beatles harmonies and production, twee psychedelia, melodrama and "no bullshit here, just unblushing romanticism." Miller misses the point. The weak Bee Gees cuts might fall prey to his list of symptoms, but the strong ones prove him wrong. Being wrong did not stop Miller's view from becoming the prism through which American critics viewed the Bee Gees for decades to come.

In mid-January, Lulu was a bit smitten with Davey Jones of the Monkees. They wrote one another and spoke on the phone when

Davey was able to sort out the time difference between LA and London. Maurice was chasing Lulu by phone as well. He flew to Las Vegas to see Lulu and then flew back to Germany to do a TV show with the band. "A few days after that," Lulu wrote, "Stigwood was quoted in the press saying I was madly in love with Maurice and had pictures of him plastered all over my walls." Lulu knew exactly what Stigwood was up to. "I called him and raged down the phone. 'How dare you use me like that? I'm not stupid. I know what you're doing' . . . I slammed down the phone."[83]

Stigwood was both trading on Lulu's name to get the band more publicity and pressuring her to give in to Maurice. Lulu gave Maurice hell even as she acknowledged that he wasn't behind the ruse. Lulu feared the atmosphere of manipulation and control she saw around Stigwood. When she did a two-week stand in London, Maurice showed up every night.

While Maurice chased Lulu, Barry chased fame, for himself and for Stigwood's other clients. In an interview with *Melody Maker*, Barry dissected the current state of pop music. "It's not groups that are selling records now—it's songs," he said. "If the Stones recorded something bad, it wouldn't go. People are buying the song: the performer is almost incidental now. They'll [*sic*] be a lot of new groups making it in a big way this year and a lot of the established ones will fall by the wayside. I think the Traffic and the Cream will really be big this year. (Both Traffic and Cream were managed by Stigwood.) The Cream will establish their place as the world's number one blues group. It's still possible to make it big in the pop world, if the group is good and they are promoted properly. After all, good promotion is the most important thing, as well as the material.

"The Bee Gees have set a target—you have to or you'd never do anything. We know what we want to do this year and we are going out to do it. If we fail, we'll set another target and try again. We are confident. You must never feel 'we've made it to the top.'

That's fatal. It's a mistake to become egotistical about success because it can turn sour. We've been lucky. And we're glad that no one person has been singled out of the group as the 'star' or the person at which all the attention is directed. Because the public can build up a person and then turn against him. They are less likely to do it with a group. But the public is fickle and you have to be prepared for it."[84]

As "Words" climbed the charts worldwide, the band never rested. In late January they did their first American show in Anaheim, California. In early February they lip-synched "And the Sun Will Shine" on *The Smothers Brothers Show*, an American variety hour noted for its pro-drug and anti-Vietnam humor and to-the-moment taste in musical guests. Two days later the Bee Gees performed in Copenhagen and Stockholm. In late February, a long series of German shows began that ran into middle March. Their mini-tour concluded with a concert in Berne, Switzerland.

Stories circulate from the European tours of Barry's curious seduction methods. In the Bee Gees' autobiography, a book ostensibly written to burnish their image with their fans, Dick Ashby tells of Barry's carrying a collection of cheap engagement rings. Barry told his potential one-night stands that he had fallen in love with them at first sight and wanted to marry them. He already had a reputation for saying that to every girl he wanted to take home in London. Ashby tells of multiple German girls showing up backstage, each wearing a ring and trying desperately to see Barry. It was up to Ashby to put them off.

Why did Barry think the girls needed extra convincing? Did he not know, or not want to own, how big a star he really was? All Barry had to say was: "Hi, my name is Barry." His Alpha-ness with the band seems at odds with his romantic technique. Those around him knew he hated to give bad news in person. He might tell people exactly what he wanted them to do, but he preferred to have proxies swing the hammer. Maybe he thought his conquests needed an excuse to sleep with him; maybe he couldn't bring himself to simply say: "Do you want to come back to my hotel?" Or maybe it goes to Barry's refusal to deal with emotion in his music. Maybe Barry had to conceal his motives, no matter what the situation. Or maybe he got off on deception.

That such a story—and a later story about their real reasons for cancelling a long-awaited tour—appears in the Bee Gees' official autobiography illustrates their career-long juxtaposition of ill-conceived oversharing and dunderheaded transparent image-polishing. They never figured out how a spoonful of truth helps the hype go down or how a wagonload of hype hides an unpleasant fact. They never learned what not to say, and seldom understood the effects of what they did say. In other words, they began, and remained, clueless.

Lynda, Barry's future wife, told of the aftermath of one of Barry's tour conquests. "Barry was doing a TV thing. I was at home feeling a bit flat, so I was in a scruffy old dress and wearing no make-up. The doorbell rang. We lived in a penthouse and the door wouldn't open unless I buzzed the person in. You could look through this eye and see who it was. I saw this chick there and thought: 'Oh!' because she looked as if she was expected. I opened the door and said: 'Can I help you?' She said: 'Oh yes I have come to see Barry.' I knew there was some press expected that afternoon so I said 'Come on in—he won't be long.' She made herself very at home, took her coat off and threw it over the chair. She lies back on the chair and says: 'Barry and I, we are so in love.' Biting my tongue, I said: 'Oh really?' She said: 'Oh we had such a wonderful time last night at the *Top of the Pops*.' I said 'Oh, you did, did you?' Getting very mad. She said: 'Are you the girl who answers the phone and does things for Barry?' I answered: 'I've just stopped.' I got on the phone. 'Who is this girl?' I screamed. Keith, Barry's assistant said: 'What are you talking about?' I said: 'The girl who had such a wonderful time with Barry. I'm going to pack my bags and go. Then Barry came to the phone and said: 'Are you all right, love?' 'Barry,' I said: 'There's some Swedish girl telling me about you and her last night.' He said: 'Oh, she arrived at *Top of the Pops* last night, it wasn't my fault. It happened on a tour before you were around. I said, like I usually do: 'When you come to England, come to see me.' I said: 'I don't believe you.'" Barry eventually managed to persuade Lynda that he was telling the truth.

Lulu went to LA and indulged in romantic dinners and long nights of "necking" with Davey Jones while they tried to figure out if they were going to become a couple. At the time, Monkee Peter Tork's LA swimming pool was surrounded daily with lounging naked girls waiting to be taken up by any Monkee who passed. When it came to Lulu, Jones showed remarkable patience.

On March 17, the Bee Gees were in New York for that crucial rite of passage, *The Ed Sullivan Show.* "Maurice got locked in the toilet of the St. Regis Hotel," Robin said, "and we only just got him out in time." Sullivan's variety hour had introduced Elvis and the Beatles to mainstream American audiences. It was at that time the single most important entertainment marketing venue in the country. Sullivan seemed comatose, a not unusual state for him. "I think Ed had some kind of dementia," Robin said, "because he introduced us with the words, 'And now, a great group from England: Cary Grant.'" Actually, Sullivan introduced the band as "a great soloist, Barry Gibb." "He really didn't seem to know who we were," Barry said. "He would say things that made no sense, these strange statements, as if there was something wrong with him."[85]

Robin slumps at the piano, hair hiding his face, with a sheepish grin and limp hands on the keyboard, looking like the biggest dork in the universe. Maurice sports a Keith Moon bowl haircut and a tight, shiny, bright-green Mod suit. Despite that description, he looks really good. Barry, in a screaming light-blue blazer, leopard-pattern waistcoat, yellow high-collar shirt and maroon ascot tied at this throat like a necktie, is the total pop—not rock—god, a young version of Englebert Humperdink. The band disinterestedly feigns playing to the recorded track. Barry's flanked by a string and horn section, all faking it like mad. Barry sings live, though, which took courage. The band, with nothing to do, comes off awkward as hell. Barry, radiating confidence, nails it.

Lulu watched the show from her hotel room in LA, worrying that Maurice might have heard about her carrying on with Davey Jones.

In late March, the band released "Jumbo" as their new single. It tanked, reaching only #25 in the UK and #57 in the US. It's a lightweight nursery rhyme and shockingly insubstantial after the weight and power of "Words." It was the worst possible choice for a follow-up single. Andy Warhol famously said: "Always leave 'em wanting less." Stigwood—whether he heard Warhol say it or not—always operated via excess. He abhorred a vacuum, and kept singles rushing to market not one after another, but one atop the other.

"Any criticism of 'Jumbo's' failure is really my fault," Stigwood said, speaking the truth. "I pick their singles and so in this case it was my judgment at fault."[86] "I can only lay it down to one reason," Robin said, "Not because it was the wrong choice of song, it wasn't the wrong choice and could easily have been a hit. But (a) because we released it while 'Words' was still in the Top Thirty and (b) because we were releasing too many singles far too fast, which gets people confused." Robin's right about (a) and (b), but wrong about the rest. "Jumbo" shows a lack of perception of the band's strengths, and what audiences liked about their earlier singles. "You see," said Colin, "the Beatles will put out a record which isn't obviously commercial and takes a lot of plays. People feel obliged to play it and play it until it clicks. For other groups, us included, if a record isn't obviously commercial at first they won't play it again and again."

Barry, changing his tune from a few months before, when it was all about the song and not the group, said: "I think something's changed in the past year as regards groups or any artists because you can have a flop record and still retain the popularity you had in the first place. Because the kids now pick a group they like and then buy the song if they like it. If they don't like it, it doesn't mean they don't like the group. There are usually dozens of kids around our door and those kids haven't faltered in any way. They haven't drifted away because we've had one record that hasn't done well. They're still there and they're waiting for the new single."[87]

Stigwood might have been a little distracted. He was preparing to open his own production of the groundbreaking hippie musical *Hair*—with its notorious all-nude finale—in the West End of London in September. *Hair* would go on to run for five years.

The band played England's holiest of holies, the Royal Albert Hall, in late March. Sharing the bill were the Grapefruit, the Foundations, and Dave Dee, Dozy, Beaky, Mick and Tich. The last six names were, in fact, one group with a long handle and two million-selling singles. They gained an extra moment of fame when their rocking hit "Hold Tight" provided the soundtrack for a spectacular car crash in Quentin Tarantino's exploitation-redux, *Death Proof.*

The Bee Gees were accompanied by an orchestra, a hundred air force and army brass players, and a hundred-person choir "who appeared vastly amused at their inclusion."[88] When the Bee Gees hit the stage, their women fans ran screaming down to the front and stayed there, shrieking throughout the show. One rather pissy critic wrote: "The Bee Gees are a precocious talent who deserve to be encouraged to realise their full potential, but there is really little point in having a 67-piece orchestra (two harps!) if you are going to drown them with amplified guitars and the incessant screaming of several hundred fans."[89] "We really did not expect all that excitement. You have to remember our previous concert was at the London Saville Theatre which was very sedate," Barry said. "We just did not know what to expect. We made a tremendous effort to give fans value for their money. We proved that we could produce the live sound on our albums on stage and draw a big crowd."[90]

In April, Stigwood recruited Johnny Speight, a many-credited British sitcom writer, to write the screenplay for a film, *Lord Kitchener's Little Drummer Boys.* Stigwood, as executive producer, had a £500,000 budget and the Bee Gees were to write six new songs for the film. Speight also had "major roles" for the Bee Gees in a TV special called *If There Weren't Any Blacks, You'd Have to Invent Them,* which had been commissioned and then decommissioned by the BBC for being "too offensive."[91]

"We are not going out to do another pop group in a film feature," Colin said. "We all play different characters, but we are not aware of the details because Johnny Speight is still sitting in his bath typing the script." Speight, with a little desk hanging from the rim, really did type in his bathtub. He claimed it unleashed his creativity. Stigwood responded to criticism of both projects by saying: "This business is rife with jealousies and frustrations and little managers whose groups are still 'puddling' around obscure ballrooms. Many of them are jealous of the fact that this group is going places and has places to go. They have a tour of America and Japan soon after this British tour is completed and a $500,000 film to start work on."[92] It all came to nothing: no movie, no TV show and the American tour was scaled back.

Between the Royal Albert Hall and mid-May, the Bee Gees did over thirty shows around England and Scotland. The pace never let up. In May, they won the prestigious Ivor Novello award and did three concerts in Ireland. When they stopped touring they went straight back into IBC to cut songs for their next record. Stigwood was busy planning a major tour of America to begin in August. The tour was timed to the release of their next album, *Idea*, and its first single, "I Gotta Get a Message to You."

The Bee Gees set out for their first tour of America with high expectations. Everywhere they went in Europe they were mobbed; girls lined up by the thousands outside their hotel rooms; their singles hit the top 20 in every European country. They had good chart results in the US and had done the necessary television and concert groundwork. The band booked a thirty-piece orchestra for every show and was guaranteed a million dollars for the tour.

They were to be bitterly disappointed.

The first shows, in Los Angeles and Sacramento, were sparsely attended. San Francisco was little better. "I Gotta Get a Message to You" was released in the US between the Sacramento and San Francisco shows. Though the song became their next #1 in the UK and scored a #8 in America, it did nothing for ticket sales. The one bright spot was a sold-out concert in a howling rainstorm in Forest Hills, Queens. Bee Gee fans stood in the downpour for the duration, screaming and cheering as they had in England, Ireland, Sweden, Denmark and Germany. The drenched fans' love and stamina raised the Bee Gees' spirits. But after one more empty hall in Providence, Rhode Island, Stigwood pulled the plug. Phoning around the country to cancel shows, he could hardly admit to the world that the US public had no interest in paying to see the Bee Gees. Such brand damage might be fatal. Stigwood fell back upon a tried and true solution to disappointing ticket sales: nervous exhaustion.

Robin took one for the team, though he was pretty exhausted at the time anyway. Stigwood made the announcement: Robin was nervously exhausted. He had to go home and be taken care of.

One amusing aspect of this deceit is that books and websites that describe Stigwood's ploy are careful to say "rumors persist" that Robin wasn't really sick. But it's the farthest thing from a rumor; the Bee Gees state plainly—in their own authorized auto-biography—that sales were disastrous and that Robin faked exhaustion to save the band from disgrace.

The Bee Gees would—Stigwood told the world—in the name of brotherhood, regretfully bail on the tour, eat the financial losses and make plans to return when they could. "I hope we will be able to pick up the tour somewhere along the line," Stigwood told the press, "and play the missed dates later. But I can't say anything until I have conferred with Robin's doctors."[93]

odessa

The late Sixties were the worst time to be a pop star.

—Robin Gibb[1]

In late September, "I Gotta Get a Message" peaked at #8 on the US charts and held that spot until October 19. Robin had written most of it; the song sprang from a lover's quarrel with Molly. Robin, longing to speak to her, wrote of his yearning from the next room. Barry honed the song with an eye toward offering it to Percy ("When a Man Loves a Woman") Sledge. As with "To Love Somebody," Barry's instincts were spot on; Percy's version, recorded years later, is definitive.[2]

Robin sang lead, a fact not unnoticed by Robin, Barry or Stigwood. Tensions were building. Who was the boss, who was the star, whose ideas would dominate and who got to sing lead?

"One of the other things was the difficulty over composer's credits for songs," Barry told Australia's *Go-Set* magazine. "One of us would write a song which would go down on the record with B., R. and M. Gibb credited; that's okay, the same as when Paul McCartney writes a song and John Lennon automatically gets a credit. The problem comes when the song becomes a hit, then that person who actually composed it realizes that, not only is he missing all the prestige of having individually written a hit song, but he's also missing two-thirds of the royalties as well."[3] And usually, it was Barry who wrote most of the songs.

Work began on *Odessa* in late July 1968. Cream's *Wheels of Fire* came out in July and lit up the charts. *Wheels* was a double album. The Beatles' upcoming *White Album*, which would be released in November, was a double album. The Who's *Tommy* was going to be a double album. Stigwood urged the Bee Gees to make a double album. Worse still, he requested one with a concept.

"*Odessa* was an attempt to do a rock opera," Barry said. "It turned itself into a bit of a mish mash, but our intentions were honourable. We wanted to do something that could be put on stage. There was supposed to be a thematic thing, but it kind of wandered off into the distance."[4]

Odessa's concept wasn't the only thing wandering off into the distance. After the cancelled tour, Vince spent a week playing at Atlantic Studios in New York. When he got back to the UK, he was ready to leave the band. There are few songs not written by a Gibb in the Bees Gees' discography, but Vince had a track on *Idea*, the rock and rolling, early Stones-ish "Such a Shame." Vince sang lead—an even more rare occurrence in the Bee Gees canon—and the song features an uncharacteristic blues-harp break. It doesn't sound like anything else on the record. "Shame" appeared on the UK release of *Idea*, but was omitted from the US edition in favor of "I Started a Joke." Vince couldn't argue with the commerce of that decision from the Bee Gees' vantage, but the omission cost him a lot of money, and it rankled.

"He'd have to be mad," Stigwood said, meaning "insane," "to walk out on a successful venture like this."[5]

"I have never really felt 100 per cent a Bee Gee," Vince said. "Because the talent that I have doesn't come up to the standard of the Gibb brothers' talent and I don't think I am adding as much as they are. I realise that my ideas don't augment their ideas."[6]

Vince worried that he wasn't getting enough solo guitar breaks and that his chops might be slipping. He wanted to play more. That not unreasonable desire foreshadowed similar desires from everyone else in the band.

"Vince felt stifled because the rest of us are only interested in playing commercial numbers," Barry told the press. "It's no good having somebody in the group who's not really with you."[7]

Vince had his complaints: "The first three albums were really rushed," he said. "We never spent much time on arrangements or perfecting sounds. The boys would come to the studio and work up a song with Barry's guitar and the three voices, while Colin and I played chess outside. Then we'd all record the basic tracks. Bill Shepherd would take away acetate and write the string parts. Occasionally Stiggy (Robert Stigwood) would come in and say: 'More strings here,' but generally he let us do our thing."[8]

Vince's leaving worried Colin. "I think Maurice felt it as much as I did," Colin said. "But I don't think I'm any more on my own now Vince has gone. Possibly if we went on tour I would feel more of an outsider. None of us see each other much and I see Maurice more than the others. It's a job and you're with each other enough when you're working. To be together all the time could be bad for a group." Colin was not going anywhere, if he could help it. "I think visually the drummer is important in a group. Vince's leaving did more damage than people think and the Bee Gees couldn't stand another person leaving. It wouldn't be possible for any of us to leave now without breaking the group up."[9]

As feelings worsened between the brothers in the studio, Barry gave an interview in early September that fanned the flames. "Sure, I'm leaving the Bee Gees," he insisted. "I'm going into films. But it will be at least two years before it happens. I had film offers about four weeks back when we came home from America," he said. "I can't be specific but they were strong, attractive offers. I don't want to do it now, but today is the right time to think about it."[10]

This was not what the two not-so-movie-star-looking brothers wanted to hear—that their fearless leader intended to abandon them for Hollywood. Barry made it clear that only a legal quibble, not band or family loyalty, stood in his way.

"I have to fulfill contracts for the next two years," he said. "So the Bee Gees won't be splitting for at least two years. I wanted to move into films before I got too old to make pop records. And, let's face it, that can happen."[11] I'd like to do whatever I'm capable of doing, writing or acting."[12] Then, in case Barry hadn't been a big enough dick about it already, he told the *New Musical Express*: "I shall honour all contracts, but will not sign any more as a member of the Bee Gees."[13]

To underscore his independence, Barry produced a single for new Stigwood signees, the Marbles. The Gibbs wrote "Only One Woman," which reached #5 in the UK. It was the Marbles' only hit.

To stop the band from communicating through the press, Stigwood weighed in, cool and businesslike: "I already have commitments for the group running well into 1970," he said. "We are hoping Barry can be persuaded to change his mind."[14] When asked how his brothers might feel about him bolting, Barry said: "They know that no group lasts forever. Can you see us like we are now when we are all thirty? I could not leave pop music altogether. I love making records; I love making music; I love writing songs. It's like the sex force. I like every part of the pop business—though I'm sick and tired of backbiters."[15] The backbiters in this case were likely the Marbles, whom Barry had found insufficiently grateful for his efforts and their #5. Apparently the Marbles talked smack about Barry to the English music press. They never charted again.

Someone inside the studio at this time said: "There was intense rivalry and in-fighting—major ego-clashes which were fed, used and manipulated."[16]

Barry made things worse: "I want to get out of the pop business because it's too petty," he claimed. "There's too many little people trying to talk big! A film star is more solid. Pop singers get no respect. Their lives are filled with drugs, bawdiness and no religious beliefs. They don't know anything about the rest of the world, just their own narrow little lives. The men behind the desks in the film business are more realistic."[17]

In the meantime, the band was groping through *Odessa* and running off to play concerts here and there. Robin and Molly grew ever closer to marriage and Barry ever nearer to divorcing Maureen. He and Lynda were living together.

In the studio, the arguments boiled down to who could impose his will on the others. If *Odessa* ever had a concept, it got lost in the logistics of whose song would get worked on and who would sing what. Vince claimed that Stigwood believed that "Barry's voice worked better on the hits."[18] But Robin sang lead on "Message," which had staying power in the charts. Seeking some kind of order, Stigwood appointed Barry as "coordinator." That pissed off Robin and Maurice all the more. Barry had always been their boss—they'd looked up to him and followed him. Now, in their view, they were grown men and wanted equality. Barry behaved as if nothing had changed. The twins became resentful.

As they bickered and created and played live, sang and played and feuded with no escape from each other, Colin ran the brothers down: "Robin is temperamental and highly strung. He won't take criticism. Maurice is a different character—a sort of romantic figure. Barry is easy going and not as single-minded as Maurice or Robin. He changes his thinking to the situation. As brothers they are alike in a different way, a vague sort of way. I'm not like any of them. I'm tighter with money than them, in that I worry about the future. The brothers mostly live for the day."[19]

As always, the guy with no piece of the songwriting or publishing has to be tighter with money and can't "live for the day." "I am closer to Maurice," Vince said. "Maurice takes interest in the interests I have apart from the group. He'll come over and we'll wash my car together, which I cannot imagine Robin or Barry doing."[20]

Barry washing anybody's car, including his own, is not an image that comes easily to mind. Vince was closer to Maurice because Maurice had chosen to become the middle brother—the conciliator communicating both ways in every struggle: between Barry and Robin, between Robin and Vince, between Vince and Barry. Maurice would end up stuck in that role the rest of his life. It did him little good.

"Maurice learned to play chess," Colin said. "Barry would get as far as the pawns and give up and sit down to write a song. Maurice will listen to me if I have musical interests that are not à la Bee Gee." Colin claimed to be the source on *Odessa* of a discernable country music influence and of an imitation of the Band's first album—the Americana-rootsy *Music from Big Pink*. "It was my idea that we do that sort of thing," Colin said. "Maurice listens to what I have to say. Although within the group the okay has to come from Barry."[21]

Maurice and Lulu became more serious. Lulu's friend Joanne Nuffield got engaged to Colin. Lulu came down to the studio at their invitation; Maurice was hanging out. "As soon as I saw him I realised how much I'd missed him," Lulu wrote. "The chemistry was still there, only stronger."[22]

At times, Maurice had difficulty with Lulu's fame. Her fans would besiege her for autographs, then dutifully ask Maurice for his, saying: "Yours, too, Barry."[23] Their romance was a natural for the tabloids. Stories appeared about them daily. The photographers that swarmed Lulu would often yell at Maurice to "get out of the way!" Maurice proposed in October. Lulu wanted a long engagement. Both their schedules were so crazed that neither had time for a wedding, or to be together if they were married. "I really wanted to make it official," Lulu wrote. "I had remained a virgin, despite all the obstacles, temptations and some marathon kissing sessions. The sixties were nearly over. I was nineteen, going on twenty. Talk about now or never."[24]

Lulu's knowing innocence underscores how incredibly young they both were. Maurice was only nineteen. No wonder his and Robin's battles with Barry felt like the end of the world. They were shedding a family model and hierarchy that hadn't changed since they were five. Finding a path to adulthood meant cutting the cord. Barry, naturally, resisted any reshaping of the dynamic.

Stigwood played the father figure in this archetypal drama. Stigwood, unlike Hugh, had power to share and blessings to bestow or withhold. Like the potentate he was, Stigwood made everyone vie for his good graces. The brothers were young enough to fall into that game without realizing they were. "He is a Svengali," Komlosy said. "He dominates you. He dominates your mind. He imposes his will. He is like a father, and the children are all jealous of the father's attention. They all respect and admire him."[25]

Stigwood said of the in-studio feud, as if he wasn't stirring the pot daily: "It was three brothers fighting, and when brothers fight that is really terrible."[26] Despite the battling, there was no letup in their schedule. The boys played concerts in Germany and returned to *Beat-Club*.

Lulu wouldn't live with Maurice until they were married. Robin and Molly had lived together since shortly after the train crash. Barry thought marriage was bad for a pop star's image and commercial prospects. He had kept his marriage to Maureen secret. He feared young fans would turn against him if they thought he wasn't somehow available. He had not lived with Maureen since shortly after he arrived in England. Barry was now always with Lynda and slowly laying the groundwork—or getting up the nerve—to divorce Maureen. Barry had the gall to tell the papers that Maurice and Lulu were too young to wed. Lulu, whose relationship with her brother was mutually supportive, was surprised by Barry's sniping. Maurice, as he had learned to do, ignored it.

In early December, *Odessa* was finally done. "By the end we weren't on speaking terms," Barry said. "We'd go into the studio one at a time. But at least we finished it.[27] "[On 'Never Say Never'] I wanted a line to go 'I declared war on Spain,'" Robin said, demonstrating that, as usual, in-band arguments made little sense to outsiders. When Robin and his demands were involved, they befuddled insiders, too. "Instead Barry wanted something so normal it was ridiculous. He said my words were unromantic. But what could be more normal than a man in love wanting to declare war on anything that was to him unlovely?"[28]

"*Odessa* marked the period when we were breaking up," Barry said. "We weren't talking to each other, so we weren't in the studio together half the time, with some of us cutting parts of it in New York while others were in London. We weren't as friendly toward each other. So the record took three or four months—a long time."[29] "We never got to the end of *Odessa*. I was the last person in the studio with Mike Wade mixing 'Lamplight' and I left before we'd finished. I thought, 'What's the point of this? There's no one else there.'"[30]

For once, the Bee Gees were ahead of the Beatles. Barry's description of their process sounds like what the Beatles went through on the *White Album*: everyone in different rooms working on his own songs; everyone playing and recording his parts by himself; everyone doing his best to avoid everyone else and everyone aware and regretful but too resentful to offer a truce. The Bee Gees were ahead of the Beatles, too, in that *Odessa*, like the *White Album*, was a widely ranging, eclectic mix of ideas and songs that defied any single group identity.

Molly and Robin married on December 4. Both wanted a private wedding, but the press found out and a mob scene ensued. Robin stridently proclaimed his lack of religion; they married at the registry office in London's Caxton Hall. A scrum of photographers and fans awaited the emerging couple. Robin blamed Stigwood. He claimed that most of the guests at his reception were journalists. While Robin and Molly were honeymooning, Maurice and Lulu announced their engagement on Lulu's television special. Robin felt upstaged.

"Robin has an incredible persecution complex," Stigwood said. "He tends to think the whole world is against him. He has no confidence and can be hurt by the pettiest of remarks, which is silly since every artist must expect a few knocks. Robin, though, gets unbelievably upset. For example, if a journalist with whom he is friendly turns round and says something bad about his performance, Robin takes it as a personal grudge against him."[31]

Robin's—mostly Robin's—composition "I Started a Joke" came out on December 21. It went to #6 in the US and was the second hit in a row on which Robin sang lead. Robin argued that the first single from *Odessa* should feature him as well. "Joke" is pure Robin; maudlin, self-indulgent, adolescent, and yet, moving. A perceptive critic wrote of Bob Dylan that he did not use words to make meaning, but instead used words to escape meaning. Robin's lyrics, like those of "Message" or "Joke," make little narrative sense. The Bee Gees don't use words to make meaning; they use words to make feelings. Robin and Barry wrote, with little self-analysis, lyrics that stir emotion.

Robin was quoted on that issue in the *New York Times*: "While other guys, like Ray Davies of the Kinks, were writing about social problems, we were writing about emotions. They were something boys didn't write about then because it was seen as a bit soft. But people love songs that melt your heart."[32]

"Joke" was the last single from *Idea*, a frustrating, revealing LP forgotten in the uproar over *Odessa*. *Idea* suggests the variety of styles the band would showcase on *Odessa*, but sounds like outtakes of notions even more grandiose than those on the later album. *Idea* opens with the now usual caterwauling over strings from Barry in "Let There Be Love." Maurice and Barry harmonize on "Kitty Can," the band's first blatant cop of Simon and Garfunkel. Three full-on warbling tracks by Robin follow — "Indian Gin and Whiskey Dry" suggests new motifs and directions in Robin's songwriting. "In the Summer of His Years" and "Down to Earth" are the usual Robin with orchestration. "Down to Earth" might be Robin's version of a protest song, but the lyrics, even for him, are too opaque to tell. Side one ends with Vince's "Such a Shame," which, like "Joke" and "Message," has nothing in common with the rest of the record. Barry sings lead on four of the six tracks on side two. "Idea" shows that the Bee Gees, at this stage, still had no instinctive grasp of beat or rhythm, which makes their later dance music all the more surprising. Their attempts to rock always fall short, though Vince gets in a few Yardbirds-style guitar licks. The final cut, "Swan Song," shows that Robin could write and sing yearning, but Barry had, for the moment, lost the knack. The band sounds worn out and reaching for ideas. The twin hit singles buoyed *Idea* and it sold a million copies worldwide.

Everything came to a head in January 1969.

Robin thought Stigwood was the instigator. Stigwood thought it was business as usual.

Robin believed he had been promised that his opus "Lamplight" would be the A-side of the first single from *Odessa*. Stigwood instead made Barry's "First of May" the A-side, with "Lamplight" the B.

"We never decide on what we are going to release," Barry said, "until we have finished in the studio. We always let Robert Stigwood decide what to release — he has the knack of picking the right one and it saves any argument."[33] "I worked and worked and worked on that 'Odessa' track," Robin said. "I got a ring from Stigwood to say it was the greatest pop classic he had ever experienced. He said it was stupendous, and I used to get calls from him at three and four and five and six in the morning telling me the same thing. I thought it was going to be the new single."[34]

Barry tried to cast it as a misunderstanding between Robin and Stigwood with himself as a powerless, neutral observer. "I had thought that it might be 'Melody Fair,' but if Robert says 'First of May' then 'First of May' it is, whether it is a flop or a hit."[35] By February, Barry, trying to save the band, backtracked from his talk of leaving. "When I said that it was after the failure of 'Jumbo' and it was a frustrating time. I thought the time had come when we should make some kind of move . . . not leaving pop entirely but going into films. That way you can stay with the kids but be seen by more people. I had the offers and I thought why the hell not— why not for me, why not for the brothers and Colin? Instead of us doing this we have found a more sensible way. Like Maurice was on Lulu's show playing the piano with an orchestra. None of the kids would have expected to see him there without the Bee Gees. Another time it may be Robin on his own."[36]

"First of May" did well, but not as well as "Message" or "Joke." It reached #6 in the UK but only #37 in the US.

Maurice and Lulu married amid a media circus on February 18 at St. James's Church in Buckinghamshire. Three thousand fans surrounded the church and blocked the local roads. Barry, the best man, hindered by the insanity, showed up late. Siblings Andy and Lesley Gibb and Lesley's daughter Berri were among the pages and bridesmaids.[37] The morning after, Lulu was back at the BBC rehearsing.

Maurice was drinking heavily. He wrecked his Bentley convertible, bashed up his face and passed it off as nothing. Lulu was astonished by the constant arrival of checks for Maurice—"some of them for hundreds of thousands of pounds." Maurice paid them no mind, cramming them into drawers and forgetting them. He liked to buy stuff, and his brothers fought to keep up. "The rivalry between the brothers was obsessive," Lulu wrote. "One couldn't have something without the other wanting it, whether it be a house, a particular car, or even a dog. At the same time there was a bond that was impossible to break. They could say anything they liked to each other, whatever the criticism, but heaven help anybody from outside the family who did the same. The boys would immediately leap to each other's defense."[38]

Odessa was released in early March 1969. It eventually went to #10 in the UK and #20 in America. The album is an earful, an eyeful and a handful. The original double gatefold jacket was clad in heavyweight, maroon, fake flocked velvet; the band's name is rendered in gold to evoke the era of *Odessa's* supposed narrative. The velvet had an unpleasant, cloying feel, but it did give the jacket heft. That heft cost a fortune to manufacture, and caused allergy problems for those packaging the record. There are no group photos.

In their groping after profundity, the Bee Gees predicted an era of pretension in album covers and content. The Beatles were moving on, but everyone else seemed stuck trying to match their earlier, more ponderous achievements. *Odessa*, though featuring several stellar songs, collapses under the weight of its own baggage. The endless opening and closing tracks are sentimental and derivative, harder to sit through than "Number 9" on the *White Album.*

Those tracks, and the weaker cuts, though never worthy listening on their own terms, prove fascinating in a career-plateauing, band-imploding sort of way. Somehow glossing over the overreaching orchestral horrors that take up half the LP, Bee Gees' fans and revisionists cite *Odessa* as a masterpiece. As the record stands, it's hardly that. The Bee Gees' gifts don't incline toward masterpiece albums. They're pop synthesists: hit makers. They write singles.

In the British film *Chariots of Fire*, a sprinter—who's wound a little too tight—hires a coach. He tells the coach that he wants to give up the hundred-meter dash and become a miler. The coach shakes his head with rueful insight. "Sprints," he says firmly "are for neurotics." The coach is telling the sprinter: There's too much in your head for you to focus for an entire mile. You're a neurotic and best suited for brief, immersive experiences. As are the Bee Gees.

In the course of their career, the Bee Gees have proven themselves ultra-marathoners of the highest order; no one has shown their stamina over the long haul. But in the studio, album by album, they've always been sprinters: one song at a time. For *Odessa*, each was sprinting on his own.

If *Odessa* had been released as a single album instead of a double—featuring only the best songs—it would be the greatest record of the Bee Gees' career; the nearest thing to a masterpiece they ever produced.

"The Bee Gees' image—adolescent and sentimentally moral—obscures the reality of their artistry and the true depth of their work," Bruce Harris wrote in *Jazz & Pop*. "On the surface, the Bee Gees might appear to be any other Top 40 bubblegum band, augmented by a flashy arranger, an oversized string section, and their own precocious habit for writing lushly pretty tunes."

(Clearly, what makes a top 40 bubblegum band has not changed much since 1970.)

"The problem lies in the fact that the group's image keeps interfering with what the lyrics to many of their songs are actually about," Harris goes on with uncanny accuracy. "The Bee Gees are most widely known through their hit singles which, though often rather morbid for AM Radio ("New York Mining Disaster 1941" and "Got to Get a Message to You"), are still their lightest material. Even in some of their most brooding work, throughout the *Odessa* album, their music remains uncomfortable and paradoxically melodious, thereby belying the murkier aspects of the lyrics. The central difficulty in analyzing the Bee Gees' lyrics is that in order to understand them, you have to forget that the Bee Gees wrote them."[39]

Odessa's title/opening track functions like the overture to *Lawrence of Arabia*; it insists that something big and serious is about to happen. A preciously orchestrated, Beatles-esque, literal-minded story, "Odessa" is warbled (and warbled and warbled) operatically by Robin from the perspective of a lost sea captain, or someone. Lacking lyrical sense, melody and a hook, "Odessa" sounds exactly like something composed by someone determined to out-music his bandmates. Lyrically, it wants to set the stage and context for the songs that follow, but no narrative unites the disparate tracks. While compelling as a curiosity—like the more ornate, "conceptual" cuts or the orchestral/choral tracks—"Odessa" remains pretentious and unlistenable.

Barry's "You'll Never See My Face Again" lays out the family feud and Barry's feelings plain as plain. It's his most bitter song, and, incongruously, one of his most lovely, with a hummable melody and lilting strings. Barry strums that acoustic hard, his anger apparent in every chord, but sings with uncharacteristic relaxation and patience. He cites all possible words having been spoken, all vows having been broken and how he laughs when someone claims friendship. It's over, Barry says, and he won't be around anymore. For a lesser ego, the finality of "Face" would suggest it be tracked as the album's closer. That would not do for Barry. He disassociates himself from the ensuing record and from his brothers on the second track.

On "Black Diamond," a naked plea for inner peace, Robin sings without his usual quaver over—for him—simple, clean production. The song's driven by Maurice's unusually forceful bass.

There's no mistaking the pain in Robin's voice as he sings about someone who's about to leave either him or a place he loves. The song is a testament to the beauty and power of Robin's voice, especially since he doesn't bury it in his usual rococo arrangements. "Black Diamond," Robin's hymn to leaving the band, is placed on the album as an immediate response to "Face."

"Marley Putt Drive," Barry's and Colin's homage to the Band's "The Weight," is a remarkably whimsical collaboration between Barry and Robin, given the circumstances. The song features the drum opening, cadence, vocal patterns and melody of "The Weight." Barry enlisted soulful picker Bill Keith—who played banjo for Neil Young—for that rootsy feel. Barry performs an able impression of Rick Danko, one of the Band's four lead singers. The lyrics—another of Barry's nursery rhyme sagas with an O. Henry ending—are beyond idiocy.

"Edison" is an eccentric, haunting Gibb tour de force; Barry and Robin harmonizing beautifully in an ode to, of all things, inventor Thomas Edison. The arrangements are strange in that Bee Gee way—they sound like nothing else yet register as almost familiar. The melody drops away for a segment of uncharacteristic 4/4 followed by exquisite a capella harmony. The repeated hook of "Edison came to stay" is one of their most unforgettable. "Melody Fair" is twee to the tenth power, a pop take on Fairport Convention and the like, but the chorus offers lovely harmony from Barry and Maurice. *Odessa*'s sophisticated arrangements and shimmering production are a leap forward, and grant even the weaker tracks staying power.

Maurice, too, was developing his own ideas and musical identity. "Suddenly" is Maurice's only solo lead vocal and asks the musical question, which seems appropriate in his circumstance: "How can you tell if humans are real?" It's the most rocking and singable cut on *Odessa*. Maurice's interest in American rootsy sounds is clear, but foremost, "Suddenly" is a perfect Donovan cop; its slow build, thick drums, jaunty guitar and conversational vocals evoke any of Donovan's hits. Maurice's vocal is so immediate and straightforward, sung with such ease, lack of affect and good humor. His voice is a treasure; it's a shame Maurice sang so few leads.

"No record encapsulated the Gibb brothers' majestically skewed pop vision like *Odessa*," Alex Petridis wrote in the *Guardian*. "Which amid the usual gorgeously orchestrated heartbreak, featured mock national anthems, country and western, and a title track that set a new benchmark for their magnificent oddness: harps, flamenco guitars, mock-Gregorian chanting, a burst of Baa Baa Black Sheep, lyrics about icebergs and vicars and emigrating to Finland. Quite what *Odessa's* concept was supposed to be remains a mystery, but it's the kind of album you listen to rapt, baffled as to what's going to happen next."[40]

"Give Your Best" is Barry's further venturing into his concept of American country-influenced roots music. It's a song of further, angry separation. Barry claims he's ready to fight, and will offer his best only to his friends. There's no mention of family. The song, in a departure for Barry, really swings, with a clippity-cloppity rhythm that evokes Tony ("Knock Three Times") Orlando collaborating with Jim ("Spiders and Snakes") Stafford. The vocal melody seems inspired by the New Seekers' "Look What They've Done to My Song, Ma," which was a later hit for Melanie.

"Lamplight" is not as strong a single as "First of May." It's ponderous, with soaring hymnlike harmonies. There's no hook; "Lamplight" takes a while to get to the point. "Black Diamond" feels more immediate and true, but Robin belts out the vocal of "Lamplight," hitting impossibly high notes. The complexity of his arrangement, with its stop-start guitar, would transfer poorly to AM radio or the tinny speakers of 1969 cars. It's not a likely single.

"First of May" suffers from Barry's cornball tendencies, here indulged to the fullest. He cites childhood, Christmas trees and the vicissitudes of fate as the source of a lost and yearned-for Eden.

The strings are unabashedly sentimental, ladled on with a trowel. Lyrically, it's a nursery rhyme, but the melody would make this a much-covered number, one that burrows into the listener's head. In opposition to the frank rage of "Face" and "Friends," "First" is Barry's lament over the estrangement between his brothers, and his fervent declaration that their "love would never die." Barry's superb—and for him, restrained—singing, coupled with the poignant vocals-only fade-out, make the song an obvious choice for *Odessa*'s first single. What's really weird is that "First" sounds so much more like a Robin song than a Barry song. At first it seems reasonable to think that Robin's real beef was that Barry took Robin's song away from him and sang the lead. On further reflection, though—in the prescient words of musical scholar Devin McGinley—"If Barry can demonstrably write in almost anyone else's style, why not his brother's?"[41]

"First of May" was a killer single, a hit waiting to happen. Any objective assessment would conclude that Stigwood was not being unfair to Robin, but making a reasoned commercial choice.

Molly, Robin's wife, thought he was getting screwed. She committed the cardinal sin of band girlfriends/wives; she inserted herself in the process by going public. She spoke to the *Daily Mirror*, commencing a pattern of the band communicating through the press, often to the same reporter in the same article. "Robin doesn't want the glamour," Molly said. "But he does want some credit and is being ignored. I can't take it anymore. Someone has to say something."

"There is a rift between us," Robin told the paper. "I am not on talking terms with Stigwood. I wish I knew where we were all heading. I am talking to my brothers but the relationship has been strained lately and this is not good for the group. As for Molly, she has got the right to say what she wishes although I am not worried about who gets credit myself . . . It's the Bee Gees as a unit I'm more worried about."

Barry, condescending as much as he could, said: "These are the aches and pains of growing up and of life in the pop world. Robin's getting into manhood and marriage has a lot to do with changes of attitude. When you've got a wife you've got her views and thinking to consider. Molly is a nice person and I like her a lot. I don't want to say anything more because she's married to my brother and we're not going to fall out." "I'm sorry Molly feels this way," Stigwood said, in the opening salvo of a campaign to cast Molly as a band-disrupting Yoko Ono figure, "but the rule is I don't consult wives in the business affairs of the group. It is untrue to say we don't give Robin enough credit or that he is ignored."[42]

Robin felt differently. On March 19, 1969, he left the Bee Gees.

"nervous wrecks"

I have no intention of returning to the group. I would rather sweep roads or lay carpets.

—Robin Gibb[1]

etween their arrival in England in February 1967 and their breakup in March 1969, the Bee Gees created, recorded and pretty much produced four albums—*First, Horizontal, Idea* and the double album *Odessa*—while writing every song for every record, save one cut by Vince. They toured, did TV, radio and press, dealt with contracts, saw America and Europe, hit #1, went quintuple platinum, fell in love, married, fell out of love and got divorced.

The pace of their output seems impossible and self-destructive by today's standards, but was considered normal for the time. In the same period, the Rolling Stones released *Between the Buttons, Their Satanic Majesties Request* and *Beggars Banquet*. The Beach Boys, suffering a breakup themselves, released *Smiley Smile, Wild Honey, Friends* and *20/20*. Dylan, who barely survived a frantic period of his own, released only *John Wesley Harding; Nashville Skyline* appeared a month after *Odessa*. Meanwhile, the Beatles, incredibly, put out *Sgt. Pepper's, Magical Mystery Tour, White Album* and *Yellow Submarine*.

Toward the end of this era of frenzied production, the Stones dumped Brian Jones; Brian Wilson, heartbroken over his band-mates'—his brothers' and cousin's—refusal to record vocals for his masterpiece *Smile*, quit the Beach Boys; the Beatles were hardly speaking and Dylan was emerging from a self-imposed isolation. Nobody survived intact. And here were the Gibbs; kids keeping pace with the greats. The strain was intolerable.

The Bee Gees were younger than any of those bands. In March 1969, the twins were only nineteen and Barry twenty-two. Unlike the Stones, Beatles, Beach Boys or Dylan, they grew up as exiles with no home in rock and roll and no understanding of the emerging lunacy surrounding the music. They arrived in the UK as naifs. They landed in the heart of Swinging London, a Darwinian youthquake of music, drugs, alcohol, fashion, sex, young success and the systemized destruction of existing notions of adult behavior. Those raised in England, and more accustomed to its ruthless, unending status wars—like the Stones—functioned well. Others arrived better equipped to star in such a scene. Before Jimi Hendrix hit London, he'd served in the 101st Airborne and played a million dates on the chitlin' circuit backing, among others, the Isley Brothers. Hendrix arrived knowing exactly who he was. The Gibb brothers didn't know shit. They had to figure it all out for themselves, remain productive and cope with an avalanche of distractions.

The Stones, Beatles, Beach Boys and Dylan grew up in the countries of their success, surrounded by family, friends, bandmates—a larger community of identity and support. Scenes coalesced around each band or performer. Each had lives outside their bands, and each had people to lean on who had nothing to do with their music or their families. Not the Bee Gees; they landed in England as strangers from a strange land. Their London community was a product of their success. Throughout this tumultuous time, they only had each other; no safety valves, no completely disinterested allies. It's a wonder they stayed together as long as they did.

Like everyone else in Swinging London, along with money, sex, fashion, liquor and unimaginable freedom, the Bee Gees discovered drugs. "We were known affectionately throughout the music business as Pilly, Potty and Pissy," Maurice said. "I was the piss artist, Barry was the pot-head and Robin was the pill-head."[2] By "piss artist," Maurice means alcoholic. Barry blew his share of weed, though to little visible effect. Robin liked pills. In those days, "pills" meant speed: amphetamine in a variety of forms and doses. If you did "pills" and stayed awake for days, then you needed the opposite "pills" to get to sleep. Those doing speed also did downers. It was a hard cycle to break and regular—or, as in Robin's case, continual—consumption of "pills" did not improve anyone's disposition. Those with a tendency to paranoia or a persecution complex—or those who had to collaborate with others in high-stress situations—grew increasingly sensitive, impatient, unreasonable, suspicious and solitary.

That's not to say that Robin hadn't been put through the wringer by Barry and Stigwood. But when band members under stress are all on different substances, they inhabit different universes, and communication breaks down.

"Robin tried to leave the Bee Gees in a peaceful way," Robin's spokesman told the press, "and bring about an amicable solution, but negotiations finally broke down last weekend."[3]

"We can't even get him ourselves," said an RSO spokesman. "When we phone him," Barry said, "we get Molly and she won't let us speak to him."[4] Barry was following Stigwood's lead—casting Robin's wife, Molly, as a manipulator and claiming that Robin was under her control.

"I picked up the paper like anybody else and I wondered what it was all about," Barry said. "I phoned [Robin] and was told to bugger off. He wouldn't speak to me. Many attempts have been made to contact him but he has made no answer. So we have stopped. Robin wants to sunbathe in the spotlight while the rest of the group stand in the shadows. The things he has said have been extremely rude, from my own brother, and I would not forgive him for that. I would say that he is unwell. He has got a big persecution complex. He thinks everybody hates him."[5]

When Robin wouldn't respond, Barry went after Molly again. "The wife should have nothing to do with the husband's business affairs. I've never got on with Molly. I tried hard because she is my brother's wife. He is being pushed around."[6]

"I make my own decisions," Robin rejoined. "I love her, but my wife is second to me in my own house. Molly and I have a partnership, not a dictatorship. She's a wonderful person and these stories that she's some kind of demon . . . they make me sick."[7]

"Molly and Lulu nearly split us up," Maurice said. "One wife would be jealous if another Bee Gee was getting attention. They even counted how many close-ups we each got on *Top of the Pops*."[8]

Stigwood wasted no time having a writ issued against Robin by the High Court for breach of contract. Stigwood's claim was that Robin was obligated to record and perform only with the band for another two years. This was the same legal hammer Stigwood threatened Barry with when Barry wanted to make movies. Barry had yielded before Stigwood actually got the writ. RSO, Maurice and Barry claimed that Robin once more had nervous exhaustion. They did not want the public to discover the split before it could be healed, and, like a couple going through a divorce, they did not want to lose face by appearing to have been abandoned by Robin.

At an April 27 BBC taping of *Talk of the Town*, Lesley Gibb, the seldom-seen sister, replaced Robin on vocals. RSO told the BBC that Robin had given them a doctor's certificate proving he suffered nervous exhaustion and so could not make the gig. Robin's lawyers weren't playing that.

"Robin Gibb did not submit a doctor's certificate to excuse himself from appearing on Sunday," said Robin's attorney, Michael Balin. "And it is not contemplated that he should supply such certificates for future agreements. His decision not to appear is one which he feels is legally justified."[9]

In early May, Robin told the *Mirror*: "I've never felt happier. I'm broke—but I'm happy. Happier than I've ever been. My health doesn't come into this. My family are involved in a High Court action against me. So how can I answer my door to them? Or take their calls? I hate doing this to them but I have no option. Until the case is heard I can't say a thing to them. I intend to defend the case and tell the High Court all that has been happening. I want to sing on my own, write my own music and create my own little scene. I only wish my family would get round to realizing this. I haven't been 'got at,' as some people may think. I came to my own decision. My family make me feel as if I am the black sheep of the fold, but I have to act for my own good as I see it, and I don't share their outlook on the future. Already I feel free. Free of all the restrictions that one finds as a member of a group. Now I can decide everything for myself."[10]

"The last time I slammed out," Barry said, "was three months ago when I said I couldn't work with Robin again. Since then, he's had the daggers out for me. I didn't know he had left until I read it [in the papers]. He didn't say goodbye or tell our parents he was leaving. That's what annoyed me."[11]

Once Stigwood understood that Robin intended to record, he turned to the *New Musical Express* (NME) as a forum for threats. He wasn't worried about making things worse; Stigwood knew that no matter what happened, the band's public squabbles would only spur sales. In the same issue of *NME*, an RSO spokesman said: "We have not heard from Robin Gibb since we read of his announcement in the newspapers that he intended to leave the group, so it is impossible to see how he can say there have been negotiations. Myself, his brothers and his parents tried to contact him well before litigation started, but his wife would not let anyone speak to him. There is no real reason why he cannot talk to myself, his brothers or his parents since litigants can always speak to each other. Immediate proceedings will be instituted in the UK and USA against anybody who purports to issue a recording by Robin Gibb, in breach of the Stigwood Group of Companies' exclusive rights. It is believed that the proposed recording may contain material by Maurice Gibb and, if so, he will join in any proceedings to restrain the record's issue since he and Robert Stigwood have given no consent. Meanwhile, the action against Robin Gibb is proceeding."[12]

When Robin's lawyer denied the nervous exhaustion excuse, Barry rushed to get his version into print. "He has said that he was not getting enough credit but he never said anything to us. If we had sat down and discussed it . . ." Barry said. "It is getting to the stage where we should be thinking of going round and smashing the door in. If Robin wants to come back he will be welcomed with open arms. But I won't speak to him again unless he speaks to me first. If he doesn't come back we will continue as a trio. There is no question of us breaking up.

"The Press are closer to him than we are. I just get abused. But I would remind him that he only wrote four songs on this new LP. I have been writing for the past nine years. He has been writing only a few years. Over the past year we never argued about him not getting enough credit. I saw something coming because we were arguing a lot. We have grown up together and never been out of each other's sight. Three brothers are not usually like that. That is one of the reasons this happened. Robin was lackadaisical about sessions. He would turn up at the last minute or an hour after we had finished. So we didn't get anything from him to put down. He still has one of the greatest voices I've ever heard. He has a far better voice than I have. And he is a great songwriter too. I don't think he knows what is going on. One day he is going to find out the truth. He has not only made a mistake; he has ruined his career."[13] In June, Maurice took his turn, discussing how he and Barry were getting along, and the state of their musical collaboration. "Barry and I are a lot closer," Maurice said. "We're working much more together. We're having a ball. We know we don't want to split up."

As far as replacing Robin, Maurice said: "We've only seen two people. We're getting tapes from Wapping and Nottingham and Stoke and all over, but . . . we want to get someone who can sing nice, we can take care of the hair and the clothes and all that. At the moment we'll go on as a three piece and if we find someone suitable to take Robin's place, we'll take him on. We're not looking for a copy of Robin. I did the majority of the backings anyway, even when Robin was with us, but there's more work for me now. It's bringing me out more—I do six leads on the next album, before I think I only sang three all told."[14]

In May, the Bee Gees—Maurice, Barry and Colin Petersen—released their first single, "Tomorrow, Tomorrow." It tanked, reaching only #54 in the US. "Tomorrow" is a strange, appealing amalgam: Maurice's opening vocals, the funky beat and the Muscle Shoals–Burt Bacharach horns reflect Maurice's love for the southern soul of Tony Jo ("Polk Salad Annie") White or Joe ("Games People Play") South. The drums are further forward in the mix than in almost any other Bee Gees number; that must have pleased Colin. Just as the swamp groove gets cooking, though, the song comes to a screeching halt and Barry sings over a piano and strings that "tomorrow everybody's going to know me better." The co-written lyrics reflect Barry's worries over the split and his crowing over triumphs he knows will come. It's off-putting, and seems, especially for Barry, a little desperate.

Despite Stigwood's attempt to stop it, Robin's single "Saved by the Bell" dropped on July 12, as Barry and Maurice's "Tomorrow, Tomorrow" faded from the charts. Robin's spokesman maintained that Robin could not wait for a legal settlement before releasing the single. Waiting too long, Robin felt, might make him fade from public consciousness and he would be unable to resume his career.

"The controversy hasn't harmed us," Maurice said, playing the middle brother for all he was worth. "I hope his single is a hit. I wouldn't stop it. I read somewhere that I was supposed to be against it, but at the moment we're all happy with the way things are."[15]

"I have left the Bee Gees," Robin said. "There won't on any account be any get together with them again. I don't regret leaving and I don't think they will miss me. The only thing I do regret is that we couldn't have come to a compatible settlement when I first left. I haven't heard from them for a long time. The reason we didn't talk during the split was because my lawyers advised me not to make contact. The first time I met Maurice after that was at the *NME* Poll Concert in May and we were friendly and chatty. He asked me if I was coming back and I said no. That was that as far as he was concerned."[16]

"Robin's popularity as a solo singer is an unknown entity," the *NME*'s reviewer wrote. "In terms of quality this has the makings of a largish hit. And it should be doubly interesting to compare its chart fortunes with the current Bee Gees release. Something of a do-it-yourself single, this was arranged and produced by Robin and written the night before he went into the studio to record it, just a few days after his departure from the Bee Gees. There are really no surprises. It's very Bee Gee-ish in conception, with orchestra and particularly strings prominent, and Robin sings it in that marvellous tear-racked voice of his that always to my mind made him the most vocally interesting Bee Gee."[17]

"Saved by the Bell" reached #2 in the UK, and only #87 in the US, but Robin took the UK sales as vindication. "I am absolutely thrilled about it," he said. "I always expected it to go in [the charts], though I thought it would either do it very quickly or I would be in for a long wait. But I always had the confidence in it."[18]

Over lush orchestration that evokes Frank Sinatra's arranger (and inspiration to Brian Wilson) Nelson Riddle, Robin opens on a refrain of loss, repeating: "I cried for you," over and over and over, like a man devoured by grief. The rich production and Robin's emotive, straightforward singing—free of his overwarbling on *Odessa*—create an atmosphere of overwhelming inner pain. The emotion, if not the music, conjures up Phil Spector's teen operas. Robin always did obsess about his own suffering in a way Barry never seems to have understood. Perhaps Barry was embarrassed by so much sentiment, and could never present such straight-up anguish in his songs. As Robin intended, his beautiful wallowing in suffering grants the listener a powerful sense of redemption.

Barry was always a human jukebox, pouring out material shaped by the sounds of the day or by his perception of what a song-writing client should be singing. Barry had a gift for being in the moment of current music. Robin's aesthetic sprang from the late 1950s and early '60s. His sound, even when it sold well, was always out of style. His voice belonged in the early '60s. Barry, awash in the sounds of London from the moment he arrived, synthesized and regurgitated everything he heard. He was attuned to trends and adapted them for his sound. Robin paid no attention to contemporary rock. The solo and duo singing models for Robin's vocals and themes were being overtaken by group rock and roll even before the Bee Gees hit England. Robin's evocative—never specific—lyrics and his exaggerated emotion show the powerful influence of Gene Pitney, Roy Orbison and the Walker Brothers. All three sung songs of heartache, emotional deprivation and bad luck in heartbroken voices; all three preferred—no matter what the time signatures—operatic song structures that showcased their astounding vocal range and ability to evoke pathos. As with Robin, their best vocals hover on the edge of hysteria.

No other rock artist would cover "Saved," but it's easy to think of, for example, Céline Dion wielding it to bring down the house in Vegas. The power and beauty of "Saved" suggests that Robin's leaving the band unleashed strong creative forces. It would be ungenerous to suggest that Robin might have held back one of his best songs from *Odessa* for his solo album.

Robin took the occasion of his success to bolster himself in the press. "I could not take the Bee Gees any more," he said. "I felt like a prisoner, like I was in a whirlpool. We used to be compatible on everything and then we started to clash. I'm not saying they became big-headed but I found the simple things we used to talk about were not happening. In Australia we used to work till four in the morning for usually £6. Barry had £1; we got 10s each. On the ship over here we were going to try and become the biggest group in the world. Success changes people and I think it left me alone in the Bee Gees. Where it did change others, maybe unfortunately it didn't change me. There became this false aura in the recording studios where they were more publicity conscious than work conscious. I found myself working by myself for half the time. It turned slowly to hatred after a while because they didn't care if I was interested in the work or not. Their heart wasn't in their work, but it is now, because I have left."[19]

In August, Barry and Maurice released "Don't Forget to Remember," from their forthcoming *Cucumber Castle*. It's a Nashville mainstream country ballad with (legendary Nashville producer) Billy Sherrill–style weeping strings. The lead vocals' put-on drawl sound like parody, but Barry and Maurice were dead serious. Lyrically, it's pure Boudleux and Felice Bryant, authors of

"Love Hurts," and most of the Everly Brothers' hits. "Don't Forget" also evokes the great Mel Tillis, a singer-songwriter who wrote for country star Web Pierce. The critics trashed "Don't Forget," but in the hands of Tammy Wynette it could have been a hit. "If they'd only taken this to Nashville and given it to people who really understand this kind of music," said music critic Jené LeBlanc, "it would have been a #1 on the country charts."[20]

"Don't Forget" got to #2 in the UK but only #73 in the US. Robin told *Melody Maker*: "We never did anything like this when I was part of the group, although we used to jam on this type of number. I think it's great. I've always liked country music. I think it might be a hit. I am not saying that because they are my brothers. I love the arrangement and it is one of the best records the Bee Gees have ever done."[21]

Barry leapt into *Melody Maker* to refute the bad reviews and get his licks in on Robin. "I can only beg to differ with the critics," he said. "They made some pretty insulting remarks—remarks that would have been uncalled for even with a new group. As for your critic's remark that our record 'wouldn't stand a snowball's chance in hell'—then just wait and see. And why criticize it for having a country and western flavour? You may as well be just as critical about Glen Campbell and Dean Martin for doing country and western type songs. But they've had big hits with them. The last Stones record was a flop. They came back with 'Honky Tonk Women' and made No. 1. We don't mind critics, but to use a phrase like 'not a snowball's chance in hell' is a pretty low comment."

Addressing questions of whether he and Maurice would keep working together, Barry said: "Lennon made a film but that didn't mean that the Beatles were splitting up. Maurice is making a film, and I will be making films. We shall be doing a lot of work individually—but we will stay together as a group. Eventually, we shall be going on tour." When asked about replacing Robin, Barry's hackles rose: "A replacement for Robin?" he said. "I don't believe in replacements when someone leaves a group. It doesn't matter who joins when a person leaves, he is never really accepted. Mick Taylor, who joined the Rolling Stones, is not to my mind a Rolling Stone. He's not one of those five guys who started together. He will be accepted by the fans—but the Stones are the Stones, the Hollies are the Hollies, and the Bee Gees are the Bee Gees. We're certainly not desperate for anyone to join in place of Robin."[22]

Shortly after "Don't Forget to Remember" came out, Colin Petersen got fired.

"I did not leave," Colin said. "I was sacked. I was happy to continue with the Bee Gees. We were working amicably together. I got a short letter—not even a phone call. The letter was delivered by a driver. It was four lines and signed by Maurice, Barry and Hugh Gibb—their father. The letter said they no longer wished to be associated with me, therefore my association with them was terminated."[23] "Colin's departure is all part of our natural progression," Barry responded. "He has been spending an increasing amount of time on his management activities, and we have been aware for some while that he would eventually leave the group."[24] "The only way to continue as the Bee Gees is to continue as two people. A lot of songs on our albums haven't had a drummer at all. That's no reflection on Colin, but they haven't needed a drummer."[25]

The next week Barry and Maurice went on *Top of the Pops* as the Bee Gees and performed "Don't Forget to Remember." Colin's attorney demanded an apology from the BBC, telling it that Colin was a partner in the Bee Gees' name and that Barry and Maurice had no right to perform as such without him. The BBC shunted his complaint into legal limbo, and the Stigwood office basically told Colin to piss off. Their statement read: "The Bee Gees will go on performing as the Bee Gees, and if Mr. Petersen instructs any proceedings they will be turned over to their lawyers. If Mr. Petersen wishes to try and form a group known as the Bee Gees, that matter will be dealt with in due course."[26]

"When Colin Petersen joined the Bee Gees in 1967, the brothers Gibb had been appearing under the name of the Bee Gees—which are Barry Gibb's initials—for many years. The brothers Gibb have no objection to Colin Petersen performing under his own initials, or any other name. The Bee Gees name predated him by years."

"Colin lost interest in the group," Barry said. "During the first week of the last recording session he didn't turn up once. He said, 'Call me if you need me.' A dedicated Bee Gee doesn't do that. He also told some press people that he was only interested in the money. He said the Bee Gees wouldn't survive when Robin left—I was never under the impression that Colin Petersen was a fortune teller!"[27] The *NME*, in reporting the contretemps, wrote: "By Christmas it will be THE Bee Gee."[28]

While Barry and Maurice were dealing with Colin, Robin was savoring the rewards of going solo. In late August 1969, Robin received a £30,000 payment from Polydor as part of his £200,000 recording contract. Robin sold his shares in a song-publishing concern to RSO for £40,000. He also wrote six songs for Tom Jones. "I put it straight in the bank," Robin said. "I'm not going to spend it just because it's there. When I see something I want then I will go out and buy it. I don't drink, but I might go out and buy a few thousand records. I'm quite a record collector."[29]

Robin may well not have been drinking, but his amphetamine consumption continued unabated. In September, his parents tried to have Robin designated a ward of the court. Since Robin had not yet come of age, Molly had been signing his contracts. Robin was "surrounded by a lot of bad influences," Barbara said, "and started taking all those pills. We didn't see Robin for 18 months. I think it was something he had to get out of his system—but he worried us sick."[30]

"I am very concerned," Hugh said, "with my son's welfare and finances. I think he is being pushed around by the wrong people. My wife Barbara and I are being kept away from our son Robin. We believe he is almost a prisoner in his own home, and we are consulting with our lawyers to have him made a ward of court as soon as possible for his own good and protection. I believe today my son is penniless. I'd like to know where all the money has gone." Stigwood had apparently given Robin a check for £5,000 just before he quit the group. "I want to know," Hugh said, "where that £$5,000 has gone. I don't want anything. And making him a ward of court is the last thing I want to do." Demonstrating his usual flair for understatement, Hugh Gibb finished by saying: "I have never been a stern father."

"I was told," Stigwood said, "that he had gone through an extraordinary sum of money." "I feel sorry for my father," Robin said. "He is making something out of nothing for himself. I have made my own career, and my own family. For a father to interfere is ridiculous—he is making a fool of himself."[31] Robin further claimed that Hugh had been receiving a 2 percent royalty from Robin's songs since Stigwood signed the Bee Gees.

In September, Robin signed a management deal with Vic Lewis, a former jazz drummer. Molly had to countersign; Robin was still a minor. Stigwood and Lewis went back and forth in the press. "We always take [legal] advice about all our contracts," Lewis said. "And I am satisfied that the one I signed with Robin is completely valid." "I don't think Robin is at all well at the moment," Stigwood replied. "He is not capable of making decisions."[32]

Barry and Maurice began filming the disastrous *Cucumber Castle.* "We have got to have twenty or thirty screen tests in Los Angeles," Barry said of his ambition to be in pictures. "You always have to do them because if your nose isn't the right shape, they'll throw you out. They have to decide what part you're going to play, you can't decide to be a hero. It's a far bigger rat race, dog eat dog. Especially in Los Angeles you have to keep looking round to see if there's a knife coming! I'd like to do a musical film and I would like to do drama, but I feel I need a lot more experience and you can only get that by doing what you know first."[33]

It's difficult to describe the plot or substance of *Cucumber Castle* because no one has ever been able to sit through more than five minutes of it. The brothers cavort in head-to-toe armor; there are comedy skits and songs by Blind Faith and Lulu. Barry and Maurice perform several numbers from their album of the same name.

On September 27, the courts thwarted Colin Petersen by allowing Maurice and Barry to perform as the Bee Gees. "It seems you are asking the court," the judge said, "to destroy something of value for the sake of the wounded pride of a litigant who enjoyed some personal fame under this name." The judge, no stranger to cliché, also said that Petersen was "cutting off his nose to spite his face."[34]

"It's given us a lot of freedom both musically and personally," Barry said. "Maurice and I will become a complete partnership in business and in everything else we do. Out of the whole mess comes the new true Bee Gees. We intend to stick together like glue. There are only two of us now, we don't [want to] be fighting each other. We've [always] been the closest, he's always talked about the personal things with me, he discussed his marriage with me. Maurice and I love ballads, you can't make us do rock and roll. We listen to rock and roll, we like it, as we like all forms of music, especially Chopin and Beethoven, but we'll stick to what we can do with our hearts, not our heads. I write the lyrics and Maurice comes up with beautiful chords. Robin is a strong songwriter and a strong singer, but Maurice is the backbone musically of the group. He always has been. Robin's leaving the group hurt me a lot. It's a shame he's not feeling the same ambitions now that we held together as three brothers. He's left me bewildered but I think his success is fantastic and I hope Colin succeeds."[35]

"Maurice and I could be the Bee Gees for the next five years," Barry told another interviewer. "Though we've given the public a confusing time, we should have the chance to prove that we are the Bee Gees. The Bee Gees are not dead and don't intend to be. I just ask the critics to back off a bit and give us a chance, we want a little leeway. Most of the dee jays and critics crucified the record. They didn't give it a chance. We're still capable of making the same records we did before. They forget Maurice is capable of playing about seven instruments, most of the backing tracks on the records were all him, and I sang lead on four or five of the hit singles. So how can the Bee Gees' sound be finished? Robin has a more heartbreaking sound in his voice, it's more emotional. Whatever he does now is his business. The critics may say we can't do it with the next records. They will, you watch. They've had their fun, but now it's a bit of fun for me. They obviously still don't know who writes the songs. They will realise that we both write songs."[36]

Robin's increasing dependence on speed began to show. He gave interviews that were not exactly public relations gold; they were flat-out hostile. "You should not try to mix too much with your record buying public," he said. "You should talk to them only from stage, through television, radio or the papers because fans want it that way. Familiarity breeds contempt. Once they know you get tired like them, eat and drink like them, get ill like them and breath the same air as them, then you are no better than Harry Blogsworth." He also talked paranoid nonsense. "Britain is making her own nuclear warheads at a secret and very well-guarded establishment near Bath," he said. "They're turning them out like mad, and M.I.5 are behind every tree."[37] Another interviewer commented on Robin "stringing his words together in a bewilderingly rapid flow."[38]

November saw the release of "One Million Years," the lead-in single to Robin's solo album, *Robin's Reign*. "One Million Years" failed to chart in the US or the UK. "Years" is worked to death and structured like Barry's most indulgent numbers. It's incongruous to hear Robin singing what sounds so like a Barry song. Maurice began working on his solo album, *Loner*, in early December and continued through January. He played most of the instruments himself. Maurice's main songwriting collaborator was his brother-in-law, Billy Lawrie, Lulu's younger brother.

In December, Barry sounded weary from the whole sorry saga. "I'm fed up to the teeth," he said. "I'm miserable, disappointed, and completely disillusioned. I'm heading for a breakdown because I have simply had enough from everyone. I don't want any more family arguments. I have taken all I will take and that's it. I started the group when I was nine years old. Would I want to break up something I started? It happened, but it wasn't me. As from today, I'm solo. Whatever Maurice does is his business."[39]

At this point, the *NME* joke appeared to be true: Maurice was the only Bee Gee left.

"I have never been pushing or jealous," Maurice said. "My biggest asset, I suppose, is that I get on with people. I keep my mouth shut and stay in the background."[40]

"I couldn't see them carrying on as a duo," Colin told the press. "I think the public will more readily accept Barry as a solo artist than they would two Gibb brothers who are nothing more than remnants of the Bee Gees."

Barry said he was leaving Britain for America, and that he had nothing left in his bank account, only shares in RSO: "I am reluctant to leave Britain," he said, "but I can't sit here any longer."[41]

"We've always been together up until now," Robin said. "When we found that we had natural harmonies at an early age, we became almost desperate to achieve stardom. We were always enthusiastic and faced with the same situations. There are certain feelings that you can convey only to brothers and relatives. There might have come a time when we'd all have been having a good time together. But that certainly wasn't the situation when I left, and I'm much happier now. At last I've got to make my own decisions, and can attract individual attention, rather than being part of the Bee Gees. There's much more scope, and the horizons are far wider. By leaving, I didn't do anything to jolt the cog of the working harmony. It was for the benefit of all, really."[42]

Robin's solo album, *Robin's Reign*, came out on December 16, 1969.

"I'm completely happy with the album," Robin said. "The only regret is that it couldn't have been longer. The album contains all my own material, including a kind of carol with a Christmas flavour, entitled 'Lord Bless All.' It's not religious really, but simply about winter life, with a lot of pathos in it. It's got a forty piece choir behind it, consisting of forty Robin Gibbs."

"Lamplight" on *Odessa* prefigures much of the material on *Reign*, which showcases Robin's tropes: unchanging beats, exquisite voice, self-harmonies, lots of room sound in the production, orchestral strings, laments for absent love, for absent friends and for missed opportunities. Themes of abandonment run through every song. "Give Me a Smile," peppered with Tijuana Brass horn choruses, includes the lyric, clearly aimed at his brothers, "You may not know, but I miss you earnestly." "Most of a Life" features a quieter arrangement with a lovely melody. For once, Robin directly addresses his wretchedness by citing an event: a woman walking away. "One Million Years" offers a switcheroo—Robin singing a lead that seems tailor made for Barry. The lyrics express bottomless yearning, desires that will never be fulfilled, even if the singer waits a million years for the unnamed object of the song.

In song construction, vocal performance, arrangement and production, Robin joined Scott Walker and Syd Barrett in the avant-garde of pop. *Reign* also evokes the little-remembered work of Curt Boettcher, a producer and writer for the Association ("Along Comes Mary") and Tommy ("Sweet Pea") Roe. Boettcher's grand opus, *Begin*, was released in 1967 and presents heartbroken lyrics over ornate strings and complex arrangements. *Begin* and *Reign* also suggest the lush strings of Brian Wilson's *Pet Sounds*.

Robin's Reign is a heartbreaking collection, overflowing with orchestration. Robin lacks Barry's gifts for melody, hooks and climax. But he surrenders to and owns his feelings as Barry never could or would. Robin hits crazy high notes throughout, belting out at full strength cut after cut. The record feels conspicuously effortful, as if Robin feared this was his one chance to get all his ideas out just the way he wanted. The overproduction seems intended to camouflage Robin's insecurity about any weakness in the material, as if piling on orchestral effects might hide a lack of melody. The massed strings provide an incongruously soft bed for Robin's suffering, and give his emotions great power. They also might be a product of his methamphetamine use. Those on speed love embellishment, get lost in detail and never leave well enough alone. Every square inch of aural space on *Robin's Reign* is packed with horns, woodwinds, strings, guitars, keyboards and endless tracks of Robin's voice.

Even the best the songs seem to lack something, an unidentifiable element, a uniting factor. In one song it might be melody, in another a relief from overproduction, in another the need for a new voice to harmonize with Robin's. This sense of something missing pervades the record, and suggests how Robin's brothers strengthened his work. To make up for what's missing, Robin bombards the listener with more, when so much of the material cries out for less.

Despite all this, the influence of Robin's singular vocals and arrangements on *Reign* can be heard clearly in the future work of many English singer-songwriters, in particular, surprisingly, Cat Stevens's *Tea for the Tillerman*.

Robin put out "August October" as a single in February to bolster album sales.

In late January, the pathos of going solo was made plain to Robin. During New Zealand's first rock festival, Robin performed with a small orchestra in Auckland. He looks so alone, unsure and tiny in the center of a huge, curved outdoor stage. As Robin begins "Massachusetts," vegetables fly from the audience. One strikes Robin in the chest, others whizz past his head. Robin backs up a step, looking deeply wounded, and keeps on singing.

This moment perfectly encapsulates the beating Robin took during the breakup. The ego tradeoffs he faced were brutal: stay solo and get pelted with food, or rejoin Barry and likely never sing lead on a new song again.

"After his triumph with 'Saved By The Bell,' the failure of Robin Gibb's follow-up came as something of a shock," wrote the *NME*. "It also accounts for this, his third solo single, being rushed out so quickly. This casts aside the cloak of quality which has previously surrounded his work, and resorts to sheer unashamed sweet corn. Set to lilting waltz-time, with mandolin effects providing a continental flavour, it erupts into a hummable sing-along chorus. Extremely well scored, it's the sort of disc that strikes me as a logical hit—even though it's a bit out of character for Robin, and his last release was a flop. I think it'll do it!"[43]

It didn't. "August October" fared no better than #45. In April, Maurice released the one song from *Loner* that would see the light of day. "Railroad," an eccentric mashup of Bee Gees strings and loping country waltz, reflects Maurice's continued interest in Nashville country and the Band—though in performance it's most reminiscent of folksinger-actor Burl Ives. RSO put out an early music video, a promo clip to accompany the song. A lyric goes: "'Cause I'm walking by the railroad till I'm home," so, of course, the clip consists of Maurice walking by railroad tracks. The song did not chart, which is a shame. Maurice, with his expressive, earnest voice, doesn't imitate the emotion of a song like Barry, or wallow in angst like Robin. Maurice inhabits his material; he has a wonderful timbre. He was never heard enough.

Robin almost finished a second solo album, *Sing Slowly Sisters*; it was never released during his time with the Bee Gees. Treasured by Robin aficionados for its frank expression of desolation amid lilting melodies, *Sisters'* production echoes *Robin's Reign*, only with more oboes. "Everything Is How You See Me," with its western-movie, theme-song chorus arrangement, is a rare Robin moment, a song of pure romantic adulation. Robin describes himself as existing only in his lover's eyes. "See Me" has a stronger, more commercial and memorable hook than anything on *Reign*.

Sisters' most unforgettable and wrenching track is "Avalanche." Robin sings—in an uncharacteristically high octave—a naked, unrelenting expression of misery and isolation. The production is brutally simple, possibly because this version is only a demo, and Robin intended to add orchestration later. Over a primal drumbeat—which sounds like someone playing an empty suitcase—and strummed guitar, Robin sings multiple harmonies with himself, begging someone to "cure my broken heart" and "free my lonely life." He chants mournfully of change and of things "locked apart." The construction and sound of the song—while possibly a nod to the *White Album*—are simply deranged. Robin never sounded so grief-stricken and unhinged, or stood so exposed. It's a daring, courageous and even frightening piece of writing, production and performance.

The placement and treatment of voices prefigures production methods that gained praise for their forward thinking years later. Robin sings in the foreground as his voice shouts out the chorus and another of his voices speaks under the shouting in the background. This was a signature of, most notably, David Bowie's "Heroes," which didn't come out until 1977. Robin's torment, and his commitment to expressing his internal agony, is almost more than the listener can bear. He evokes and matches other singers of un-bearable wretchedness, like, incongruously, the Louvin Brothers ("Satan Is Real") or Gram ("Hickory Wind") Parsons. "Avalanche" is Robin's least pop, most moving composition.

In July of 1970, RSO went public. The pre-tax profits for RSO had been estimated at $1.2 million, so those owning a piece of the company anticipated a hearty windfall. Just prior to the sale, RSO freed Barry from his recording and management contract with the company. Barry and Maurice remained contracted as songwriters for RSO under a deal that lasted until 1975. That deal paid RSO publishing royalties from anything Maurice and Barry wrote.

The initial share price was $00.90 but quickly dropped to $00.72. Three-quarters of the available shares remained unsold. The offering was a disaster for Barry—who was reputed to be near destitute at the time—and for Maurice. The brothers were the two largest stockholders in RSO among the artists who held shares. It's never been clear what the various RSO artists gave up for their stock, but supposedly Barry had all his cash in the company. He lost £36,000, Maurice lost £24,000 and Robin, who had cashed out before the sale, was also bust.[44] Eric Clapton, Ginger Baker and Jack Bruce—Cream—were also shareholders.

By August of 1970, the corporate financial implications of the split were weighing heavily on all three brothers. Rancorous nego-tiations between NEMS and RSO seemed destined for the courts. There were rumblings about physical threats being made against Robin, and hoodlums turning up who were somehow connected to monies flowing to the Bee Gees. These rumors could be dis-missed as early symptoms of the paranoia that slowly overtook Robin, but hoodlums threatened the other brothers, too.

The Gibbs were learning that without each other they could not express themselves. Nobody was happy with his solo output, or performing without all his brothers. Even Barry, the ultimate unstoppable professional, never got his solo career going as an actor or a singer. The irony is that all their solo work created during the breakup, however it fared in the market, has proven over the decades to be arresting and worthwhile. Too bad neither the brothers nor their audience realized it at the time.

In the brothers' view, their solo careers had failed. The RSO stock sale had tanked. Thugs appeared after the sale failed to meet expectations. The brothers were broke. Maurice was living above a fish and chips shop.

Those unfamiliar with rock economics might wonder how a band that sold so many records in such a short time could be destitute. The answers are simple, and lie in the pitiless contractual practices of pre-Napster rock and roll. (Post-Napster, the financial prospects for 99 percent of working musicians are even worse.) Bands signed with managers. Managers took 25 percent of everything the band made, off the top, prior to taxes or expenses. Bands signed with record labels. Record labels gave bands advances—sometimes enormous signing bonuses—from which the manager, of course, took 25 percent.

Monies paid on signing are advances against royalties—against future earnings. Every penny of an advance must be repaid—or, as the terminology has it, recouped—before the artist sees another payment from a label. A band receives only 75 percent of their advance money, but they have to pay back 100 percent. Taxes took whatever percentage taxes in England took in 1967–69.

Labels have perfected the practice of ensuring that few albums are ever profitable—that few albums earn more than they cost to record, manufacture, package, ship and promote. Any parties the label throws for the band, any promotional expenses they incur, all touring costs, any lunches the label buys for a DJ or music writer: it all gets charged to the band. That's why many best-selling bands are in deficit to their record labels while their managers thrive. And that's why, with few exceptions, the richest people in rock and roll are managers and not musicians.

A musician's strongest source of income is his or her publishing or songwriting copyrights. But from the earliest days of record labels, musicians had to surrender to their label a hefty percentage of their publishing as part of getting signed. For decades, the publishing and copyrights of successful bands funded the speculative signing of all the other bands that would never earn a dime.

The Bee Gees signed away 51 percent of their publishing at the start of their relationship with Stigwood. The most—and it's likely that they signed away other percentages of their songwriting, too—they could possibly earn was 49 percent of their own songwriting royalties. Add to this disheartening formula that the brothers spent like what they were—newly rich teenagers—and it's easy to see where the money went: into thin air.

It was time for a reunion. Part of the thinking was that a reunion would give new life to RSO's stock. "This is a real challenge," Barry said. "One hit from us could change the whole situation. Shareholders and speculators apparently need some confidence. Well, they are going to get it." "All that matters is that we're back together," Maurice said, "and with the same objective—to get the good vibrations into the company." "For some reason best known to itself," Stigwood said, "the City (England's financial market) looks upon the show business world as a poor relation. But we are going to show how wrong the pundits can be and make them eat their words."[45]

Before Barry could fully embrace his brothers, however, he had old business to attend to: Barry's divorce to Maureen Bates was finalized on August 27.

The Bee Gees' reunion was consummated on August 21, 1970. It was announced to the public on August 28. "We had all been together the night before—but with our lawyers, arguing about the same things that we had been arguing about for months," Robin said. "The next day we met in Robert Stigwood's office to carry on the argument, and suddenly it was all over. We threw it all out the window and decided to go into the studio that afternoon. But before we did we had a bit of a thrash with champagne on the roof garden."

"We know that there are people in the business who have to be convinced that we mean what we say," Barry said. "Over the next few months we will be able to convince them that we haven't lost any of the old spark." "Everything had been too emotional," Maurice said. "It had been almost two years since the first signs of a split, but it seemed that afternoon in the studio it had been yesterday. Everyone asks about the rows, but I have honestly forgotten what most of them were about. We reached the stage where we believed what we read before we believed what we said to each other. Now I think we all have more stability, and are more mature. Before we were so wrapped in the Bee Gees that even minor arguments seemed to fill our whole world."[46]

"If you had to find a reason for the reunion," Robin said, "all I can say is that I've been Robin Gibb since I was born, and a Bee Gee since I was six. When I was an ex-Bee Gee all my records sounded like the Bee Gees, because that's what I am. Now it's like being back at school with no worries." In keeping with his role as peacekeeping middle brother, Maurice said: "We discussed it and reformed. We want to apologise publicly to Robin for the things that have been said. We want to stop boring the public with our squabbles and do the music. We intend carrying on with our solo careers but we want to start things as a group again. There will be the three of us and we will use a session drummer. We will go into the studio to record a new single and an album in the near future."[47] "There were some misunderstandings between us," Robin said. "But that's all in the past now." "Individually they are creative people," Stigwood said. "Collectively they are, for my money, the best pop group in the world."[48]

"I think we re-formed because we were tired of being on our own," Barry said. "We didn't split because we wanted to be solo acts; we wanted to be alone for a while because we had been together for ten years. Robin rang me in Spain where I was on holiday and he gave me his views on being alone. When I got back we had two meetings and we realised we had forgotten our original arguments."[49] "We hope we haven't lost the public's confidence," Robin said. "I think we were afraid of losing each other as brothers. When brothers fight it's worse than friends fighting and we were making mountains out of molehills."[50] "Robin and I were the people who really fought," Barry said. "Maurice was always on the outside getting the flak. We two were at loggerheads cause he was a songwriter and I'm a songwriter, and his voice and my voice are different. It was too much for us: who was getting credit on the songs, who was getting voice credit, who should be *singing* what song. Nowadays we don't care, we discuss and then do. But our problems were very destructive."[51]

"There would be a reporter at my door every morning," Robin said, "telling me what Barry had said. The phone would ring at midnight and it would be Barry telling me he'd never said such things. And I wouldn't believe him cause I'd read it in print."[52]

"The 15 months we were split up was the best thing that could have happened," Maurice said. "We were okay separately, but together we're something else. In the old days, when the publishing credit said, 'B., R. & M. Gibb,' and I had nothing to do with it, they would say, 'What's Maurice's name doing on it? Why's he getting paid?' We went through all the little stupid crap. 'Who sings lead?' Who cares as long as it's a hit? I don't care if I don't have a solo track on the entire album. It's still a Bee Gees record. All the bullshit is past; now we can handle it. After almost a year and a half apart, we wrote 'Lonely Days' and 'How Can You Mend a Broken Heart,' in the studio and cut both right away. The roadies were clapping; it was happening again."[53]

"You become famous for the first time," Barry said, showing a new maturity. "You're about 20 years old. You suddenly have more money than you've ever known. You suddenly believe everything you read about yourself. You suddenly believe that maybe you've been sent on a special mission by God, that you have a philosophy for the world, 'cos you write songs, so there must be some great mystical purpose in your being. All of these things are quickly dashed when you've had about half a dozen hit records and you realise that everyone's a bit fed up with you."[54]

"They all learned their lesson," Barbara Gibb said. "Those days frightened the life out of Robin. Now he hardly even takes an aspirin."[55]

"We had a lot of ego problems, and we were green," Robin said. "And the press were saying that maybe Barry should be going into films or maybe Robin should be doing this. We were being isolated by different people who said: you're better doing things on your own. And it goes to your head."[56]

"It was a dreadful time seeing the children you'd brought up not even talking to each other," Barbara said. "Barry kept most of the bad things from us. Even today we don't know half the things that went on." "People talk to me about the strain of the rock world," Hugh said, "and I say 'rubbish.' I tell the boys how we used to play the Mecca circuit twice a night six days a week and all we ever had was a couple of pints in the interval. So don't talk to me about the pressures of the rock world. There's more strain involved in driving a double-decker bus round London."[57]

"We were nervous wrecks at the end of the Sixties: touring, recording, promotion," Barry said. "I was living in Eaton Square and my neighbours must have thought I was a bit freaky. I can remember a time when I walked out my front door and there were six cars and they all belonged to me. That's madness. The break up was a traumatic experience. Long after we fought, the press had us fighting and reopened wounds."[58] "We are best friends with rivalries. We accept that within each other, because that is what brothers are. Now we reached the age when we can see each other clearly, understand each other rather than fight."[59]

"The speed (methamphetamine) took Robin hard and he was seriously ill for a time," Barry told Mitch Glazer of *Playboy*. "The pressure and fame got to Robin. He's a deep thinker with a serious, sensitive side. He gets in moods that last quite a while. I couldn't go as the big brother and tell everyone to calm down. It was impossible with that speed going around. We were too green to see the dangers, the paranoia and illness. Maybe I was guilty. They all said I was responsible. Maybe I could have kept us in line. Maybe."[60]

On September 1, 1970—Barry's twenty-fourth birthday—he married his dream girl, Lynda Gray. Robin had wed his boss's receptionist; their marriage and divorce would become public and desperately rancorous. Maurice had married a pop star; their marriage lasted about as long as a union between million-selling celebrity teenagers might. As the Alpha brother, Barry secured an Alpha wife while his brothers struggled through starter marriages. Barry and Lynda lived happily ever after. No hint of scandal or serious discord ever attached to their union. Lynda usually toured with Barry; they don't like being apart and they're still together. They have five children.

On September 2, the newlywed Gibb bailed on his planned honeymoon and went into the studio with his brothers. As per their prior work habits, they recorded six songs in the first session.

One of the tracks cut the day after Barry's wedding was "Lonely Days." Stigwood wasted no time getting it to market. It's the Bee Gees' strongest, most exuberant song in years. Maybe shedding Colin was good for them—"Lonely Days" has a true rock beat. Opening over a Beatles-esque piano and the brothers singing a Beatles-esque intro over Beatles-esque strings, "Days" breaks wide open into a passionate, joyous sound. A driving piano, handclaps and on-the-one drums support the repeated chorus. Though referencing the loneliness of being without one's woman, the song is obviously brothers telling each other how glad they are to be back together.

Released in October, "Lonely Days" was a smash in the US, reaching *Billboard*'s #3. Worldwide, it went #1.

> "It was a lot nastier in the press than it was in actuality."
>
> —Barry Gibb[61]

"please pretend it's not them"

he Bee Gees were busy. They started recording *Trafalgar* in January. As they worked on "How Can You Mend a Broken Heart," guitarist Alan Kendall joined the band as lead guitarist. In February, they commenced their Two Years On tour in Albany, New York. In March, drummer Geoff Bridgeford came aboard. After a June appearance on *Top of the Pops*, the band set off for a July tour of Australia. In August, they came back to the states to tour in support of *Trafalgar*, which came out in September.

A measure of their joy at reuniting is that in two days the brothers wrote and recorded two of their most storied songs: "Lonely Days" and "How Can You Mend a Broken Heart." Each now understood that he did not have the voice or material to make hits alone. They cherished their collaboration as they had not in years.

Trafalgar opens with "How Can You Mend a Broken Heart," their first #1 in the US. Demonstrating how estranged the Bee Gees were from their UK audience, "Heart," did not chart in their home country. After "Heart," *Trafalgar* is slow paced, orchestral, straining for majesty and mournful. The single "Trafalgar" takes much from the Kinks, which is good news. It's a grand, plodding affair; *Trafalgar* reached #34 in the US and failed to chart in the UK. "They had American hits for a while," Stigwood said, "but the British public was cheesed off. I think the public's attitude was that they were lucky to be so successful."[1]

Barry played guitar on the album and, setting the course for their future records, Robin provided only vocals. Maurice played bass, piano and guitar; he also helped build the arrangements and taught them to the new players and studio musicians. Bee Gees scholar Joe Brennan wrote of this period: "The Gibb brothers' abstract and indirect lyrics deliberately avoided telling specific personal stories. The Bee Gees continued to be much more interested in the sheer sound of a record and the feeling it conveyed as music."[2]

Lulu discovered Maurice's disturbing penchant for fantasy. "I don't know why he felt the need to embellish or exaggerate incidents. Maybe it had something to do with the influence of Robert Stigwood, who never let the truth stand in the way of a publicity coup for the Bee Gees. If you do this often enough you start forgetting what's real and what's invented."[3] In interviews and in conversation Maurice would make up events, pass them off as the truth and defend them staunchly. His refusal to own up infuriated Lulu, who would end up slapping and shaking Maurice, to no avail. He never struck back. Their life was a whirlwind of social encounters and drink. "It wasn't a marriage," Lulu wrote, "it was party planning."[4] Their constant boozing and fighting upset Lulu, but Maurice took it as normal married life. Maurice and Lulu, both performers since they were children, had been deprived of childhood. As the family breadwinners, they never saw adulthood modeled in a functional way. At nineteen and twenty respectively, they had to invent what a marriage might look like. It ended up looking a lot like life on the road.

The Bee Gees spent 1972 touring and wrestling with songwriting. In September, recording began on both *Life in a Tin Can* and

A *Kick in the Head Is Worth Eight in the Pants*. These were intended to be the first releases on Stigwood's new RSO—Robert Stigwood Organization—label. To finish *Tin Can*, the band moved to Los Angeles. The record came out in January of 1973. It did not chart in the UK and reached only #69 in the US. There were no singles on the album. But there are two country-influenced songs, "South Dakota Morning" and "Come Home Johnny Bridie." The latter mimics early 1970s LA soft country-rock and showcases superb pedal steel guitar by steel savant and visionary Sneaky Pete Kleinow. Kleinow played with Gram Parsons and Chris Hillman in the pioneering Flying Burrito Brothers.

Tin Can finds the band reaching for genres in which to hide and writing shorter, more lyrically direct songs. Though it never sold, and was despised by Atlantic, *Tin Can* offers several worthy cuts. Barry's in good voice, and embraces the straightforward material. Maurice plays his usual bass, guitars and keyboards, but does not sing. The fervor of Barry's country rock makes his upcoming forays into modern funk seem all the more unlikely.

After another drunken row in late 1972, Lulu left the marriage. She and Maurice announced their split in '73. The announcement cited an amicable, mutual parting and provoked a firestorm of press and photographers lurking in the bushes outside Lulu's house. A few days later, Maurice contradicted the statement and told the press the separation was due to Lulu's career, that he loved her, missed her and wanted to be with her again. Lulu, enraged that Maurice had broken their privacy agreement, issued her own statement that closed with: "Typical of Maurice is his reported remark that if we met now we would go out and get a drink."[5]

Then, the unthinkable happened: Atlantic refused to accept or release A *Kick in the Head Is Worth Eight in the Pants*.[6] Between 1967 and 1972, the Bee Gees sold 25 million records. Now their label was telling them their new album wasn't worth releasing. "Part of the problem," Maurice said, "was that our manager, Robert

Stigwood, had become so involved with movies and stage shows like *Jesus Christ Superstar*, that he's taken his eye off us, and we were kind of drifting."[7]

Ahmet Ertegun, the co-founder and co-head of Atlantic Records with Jerry Wexler, made a fateful recommendation. Ertegun is rightly worshipped for his musical and business instincts, for his ear, and his understanding of how to put the necessary elements together to make—not necessarily hits, though Ahmet always liked hits—but the best possible music. Ahmet suggested to Stigwood that Atlantic house producer Arif Mardin work with the Bee Gees. Actually, it was not a suggestion.

"When we discovered," Ertegun said of Mardin, "that we had great arranging talent in-house, myself and Jerry Wexler availed ourselves of his services."[8] "In the old days," Mardin said, "someone like Phil Spector had a certain sound, and different artists that he used would be featured within that soundscape, and they were great. I'd usually go with featuring the artists, build the arrangements around the artist. I didn't want to bring the artist into a preset situation. I guess that's why I was able to work with various artists of different styles."[9]

Mardin, over his forty years at Atlantic, produced Aretha Franklin, Willie Nelson, Bette Midler, Dusty Springfield, Laura Nyro, the Average White Band, Hall and Oates, Chaka Kahn, the Young Rascals, Carly Simon, John Prine, Doug Sahm, David Bowie, Culture Club, Ringo, Barbra Streisand and Roberta Flack and is credited with the success of Norah Jones's multi-platinum *Come Away with Me*. He worked with jazz artists Freddie Hubbard and Mose Allison, among many others. As a producer, Mardin found jazz limiting. All the producer does, he said, "is turn up the mic when there's a good solo."[10] Arif understood every kind of music and performer. His heart, like that of Atlantic's, belonged to R&B, a term coined by Jerry Wexler. In the 1950s, black music was classified under "race records," and Wexler was determined to create a less racist term.

The relationship between musician and producer is delicate and fraught. Phil Spector and Motown's Barry Gordy invented their own universes that performers had to fit within. Other producers so understood the essence of the musicians in their care that their collaborations lifted both to new heights: George Martin and the Beatles; Jimmy Miller and the Rolling Stones; Brian Eno and the Talking Heads; Pete Anderson and Dwight Yoakam; Brian Eno and David Bowie; Nick Lowe and Elvis Costello; Elvis Costello and the Specials; Chris Thomas and the Pretenders; Billy Sherrill and Tammy Wynette; Willie Mitchell and Al Green; Ray Manzarek and X; Theo Macero and Miles Davis. Arif Mardin and the Bee Gees would prove a similarly magical pairing, even if it took a while for the magic to happen.

"Our studio tactics had become lazy," Barry said. "We had to own up and Jerry Wexler recommended Arif."[11]

Arif took the band back to London and IBC studios, where they'd done all of their early work. Their first effort, 1974's *Mr. Natural*, showed progress, and proved a transition, but the material is not entirely new. Some of the songs were reworked demos from 1968. "Down the Road" is an almost-traditional blues shuffle; "Dogs," made as the hit single, builds like classic Atlantic soul, with a lagging soul beat, blues guitar intro, "Spanish Harlem" vocals and Young Rascals' piano motif. Robin demonstrates the band's future ability to sing R&B. His vocals on "Dogs" align with the drums—as R&B vocals must—as in few other Bee Gees songs. *Mr. Natural* has a lot of soul, with Barry doing his best Maurice impression. At this point, there's little point in asking why Maurice didn't get to sing lead on songs that suited him perfectly. Despite sincere attempts to create a new sound, and heartfelt material, *Mr. Natural* proved a commercial failure. "When we did *Mr. Natural* we didn't have a positive direction," Maurice said. "We were thrashing about."[12]

On the night of April 28, 1974, the Bee Gees were not in the Royal Albert Hall. They were at a grubby, second-rate supper club—Batley's Variety in Leeds—on a tiny stage. They sang while around them the working-class mums and dads of England's north tried to enjoy the band and the full-course meal they had to order to get into the show. Batley's was the only gig the band could get. "We ended up in—have you ever heard of Batley's the variety club in England?" Barry said. "It was a little club up north, and if you ended up working there it can be safely said that you're not required anywhere else. In those days that was the place *not* to work in and we ended up working there. I remember us talking about it backstage at that place and I said, 'If this is the bottom, there's no further we can fall. Something's gotta happen for the positive.' It was positive thinking that got us back to where we are now, refusing to accept anything negative. It was a frightening time."[13]

The Bee Gees had always been a singles band. When they had hit singles, they sold out shows. When they didn't, their audience went elsewhere. It wasn't only having to play miserable dives that unnerved the brothers. It was the thought that all their work had generated so little long-lasting audience loyalty.

One good thing came of the humiliating tour. After the April 28 show, Maurice met Yvonne Spencely, the manager of the steak restaurant attached to Batley's. He fell instantly in love; Maurice said it was her smile. "There was a pure innocence about her that I loved," Maurice said. "I suppose you could call it love at first sight. I was quite thrilled. It changed my life as quickly as that."[14] Part of his immediate attraction might have stemmed from Yvonne being the spitting image, the young twin, of Maurice's mom, Barbara Gibb.

Despite Maurice's proclamations that he would never marry again, he rapidly finalized his divorce with Lulu—both had been too busy to bother with it. He married Yvonne in Sussex on October 17, 1975. Yvonne was pregnant with their first child, Adam, when they married. They had a daughter, Samantha, and were together for the rest of Maurice's life.

After their week at Batley's, things got worse. Sparse attendance at the Golden Garter in Wythenshaw and the Fiesta Club in Sheffield led to the cancellation of a week at the other Batley's club, in Liverpool. They could not sell out the least desirable venues in England. The Bee Gees' nadir was a grim spectacle.

"We'd lost the will to write great songs," Barry said. "We had the talent, but the inspiration was gone. We decided right then we were going to [start writing again] and, honestly, it took us five years to get to know one another again. Those five years were hell. There is nothing worse on this earth than being in the pop wilderness. It's like being in exile. The other artists treat you like crap. They say, 'Hey, I didn't know you were still together.' You realize they haven't thought of you for years. It's all ego. This whole business is ego."[15]

In December of 1974, multi-instrumentalist keyboardist Blue Weaver joined the band. "The Bee Gees' drummer then was Dennis Bryon," Blue said. "He rang me up to ask if I'd be interested. They'd realised they had to change direction and were trying to inject some fresh ideas. In December 1974, I had a meeting with them where they lived, for tax reasons, on the Isle of Man. I agreed to start work at Criteria Studios in Miami on January 2. [Criteria] had been recommended to them by Eric Clapton . . . We all moved into the house at 461 on Golden Beach and started writing. Basically we'd lie all day on the beach, work over at the studio in the evening, and late into the night."[16]

The band felt comfortable at Criteria, where Clapton had recorded 461 Ocean Boulevard and Layla and Other Love Songs. Criteria would become their home for decades, and Miami would become home to Barry and Maurice. "Ahmet [Ertegun] was so quick to turn off to us," Robin said. "We thought, Fuck it. They aren't even going to give us a chance. They were burying us. Only Arif, of all the Atlantic people, kept faith in us."[17]

"The brief, from the start, was to find a new direction." Blue said. "But the first songs we worked on were in the same old Bee Gees ballad style, and when Stigwood heard the tapes, he wasn't impressed." "One of the first four songs we came up with and played to Arif was 'Wind of Change,'" Barry said. "He took those songs to Atlantic, and they didn't like them."[18] "I got the feeling," Stigwood said, "they weren't listening to what was happening in the industry anymore. So I flew down and had a confrontation with them."[19] "We were devastated," Maurice, said, after Stigwood vented his displeasure, "but Stigwood sat on Golden Beach with us and apologised for having been so distant from us, and said, 'I'm determined to get involved again.'"[20]

When they arrived in Miami the following year, Mardin said, "We started to record and some of the songs were *still* in their old ballad style. But the Bee Gees were listening to American groups, especially R&B groups, and since my background was R&B, I was well suited for the affair."[21] "Arif was incredible to work with," Robin said. "Especially with Maurice. He changed our style of recording. We would start with one instrument and build up from there, as opposed to all playing at once. It is a clearer process."[22]

"The drink and drugs didn't stop when we went to Miami," Maurice said, "but we were determined to change."[23] "It was more about getting back into the music we were always into," said Barry, "which was R&B. When we arrived in Florida, the place teemed with it. Here was a new culture to absorb, to base our music on. That's basically what we've done all our lives. Everything sprang from our deep love of R&B—Al Green, Otis Redding, the Stylistics. So we went to work with Arif and he said, 'I'm going away for a week and I want you to write while I'm away.' During that week we wrote 'Jive Talkin',' 'Nights on Broadway,' 'Edge of the Universe.' All those songs we wrote in one week, simply because we knew that this was it. If this album doesn't work, it's the finish for our recording career."[24] Their career was certainly on the line, that much is true. But, if their love of R&B was so deeply rooted, why did it take Arif Mardin to get them to play it? The Bee Gees had twelve years in which to make R&B records and never did. Mardin saw their potential for funk music and explained to them how to embrace it. Afterward, Barry characteristically took all the credit.

"They started writing different songs," Arif said, "like 'Jive Talkin',' and we had a fantastic rapport. We spent fifteen or eighteen hours in the studio every day for two months and it became like something out of a movie, with everybody being incredibly creative and dynamic. We would try many things, like synthesizers, and probably because of my background with Aretha Franklin and all the R&B greats, I said, 'Hey Barry, why don't you sing a *high* note here?' He said, 'Okay, let me try it.'"[25]

"I asked Barry to take his vocal up one octave," Mardin told an interviewer. "The poor man said, 'If I take it up one octave, I'm going to shout, and it's going to be terrible.' He softened it up a little bit, and that was the first falsetto, which he sang on 'Nights on Broadway.'"[26]

"It all happened in the course of a day's work. So when people say, 'How did you bring it about?' I must say we all did it together. It shouldn't sound like the *Glenn Miller Story*, or something where someone discovers a new sound overnight. The Bee Gees have always had an unmistakable sound. It's their collective singing and beautiful vibrato and their unique solo vocal strengths. There was a happy marriage of their sound and the orchestral strings punctuated by a strong beat, which is part of my style."[27]

"He hears everything and immediately knows what's right or wrong with the voices, the instrumentation and the tempo," Maurice said. "He showed me riffs for my bass I never dreamed of."[28]

"I didn't say 'Hey, sing falsetto, I'd like to invent this sound for you.'" Mardin said. "But there was a melody in one of the songs—

it might have been 'Jive Talkin'' — and Barry said 'Let me sing it in a soft voice.' He sang it in that voice and the brothers and everyone were saying 'That's great, that's great, keep that.'"[29] "It was a revelation," Arif continued. "We had already heard 'Nights on Broadway,' so I could see the new direction. But when Barry walked in with 'Jive Talkin',' it proved we were on the right track. Those were some of my most memorable sessions; some of the touchiest, at least in the beginning, but also the most rewarding."[30]

"It's a matter of arriving at now," Barry said. "We had always done things out of time. All our lives. When we were kids, we had a sound similar to the Beatles', melodic, with harmonies. So they came along first and it was their story. We worked in nightclubs when we should have played to kids. We've always done things strangely. At last, we are *now* doing things for *now* in a whole sphere of *now*.[31] We were getting into something we didn't fully understand. It was a certain experimentation which was based on black groups, based on R&B groups. *Mr. Natural* was whiter. With *Main Course* we started to turn black . . . or blacker. A healthy shade of brown."[32]

The music may have been turning brown, but the boys and their cultural references remained whiter than white.

"We were calling it 'Jive Talkin'," Maurice said. "But, being British, we thought jive was a dance, so the opening line was 'Jive Talkin', you dance with your eyes . . .' It was Arif who said to us, 'Don't you guys know what jive talk is?' He explained that it was black slang for bullshitting, so we changed the lyric to 'Jive Talkin', you're telling me lies.'"[33]

"Arif showed us the right track," Maurice said. "*This* was the track leading to R&B and hits, and *that* was the track leading to lush ballads, and he shoved us off that track and right up this one."[34]

"I played a synth bass line on ['Jive Talkin'']," said Blue, "which was unusual at the time and gave it a distinctive sound, but that happened by accident. Usually Maurice would play bass guitar, but he was away from the studio that night, so I found a bass sound on the ARP 2600 and laid down a guide bass line for him. It sounded pretty good. When Maurice came back, we let him hear it and suggested he re-record the bass line on his bass guitar."[35] "I really liked the synth bass lines," Maurice said. "I overdubbed certain sections to add bass extra emphasis."[36]

Even Ahmet Ertegun did not understand what the Bee Gees and Mardin had wrought. "We were over the moon about 'Jive Talkin'," Maurice said. "But when we played it to people at the record company, they didn't want it. They said it wasn't a good single because it was so different to what we'd done before. Yet they were the very ones who'd told us we had to change. Stigwood was fighting with them, telling them they were mad and it was a guaranteed Number 1 single, and we were getting secret phone calls from the record company asking us if we could talk Stigwood out of [releasing it]. Robert came up with a way round it, which was that he sent out some unmarked cassettes to DJs and critics. They wouldn't know who it was, so they'd only come back to us if they liked the music. Then, having said they liked it before they discovered it was The Bee Gees, it was hard for them not to play it."[37]

That story has been told so many times in so many different ways it might well be true. And if not, it's such a perfect record business legend that it has more resonance than any fact. Stigwood had records and cassettes made of "Jive Talkin'" with blank white labels and sent them around. *Rolling Stone* reported that only 20 percent of English DJs could identify the unlabeled test pressing as a Bee Gees record.[38] Further proof of Stigwood's marketing savvy is that the RSO pre-release press statement said right up front that RSO knew that most people wanted nothing to do with the Bee Gees: "If you've never liked the Bee Gees before, and there seems to be some who now have a mental block when it comes to their records, please give this single a chance. It is totally unlike anything they have recorded in their entire career. That's a bold statement but it's not wrong. Produced by Arif Mardin, this is actually almost unrecognizable as the Gibb brothers and is an extremely funky piece of music . . . If you don't like the Bee Gees (or rather if you haven't in the past liked the Bee Gees) please pretend it's not them."[39]

Main Course was released in the US in August 1975. The album made it to #14 US. "Jive Talkin'" was the first US single and was released in July. "Nights on Broadway" came out in September and spent sixteen weeks on the charts, reaching #7, and "Fanny (Be Tender with My Love)" followed in January of 1976 and peaked at #12, though it quickly dropped away.

"*Main Course*," wrote one reviewer, "is the best sounding Bee Gees album ever, represents a last ditch effort to reestablish the group's mass popularity in front of their upcoming US tour. My guess is that it should succeed, due to Arif Mardin's spectacular production, which presents the Bee Gees in blackface on the album's four genuinely exciting cuts. 'Nights on Broadway' and especially 'Fanny (Be Tender with My Love)' boast spacious disco arrangements against which the Bee Gees overdub skillful imitations of black falsetto. 'Jive Talkin'' approximates the synthesized propulsion of Stevie Wonder's 'Superstition,' while the song itself offers an inept lyric parody of black street argot. In 'Wind of Change,' also synthesized Stevie Wonder style, the Gibb brothers dare to pretend to speak for New York black experience. While I find the idea of such pretension offensively co-optive, musically the group carries them off with remarkable flair. For all their professionalism, the Bee Gees have never been anything but imitators, their albums dependent on sound rather than substance. In this respect, *Main Course* is no different from its predecessors."[40]

This review, while in substance in accord with most other reviews of *Main Course*, proves to be a comparatively reasonable assault. Other reviews were openly contemptuous and vituperative. In its almost perfect wrongness on every point, this review encapsulates the entrenched critical hostility to the Bee Gees, and how determined critics were to defy the evidence of their own ears. This critic, and others, failed to grasp how revolutionary and enduring *Main Course*'s better songs would prove to be.

"Jive Talkin'" is, simply put, one of the best singles ever cut and has outlasted all the songs it's accused of imitating.

The critic is right about one thing: *Main Course* was and remains the Bee Gees' best-sounding record, and likely their best LP overall. As usual for the band, it has two great cuts, two decent cuts and the rest are, for the Bee Gees, high-grade filler. But the great cuts are game changers. "Jive Talkin'" is the pinnacle of their career. It does cop, in the most intelligent way, Steve Wonder's clavinet riffs from "Superstition" and the pre-disco ascending and descending bass lines from underrated bass futurist Freddie Graham. Graham first blew the music world's mind with those riffs on Sly Stone's "You're the One" by Little Sister and later made them a household sound on Sly's *Fresh*. If you have to steal from someone in art, it's wise to steal from the best, and for once, the brothers did.

These are not straight thefts; they are appropriations in pursuit of an original sound. Barry's languid strumming reveals a gift no one knew he had. It's a smoother version of Kool and the Gang's signature chicka-chicka and a more Funky Nassau version of KC and the Sunshine Band's homogenized Caribbean strumming. Nothing that came before from Barry's right hand sounds like that, though it does evoke the immortal rhythm riff from Shirley and Company's classic dance track "Shame, Shame, Shame." These are earmarks of the song, and worth commenting on, but they remain part of a complete whole. "Jive Talkin'" cannot be reduced to its component parts.

No one in his or her right mind, save the Bee Gees, would have broken up all that smooth dance funk for a whimsical, seemingly pointless, 9/16 break. But it's the break that marks the song's singularity, makes it so eccentric and lets DJs sort out the timing for endless club versions.

"Jive Talkin'" is also a stutter song, a prized pop pigeonhole, and joins the company of other great stutter songs: "My Generation" by the Who, "Changes" by David Bowie, "Benny and the Jets" by Elton John and Bob Seeger's "Katmandu."

As for the critical charges of "blackface," or the Bee Gees attempting to sound black, the most astonishing aspect of "Jive Talkin'" is its racelessness. Within the first ten seconds of any Kool and the Gang song, it's clear they're African American. Within the same time frame of KC and the Sunshine Band, it's clear their intention is to make a white sound. Ten seconds of the Average White Band might fool you, but thirty seconds in there's no doubt that they are correctly named. "Jive Talkin'" sounds neither black nor white; it exists in a whirling limbo of all the sounds in the air at the time of its making; the result is pure Bee Gees.

"It was a departure from the ballad style we were most often associated with," Barry said of "Jive Talkin'." "When it became a hit, people started saying that we had stepped down to be a disco group which was a put down to disco music as well. We don't think disco is bad music; we think it's happy and has a wide appeal. It's for people to dance to; that's what it's all about. We decided to try something lighthearted, and we did. We didn't cunningly go into disco music to gain greater strength in the record market as some people implied. We simply try to embrace all kinds of music, whatever music there is."[41]

"Nights on Broadway" melds old-school Bee Gees bombast with a gentler vocal approach over contemporary synth riffs. The introduction of falsetto into their familiar soaring harmonies makes the song leap out of the speakers. On an AM radio in a moving car, it sounded totally new. "Wind of Change" is pretty much a Spinners ("Rubber Band Man") backing track with the Gibbs singing over it. That is not necessarily a bad thing. Barry's vocal approach is much influenced by Eddie Kendricks's proto-disco "Keep on Truckin'."

After those first three cuts, the discernable influences really get eclectic. "Songbird" and "Country Lanes," with their hesitant piano lines and country-tinged guitars, mimic Elton John's *Tumbleweed Connection*. "Edge of the Universe" proves to be the second-best cut on the album. It doesn't sound like anyone save the Gibbs, though an argument could be made that the driving piano comes from Bob Seeger. Arif Mardin figured out how to take ideas that had failed the band on their last three records and make hits out of them. The less said about "Fanny," the better. It's a Robin one-off dirty joke, either for the benefit of, or at the expense of, their gay audience.

After *Main Course* exploded, plans were made to record the follow-up, *Children of the World*, with Arif at Criteria. But RSO severed its distribution agreement with Atlantic; Arif was an Atlantic employee and Atlantic was not going to loan him out. The Bee Gees went to LA to work with producer Richard Perry, famed for his bright, shiny production on albums by Harry Nilsson, Linda Ronstadt and Carly Simon. Perry was not a good fit.

The Bee Gees' future producer Albhy Galuten said, "They decided that they would come back to Miami and try to make the record with [Criteria engineer] Karl Richardson. At the time, I was in the UK producing a band named Bees Make Honey. I had been dropped by Atlantic [as an in-house producer] and was hired as a producer where I had a budget and a hotel room and a meal allowance and could actually hang out and make a record. I was finishing the last mix when I got a call from Karl Richardson. Karl said, 'I'm here with the Bee Gees. We're trying to make a record, and they could use a producer. When are you coming back?' I said, 'I'm on a plane in a few hours.'"[42]

Before teaming up with Karl to become the fourth and fifth Bee Gees through their most productive and popular years, Albhy Galuten had a remarkably full and varied career as a sideman and producer. Whenever music history was made, Albhy was there. A dropout from the Berklee College of Music, Albhy played with the legendary southern soul studio outfit Charlie Freeman and the Dixie Flyers; he worked as an assistant on *Layla* and played keyboards on a couple of *Layla* cuts as well; he played on "Rock Your Baby" by George McCrae; played keyboards for Jackie DeShannon; produced Jellyfish, Kenny Rogers and Dolly Parton and played with Aretha Franklin, Rod Stewart, Kenny Loggins, Wishbone Ash, Chris Hillman and the Eagles. Albhy's perfect pitch, wide-ranging experience, determination, patience and relaxed perfectionism made him the dream producer for Barry.

Albhy first heard the Bee Gees, like most people, on his car radio: "I was driving in the car," he said, "and heard 'Mining Disaster' for the first time, I thought it was a Beatles song. Because at the time, being a Beatles song meant 'Here's a song that sounds like nothing I've ever heard before, it must be the Beatles' because they were the only ones who broke ground."[43]

Albhy said, "I got off the plane and came directly over. They were already in the studio. They were tracking 'You Should Be Dancing.' I don't remember my comments. I think I probably thought it was good. I was pretty tired. I wouldn't have been nervous. Had I known what it was going to become in my career, I might've been nervous. To me, after working with Eric Clapton or Rod Stewart, the Bee Gees were just another band. I remember I left early that day. They said, 'We'll see you tomorrow.' So I came back and began coming in every day and working on what I do as a producer."[44]

Children of the World came out in September of 1976. It went to #8 in the US. "You Should Be Dancing" became a #1 hit, spending twenty weeks on the *Billboard* charts, along with charting worldwide on pop and adult contemporary lists, and "Love So Right" reached #3, maintaining its place for fourteen weeks. "Boogie Child," the weakest single, still made it to #12 and spent fifteen weeks on the charts.

"We wanted an album that was more nervous," Maurice said. "We felt *Main Course* was too varied. There were too many directions. We wanted to take the R&B flavour a step further with *Children*."[45]

"From mushy pop ballads," *Rolling Stone's* critic wrote of *Children of the World*, "through late-Sixties psychedelia and low-key rock, the Bee Gees have demonstrated a chameleon like ability to adapt to disparate pop trends. These days, as they said on the *Tonight Show* with their best Cockney accents, 'Rhythm & blues is what's happening.' Audacious, right? Well, not exactly. Some of their stuff is really good, better than poseurs like Wild Cherry, AWB and Kokomo."[46]

The critics didn't see that these songs, however they were aimed at the time, would reach way past disco. The champion of the album is "You Should Be Dancing," with its bottomless stack of layered guitars, old-style funk horns and a guitar solo that prefigures "Thriller." "Boogie Child" is an embarrassment; the group does try to sound like AWB or Wild Cherry—precisely the limited white funk–imitators that the Bee Gees transcended with "Jive Talkin'." Here, for the only time, an accusation of blackface might not be inappropriate. The rest of the album falls somewhere between those two poles: original and groundbreaking takes on funk and poorly conceived imitations of it. Alan Kendall's lead guitar work stands out, and Barry chicken-scratches with the best.

When *Children* broke huge, Robin said, "We're becoming bigger now than we ever were before. No-one would ever have thought that it would happen."[47] "We were always writing the kind of music we do now," he claimed. "But we weren't putting it down right. We were writing R&B, but we weren't going in an R&B direction."[48]

"[Record labels] were the same as they are now—they want to tell you what to record," Barry said. "When 'How Can You Mend a Broken Heart' became a No. 1 record, they didn't want to hear us do anything else but ballads."[49]

"We've always been able to play different kinds of music," Maurice said. "But we never had the backing. When we were going with softer material like 'How Can You Mend a Broken Heart?' and 'Run to Me,' I think that's all people wanted to hear from us. I don't believe that our audience would have accepted our new songs then. We were not devoting enough time to our albums. We recorded *Mr. Natural* while on tour. Every time we had a few days off, we'd be shooting back to New York to do a few tracks. When we finally finished, we knew we could do better work."[50]

"We'd been doing this new sound for years," Robin insisted, unconvincingly. "In dressing rooms, planes. Just never on record. The black influence was our original one. Long before the pop ballads. It's the way we thought and felt, so we were, in a sense, going back to our roots. 'To Love Somebody' was written for Otis Redding. Otis came to see Barry at the Plaza in New York one night, said he loved our material and would Barry write him a song? We were stuck in a niche; and after a couple of ballads— 'Lonely Days,' 'Mend a Broken Heart'—went to number one, we couldn't get out of it. But first and always, we are songwriters; we explore all avenues."[51]

"He pointed us in the right direction," Barry said, speaking of Arif Mardin. "We love that direction, it mustn't be the be-all and end-all. We're going to continue in that direction, but if we keep doing it for another five years, we'll be back in the wilderness again."[52]

Robin, Barry and Maurice in Brisbane, Australia, 1960.

Maurice, Robin and Barry, 1966.

Barry, Robin, Vince Melouney, Maurice and Colin Petersen, 1967, on *The Simon Dee Show* in the UK.

Barry, 1967.

Maurice, 1968.

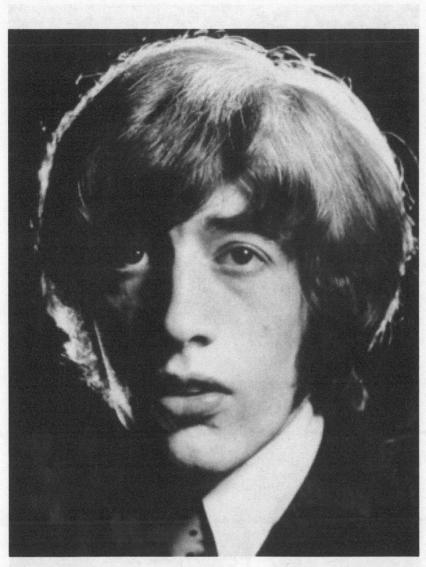

Robin, 1968.

Barry and his Lotus, 1969.

Maurice and Lulu, 1969.

Maurice, mid-1970s.

Maurice, Barry and Robin with Hugh, Andy and Barbara, 1970, backstage at *Top of the Pops*.

Barry, Maurice, George Burns, Peter Frampton and Robin on the set of *Sgt. Pepper's Lonely Hearts Club Band,* 1978.

Maurice, Barry and Robin, 1978.

Andy, 1979.

Maurice, Barry and Robin, 1979.

Bee Gees' manager Robert Stigwood, 1979.

Maurice, Robin and Barry; *Spirits Having Flown* tour, 1979.

Andy and Victoria Principal, 1983, promoting their single "All I Have to Do Is Dream."

Dwina Gibb, Robin John and Robin, 1986.

Andy's wife Kim Reeder and their daughter Peta, 1988.

Maurice, Robin and Barry, Sydney, Australia, 1999.

saturday night fever

> People crying out for help. Desperate songs. Those are the
> ones that become giants. The minute you capture that on
> record, it's gold. "Stayin' Alive" is the epitome of that.
> Everybody struggles against the world, fighting all the
> bullshit and things that can drag you down. And it really is
> a victory just to survive. But when you climb back on top
> and win bigger than ever before—well, that's something
> everybody reacts to. Everybody.
>
> —Barry Gibb[1]

> None of us expected it to be so big.
>
> —Maurice Gibb[2]

*D*isco is not the Bee Gees' fault.
They are not to blame.

In an episode of an American sitcom, two students—a straight
African American girl and a gay white boy—sit down to talk to a
teacher. The boy says: "She's black. I'm gay. We make culture." In
America, truer words were never spoken. The brothers Gibb are
demonstrably neither, and were never part of the thriving underground then increasingly overground black, gay and jet-set club
scene based on dance music (and sex and drugs) that exploded—

as ever, in a diluted form—into the mainstream. The Bee Gees' only crime was to help make disco popular. Very, very popular.

They did this by selling 25 million copies of a double album between 1977 and 1980, at the time the most copies of any sound recording sold since the advent of sound recording. It's one thing for, say, Lady Gaga to get 80 million hits on YouTube. It's nice, but her audience didn't have to do much. To move 25 million double units in the late 1970s, about 20 million people had to get in their cars, drive to a record store, take out their wallets, buy the damn thing, carry it home, undo the shrink wrap and slap it on the turntable. Then their friends all had to go out and do the same thing. To date, over 40 million copies of *Saturday Night Fever* (*SNF*) have sold.

Saturday Night Fever was a hit like nothing before and hardly anything since, spending twenty-four consecutive weeks at #1 from January to August of 1978. The single "How Deep Is Your Love" stayed in the top 10 for seventeen straight weeks. No other *Billboard* single had ever done that. In February and March of '78, three singles from the record made the top 10 twice. During March and April, "Night Fever" and "Stayin' Alive" both hit #1 and spent time at #2. "Night Fever" was #1 for eight weeks in a row and "Stayin' Alive" was #1 for four. Yvonne Elliman's cover of the Bee Gees' "If I Can't Have You"—the fourth single from the album—charted for six months and made #1; the Tavares' cover of "More Than a Woman" stayed in the top 100 for five months. The *Saturday Night Fever* double LP remained in the top 200 from November 1977 to March 1980: twenty-nine consecutive months.

Some of the songs have aged poorly, some well and one is immortal.

"Fleetwood Mac's *Rumours* sold between 9–10 million units at $7.98," Al Coury explained in 1978, citing then-current prices. "Before that the big album was Peter Frampton's *Frampton Comes Alive*, which did 7–8 million at $6.98 originally and then $7.98.

Before that it was Carole King's *Tapestry*, which did 10–12 million, with most of the sales at $5.98. *Saturday Night Fever* became the top-grossing album of all time when it hit 8 million units (because of its higher price)."[3]

The soundtrack proved such a monster because, Bee Gees aside, it was packed with known disco songs from brand name bands in a range of dance styles and demographics. KC and the Sunshine Band, Kool and the Gang, the Trammps, M.F.S.B., Yvonne Elliman, Ralph McDonald, Tavares, Walter Murphy: you could put on *SNF* and have a dance party without lifting the needle. When you needed to sit down and cool off, you could ignore the unlistenable soundtrack cuts from hack composer and Francis Ford Coppola brother-in-law David Shire, who had to be the luckiest man in show business to get his clueless disco-lite onto the LP.

Saturday Night Fever—the movie and the double LP—demonstrated the scale of the disco market and others rushed in to service and earn off that market. The soundtrack hit first and fueled the movie; then the movie hit and refueled the soundtrack. In that way, *SNF* is analogous to *Woodstock*—the event, the movie and the soundtrack album.

The message of *Woodstock* was not that 400,000 longhairs could come together peaceably for three days of music and love. The real message of *Woodstock* was that there *were* 400,000 longhairs, and all of them willing to travel and spend to revel in longhairdom. And if 400,000 would travel, then millions more must be waiting at home, along with their younger brothers and sisters, all ready to pay to demonstrate their longhairedness. *Woodstock* showed mainstream and niche marketers alike that profits awaited on the hippie bandwagon, and everybody got on board. No one had any idea of the scope of the sales opportunities until *Woodstock* hit. Suddenly, longhairedness was not aberrant. It was the new normal—the everyday face of the youth market. And so it was with *Saturday Night Fever*.

Disco haters talk about *SNF* and disco as a pernicious, undermining of the popular will. They should instead recognize *SNF* as the absolute manifestation of that will. Bill Oakes—then head of RSO and husband of Yvonne Elliman—believes that disco was not only well entrenched in America before *SNF*, but had already peaked. "These days," Oakes told W magazine, "*Fever* is credited with kicking off the whole disco thing—but it really didn't. Truth is, [SNF] breathed new life into a genre that was actually dying."[4]

Saturday Night Fever showed how nationwide the disco market could be. Not only for disco music, but for discos themselves, disco sound systems, disco dance floors that lit up, rotating mirrored disco balls for clubs, homes and cars, disco clothing, disco haircuts, disco dance lessons, anything that cohered to disco. How could it not be huge? American white people love dancing that involves simple moves repeated over and over and over to a beat that never changes—like punk rock and the pogo, or country line dancing. That's why disco took over mainstream America, black and white, while, say, Parliament-Funkadelic took over people who could actually dance.

Discotheque culture had been around a long time before the Bee Gees put it in every home. Discotheques, or at least people dressing up and going out to dance to records, had been around for decades.

Dancing to records—rather than to live music—in clubs began as a counterculture of resistance in pre–World War II Nazi Germany. In Hamburg, in the 1930s, the Swing Kids—mostly high schoolers—rejected National Socialism and the forced regimentation of the Hitler Youth by meeting in clubs and rented halls to swing dance to American jazz. Nothing could have been more verboten; jazz was the antithesis of the Nazi credo. It was individualist "degenerate" jungle music played by "Negroes" and distributed by Jews. The Swing Kids' preference for "effete" English fashion, long hair on the boys and learning enough English to decipher song lyrics was further proof of their anti-German, antisocial "decadence." The scene revolved around records because German radio never played such music. As the Swing Kids movement spread, underground dance clubs popped up in other cities. A crackdown in 1941 greatly reduced the number of Swing Kids but increased the determination of the survivors.

In 1942, leader of the SS and German police chief Heinrich Himmler sent a memo regarding the Swing Kids to his underling, Reinhardt Heydrich—the feared organizer of the Final Solution—that read, in part: "My judgment is that the whole evil must be radically exterminated now. All ringleaders . . . into a concentration camp to be re-educated . . . It is only through the utmost brutality that we will be able to avert the dangerous spread of Anglophile tendencies."[5] After that, anyone caught swinging, or looking like they did, ended up in death camps.

From its earliest days, then, dancing to records in clubs involved an underground culture, a forward fashion sense, secrecy and danger.

French citizens blasted American "Negro music" at top volume in below-street-level clubs and restaurants during the Nazi occupation of Paris. Playing the records as loud as possible meant that Germans outside the clubs couldn't hear anything anyone inside was saying. Devout Nazis were repulsed by the music and wouldn't come near it, and the less devout didn't dare. Loud jazz provided perfect security.

At the end of World War II, urban Europeans were vested in a culture of records—rather than dance bands—playing in clubs. The first commercial disco, Paris's Le Whisky à Go-Go—not to be confused with the LA rock club of a similar name—opened in 1947. The walls were made from whiskey crates decorated with labels of various scotches, stacked floor to ceiling. A whiskey bar was an anomaly, and an instant hit, in a wine-drinking nation. Remarkably, there were two turntables, playing 78 rpm records.

Régine Zylberberg worked there, became manager, and in the late 1950s opened her Chez Régine in the Latin Quarter of Paris. It became a legendary place for dancing to records and introducing new jazz cuts at the height of the era of the American expatriate jazz musician in Paris. Régine's featured a professional DJ.

Discotheque invaded New York City via the Peppermint Lounge, a seedy gay bar and sailor hangout on Forty-fifth Street and Eighth Avenue, pretty much the epicenter of seedy New York nowhere at the time. The rise of the dance the Twist in 1960–61 helped make the Peppermint Lounge a success. The Twist was a worldwide phenomenon in its day, like *Saturday Night Fever*. Hank Ballard did the first version, then Chubby Checker broke it nationwide twisting on Dick Clark's *American Bandstand*. The celebrities of the day would go slumming at the Peppermint Lounge to twist the night away. The DJs played mostly early sixties pop soul records, the various twisting hits like the Isley Brothers "Twist and Shout" and selections from easy-listening compilations sold at supermarkets, like Enoch Light's 1964 *Discotheque Dance . . . Dance . . . Dance.*

The next significant discotheque was Arthur, created by actor Richard Burton's ex-wife Sybil. Opening in 1965, Arthur epitomized the jet-set disco. The initial investment came from Sybil Burton's alimony. Eighty-eight celebrities—including conductor-composer Leonard Bernstein, composer Stephen Sondheim, director Mike Nichols and actors Lee Remick, Julie Andrews and Rex Harrison, among others—ponied up $1,000 each to provide the rest of the funding. The club was named for a moment in the Beatle's first film, *A Hard Day's Night*. A square from Squaresville asks George Harrison: "What would you call that hairstyle?" George replies: "Arthur." Arthur broke new ground with its linked turntables run through a mixer connected to the amplification system. The renowned sound and lighting designer Chip Monck—

who gained a different sort of fame as the voice of *Woodstock*—set up the Arthur sound system in stereo.

Arthur served as a model for Studio 54. For the first time, patrons had to pass an overt inspection at the door, and risk being rejected on the sidewalk. Mickey Deans, who would go on to be Judy Garland's fifth and final husband, was the night manager and believed in "body fascism," that is, the natural social supremacy of the smoking hot. His door policy sought to create a precise mix of titled Europeans, beautiful young things, celebrities, New York bluebloods and outrageous night people. Arthur showcased New York's mixed after-midnight universe, where stars mingled with gay culture and really good-looking "normal" New Yorkers. DJ Terry Noell had two turntables and played mostly soul music—with Motown dominant—and the sounds of Swinging London and Carnaby Street British Invasion.

The disco-defining game-changer was the Church, in Hell's Kitchen, later known as the Sanctuary. In 1969, Francis Grasso— a kid from the outer boroughs like *SNF*'s Tony Manero—became the precursor of all modern DJs when he created the first extended mixes by switching between two copies of the same record on two turntables. Because he could best run the switch during drum solos, his sets were all about the break. Grasso played African music like Babatunde Olatunji's "The Drums of Passion," and conga-heavy Latin music. Another crowd favorite was the long version of the Chambers Brothers' "Time Has Come Today," with its tick-tocking cowbell—which made switching between turntables easy to time—and extended psychedelic drum break. Grasso could make the song last as long as his crowd wanted to dance. The Sanctuary is supposedly the birthplace of the dance the Bump. Around this time in 1969, the first song appeared featuring the distinctive chugging disco bass-line, unchanging shuffle beat and soaring strings, the Four Tops' "Don't Bring Back Memories."

Another proto-disco cut was written and produced by Sly Stone: Little Sister's "You're the One." Larry Graham, Sly's bass player, created what would become a widely copied, thumb-popping, disco-style bass line on several cuts on Sly's 1973 album, *Fresh*.

The next important scene was the Loft, conceived and run by David Mancuso, on Broadway in Manhattan's Soho neighborhood. In 1970, Soho after dark was a deserted wasteland, a desolate, garbage-strewn backwater. Because the Loft had no liquor license, it was spared the vice squad entrapment seductions and harassing police presence suffered by most gay bars. The Loft served no food or drinks; the crowd was young and liked LSD. The psychedelic mind-set didn't sit well with songs that ran only two minutes fifty-nine seconds. The Loft DJs sought out and showcased longer tracks, like Eddie Kendricks's groundbreaking, eight-minute "Girl You Need a Change of Mind," and his equally epic "Keep on Truckin'." The most legendary and influential proto-disco track was "Soul Makosa" by African saxophonist Manu Dibango. After the Loft's DJ David Mancuso put it into heavy rotation, "Soul Makosa" became an underground smash and widely imitated.

Studio 54 opened in an old CBS radio and TV Studio on West Fifty-fourth Street in Manhattan in 1977. Steve Rubell and Ian Schrager had a specific, but wide-open concept: to bring the energy and glamour of the underground gay clubs out in the open and to meld that with show business, international society, fashion and New York money. The atmosphere was glitzy and decadent, the decorations lavish and the bartenders and waitresses all famously beautiful. Author Truman Capote said of the staff: "You can't have a candy store without candy." The door policy was—by design—capricious, ruthless and humiliating. Steve Rubell said, "We turned away the president of Cyprus because he looked boring."[6] According to cultural commentator Sara Stosic: "Schrager/ Rubell . . . were famed for a selective screening policy on who was allowed into their venue, building on the idea of 'inclusive exclusivity'. . . . where access was granted on an economic factor, looks, or social standing. Schrager/Rubell pioneered the 'velvet rope'—in their opinion a 'democratic process to exercise the same discretion people exercise when inviting people into their home.'"[7]

"The criteria for entrance are unwritten and, at best, whimsical," wrote rock critic Dave Marsh. "Prestige is at stake, so fame counts, but conformity to certain sartorial standards also plays a part. Sometimes the owner himself is perched at the door to make these key decisions, guarding the Studio gate like St. Peter on Quaaludes."[8] Model and *Vogue Italia* editor Bethann Hardison said: "Studio 54 changed the world. That's why you could go to Bosnia or some small, obscure place and there'll be some fool standing outside with a red velvet rope."[9]

"I've been to a lot of night clubs," Truman Capote said, "and this is the nightclub of the future. It's very democratic. Boys with boys, girls with girls, girls with boys, blacks and whites, capitalists and Marxists, Chinese and everything else—all one big mix!"[10]

"By going to this venue at midnight," Stosic wrote, "one knew that everybody they wanted to see would be right there, and that seems to have been the beauty of it. One didn't have to go to five restaurants and three clubs and six parties. It was midnight and everybody was at Studio. Everybody perceived [Studio 54] to be immune to the law and whatever one did would not enter into the rest of their lives. There seemed to be no concept of punishment and morality. In the words of Studio 54 co-owner Steve Rubell (who was paraphrasing William Blake): 'The path of excess leads to the palace of wisdom.'"[11]

That freedom extended only so far, it turned out. One of the owners bragged during a TV interview of out-earning the Mafia and said: "What the IRS don't know won't kill it." Unsurprisingly, the IRS subsequently raided the club and convicted the owners of tax evasion. Each served thirteen months in prison.[12]

Studio 54 lured folks from every borough of New York, hence the lines around the block. For the working-class aspirants in those lines, 54 was the big-time, Manhattan version of the infinitely less glamorous discos and dance clubs that operated in neighborhoods around the city. *Saturday Night Fever* had its genesis in one of these clubs even before 54 opened. Or, more accurately, SNF's genesis came from a great fraud spun around one of those clubs, a bold lie that could never be perpetrated today, an article about a real dance club and a scene that never existed.

On June 7, 1976, *New York* magazine published the article "Tribal Rites of the New Saturday Night," by English pop culture observer Nik Cohn. Cohn wrote one of the first books of rock criticism, 1969's *Awopbopaloobop Alopbamboom*, featuring capsule biographies of James Brown, Bob Dylan, the Who and other founding figures. Cohn's friendship with the Who and willingness to shoot his mouth off led him to be credited by Pete Townshend as the inspiration for—or at least the suggester of—"Pinball Wizard." He worked with Dutch artist Guy Peellaert on the seminal, licentious illustrated volume of imagined rock-star fantasies *Rock Dreams*, wrote collections of essays and, later, an in-depth, loving exploration of New Orleans rap and hip-hop. "Tribal Rites" was Cohn's first piece for *New York*. In the introduction he writes: "Everything described in this article is factual and was either witnessed by me or told to me directly by the people involved." Nothing, however, in the piece turned out to be factual; Cohn made it all up.

Stigwood, never shy about taking credit for anything that ever happened anywhere, claims to have been contacted by Cohn some months before the article appeared. Cohn wanted to write a movie for Stigwood but had no firm ideas. Stigwood told him to keep in touch and send him whatever he wrote. Stigwood frames the story to present himself as having his finger on the pulse not of what was happening, but what was going to happen. And, as usual, Stigwood actually did.

Cohn posits a young working-class Italian, Vincent, from the insular Brooklyn Italian neighborhood of Bay Ridge. Vincent works in a hardware store by day, stocking paint. By night he's the best dancer at the Bay Ridge disco 2001 *Odyssey*. Cohn writes that Vincent is known as a "Face" and his dancing gang of buddies as "Faces."

Cohn copped to "Tribal Rites" being fiction in 1996. "My story was a fraud," he said. "I'd recently arrived in New York. Far from being steeped in Brooklyn street life, I hardly knew the place. As for Vincent, he was largely inspired by a Shepherd's Bush Mod whom I'd known in the Sixties, a one-time king of Goldhawk Road. All I'd intended was a study of teenage style. Even its fakery had been based on the belief that all dance fevers were interchangeable."[13]

A "Face," as anyone who's seen the movie adapted from the Who album *Quadrophenia* knows, was a cool Mod—natty, tailored, speed-taking, customized Italian motor scooter–riding urban English "youth" dandies from the early sixties who made the pages of *Life* magazine engaging in fistfight riots on Brighton Beach with the Mod's archenemies, the leather-jacketed Rockers. The "Ace Face," as portrayed in the film by Sting, had sharp, raw silk suits, a buff Vespa and to-the-minute razor-cut hair. Cohn so transposed his Mod from Shepherd's Bush that he had the Bay Ridge kids slinging Mod slang.

Cohn's gang of Faces are dead-end guys who spend their menial-job pay on plumage for the club. What makes them different, what allows them to believe that they are different, is that they really can dance and they dress with what passes for style in Bay Ridge. As Cohn puts it: "To qualify as an Odyssey (the name of the club where the Faces dance) [one] needed to be Italian, between 18 and 25, with a minimum stock of six floral shirts, four pairs of tight trousers, two pairs of Gucci loafers, two pairs of platforms . . . and he must know how to dance."[14]

The dance floor was sacred. Anyone who came in wearing the wrong clothes or pulling dated moves wrecked the vibe and was quickly made unwelcome. That atmosphere was straight out of Mod culture, whose in-club competition to be styling in the proper manner was ferocious. Cohn describes a Darwinian hierarchy in which the threat of public humiliation maintains the club's standards of cool, dress, dance and decorum. Vincent led every dance, calling out moves, counting the beat, directing traffic. Off the dance floor, the girls chase Vincent, but he keeps his remove. When he worries, he worries about his nonexistent future. That one day he'll be too old to dance or somebody will dance better and he'll be left with nothing but the hardware store. The article ends with Vincent and the Faces heading off into the night, deeply dissatisfied with themselves, looking for somebody— anybody—to beat up.

It's a good story, a classic tale of a doomed gunslinger. He became the fastest gun in his little town, but outside his little town, his skills not only mean nothing, but come with an expiration date. The movie's plot expands on Vincent and his terror of a dead-end life, of being unable to love and of yearning for a shot at a future, possibly as a dancer, in the real world, namely, Manhattan. In the screenplay by Norman Wexler, who won an Oscar for the screenplay for *Serpico*, Vincent gets renamed Tony Manero.

"[Robert] called me and told me to pick up *New York* magazine with an article in it by Nik Cohn called 'Tribal Rites of Saturday Night,'" Al Coury said. "I went down to the lobby to get it and [Stigwood] called me back and said: 'I'm going to take that story and make a movie and you are going to have the biggest soundtrack ever.'"[15] Stigwood bought the screen rights to the story less than twenty-four hours after it appeared in print. Cohn got

$90,000—pretty big potatoes in 1976—and wrote the first draft of the screenplay. Some versions of the history have Stigwood so intent on securing Cohn's article that he gave Cohn a big fee and a percentage of the soundtrack royalties. If true, Cohn certainly never had to work again. The rationale for this version is that Stigwood didn't think soundtracks sold that well and so had little to lose. But that doesn't sound like Stigwood: he never gave away percentages, he kept his partnerships to a minimum and he was adamant from the start that the movie and the record would be enormous.

"Disco was happening," said Freddie Gershon. "But it was not yet the worldwide craze. It was the smart set and the gay set. Which was sometimes the same set. It hadn't spilled over. But Robert saw what was happening in Brazil. We went on the maiden voyage of the Concorde from Paris to Rio. Rio was rough, and exotic and the music never stopped. Stigwood saw it in England, France, Germany. [Disco] was going down the social strata. Five years earlier it would have been effete for men to even be on the dance floor. Now men were becoming peacocks. It was Robert's instinct that a Tony Manero existed in every community in the world."[16]

Legendary music producer Sam Phillips always said that if he could find a white man who sang like a black man, he would make a million dollars. Then one day Elvis Presley walked into Sam Phillips's Sun studio . . . Stigwood's vision paralleled Phillips's. If only he could create a straight dancing idol and a credible world in which straight guys vied to be the best dancer, he would make a lot more than Phillips's puny million. Tony Manero—as portrayed by John Travolta—was that guy.

The Bee Gees flew to France in January or February of 1977.[17] They did not go there to record *Saturday Night Fever*. At the time, they knew nothing about it. What they knew was that they needed to write and record tracks for a new, as yet unnamed, studio album, their follow-up to *Children of the World*. They also had to mix a double live album from their recent LA Forum show. A combination of factors landed them outside Paris, at the Château d'Hérouville.

"For tax purposes," Karl Richardson said, "they needed to make records outside the United States or the UK." Dick Ashby booked them a month in Hérouville.[18] The eighteenth-century château was a live-in work environment featuring the sixteen-track Strawberry Studios, built by film-score composer Michel Magne in 1970. Elton John recorded there in 1972. After his LP came out, the place became forever known as Honky Château. It's an idyllic spot. Van Gogh painted in the meadow below the château, and composer Frédéric Chopin and author George Sand (real name: Amantine Dupin) used the château for their secret trysts. Sweet, Cat Stevens, T-Rex, Iggy Pop, David Bowie, Fleetwood Mac and Pink Floyd all recorded at the Honky Château.

The rundown, mangy atmosphere quickly dashed whatever fantasies the Bee Gees might have had of a luxurious retreat in a continental castle. The château proved something of a shithole—poorly heated and badly furnished. Maurice, in particular, hated the place. The winter weather was oppressive; there was no television and nothing to do. There were only two functioning showers. The band, the crew and the few wives that had come along all queued up for the bathrooms. Recording began around two in the afternoon and usually lasted until three or four in the morning. No one wanted to play before they'd showered to get warm, and it took until midafternoon for everyone to stand in line and get their bathing done.

The studio itself was no marvel. "After Elton John left," Richardson said, "the owner of the studio smashed it to smithereens and rebuilt what was left in a second-story loft within the castle. When I arrived there was a terrific buzz on everything—it was all ungrounded. So I spent the first two days grounding the place."[19]

Robin had a different take on the vibe in Hérouville. "There were so many pornographic films made at the Château," he said. "The staircase where we wrote 'How Deep Is Your Love,' 'Stayin' Alive,' all those songs, was the same staircase where there've been six classic lesbian porno scenes filmed. I was watching one called *Kinky Women of Bourbon Street*, and all of a sudden there's this château, and I said, 'It's the Château!' These girls, these dodgy birds, are having a scene on the staircase that leads from the front door up to the studio. There were dildos hanging off the stairs and everything. I thought, 'Gawd, we wrote "Night Fever" there!'"[20]

Robin was known for his constant drawing of explicit stick figures featuring exaggerated male sexual organs. He left plenty of them on the walls of the Honky Château. One writer described them as "grotesque, elflike creatures who scurry about with enormous genitals and ravenous stares."

The studio was jury-rigged at best. The control-board fader knobs were painted with different-colored nail polish, and some had contacts so worn the audio would drop out if they were slid past a certain point. The playing musicians—Maurice, Blue, Dennis, Alan and Barry—set up in a main room with overhead beams, a space offering little of the expected studio sound-baffling.[21] It was a tough space in which to get a clean recording. There was no easy way to isolate the instruments and Karl Richardson remembers a lot of "leakage."

But the château was self-contained, far from distractions and inexpensive. Management had paid for a month in advance.

"It was a serviceable studio, a little tricky," Albhy Galuten said. "The piano was near a window that was generally open, so it wasn't in tune much. There was a control room that looked into the studio, and a sort of an anteroom you could use like a vocal booth. It was not highly maintained in the technical sense. They did have an ATI console, which was considered a high quality, high fidelity [board]. We took advantage of the liveness [of the room].

"The musician is more important than the instrument, which is more important than the microphone, which is more important than the console, which is more important than the tape recorder. The further you get from the performer the less important it is.

"You could make great live recordings there. It's a matter of the engineer's capability."[22] "Since I started working with Karl, I've never had to worry about the sound. I get a buzz on with the people we're working with and concentrate on that. Karl never has to worry about the production and arrangement of the song. We don't get in each other's way."[23]

However uncomfortable or unhappy with their surroundings the Gibbs might have been, they let Albhy and Karl figure out how to make the studio suit their needs. The band sat down and got to work. Barry, the driving creative force, was writing funk pop songs. The song structures are based on repeating figures or figures of constant, repeating change or both—similar to the song structures from the heyday of Motown. The parts fit together schematically, layered with care, and there's little room for improvisation. On first hearing or on the thirtieth, the songs remain hard, glossy objects—polished to a high sheen. Bee Gees detractors talk about a mechanistic quality; an almost inhuman perfection that suggests studio musicians running down carefully orchestrated charts. Maybe it's the overly finished aspects of the songs that lead people to forget that the Bee Gees were a real band.

Barry was in charge and Maurice was often drunk, passive and ineffectual; Robin made "suggestions," as one studio presence put it, and his suggestions were heeded, by and large. "Robin had great instincts," the studio source said. The brothers had worked with the same musicians—Blue, Alan and Dennis—for at least two years and two albums and two tours. They enjoyed the instinctive mutual understanding and chemistry that only comes from extended, repetitive studio work and close listening. Blue, Alan and Dennis were not hired guns. They played on the road, they played with the brothers for fun, they trusted one another and were vested in the music. Albhy and Karl were integral members of the band.

There endures a jumble of assertions—a lack of a definitive version—about who did what and who should get credit for which finished part. "That is me playing the "Stayin' Alive" lick," said Alan, "although several people lay claim to coming up with it. Dennis says it was me. Maurice used to say it was him. My recollection is extremely hazy due to my drug and alcohol abuse."[24]

Everyone had ideas together and everyone figured out how to make those ideas come alive. For example, the musical track for "How Deep Is Your Love" came mostly from Blue. But for some reason, Albhy played Blue's piano part on the recordings made at the château. Maurice later claimed to have played both the bass and the synclavier strings; he tried to deny credit to both Ahlby and Blue Weaver.[25]

The Bee Gees had a sound, a product of seven musicians working together. Barry dominated the sound, not only by his falsetto, his songwriting and his willpower, but also by his underrated rhythm guitar. "A lot of that was Barry's right hand," Richardson said. "Every one of those records has some form of acoustic guitar with Barry going ching-ching-ching. Whether it's hidden or not, it's there, driving the track along."[26]

"Somewhere along the line," Arif Mardin said, "Barry became completely in tune with the times. That's the phenomenon. It hasn't happened many times before, but he has totally locked into what people are hearing. And what they *want* to hear. This is surely his time."[27]

The work was collaborative, dominated by Barry. The songwriting began with Barry's ideas, and those were sometimes a lyric line looking for a melody, and sometimes a finished song complete in every detail. "[Blue Weaver] had a lot to do with the creation of 'How Deep Is Your Love,'" Albhy said. Barry asked Blue: "What's the most beautiful chord you know?" Blue replied: "E flat." Barry had Blue play the chord and Barry's lyrics tumbled out. "In other times he might've been a co-writer on that song," Albhy said. "Barry would sit down at the piano, and the song would spew out of him. He didn't like the process of saying 'Well, you wrote 10% of this song.' You were either in for 50% or not in at all. Blue's misfortune for 'How Deep Is Your Love' was that he was not in."[28]

"The songwriting was exquisite," Karl said. "At that point all we could do was screw it up. Barry came up with the initial idea, and he and Blue Weaver developed it. Blue was on electric piano, Barry on acoustic guitar, and in an afternoon they wrote 'How Deep Is Your Love.'" The music was written in a couple of hours. Barry, Robin and Maurice huddled together and came up with most of the lyrics later that day. I think the second verse still needed to be written—there was a lot of 'hummeny, hummeny, hummeny'—but three or four days later we were doing the vocals."[29]

Barry—like Robin and Maurice—never wrote down what he heard in his head. "When I walk into the studio, I have a complete picture of what the song will be like as a record," Barry told Mitch Glazer for *Playboy*. "I know when and where the strings will be, what the horns should be like; the finished product. You try to share your picture to a certain extent, because whoever wrote the song can't give the picture away; it's impossible. My original struggle with Albhy was about this. I would play him a song on the guitar and he couldn't hear how it would come out. He'd say, 'I just can't see it.' But what made it work was that he trusted me and went along blind in some cases. That's how our production started. On a song like 'Stayin' Alive,' I could hear the choir and the orchestration, but I couldn't put it into practice, translate it for the musicians. That is what Albhy does."[30]

"The Bee Gees have this tendency to disobey the laws of music because they are not formally schooled in it," Karl said. "They don't even know the names of the chords they write with. But if they'd studied formally, they'd have never sung the melodies they do."[31]

"We can't write music," Robin said. "Semi-quavers and all that stuff, I wouldn't know a semi-quaver from a black hollow!"[32] "At this point in our lives," Barry said sensibly, "learning to read music might take something away from us that has been natural all our lives."[33]

Barry likes to toss this off as normal procedure and Albhy understates everything. But the images that arise are near to incredible: Barry playing a little of what he hears — and to paraphrase rock critic Robert Christgau writing of folksinger Phil Ochs: Barry's guitar playing would not suffer were his right hand webbed — stopping, explaining, moving on. Imagine the frustrations built into this scenario, and Barry is not the most patient of men.

Also imagine the trust between Barry and Albhy, between Barry and the band, between the band and Albhy, between Albhy and Karl. And the awe that Barry must inspire, walking into this crappy, freezing, underequipped studio, three thousand miles from home, undaunted, with a hit song in all its parts running like a movie in his head. Barry hummed the string parts he wanted; he guided Blue, Alan and Dennis, Maurice. When Barry had an idea, everybody knew they would manifest that idea in its complexity from Barry's head onto the tape. They also knew that Barry wrote hits.

"I distinctly remember Barry saying: 'Boy, Karl, have I got a song for you,' and sitting down to play 'Stayin' Alive' on an acoustic guitar," Karl Richardson said. "It was like a chant and it was unbelievable. I said 'Barry, don't forget that rhythm. That's a number one record.' I knew, five bars in, no questions asked. You couldn't get past the intro without knowing it was a smash."[34] Engineers always say this later about songs that turn out to be smashes. But Richardson, an engineer to his core, never engaged in hype. He's a calm and steady presence. If he got excited, then the moment of hearing the song for the first time must have been exciting.

"Blue, Barry and I would sit down and say 'That chord sounds great there, but how about when the guitar player goes "dang, watang"?'" Albhy said. "'Do you want the seventh in the chord or do you want to leave that hole there?' Those were the kinds of things that had to be worked out."

"It's obviously easy," Robin said, getting breezy about the backbreaking work of others. "We've all got the same kind of brain wave."[35] "There was a period of time when Robin was important," a regular studio presence said. "Maurice would come in with his Perrier bottle with vodka, I assume, in it. Robin would come in, maybe once a day and he'd say, 'That's not getting the emotion. This should be in two parts, that's too busy.' He would make executive producer sort of comments, which were useful."[36]

"Robin is the objective production ear," Karl said. "The rest of us—Barry, Maurice and Albhy—get so close to the music, we do so many different experiments, that we can't always tell what sounds good. Robin comes in and calls it in a moment; it doesn't work or it sounds great."[37]

"Robin's opinion was very valuable," Albhy said. "Carl and I sat in the control room all the time. Blue and Denis were there more than Maurice and Robin. The day to day in the trenches was me, Barry and Karl. It was clearly Barry's vision. If Barry felt strongly about something, Karl and I would relent. Generally one of us would agree with him anyhow, because we knew it was what Barry wanted. We were executing Barry's vision."[38]

"It was orchestrated," Albhy said. "It was a process and it was all about 'head charts'; creating in the studio. 'Gee, OK, that's the part of the verse for the keyboards.' Then we would go for the performance. All of the arrangements were done on the spot and the performance was executed until it felt good. That was the standard. It didn't matter how we got there—whether something was thrown together or it was one take—our concern was that it felt good, that it made a statement. How it's done, I don't know. I know the end product. If that's accepted, then how it came to be is just detail."[39]

"Barry," Albhy, said, in the understatement of the twentieth and twenty-first centuries, "is meticulous about pitch and meter."[40] Barry at times demonstrated what songwriter Randy Newman has described as "the greatest gift," a gift for melody. Barry also was gifted with, always relied on and had trained over decades his absolute perfect pitch. Barry heard everything. What he heard in his head, he expected to hear on the tape. Barry's work ethic made that happen and he had a team that worked as hard as he did. If Barry, Albhy and Karl were awake, they were at the control board.

"Without them," Barry said, "I doubt that I would be able to express exactly what I want on a record. It would be far too much for my little head to comprehend. Their expertise in the studio really makes things happen."[41]

"The Bee Gees usually work from about three until midnight," Albhy said. "You're not a slave to the music, but you're dependent on their inspiration at the moment, or maybe your own. If you're excited about something and something is working, you can't leave."[42]

"They went out into the studio and nailed it," Karl Richardson said. "It didn't take long. If they didn't get the execution or the balance, it was easier to do it again. It would take longer to argue about it than to redo it, as they were all natural vocalists. Barry

Gibb doesn't really have vibrato, he has tremolo, so his intensity changes but not necessarily his pitch. Whereas Robin has fast vibrato and there are lots of pitch changes. [Maurice] was somewhere in between. Depending on where he was in his range, Maurice either had a little bit of vibrato or just straight tone. So, the distinctiveness was all three voices combining to make this unusual blend that you'd never get anywhere else. Nobody was tracking each other's vibrato, I can tell you that."[43]

Then, out of the blue, in the midst of work, everything changed. Stigwood told the band to forget about writing for an album, and to adapt what they already had for his upcoming movie soundtrack.

"You've got to remember," Barry said much later, "we were fairly dead in the water in 1975. The Bee Gees sound was basically tired. We hadn't had a hit record in about three years. We had to find something. We didn't know what was going to happen."[44] "The Bee Gees were making their 35th comeback," said Peter Brown, who had been a high executive at RSO. "Robert was very close to them. He'd developed them, produced them, he'd looked after them. At the same time, of course, he owned their management, their record label and their music publishing. So when *Saturday Night Fever* hit, Robert had the movie, their management, their publishing and the record deal."[45]

"Robert Stigwood flew up and told us the basic idea of his movie,"[46] Maurice said. "It was hard to get them to read anything," Stigwood said. "So I described the story."[47] "He asked if we'd like to write the music for it," Maurice said. "In those days it was like 'Wow! Movie music!' [Back then] you would pay people to get your songs in a film."[48] "We played him demo tracks of 'If I Can't Have You' and 'More Than a Woman.' He asked if we could write it more disco-y. We'd also written a song called 'Saturday Night,' but there were so many songs out called 'Saturday Night,' even one by the Bay City Rollers, so when we rewrote it for the movie, we called it 'Stayin' Alive.'"[49]

According to the Bee Gees' autobiography, Stigwood explained the plot and the boys leapt at the chance to create pure disco material. Both "Night Fever" and "Staying Alive" were written to align with the film's themes, and as possible titles.[50] They wrote the songs and recorded rough demos in "two and a half weeks." Stigwood liked everything, but couldn't understand why the most danceable song's chorus went "Stayin' alive / Stayin' alive." He wanted a chorus of "Saturday night / Saturday night." The band told him there were too many songs out already called "Saturday Night" and they wouldn't write another one. Barry told Stigwood to accept "Stayin' Alive" or the Bee Gees wouldn't let him have their current songs for the movie. Maurice said: "Then we wrote 'Night Fever' and Stigwood changed the movie's title to *Saturday Night Fever* from *Saturday Night*."[51]

"To me," Robin said, "*Saturday Night Fever* sounds like some sleazy little porno film showing on the corner, second billed to a film called *Suspender Belts*."[52]

Maurice later claimed to be gobsmacked at how well the song lyrics fit the film; the brothers had never been given a script and they would never read one. Travolta's showcase dance number is set to "You Should Be Dancing" rather than the newer Hérouville material because the actor had been rehearsing to "You Should Be Dancing" for two months. He was reluctant to scrap his work and shift to a new number.[53] Travolta's insistence helped make the song a hit for a second time.

"We weren't looking at *Fever* as a career vehicle," Maurice said. "We got caught up in the Robert Stigwood syndrome: Anyone he managed he also wanted involved in his film projects, as opposed to keeping them separate. He asked for songs, we gave him songs off what would have been our next studio album."

Regarding the sequence of events, Robin and Barry disagree with Stigwood's chronology, the timeline in their autobiography and each other. Robin insisted that the five songs—"How Deep Is Your Love," "If I Can't Have You," "More Than a Woman," "Night Fever" and "Stayin' Alive"—were written before Stigwood told them about the movie. Barry characterized that as "quite incorrect." Since they disagree, no printed account or interview since agrees, either. Accounts also differ as to Stigwood's influence on the songwriting. "Robert would tell them what the scene was about and what tempo and rhythm to use," Al Coury said, "and the boys would write it in the way he wanted."[54] So, in the Bee Gees' version, they dictate terms to Stigwood, threatening to withhold their songs; in Coury's version, Stigwood dictates to them . . .

Melody Maker captured their gestalt in an interview from December 1976: "Barry Gibb, the best looking of the three, with his coiffured hair and neatly trimmed beard, is a natural leader, holding down most of the conversation. Maurice, who is balding slightly, is perhaps more open and honest, but is held down by Barry. Robin, of the buck teeth, fly-away hair and intense falsetto voice, limits himself to rather cynical quips, most of which include rather bad language. They all tend to talk at once, frequently contradicting each other and indulging in arguments over small details."[55]

"To be able to watch the creative process when I was with Robert in France was a thrill," Freddie Gerson remembered. "The Chateau was a cold, depressing place. [The Gibbs] were more than a little cranky. When Robert explained this plot about some Italian kids in Bay Ridge, I never thought it would come together. But as Robert played tapes of just vocals and acoustic guitar, it was clear something very special was happening. They were all hits."[56]

The songs cut at Hérouville were "roughs," guide tracks for the final versions to be recorded at Criteria. There, extra instrumentation would be layered on, the vocals sung line by line as Barry wanted and new parts overdubbed. Stigwood's description of the film and demand for soundtrack material changed the vibe at the château. The band worked with renewed purpose. The sessions caught fire.

Albhy described the setup for "Night Fever": "The group had the hook line and rhythm—they usually pat their legs to set up a song's rhythm when they first sing it—and parts of the verses. They wrote the song in the castle stairway, which had natural echo. They had the emotion, same as on the record. We put down drums and acoustic guitar first so the feel was locked in. The piano part was put on before the bass, then the heavy guitar parts. Next came the vocals. A lot of the words are left out at first. Only the chorus and key words are locked in, and the rest is scat vocals because they find nice holes rhythmically to put words in that way. So they end up putting different lyrics in unusual places."[57]

"You're using the tape machine like a composer," Richardson said. "You start with no preconceived ideas, and when you keep working, it becomes unique."[58]

"It's easy to find something that works," Albhy said. "But it's hard to find something that really helps. On 'Night Fever' the sound of the verses is heavy guitar playing, long chords, and on top a harpsichord, one electric guitar playing octaves, triangle and lead guitar with muted strings through a wah-wah. It's mathematical, calculated—but the mathematics is in retrospect. You try to communicate with people's hearts."[59]

On "Night Fever," "Maurice was playing bass with his pick," Richardson said. "Dennis Bryon was playing drums; Blue Weaver keyboards; Alan Kendall rhythm guitar; and Barry was playing rhythm and singing the pilot vocal. The drums were the only thing retained [at Criteria] from this live track—it was a complete take, not comped—and all the other parts were overdubbed, like the keyboard part that was carefully crafted. Many parts weren't there from the start.

"[But] 'Night Fever' [on the record] is the rough mix. We mixed that song in 10 minutes. We had overdubbed all these synthesizer pads, extra guitar notes, little percussion instruments and so on, and we kept mixing it again and again and again, and finally we played the rough mix and everybody said it felt better. We had a demo of 'How Deep Is Your Love' from France, with the brothers singing, Blue playing keyboards and Mo playing bass, and right up until the final mix we would play that rough mix from France to use as a guide, because feel was everything to us."[60]

Barry remembers Stigwood's instructions about "Stayin' Alive": "Give me eight minutes—eight minutes, three moods. I want frenzy at the beginning. Then I want some passion. And then I want some *w-i-i-i-ld* frenzy!"[61]

"Stayin' Alive" is among the band's most enduring songs and by far the best cut on *SNF*. It has enthralled and irritated millions through the years. Its lyric: "We should try to understand / The *New York Times*' effect on man" ranks high among the band's most gnomic, and proves a strong contender for the band's second most misunderstood. The first most misunderstood being "Let's do it in your butt" from "You Should Be Dancing" (the actual lyric seems to be "What you doin' in the back?" though some also advocate "What you doin' in your bed in the back?"). "Stayin' Alive" is the Bee Gees' best-known song, an irresistible dance track and a watershed in recorded music history.

That watershed is a powerful secret at the beating heart of "Stayin' Alive." The song marks the first appearance of what would become a staple of modern recording: the drum loop.

The drum loop is called a loop because that's what it was: a circle, a sacred hoop, an actual loop of recording tape containing one sound—the sound of one drumbeat—cycling through the recording heads of the master recorder over and over. As with many industry-changing inventions, the drum loop came about as a simple, functional solution to an immediate problem. The immediate problem was that the drummer wasn't around.

The Bee Gees got things done. They had to record the song. Dennis's father suffered a health crisis and Dennis went to England to be with him. "'Stayin' Alive' didn't sound steady enough," Richardson said. The boys wrote "Night Fever" thinking it would be the lead song of the film and the first single. "Everybody was happy with the way 'Night Fever' turned out," Richardson said. "It had spark and it sounded wonderful."[62]

But Stigwood and the film's producers thought "Night Fever" was too mellow and not strong enough to be the lead single, which—since the album was coming out in advance of the movie—would also be the lead promotional piece for the film. The band turned their attention back to "Stayin' Alive." With Dennis gone, Barry wondered if the percussion sounds built into the studio's Hammond organ could provide a stronger, livelier beat. No one had ever attempted to use the built-in Hammond rhythm tracks like that before. Albhy and Karl thought it might work if the tracks were carefully "augmented by Barry's own rhythm guitar."[63]

"We were able to get a 4/4 beat out of the Hammond, but when Barry played along to it we didn't like the result," says Richardson. "Albhy and I came up with the idea of finding two bars [of actual drums] that really felt good, and making an eternal tape loop."[64] Richardson's first idea was to record "two bars of the four-track drums from 'Night Fever,'" rerecord them over and over and over, and put all those rerecords together to make a new, separate drum track that was as long as the song itself. But, as Karl, Albhy and Barry listened to the song repeatedly to find the best single beat to rerecord, Richardson or Galuten or both decided to copy one bar for a loop.

"Back then, drum machines were really primitive," Albhy said. "I had a brainstorm and told Karl we should take a bar from 'Night

Fever,' which we had already recorded, and make a drum loop." Barry, Karl and Albhy went back and listened to "Night Fever" for another marathon session, searching for the drumbeat best suited to "Stayin' Alive." "To make the loop, we copied the drums onto one quarter-inch tape," Albhy said. "We had nothing to do [at Hérouville]. There was no TV, there was nothing. We got up in the morning and hung out in the studio all day long. The idea of spending an hour trying to make a drum loop was . . . why not? We had nothing but time."[65]

Karl: "The tape was over 20 feet long and ran all around the control room—I gaffered some empty tape-box hubs to the tops of mic stands and ran the tape between the four-track machine and a 24-track deck, using the tape guides from a two-track deck for the tension. Because it was 4/4 time—just hi-hats and straight snare—it sounded steady as a rock."[66] "Karl took a boom microphone stand, with the boom horizontal, parallel to the ground," Albhy said. "He threaded the loop into the tape machine and the loop was too long for the supply and takeup reels, so Karl taped them down so they wouldn't spin. He set the microphone boom stand a few feet from the tape recorder and ran the tape over the horizontal part of the boom stand and down across a seven inch reel. We pressed play and the drum loop played."[67]

"As we started to lay tracks down to it," Albhy said, "we found that it felt really great—insistent but not machinelike. It had a human feel. By the time we had overdubbed all the parts to the songs and Dennis came back, there was no way we could get rid of the loop. Everybody knows that it's more about feel than accuracy in drum tracks. I wish now I knew which bar it was. That's a great sounding bar."[68]

"The loop was so popular because it has a feel," Albhy said. "Live drummers sometimes slow down or speed up, but the feel inside the bar can be amazing. The feel changes based on the dynamic. It's not like sampling where you have an individual drum.

We thought that this bar would be replaced by real drums later. Because it had never been done before, we didn't know—nobody knew at the time—that a good-feeling bar repeating incessantly has an unbelievable feel. 'Stayin' Alive' has an insistent rhythm unlike anything you heard before.

"Because of the drum loop, it was the first song where we over-dubbed instruments one at a time," Albhy continued. "We'd fixed things, we'd rerecorded things, but [this was the first time] that we recorded one instrument at a time."[69]

Maurice had to be taught the "Stayin' Alive" bass line, some-one hanging around the sessions asserts. "Maurice was not a ses-sion musician. Generally, pitch is not a problem if you're playing electric bass. But meter was critical. Maurice was shown the bass part, and played along with it. Karl and Albhy marked the notes that were out of time, early or late, and Maurice would take an-other pass at it. Karl would punch in and out (meaning stopping and restarting the tape) for each note that was funny. Albhy and Karl fixed all notes until the bass part was completely right."

"The 'You Should Be Dancing' bass line is very much a Mau-rice bass line," the studio source goes on. "Whereas the 'Stayin' Alive' bass line is a healthy bass line. 'Stayin' Alive' was one of those rooted bass lines. Barry was playing guitar and Robin and Maurice were out in the studio working on the song. The key-board part was all Blue Weaver. Blue was independent. He did not like to take direction and he was a creative musician."

So, there it is . . . the recurring motif, stated as baldly as possi-ble. Maurice could not come up with a bass part complex enough for the material, and had trouble learning the bass parts he had to be taught. Unsurprisingly, nobody fought the dissemination of this idea with greater tenacity than Maurice. In 1979 he told *Rolling Stone*: "I'd like to clear this point up. I know there are rumors that Barry does more on our records than Robin and I. I don't know how that rot got started, but I hate and resent it. It's a load of shit. People get that impression because Barry's out front a lot and gets quite a bit of attention for his work with Karl and Albhy on other people's songs, and for his work with [brother] Andy. But as far as *our* records are concerned, we all contribute *equally* and all produce *equally*."[70]

Only, they didn't. They hadn't contributed or produced equally since they reunited after the post-*Odessa* breakup, and seldom before that. When the brothers got back together there was no doubt who was in charge, and one glance at the band playing live or in their music videos only confirms it. Barry ran the show. That dynamic was a harsh toke for Maurice, no doubt—and worse for Robin—but the hard truth, nonetheless. Neither Robin nor Barry ever made any strong assertions in support of Maurice's claims.

"I wouldn't call [Maurice] a nonentity," the studio guest said. "But he was more of a social entity than a musical entity."

The infinite universe of music nerds on YouTube helps back up the assertions about the difference between Maurice's "You Should Be Dancing" bass line and the bass on "Stayin' Alive." Plenty of players have posted videos of themselves playing the bass line along with the song. Hearing the bass separate from the mix is revealing. The bass on "You Should Be Dancing" has a programmatic feel. It's a relatively simple, easily memorized piece played over and over with no variation. The bass walks the 1-2-3-4 beat, comps during the bridge and tosses in a little riff under the lyric "You should be dancing." It's funky enough, if unrelated to any other instrument except the drums.

The bass in "Stayin' Alive" is aggressively syncopated and showcases a sophisticated compositional sensibility. In the early verses the bass stays simple, keeping out of the way, providing a steady bottom. As the song progresses, the bass intertwines with the equally complex guitar, suggesting that the same person wrote for both instruments with their interplay foremost in mind. The bass comps during the chorus, leaving plenty of room for the vocals. A close listen to the bass line, even as played by amateurs in their bedrooms, strongly suggests that the same musician could not have conceived the two parts.

"That steady, steady [drum] track gave us the groove we wanted, and we then overdubbed everybody to it," Richardson said. "The guys did their vocals, Alan played the guitar riff, Blue played electric piano and an ARP string synth and when Dennis returned he overdubbed the toms, crash and hi-hat. He loved it. A case of a lot less work. On the record sleeve, the drummer on 'Stayin' Alive' was listed as Bernard Lupé; a sort of French version of the famous session drummer Bernard Purdie. We received an unbelievable amount of calls looking for this steady drummer named Bernard Lupé. You know, 'This guy's a rock! I've never heard anyone so steady in my life!'"[71]

"The loop crossed the boundary, giving us music that was in time with a good feel," Albhy said. "If I had been working for a technology company then and knew what I was doing, I would have tried to patent the idea. Nonetheless, it changed a lot of things. That first loop was a watershed even in our life and times."[72]

That loop—the infectious, driving pulse of the song—had "quite a career in its own right," Karl said. The loop ended up as the drumbeat for "More Than a Woman," and for Barbra Streisand's "Woman in Love," which Barry would write and produce.

"We knew we had a smash track," Karl said. "John G. Avildsen—the director of *Saturday Night Fever*—envisioned setting one of Travolta's dance numbers to 'Stayin' Alive.'" He asked Stigwood if the Bee Gees could provide a slower tempo bridge section so Travolta and partner Karen Lynn Gorny could go all slow-mo as they fell in love on the dance floor. Once that heart-stopping moment had been established, the dance beat would return, and the two would celebrate their love with even more ecstatic discoing. Travolta didn't like the idea; he'd been rehearsing to "You

Should Be Dancing" for two months for his big solo number and to the more recent rough of "More Than a Woman" for the pas-de-deux.

"Robert wanted a scene that was eight minutes long," Barry said, "Where Travolta was dancing with this girl. It would have a nice dance tempo, a romantic interlude and all hell breaking loose at the end. I said, 'Robert, that's crazy. We want to put this song out as a single, and we don't think the rhythm should break. It should go from beginning to end with the same rhythm, and get stronger all the way. To go into a lilting ballad just doesn't make sense.'"[73]

"They did write a bridge," Karl Richardson said, "and there is a version of 'Stayin' Alive' where the song changes key and turns into a slow ballad for 16 or 32 bars. Then there's a big drum break and everything reverts to normal. After the bridge had been recorded and I'd spliced it into the track, Albhy and I stared at each other and said 'We just ruined a hit record.' We turned to Barry and said 'We can't use this. We've screwed up a number one record,' and Barry said 'Yeah, we have.' So, we put the tape back together without the new bridge and called Stigwood to say 'This is bogus. We're not doing it.' And that's when Stigwood fired the director."[74]

Poor John Avildsen. For all his experience, he did not recognize nor sufficiently kowtow to his most crucial constituency—Stigwood and Travolta. He also apparently didn't understand how to shoot dance sequences, or at least not to Travolta's specifications. Travolta called Stigwood in tears and told him he was leaving the picture. This was not movie-star grandstanding because, at the time, Travolta was not a movie star. *SNF* was his breakout opportunity, so Travolta had little leverage. His strong reaction was heartfelt passion from an actor who knew that the one moment that could change his career forever was being compromised. Coincidentally, Travolta also knew that the film itself was being undermined. This was a rare intersection of artist's vanity and practical vision. In the movies, there is no more powerful moral force.

Travolta's complaint was that Avildsen refused to shoot Travolta's big dance number from the floor up, so that all of Travolta's body—from his head to his toes—could be seen in the frame. Travolta wanted to be seen dancing. He didn't want edits going back and forth from his upper body to his feet; he wanted no suggestion that some stunt dancer was making moves for him. Travolta asked for an old-fashioned movie-musical straight-on wide shot capturing all the dancers in their disco lines, with Travolta front and center. However commonsensical the idea, Avildsen wouldn't do it.

Multiple sources claim that Avildsen did not want the Bee Gees music in the movie in the first place and resisted their songs from the start. But the Bee Gees were Stigwood's band and any director would have to have known going in that they were part of the deal.

Stigwood called Avildsen. The passing of time has allowed many different versions of that call to be cited, and the two best come from Stigwood. "The other night I fired the *Saturday Night* director," Stigwood said. "It was a terrible coincidence, too. When I was firing him, the message came through that he'd been nominated for an Academy Award (for directing *Rocky*). I had to break off and congratulate him in the middle and then carry on with the foul deed."[75] In an even better version, Stigwood claims to have said to Avildsen: "I have good news and bad news." To which Avildsen naturally replied: "What's the good news?" Stigwood said: "You've been nominated for an Oscar for directing *Rocky*." Avildsen: "And the bad news?" Stigwood: "You're fired."

In all the universe, only Robert Stigwood gets to have such conversations.

"I'm sorry the picture isn't going to happen," John Avildsen told the *New York Times*. "Why I was fired is a matter of opinion and I'd rather not dwell on it."[76]

John Badham replaced Avildsen. For the discerning filmgoer, Badham's greatest claim to fame is his sister, Mary Badham, who played the unforgettable Scout in *To Kill a Mockingbird*. Badham's sole major directing credit before *SNF* was the James Earl Jones–Richard Pryor baseball farce, *The Bingo Long Traveling All-Stars & Motor Kings*. Badham turned out to be both biddable and able to direct a cogent dance sequence. Oddly though, in the finished film, as Travolta and Gorny swirl about the floor to "Night Fever," there remain a number of shots from below, framing the two against the disco ceiling as they turn arm in arm. Could these have been left over from Avildsen's time at the helm? The dancers are shown only from the waist up. Travolta was right: they look ridiculous.

The sessions at Hérouville lasted for two months. When Karl wasn't attending to all that *SNF* demanded, he was, at Stigwood's behest, mixing the Bee Gees' next release—*Here at Last . . . The Bee Gees . . . Live*—a double LP and the band's first live album. It captured their December 20, 1976, concert at the Los Angeles Forum, which was broadcast live on the radio on the *King Biscuit Flower Hour*. A television special of the show had been planned. Wally Heider's Record Plant mobile unit, the best mobile recording studio in the world, was on-site to capture the audio. The video proved subpar and no completed version of the show has been released. The Bee Gees finished up at Hérouville in the late spring of 1977.

Timbales and other percussion for "Stayin' Alive" were overdubbed at Criteria by Joe Lala. The Miami String Section made Blue Weaver's synthesizer lines more majestic. More strings were added during sessions at Capitol Studios in Los Angeles. *SNF*'s final mix was done back at Criteria. Post-production work finished on the album in April 1977.

With only six tracks from the Bee Gees, the soundtrack needed padding. Bill Oakes was president of RSO and is credited with "Album Supervision and Compilation." That suggests he picked the other material and was responsible for the order of the songs on each side. Whoever chose it, the non–Bee Gees material on the record is mostly second-rate, both second-rate disco and second-rate compared to each band's best work.

Oakes was, at the time, married to Yvonne Elliman. Elliman starred as Mary Magdalene on Broadway in *Jesus Christ Superstar*. Throughout the mid-1970s she sang backup for Eric Clapton on record and onstage. Her voice can be heard on his "Lay Down Sally" and "I Shot the Sheriff." There had been talk of her covering "How Deep Is Your Love" for *SNF*, but Stigwood vetoed that idea. He thought more of the song than the Bee Gees did, and he insisted that their version go on the album. The band had recorded "If I Can't Have You," but Elliman's version appears on the soundtrack. Produced by disco maven and Gloria ("I Will Survive") Gaynor producer Freddie Perren, the song's both bouncy and pallid, riddled with flute flourishes, and Elliman's voice is no revelation. As with a lot of disco, the song has no climax or peak, only the same refrain repeated endlessly. Even so, it charted from late January until June of 1978 and spent a week in mid-May at #1. Compared to the Bee Gees' other songs on the album, it's weak. Their own version of the song has no more force or staying power than Elliman's.

David Shire's "Night on Disco Mountain" is a five-minute-thirteen-second argument for the horror of all music piggybacked onto disco by those who had no understanding of rhythm or dance music. A studio source maintains that Shire came in, picked up the assignment to create "soundtrack" filler, wrote his pieces and recorded them, all on the same day. They sound like it. There's no telling how much money Shire made from that one day of half-hearted effort.

M.F.S.B. had strong credentials, but their "K-Jee" is not only generic material for the band, it's generic instrumental disco.

Which is a shame; there are far better M.F.S.B. tracks to choose from. Mother Father Sister Brother or, as they were better known, Motherfucking Soul Band, had a hell of a résumé. They wrote and performed the theme for *Soul Train* and were the house band for famed Philly producers Kenny Gamble and Leon Huff at Sigma Sound. There they backed Harold Melvin and the Blue Notes, the O'Jays, the Spinners and the Stylistics, among many others. It's hard to find a worse song in their catalog than "K-Jee."

Kool and the Gang's "Open Sesame" is another convincing argument for the reverse-Midas touch of disco. Kool and the Gang was not a disco band; they played hard-core funk. This layering of disco tropes over a speeded-up version of their signature sound is dispiriting. Like "K-Jee," it did not chart as a single.

"Boogie Shoes," by KC and the Sunshine Band, sounds like every KC song, which sound like every other KC song. It's hooky, innocuous, content free and happy, reflecting KC's ingenious whitening of the Funky Nassau sound, with its calypso influences and cruise-ship version of the rock-steady beat. "Boogie Shoes," which charted for ten weeks in early 1978 and peaked at #35, didn't sound like disco then and doesn't today.

Tavares was a vocal group of long standing, whose 1975 R&B chart #1, "It Only Takes a Minute," made the UK top 10 decades later when covered by boy band Take That. The Bee Gees liked the Tavares' sound. Al Coury said:"The Bee Gees wrote ['More Than a Woman'] and gave it to Tavares. We wanted to give them a shot; they said they'd bring it home."[77] Their manager later lamented that the Tavares' version was too disco for their more traditional black R&B constituency, but it charted for fourteen weeks, reaching #32. Later, desperate along with everyone else to escape the stigma of *SNF*, their manager said: "The totality of our show has nothing to do with disco."[78]

The Trammps' "Disco Inferno" is one of the welcome exceptions on *SNF*. A classic dance track, and proof of how driving, funky and galvanizing good disco could be, "Inferno" combines archetypal disco arranging with old-school R&B throat clearing, grunting and soul shouting. The chicken-scratch wah-wah guitar, string charts, keyboard riffs and repetitive bass are pure disco, but the break, the harmonies and the shout-back chorus owe their sound to Stax-Volt and the traditions of southern soul. It charted for nineteen weeks and spent two weeks at #11.

"Calypso Breakdown" is uncut Funky Nassau run through a disco mixer. It's a not much of a track, but does offer a textbook of combining preexisting sounds to make a sure-fire club hit. The unchanging cowbell gave DJs a clear metronome to guide switching from one copy to another. The bass line and unbroken cymbal riff echo—not to say copy—"Soul Makossa," but the song never takes off. It does, however, by its inclusion, draw attention to the remarkable career of its composer and producer, Ralph MacDonald. A life-long percussionist, MacDonald joined Harry Belafonte's band at age seventeen. MacDonald co-wrote "Where Is the Love," which hit #5 for Roberta Flack and Donny Hathaway. He co-wrote "Just the Two of Us" for saxophonist Grover Washington and singer Bill Withers; that got to #2. His *New York Times* obituary described MacDonald as "the ghost behind the hit records of a multitude of 1970s and '80s pop stars." Though "Calypso Breakdown" hardly showcases MacDonald's true skills, it's nice to see him get some of that SNF money.

Walter Murphy's "A Fifth of Beethoven" is a disco novelty cut featuring moments from Ludwig van Beethoven's Fifth Symphony over corny strings, bombastic horns and secondhand clavinet riffs that evoke the worst of Deodato. And what's worse than Deodato?

The inclusion of "A Fifth of Beethoven" suggests that somebody at RSO both liked and saw the market potential in novelty tracks. Nowhere was this canniness more evident than in Stigwood's treatment of Rick Dees, the auteur behind "Disco Duck." Dees, a "personality" on radio and TV, wrote the track as a disco parody; it features in-rhythm quacking and is even more unlisten-able than that sounds. Dees released the track on a small label, expecting little. Stigwood heard it, recognized its potential and bought the master tape for $3,500. Fueled by RSO's promotion, "Disco Duck" went on to spend October of 1976 at #1. RSO secured permission to put "Duck" on the soundtrack of the film. Dees took the offer assuming his song would be on the album. Alas for him, "Duck" can be heard only as background music in one scene. Dees claims he lost $2.5 million by not being smart enough to insist that his cut make the record.

The Bee Gees' tracks, save one, have not aged well. "More Than a Woman" and "How Deep Is Your Love" are pablum. A close read of the lyrics suggests that both songs spring from Robin's juvenile sense of humor. Like *Main Course's* "Fanny," the lyrics of "More Than a Woman" seem both a wink to, and a dirty joke at the expense of, disco's gay demographic. When asked what the lyrics to "Woman" were about, Robin said, in one of his classic retorts: "Three tits, two vaginas."[79] What Robin meant is anybody's guess; he loved to blow off interviewers with those sorts of quips. "How Deep Is Your Love" addresses another of Robin's recurring obsessions, if his studio-wall drawings are any guide: penis size. Perhaps this issue stemmed from sibling rivalry. Maurice—Robin's fraternal, but not identical, twin—answered to a long-standing family nickname: Moby.

The saccharine, unchallenging production of "How Deep Is Your Love," "More Than a Woman" and "Night Fever" under-scores, as always, the packaging genius of the Gibbs and their production team. Nightclub performers would be crooning all three for another decade. The irresistible pop power of the melodies overcomes Barry's screechy falsetto and any lyrical content. The cuts are as hummable as the lyrics are instantly forgettable. Does anyone actually know a verse lyric to "More Than a Woman"? Has anyone who heard it once ever forgotten the chorus?

At least "Night Fever" changes between verse and chorus, but like "Deep" and "Woman," fights against a layer of studio gloss that holds the song at a remove. That gloss deadens the funky rhythm guitar and shrouds the nice wah-wah vamping and sustained guitar drones during the breaks. That guitar work—and these three tracks—exemplify an unsolvable problem of Bee Gees music of this era: the willful mediocrity of the second-rate songs pushes away the listener. But the popcraft, production and musicianship remain compelling. These are mediocre songs that, when broken into their component parts, prove textbooks in understanding pop, how to embellish, how to build pieces that add up to a whole. Few bands present this dilemma. Most second-rate or really annoying songs eventually fade away. Not these. Simply focusing on, say, the killer guitar part on "Night Fever" keeps the listener engaged. It's a conundrum. These songs are so part of the cultural ether, and so in everyone's heads, that a clear aesthetic read on them proves almost impossible.

No late-period Bee Gees track offers a greater conundrum than "Stayin' Alive." It's a killer song, as modern today as the day it was recorded, with that perfect funk drum-loop barely lagging the beat and the grunting chorus driving it on. Like "Jive Talkin'," it plays as essentially raceless. The song is actually slower than it sounds, which springs from the tension between the lagging beat and the pushing bass. That tension brings the funk, and some part of your body will move whenever this song comes on. Today it carries so much cultural baggage that whenever it does come on—in a TV show, on the radio, ironically on a film soundtrack, as somebody's ring tone—everybody smiles. "Stayin' Alive" is beloved, and for good reason. It sounds like the Bee Gees; nothing and nobody else.

A closer listen reveals the core problem. There is something grating about "Stayin' Alive," and the louder the volume, the more grating it becomes. Listen to, for instance, the vocal-only tracks of the Beatles, the Beach Boys or even Little Feat—something easy enough to do these days; they're all on YouTube someplace—and you hear music of the spheres. The vocals are lovely, heartfelt and transcendent even, or especially, when they're not perfect. The vocal tracks for the Beach Boys' *Pet Sounds*, and the revelations of process to be heard there, are unforgettable. The vocal-only tracks from "Stayin' Alive" are hard, ugly and effortful. The falsetto harmonies, which worked so well on "Jive Talkin'," sound forced and revved up, like the Chipmunks overdosing on Adderall. Barry shouts and grunts with off-putting aggression. The harshness of the vocals is a hidden time bomb in the song, making it hard to listen all the way through.

The problem with the Bee Gees' music during this era can be summed up in one tough question: Could Barry hear the difference? Could he tell his best work from his second best? The Spanish have a proverb which translates: "Too much perfection is a mistake." Did Barry's mania for control and pop perfectionism stifle the soul in his soul music? "Stayin' Alive" is a mechanistic artifact from a mechanistic genre, and tragically, soulless at its core.

Danceable as hell, though . . .

"Stayin' Alive" spent less time at #1 than any other #1 on the LP.

The lineup of novelty cuts and second-rate songs from bands that had done much better work suggest bottom-feeding, that RSO sought the cheapest material to fill out the record, a time-honored practice with soundtracks. *SNF*'s success put an end to that practice, as studios discovered the earnings a well-constructed soundtrack could bring. But it does raise the question of whether, despite investing so much of his own money in the project, Stigwood was having second thoughts, whether he did not believe that the record was going to have legs. This notion is reinforced by Bill Oakes's attitude when he mastered the LP.

In October of 1977, Bill Oakes ran the mastering sessions for *Saturday Night Fever*. He seems, like others, to have run out of interest in and patience for the project. He feared the cultural wheel had already turned and that *SNF* would be left behind. Oakes told Anthony Haden-Guest: "We started at midnight and went on till dawn, and by this time I was absolutely fried. I had been listening to disco for so long, I never wanted to hear the stuff again. I wanted to get it over with. The word was that people had had enough; the Deadheads were coming back. Heavy Metal was making a run at it. That's it! Let's move on. Tom Petty was auditioning for a label deal with Capitol that night. I thought that sounded interesting. But they kept calling me down the corridor with the master. 'C'mon! We've got to listen to another track! Tavares, pumping away.' Great! I won't have to listen to it again. I was going to hand [the master tape] to the record company, and they would do what they would. It was in the back of my car. I was between La Brea and Hollywood as dawn broke, sitting behind a truck with a bumper sticker that said 'Death to Disco.' I was sitting there thinking, perhaps it is. It's too boring to think of. I drove home, and left the master in the car."[80]

SNF's album packaging might not have seemed cheesy and cheap in 1976; to see the LP today is a shock. The front cover features Travolta in classic one-hand-raised disco pose, pointing upward to a shot of the Bee Gees in disco-white ensembles. The inside of the gatefold hasn't a word of text or detail about the record. Instead, there are nineteen photographs of Travolta from the film, with a montage of his most iconic moves in the center. The back of the jacket showcases a crop from the front-cover photo of the Bee Gees, and incongruous promo shots of Elliman and Tavares. It looks like Stigwood spent as little as possible on the jacket.

Making sure product kept moving through the pipeline, Stigwood released *Here at Last . . . The Bee Gees . . . Live* in May 1977. It went quadruple platinum, selling over 4.5 million copies and hitting #8 in the US. A live version of "Edge of the Universe" (from *Main Course*) reached #16 on the US singles charts. For any other group, this level of success would be a career milestone, proof that fans still cared enough to gobble up a live record in astounding quantities. And proof that the Bee Gees' fan base remained, at minimum, almost 5 million strong. But given events that were coming down the pike, *Here at Last* in the eyes of the public, the label, the band and history proved merely a footnote.

As RSO's formidable publicity machine geared up for the December release of *Saturday Night Fever*, the Bee Gees embarked on another of Stigwood's grand adventures.

sgt. pepper's lonely
hearts club band

> While we were filming *Sergeant Pepper*, we wrote songs like "Tragedy" and "Too Much Heaven," and then "Shadow Dancing," all in one day. That's three hit singles in less than 24 hours. So the drugs must have been good that day.
>
> —Maurice Gibb[1]

> It was the best of times, we had the worst of films.
>
> —Robin Gibb[2]

*I*t's not easy to make the worst movie ever made.

In cultures where cannibalism carries religious or spiritual overtones—as opposed to its occasional appearance when folks just get really, really hungry—the act of consuming your dead enemy or beloved grandpa supposedly transfers to the diner the power, soul and positive attributes of the eaten. But if certain rituals are improperly performed or righteous respect not paid, then the consumed can rise up within the consumer and, you know, consume him. In ancient myth, the daring mortal Prometheus stole fire from the Greek gods. For messin' where he shouldn't have been a-messin', the gods had Prometheus chained to a sea-side rock and summoned birds to peck out his liver for all eternity.

This is kind of what happened to the Bee Gees with *Sgt. Pepper's*.

The Bee Gees learned the hard way that you can *Meet the Beatles*—and, as the eighth-grade joke went when that album was released, you can "Beat the Meatles"—but you can never beat the Beatles. Barry seemed obsessed with trying, to slight reciprocation. Maurice met John Lennon once and ended up irritated, intimidated and moved to ingratiation.

"Robert introduced us," Maurice said. "He said, 'John, this is Maurice Gibb of the Bee Gees, a new group I just signed up,' and I said, 'It's nice to meet you, John,' and he said, 'Naturally.' So I said, 'Oh, stuff you!' A little bit later he came over and offered to buy me a drink. He said, 'I like you, you know.' I said, 'What do you mean?' He said, 'I like the way you answered that.' I said, 'Does that mean we're friends then?' And he said, 'You bet.'" They went for drinks at the Speakeasy during a Cream concert where Maurice sat between Lennon and Keith Moon.[3]

It's hard to find an interview wherein Paul, John, George or Ringo even mention the Bee Gees. Barry chose the Beatles as his nemesis, but always felt invisible to them. He told Timothy White: "George Harrison always said, 'you were four years later than us; we were four years earlier than you.' That's the way he put it to me, and I'd never known until then whether the Beatles even thought about the Bee Gees being around."[4]

"The brothers suffered greatly during the late Sixties from the Beatle thing," Stigwood said. "When their first single, 'New York Mining Disaster 1941,' was released, everyone thought it *was* the Beatles. That hurt them badly"[5]

This was a widely held, or at least widely published view, when the Bee Gees first hit. In 1967, Richard Goldstein wrote: "More than common management, this new combo shared something musical with Lennon and McCartney: their sound. 'New York Mining Disaster—1941' would have been a credible title for a new Beatle composition, and the production (intoning strings to back a sparsely tragic tale) would have been an appropriate sequel to 'Eleanor Rigby.' Even the vocal phrasing—clipped, soft and incredibly sad—had a certain McCartney quality to it. Heads shot back when the radio announcers revealed that the Bee Gees were themselves."[6] Even Barry said, well after the fact: "We were Beatlish in the early days. Our melodies lent themselves to that style. Thank God we got away from them. It could have led us further and further astray."[7]

But "New York Mining Disaster 1941" doesn't sound anything like the Beatles. Its familiar strumming guitar comes not from the Beatles, but straight out of the skiffle music scene that influenced almost every early British pop band. The Bee Gees' first #1 in Australia—"Spicks and Specks"—apes Herman's Hermits, not the Fab Four. The 1968 release of tracks recorded in Australia between 1963 and 1966, *Rare, Precious & Beautiful*, showcases songs that do sound much like the Beatles in form, harmony, guitar and mood. It speaks—like everything else—to Barry's pop genius that at eighteen he could perfectly imitate the full range of early Beatles sounds. Nobody else in England at the time—and everybody was trying as hard as they could—even came close.

Viewed from fifty years on, it's clear that the Bee Gees' first four hit singles are theirs alone. It took guts, conviction and even self-delusion on the part of the band and Stigwood to release music so idiosyncratic, so unlike the popular hits of the day. "Words," "Massachusetts" and "Got to Get a Message" take nothing from the Beatles.

How could they? The Bee Gees were never rock and rollers. Their sound did not combine American postwar R&B and seminal African American rock acts with English pub and dance-hall traditions. The Bee Gees never vested in rock's 4/4 driving beat—the signature of the Liverpool sound known as "the beat"—that served as the Beatles' namesake. The Bee Gees' music never, in any iteration, bore the foremost quality of the Beatles: raucous joy.

The Bee Gees were the least likely guys on earth to cover, let alone understand, for example, "Dizzy Miss Lizzy." They didn't holler out harmonies, seldom improvised and held themselves aloof from the emotion of their music. Unfortunate, then, that the Bee Gees undertook the deeply thankless task of covering—cannibalizing—the Beatles' least rock and roll, most mock-profound album. But mock-profundity was, after all, Barry's stock in trade.

The whole debacle was Stigwood's fault. According to the Bee Gees' autobiography, making a movie of the Beatles' album had been "a pet project of Stigwood's for a number of years."[8]

On November 17, 1974, Stigwood's production of a theatrical musical version of *Sgt. Pepper's* began a seven-week run at New York's Beacon Theatre. Tom O'Horgan, an off-Broadway experimental theater director who worked with the pioneering downtown theater company La Mama, directed. Rock critic Robert Christgau, who found the show "one-dimensional schlock," wrote: "Artistically as well as commercially (the Beacon wasn't one-third full on the fourth day of the run) 'Sgt. Pepper' is a flop."[9]

Stigwood closed the show after six weeks. Not, he insisted, because it was a commercial failure, but because it wasn't what he had envisioned. In April 1976, Stigwood sought out rock critic Henry Edwards, who would later author *Stardust: The David Bowie Story* and function as John Lennon's secretary-turned-mistress May Pang's co-author for her tell-all, *Loving John: The Untold Story*. Stigwood wanted Edwards, who had never written a screenplay, to write a *Sgt. Pepper's* movie. Shortly before *Sgt. Pepper's* was released, Henry wrote of his experience in the *New York Times*: "[Stigwood] had first tried to put 'Sgt. Pepper' on stage. The result was an evening of razzle-dazzle production numbers that tried to duplicate the sound of the classic Beatles album. It was an artistic failure, but the production was selling tickets when Mr. Stigwood closed it. He wanted to rethink it—for film. If there's one rule that stands above all others in Hollywood, it's that if at first you don't succeed, don't under any circumstances, try again. Mr. Stigwood was preparing to break this rule."[10]

Edwards told Stigwood he saw the film as a modernizing of a "World War II-era musical." Edwards loved MGM musicals from the golden age of Hollywood and told Stigwood he wanted to make "the musical of the future."[11] Edwards cited the heyday of the studio system, when lyricists would throw out ideas, studios would summon their stars and start shooting the next week. Edwards said Stigwood listened with care, "aware that giving them his O.K. would result in a film as unconventional as it would be expensive. Grinning, he said, 'It has the right feel to me.'"[12]

The Beatles had always been leery of Stigwood—back in the day NEMS paid him off to go away. Stigwood returned seeking use of their songs and for once in his life he did not get the best of a deal. "It took about a year to negotiate," Stigwood said. "Anything to do with the Beatles is complicated. But I must say, they were cooperative."

Cooperative to the point of producing a phone-book-size contract and demanding rights of approval over Stigwood's choice of screenwriter and director.[13] Stigwood also agreed that a Beatles management company rep—that is, a snitch in service to John or Paul—could attend the screenings of each day's footage. That Stigwood surrendered so completely speaks to his mad desire for the material. Had the Beatles wanted to screw him, they could have rejected one draft or director after another and kept Stigwood dangling for years. Maybe they found Stigwood's concept so farcical they said yes as a lark. Or maybe, like everyone else involved before production began, they thought Stigwood would make a mint. *Tommy*, released a year before, did; so did *Jesus Christ*

Superstar. That's what Stigwood did: he made mints. Nobody could conceive that the picture might tank.

Edwards said: "We want to create a movie that's a movie, not a Beatles film. It's even set in the present, not the sixties."[14] Edwards culled 22 songs—out of the 29 to which Stigwood secured the rights—from *Sgt. Pepper's*, *Abbey Road*, and *Let It Be* to flesh out the skeleton of his screenplay. Stigwood held a production meeting in Acapulco. "The traditional method of reducing the cost of a movie is to excise whole scenes," Edwards said. "But at the Acapulco meeting, Mr. Stigwood interrupted the discussion of which chunks should go: 'I love it all too much,' he said, 'for any of it to be discarded. Let's find creative ways to do it for less.'"[15]

The film's production designer, Brian Eatwell, was on an MGM back lot in Culver City, California, when he discovered the small-town set used in Mickey Rooney's 1930s and '40s nauseatingly innocent *Andy Hardy* films. The set had the atmosphere Edwards sought when describing a modern remake of a 1920s musical. Stigwood dispatched two hundred carpenters to work twenty-four-hour shifts to rebuild the quaint town square for *Sgt. Pepper's*. That was not exactly doing things for less.

The film generated a lot of pre-production good will. The *New York Times* reported breathlessly on invitations going out to various stars offering them parts: the Eagles, Perry Como, Frank Sinatra, John Lennon, Bing Crosby, Bette Midler and many others.[16] *Rolling Stone* reported that the Bee Gees would only narrate the film, not star in it.[17] The invitations raised the specter of *Tommy*, a kitchen-sink picture in which half the roles could have been played by anybody. The Who's rock opera, however loosely structured, gave the film something Harry Edwards would have to concoct—a coherent narrative. Anyone who owned *Tommy* the record came to *Tommy* the movie knowing how events would unfold; the movie functioned like a *Classics Illustrated* version of the album. Director Ken Russell, a madman and visual decadent, understood that *Tommy* would work best as a series of more or less disconnected musical vignettes. He threw ideas at the wall—and at Anne-Margaret—and kept what stuck. That approach worked fine for a story that audiences already knew. Stigwood's mood swings with regard to *Pepper's*—at times penny pinching and at others overindulgent—started the boulder of disaster rolling before a single frame was shot.

For his director, Stigwood chose—and the Beatles apparently approved—Michael Schultz, who came up through New York City's Negro Ensemble Company, a theater group. Schultz made his directorial debut with *Cooley High* (1975). His second film was 1976's fondly remembered, unintelligible, episodic, black stoner comedy *Car Wash*, which featured an all-star cast—Richard Pryor, the Pointer Sisters, Antonio Fargas, Bill Duke and George Carlin—and, in keeping with most stoner comedies, no discernable story line. The soundtrack did a lot better than the film. The title song hit #1; "I'm Going Down" and "I Wanna Get Next to You" both cracked the top 10. Schultz later made the episodic, cringe-worthy *Krush Groove*, an almost unwatchable yet indispensable guide to New York mid-eighties rap, break dance and b-boy culture starring Sheila E, Run-DMC, the Fat Boys, Kurtis Blow, Bobby Brown and Blair Underwood. Schultz has since enjoyed a respectable forty-year career directing television. Stigwood's hiring the inexperienced Schultz makes a certain sense. With *Car Wash*, Schultz turned an underwritten screenplay into respectable grosses and killer soundtrack sales.

But *Car Wash* starred comedians, who know how to fill the screen. Richard Pryor's director, however inexperienced, needed only to say "action" and "cut" and Pryor would do the rest. The Bee Gees, as rank amateurs, required a director they would respect and listen to. Hiring David Lean, however, might not have made any difference. Stigwood's concept ignored an immutable law of show business: rock stars cannot act—any more than movie stars can rock and roll. The two jobs demand opposite energies and sensibilities, and pretty much nobody makes the transition.

The Beatles, the exceptions who prove every rule, were charming enough in *Hard Day's Night* and *Help!* Ringo showed a flare for channeling Ringo-ness onscreen and he made a nice half-assed second career of doing just that. There is only one fully realized movie performance by a rock star: Mick Jagger's messianic, satanic incarnation of, in his words, "a projection of the director's fantasy of who he thinks I think I am," in Nicholas Roeg's hallucinatory, perverse *Performance*. Mick played an italicized version of himself, but at least he could do that. The Bee Gees showed few gifts as thespians. They, like every other musician who tried acting—from George Strait to 50 Cent—only embarrassed themselves. (Except for Queen Latifah.)

The Bee Gees' terrible performances were not their fault. They fell in with Stigwood's fantasy. When the cameras started rolling, they reverted to the baseline performance mode that had worked for them since they were children: show up and smile. No director could make film actors of the Gibbs with such craptastic, superficial material. They had no idea what they were getting into, and when they discovered they possessed no appropriate skill sets, it was too late.

"Do you realize what Stigwood's doing?" Edwards said. "He's got a writer who never wrote a movie before. The director never directed a musical or a white movie before. And the stars never acted before. Can you imagine what [the studio executives] think about this?"[18]

Whatever they thought, Stigwood's amateurish enthusiasm extended to the casting. For the female lead—named Strawberry Fields, no less—he chose Sandy Farina, an unknown singer who had never acted in a film, and appeared in only one other picture after—*The Toxic Avenger*, a Troma Studio mega-low-budget classic. She later co-wrote Barbra Streisand's #1 "Kiss Me in the Rain."

The Bee Gees can't act, but Sandy Farina simply disappears, even when delivering her lines or singing her heart out. Farina has perfectly negative onscreen charisma and often looks terrified.

To round out the inappropriate cast, Stigwood brought in another amateur: Peter Frampton, the elfin singer-guitarist who rose to prominence with the blues-shouters Humble Pie. Regarded as a guitar prodigy, Frampton achieved worldwide fame with 1976's *Frampton Comes Alive!*, a double album that became the benchmark for absurd breakout sales until Fleetwood Mac's *Rumours* and *Saturday Night Fever*. *Comes Alive!* spent fifty-five weeks in the top 40 and sold 13 million copies by the time shooting on the film began.

Controversy surrounds the album, primarily because those who worked on it claim there was nothing "live" about it. One insider said: "After six months of overdubs the only thing live was the crowd noise." The fearsome Dee Anthony, a larger than life personality who cultivated a thug image that was the opposite of Stigwood's urbane presentation, managed Frampton. Anthony managed crooner Tony Bennett for a decade; he and his brother handled King Crimson, Traffic, Jethro Tull, J. Geils and Joe Cocker, among others. In 1976 and '77, Anthony was named *Billboard*'s Manager of the Year, whatever that means. Anthony and Stigwood, the two most powerful and intimidating musical managers of their day, formed an unholy alliance. Stigwood, recognizing that Frampton was younger and cuter than the Bee Gees and, at the moment, the most popular musician on the planet, cast Frampton in the lead role, Billy Shears. Frampton couldn't act, either.

Post-production on *Saturday Night Fever* ended in April of 1977; *Pepper's* began filming in October. When shooting started, the Bee Gees had not yet sold more copies of a record than any other record since there were records. Their musical and contractual obligations had been fulfilled. They were a band between projects. *SNF* was in the can; *Here at Last* . . . was doing extraordinarily well.

The usual Stigwood hype began innocently enough. Robin, talking about the decision to record Beatles songs for the *Sgt. Pepper's* soundtrack: "When we were first signed by Robert Stigwood to Brian Epstein's NEMS firm, much of our excitement came from being represented by the same company as the Beatles." Barry: "If there is any music in the world we would record, any artists in the world we would feel pleased to be associated with, it's the Beatles. We were almost listening to our own story. It's not quite the same, not as glorious. But it is the story of a group that goes to the top." Maurice said: "Robert always pictured us as being the band. Peter Frampton was the hottest property. It was the Bee Gees and Peter. By the time we'd finished the film, we'd become the band."[19] That's what they said before the film was released. By the time the picture hit the theatres, their positions would change.

After behaving contrary to his interests in hiring the writer, director, female lead, co-star, cameos, bit players and "villain" band, Stigwood did something that was not self-destructive. In 1976 he had approached the Beatles' producer George Martin about arranging the music for the film. Martin, the incarnation of an English silver-haired eminence, had signed the Beatles to EMI and produced every one of their records. He was widely regarded, even by the Beatles, as a key component of their sound. Martin's plummy accent and bemused remove only bolstered his reputation for integrity and for being a no-bullshit personality. He put Stigwood off again and again. Stigwood's increasingly large payment offers and Martin's concerns about his legacy led him to finally take the gig. "I didn't want to do the project at first," Martin said, "but I was persuaded because Peter Frampton was riding so high back then and I admired the Bee Gees. The premise was that it was a film score and not a record album. I did the best solo job I could, and I *was* faithful to the arrangements, but they were not mere copies. The music was right for the film but wrong for the Bee Gees—and their disco sound would have been unsuitable. With all the different songs we used, it's a pity that the film wasn't called *Sgt. Pepper's White Abbey Road*. I have no regrets, though."[20] Martin was worried, for good reason, that if he did not arrange the music, someone else would do a worse job. "If the film is a total flop," Martin said, "my name will be mud. And if it's good, it will be mud."[21]

In the spring of 1977, Frampton hosted Martin and the Gibbs in Nassau to work out arrangements and rehearse. Barry told *Rolling Stone* how much he was looking forward to working with Martin and that singing the Beatles would be a joy. Barry recounts back when the band was first signed by Stigwood, and Stigwood showed up with the brand new *Sgt. Pepper's* album. "Nobody could believe it," Barry said. "It frightened us to death." Maurice said: "It was incredible. [Stigwood] put it on the stereo and we went: 'Jesus!'"[22]

Martin assembled an all-star session band. They would work at Cherokee Studios in LA and the Record Plant in New York. Martin had the musicians listen to the originals and copy them note for note.[23] The band improvised new arrangements and Martin wrote the charts for those. He recorded and produced the tracks. He brought in the Bee Gees, Frampton, Sandy Farina and others to lay down vocals. Dee Anthony said: "The songs aren't going to be changed that radically. They're basically being done the way the Beatles would probably do them today." In attempting to describe music he had not yet heard, Frampton said: "And as the film goes along they get progressively funkier. 'The Long and Winding Road' was going to be a kind of disco ballad, but George Martin pulled the reins on that one."[24] Martin pulled in the reins because Dee Anthony bested Stigwood in a squabble over who would get to sing "Long and Winding Road." Frampton won out, and Martin's arrangement mirrors the original. Barry said, of singing with

Frampton: "We were wary of each other. [Frampton] was a little worried about singing with us because we'd sung together all our lives. He didn't know how he fitted in. A lot of our sessions were done separately."[25] Even on songs in which the four harmonized, the Bee Gees cut their tracks without Frampton and Frampton cut his without them. Martin's soundtrack took over a year.

On October 17, 1977, filming began. The Bee Gees were in for some unpleasant surprises. No one had told them that movie making operated on the opposite schedule of rock and roll. The Gibbs had to get up early and be at their most creative during daylight hours. They were perplexed that, in the words of Michael Schultz, "movie making was done in pieces, not in chunks like a concert. The whole idea of performing in an acting scene was new to them."[26]

About having to share screen space with Frampton, Barry said: "It was a battle all the way for us. Robert had verbally promised us the starring roles, and this red-hot young man named Peter Frampton came along and Robert wanted him to play Billy Shears. The film didn't work for the Bee Gees. It worked for Peter but—and I think you'd have to be blind not to see it—the Bee Gees had no place in the story. We tried to point that out along the way. I just wish they'd given people a chance to act."[27] The Bee Gees' official biography has Maurice recalling that the roles weren't particularly "demanding."[28] After the filming, Maurice had a slightly different take on the experience: "It was ridiculous," he said. "I walked on to the set at 7 AM. The crew was in their trailers and I shouted: 'Has anyone got any cocaine?' Loads of the stuff landed at my feet."[29] Schultz said, of all the amateurs in the film: "They had to learn not to move around so much."[30]

The great rock critic Lester Bangs once wrote of an album: "It's stupid with none of the virtues of stupidity." The same can be said of *Sgt. Pepper's*. It's not so bad that it's good, nor some camp horror peppered amusingly with bad taste, like, say, *Xanadu*. There's no point in attempting to recount the so-called plot. The songs tumble after one another with minimal exposition. The story line makes almost no sense, and the cameos are unbearable. Steve Martin makes his film debut as a homicidal MD, singing "Maxwell's Silver Hammer" and portraying the song's title character. Martin does the shoulder-raising, grimacing, overanimated shtick he later duplicated in *Little Shop of Horrors* and most of his other pictures. He leads some extensive robotic choreography featuring hot nurses. Martin's talk-singing is no worse than George Burns's, who looks like a rotting animatronic of himself—with a toupee made of polyurethane—and staggers through "I'm Fixing a Hole," among other numbers.

The huge set that Stigwood had rebuilt is presented as the town of Heartland, and it's here that the original Sgt. Pepper's Lonely Hearts Club band performed. Frampton plays the ingénue rock-star-in-making Billy Shears. With his suspenders, open-to-the-waist shirts and perfect curls, Frampton—blank, waxen and scared shitless—looks like a rent-a-boy from Studio 54. His facial expression of confused terror never once changes in the entire picture. Billy Shears, beguiled from his small-town love, Strawberry Fields, gets spirited off on a bus full of groupies to an unintentionally hilarious depiction of Los Angeles rock decadence. The character actor Donald Pleasance, apparently determined that no one would ever recognize him in this disaster, plays a parody of a rock manager–mogul in silk pants, silk shirt and silk cowboy hats, speaking in an unintelligible Germanic Texas twang. Stigwood and Anthony must have enjoyed his performance enormously.

The Bees Gees portray Billy's band, and when Frampton lip-synchs unconvincingly next to them, Barry's look of impatient contempt is one for the ages. In the Bee Gees' musical numbers, poor Maurice gets stuck on drums, Barry has to hold a bass and

Robin a guitar. Barry stands right in front of Maurice's drum kit, so Maurice ends up with less screen time than anyone. Maurice was given the drums because Barry thought Robin would be "too stiff" and because Maurice was used to keeping time. Maurice tried to copy Bernard Purdie, who played drums on the soundtrack. Maurice later claimed that Purdie told him he never missed a beat on camera. It's hard to see how Purdie would know, since Barry almost always obscures Maurice's hands. The volume and shine of Robin's and Barry's hair defies human anatomy, but there it is, in every shot.

A diabolical team of Alice Cooper, Steve Martin and Aerosmith (!) plans to unleash a cult of zombified teens on the world, thus destroying love and perpetuating a value system based only on money—this is the "message" of the picture. Aerosmith's guitarist Joe Perry spoke of the band's concern about the script and its potential for brand damage: "Doing *Sgt. Pepper's* was hard work—12 hours a day for three days. It gave us some insight into why not to be an actor, but it was all right. Nobody was pulling any star trips, Frampton or the Bee Gees, or anything like that. But, ah, there was a few things they wanted us to do . . . . One thing was, [Aerosmith lead singer] Steven [Tyler] was gonna get killed by Frampton. Frampton was gonna kill Steven. And we're sayin', 'There's no *way* that Steven is gonna get offed by Frampton. No way. It's gotta be an accident.' So they switched it and we're killin' the Bee Gees, and Strawberry Fields pushes Steven off the stage and kills him. So it wasn't Frampton that got him." Joe said: "We were gonna mess up their hair instead of beating them, and totally fuck 'em up!"[31]

Billy Shears foils their foul plot at the cost of Strawberry Fields's life. Perry: "We killed Strawberry, so it was real cool."[32] Before she dies, Strawberry bumps Steven Tyler off his towering band riser, killing him and thwarting the Future Villains, as Aerosmith is called.

"They picked the right band for the Future Villain Band," Perry said. "There you have the Bee Gees smiling with their nice teeth and all that shit, and then you got the close-ups of me and Steven, and Steven's fried and we're both fuckin' . . . out there. My skin is all white 'cause it was last winter and we had been in Boston, and there's my face up there in close-up with my fuckin' crooked teeth and my crooked nose. We didn't think the movie was gonna bomb as bad as it did, but I don't think we suffered too badly for it as far as our image goes."[33]

One big reason they didn't is because no one remembers that Aerosmith was in the movie. Perry speaks the truth about his close-ups. He and Tyler look pasty, sleepless and wasted. They appear descended from a different show business universe than the Bee Gees, who, with Frampton, sneak up on Aerosmith for their climactic battle wearing head-to-toe satin outfits. Barry's is scarlet, Robin's orange and Maurice's purple. Frampton's features a bare midriff.

The final indignity of the film is reserved for Beatles and Rolling Stones sideman-singer-organist Billy Preston. First appearing as a wind vane, Preston springs to life after Strawberry's funeral. Using his magical powers, which appear to be vested in his jive, cartoonish dancing, golden knee-high satin boots and billed cap, Preston, singing "Get Back," zaps a magic soulful lightning bolt into Strawberry, bringing her back from the dead. Further funky lightning leads to the mind-blowing finale.

Though the film's song list isn't worth citing and neither is every plot incident, the finale begs to be explicated in detail. In keeping with their unhinged notions of when to cut costs and when to spend like drunken sailors—the film's final budget is estimated at $18 million (1977) dollars!—Anthony and Stigwood decided to invite pretty much everyone in showbiz to participate in the film's final scene. They sent the following engraved invitation out by the hundreds:

Robert Stigwood & Dee Anthony Cordially Invite
[x]
to Join
[immense Sgt. Pepper's logo]
In a day of musical celebration and to take part in
"The Grand Finale Sequence" of the film.
We will be honored by your presence at Heartland, U.S.A.
In Los Angeles between 10 A.M. and 6 P.M.
on Friday, December 16th
And at the Gala Dinner that evening
at a location to be announced.

Included with acceptance was first-class airfare to LA from wherever, and four-star accommodations, limos, champagne and the finest cuisine upon arrival. On the big day, seventy-five luminaries of various lumens gathered on a sound stage to sing "Sgt. Pepper's Lonely Hearts Club Band."

Michael Schultz figured out each person's place on a set of eight-tiered bleachers and arranged the groupings. His taste is reflected in the fact that front and center, above the Bee Gees and Frampton, stands Broadway star and difficult personality Carol Channing—someone few Bee Gees fans were likely to recognize or celebrate. Schultz explained the minimal choreography. George Martin ran the assembled through the lyrics and gave them the key changes. When Schultz said "Action," Martin directed the singing.

The guest list has to be seen in its entirety to get a proper sense of the deranged juxtaposition of entertainment-arena types and modalities: disc jockeys, harmonica players, Broadway stalwarts, actors, rockers, percussionists, soul singers, country music performers, session musicians, blues legends, guitar heroes, Las Vegas comedians and Dr. John.

Keith Carradine wears a billowing white pirate's blouse; Carol Channing—for whom the lip-synching is clearly a trial—sports her trademark platinum wig; next to her, Tina Turner wears her long golden wig; future Bruce Springsteen guitarist Nils Lofgren looks appropriately puzzled, albino bluesman Johnny Winters might be asleep on his feet and Mark Lindsay, late of Paul Revere and the Raiders, appears profoundly grateful to be included. Everyone seems either high, stoned, drunk, wasted, indifferent, baffled, overly sincere, weirdly poised and alert, or some combination thereof.

The list of performers includes Adrian Gurvitz, Al Stewart, Alan O'Day, Alan White, Anita Pointer, Barbara Dickson, Barry Humphries, the Bee Gees, Billy Harper, Bobby Womack, Bonnie Raitt, Bruce Johnston, Carol Channing, Charlotte, Sharon and Ula, Chita Rivera, Connie Stevens, Cousin Bruce Morrow, Curtis Mayfield, D. C. LaRue, Danielle Rowe, Del Shannon, Diane Vincent, Donovan, Dr. John, Eddie Harris, Elvin Bishop, Etta James, Frankie Valli, George Benson, Geraldine Granger, Gray Wright, Grover Washington Jr., Gwen Verdon, Hank Williams Jr., Heart, Helen Reddy, Jack Bruce, Jackie Lomax, Jim Dandy, Jo Leb, Joe Lala, Joe Simon, John Mayall, John Stewart, Johnny Winters, Johnny Rivers, José Feliciano, Keith Allison, Keith Carradine, Lee Oskar, Lenny White, Leif Garrett, Marcy Levy, Margaret Whiting, Mark Lindsay, Minnie Ripperton, Monti Rock III, Nils Lofgren, Nona Hendryx, Peter Allen, Peter Frampton, Peter Noone, Randy Edelman, Rick Derringer, Robert Palmer, Robert Stigwood, Sarah Dash, Seals and Crofts, Sha Na Na, Steven Bishop, the Paley Brothers, Tina Turner, Wilson Pickett, Wolfman Jack and Yvonne Elliman.

The idea behind this spectacle was to create a living tableau of the famous and noteworthy to echo the *tableau vivant* of cardboard cutouts on the original *Sgt. Pepper's* cover. It didn't quite work out. It plays as one more random element thrown into the mix. That one song—and the night that followed—provides a paradigm of late 1970s self-indulgence. "The revelry that night spilled over into three adjacent sound stages with strolling violinists, a disco dance floor, lavishly catered dinner and a garden room with private tents for each of the stars. The party continued well into the wee hours of the next morning."[34]

Meanwhile, across town, Martin was still recording. Of working with Barry, Martin showed his usual insight. "Barry Gibb was a great stickler for being dead in tune," Martin said. "I actually found myself telling him that by being so exactly in tune he was tending to spoil the nice parts of the double-tracking. He was so accurate it sounded almost like a single track."[35] Martin compared the Bee Gees' "irreverent sense of humor" to the Beatles' and said: "When it came to harmony singing, they were incredibly facile. When we came to 'Because,' from the *Abbey Road* album, I decided that the backdrop should be the authentic *Abbey Road* sound; that is, the choral structure of the voices, the electric harpsichord which I played on the original album, and the generally thin backing. So I again laid down the electric harpsichord track myself, and gave the Bee Gees the notes of all the complicated harmonies. There were three tracks, each bearing three voices, and the way the lines moved was quite complex, but they got them almost as easily as the Beatles had done. That was surprising. A group of professional singers would have had more difficulty with it, but the Bee Gees had an innate sense of where it should go."[36]

"My main criticism of *Sgt. Pepper*," Barry said, "is that the music shouldn't have flowed consistently through the film, and they should have used only *Sgt. Pepper* music. It seemed like the idea was to shove as many Beatles songs in there as was humanly possible. I don't think George [Martin] should have produced *Sgt. Pepper* again. George was religious with the original arrangements; he didn't want to change them. What the people were looking for was something totally new." Barry described how completely Martin controlled the vocal sessions. "We could have gone crazy on a lot of those tracks," he said. "We wanted to use falsettos and so on, and to some extent he let us do that. But not all the way. [Martin's] got real tight lines the way he wants to go, and he made that clear to everyone when we were doing it."[37]

The Bee Gees weren't the only cannibals on the project. Martin seems to have been determined to cannibalize his own work, and to ensure that nobody else got a bite. His overproduced, antiseptic, soulless arrangements overpower every vocal track save one—Robin's heartbreaking, dirgelike rendition of McCartney's "Oh! Darling." Robin finds tragic emotion in the song and connects to it as no one else connects to any song in the film. Even so, it takes all the power of Robin's soaring voice in top form to make a dent in the bombastic backing track. Robin's effortless range fights the accompaniment to a draw.

Elsewhere, Martin's arrangements are mixed so loudly, and mixed to sound so separate from the vocals, that the music and voices never merge into a musical whole. The numbers with weaker or more by-the-numbers vocal performances—the rest of the album, really—stand no chance against the fortress of music Martin erected. His arrangements are corny, with giant plucked bass notes, lush strings and overemphasized pauses. The musical arrangements were completed before the vocals were recorded, and the singers understood they could only belt away and hope for the best. Martin focuses an aural spotlight on his own work, and makes certain that nobody would prefer this record to any of the originals.

On December 14, 1977, the *Saturday Night Fever* soundtrack was released and everything changed. Just like that, Peter Frampton was no longer the best-selling musician on the planet, and Stigwood's Beatles' movie was no longer foremost on the Bee Gees' agenda. The Bee Gees sat back and watched the world come to them. The filming went on through January 1978, but the Gibbs were becoming increasingly detached.

SNF's sales kept going up and up. The Bee Gees held off on touring. Robin was deeply enmeshed in his amphetamine addiction, gacking himself daily and scarfing barbiturates to sleep. Maurice drank every waking moment. The band was on top of the world, and it must have been baffling. In the first year of *SNF*'s success, there was little backlash to either disco or the album's ubiquity on the charts. That reaction would come further down the road. What the first six months brought was pure validation, the kind of validation the brothers had yearned for since they regrouped. The kind of validation that might fulfill even their sense of being underappreciated outsiders. America loved them; England loved them; Japan loved them; the whole world loved them and the whole world proved it with their wallets. Nobody in the history of recorded music had ever been loved as much as the world loved the Bee Gees.

The band took a break from Criteria and headed to Los Angeles for the gala, star-studded July 18 premiere of *Sgt. Pepper's* at the Palladium Theater. Peter Frampton, badly injured in a car wreck, could not attend. Commentators later blamed the forestalling of his career on *Sgt. Pepper's*. But it was the automobile accident, not the movie, that kept Frampton out of the public eye and unable to record. Three days later, the film premiered at Radio City Music Hall in New York. The city declared *Sgt. Pepper's* Day and all proceeds from the premiere went to one of the Bee Gees' favorite charities, the NY Police Athletic League.

On July 23, 1978, the *Sgt. Pepper's* soundtrack was released. The movie came out the next day. Expectations were high. Al Coury, never one to understate, said: "It could make *Saturday Night Fever* look like a punk album; like a test run for the main event."[38] "Kids today don't know the Beatles' *Sgt. Pepper*," Robin told *Playboy*, though it might have been speed doing the talking. "And when those who do see our film and hear us doing it, that will be the version they relate to and remember. Unfortunately, the Beatles will be secondary. You see, there is no such thing as the Beatles. They don't exist as a band and never performed *Sgt. Pepper* live. When ours comes out, it will be, in effect, as if theirs never existed. When you heard the Beatles do *Long Tall Sally* or *Roll Over Beethoven*, did you care about Little Richard's or Chuck Berry's version? The only credit the Beatles get on this film is for songwriting."[39]

Despite all the *SNF* love, and despite *SNF* holding at #8 eight months after its release, it was not going to be as if the Beatles never existed. From the moment radio began playing the record, according to *Rolling Stone*, "stations reported negative feedback from listeners, who requested the original Beatles versions."[40] Capitol Records, the Beatles' US label, couldn't resist getting in a dig. "Ours," Capitol's Dennis White told *Rolling Stone*, "is doing as well as the soundtrack in a lot of areas."[41]

Sgt. Pepper's debuted at #5 on the *Billboard* charts and stayed there six weeks. Much of that chart position came from pre-orders and there would be millions of unsold returns. According to Bee Gees archivist Joe Brennan: "RSO made two million copies of the expensive two-LP set, which had an embossed front cover, special inner sleeves, and a poster. Counterfeiters who had made a tidy profit on *Saturday Night Fever* managed to get copies of the music and artwork ahead of release and added to the overabundance of product. At that time stores were allowed to return unsold albums for credit. Record business insiders said that it was the first album to 'return platinum,' and that because of the counterfeiting it returned more than it shipped. RSO destroyed hundreds of thousands of copies, and despite that the album was a familiar sight in cutout bins for years to come."[42]

"We shipped triple platinum," Gershon said. "That was unheard of. Lo and behold—the movie stiffed. The album stiffed."

Anticipating a success similar to *SNF*, organized crime record bootleggers printed untold quantities of fake copies. "The FBI," Gershon said, "told us that the word got out to the guys driving a convoy of trucks that the *Pepper's* [bootlegs] were valueless. They found them all dumped on the side of some road in Southern California. We sent out three million albums. And we probably had to take back more than four million returns."[43] Gershon means that the fakes were so good no one could tell real albums from bootlegs. The bootleggers got paid their refunds, as did the legit retailers.

"It was the beginning of the end," Gershon said. "Robert said we're a small record company. Why bother staying in a business that is no longer very profitable." Stigwood, never one to back a slow horse, said that while *SNF* was still setting records for sales. Prior to the film's opening, Stigwood had been planning a "Heartland-based amusement park, a television movie on the production of the film and a novel version of the story."[44] The film's reception put an end to those plans.

The reviews were not kind. Even Janet Maslin, who could find the virtue in any film she chose to promote, no matter how abysmal, wrote: "This isn't a movie, it's a business deal set to music."[45] Marilyn Laverty wrote in *Record Mirror*: "This film is one of the classic characterizations of the late '70's era, the quintessential statement of the cynicism and vacuousness of the corporate entertainment biz. Working from the proven commercial precept that a sucker is born every minute, those responsible for both the film and the album soundtrack can flaunt the success of their theory. The two-record soundtrack, one of the most expensive pop sets ever in the US, has an astounding initial shipment of 3.5 million copies. There are a lot of chumps out there plopping down 15.98 dollars retail cost for the privilege of hearing the Bee Gees prove THEY AREN'T nearly as interesting as the Beatles."[46] According to Paul Nelson in *Rolling Stone*, Robert Stigwood and

Dee Anthony "masterminded a double fiasco so unique it should win some kind of award for ineptness beyond even the normal call of duty. Stigwood and Anthony not only produced one of the worst movies ever made, but also managed to trash whatever rock & roll reputations such Seventies artists as Peter Frampton and the Bee Gees had before this excremental soundtrack was released. To be fair, the movie does show a certain charm in its relentlessly stupid grasp of the obvious. When Frampton sings 'The Long and Winding Road,' for instance, he is walking down a long and winding road. You keep laughing and thinking it can't get any worse. But it does."[47]

Despite the film's unspeakable reviews, Robin's revelatory "Oh! Darling" hit #15 on the singles charts; Aerosmith's cover of "Come Together" made the top 40. Earth, Wind and Fire's—they were in the movie, too—"Got to Get You into My Life" went platinum. When the movie tanked, it took the soundtrack with it. *Sgt. Pepper's* fell out of the top 100 after only six weeks.

"The movie was, to be polite," Al Coury said, "something less than an overwhelming success at the box office."[48]

Paul McCartney, after admitting he had not and would not see the movie, said: "I thought that they couldn't make a film of it. We used to be stoned all the time and talk about things like that and say, 'Hey, what a great film this would make.' But we used to say that the trouble is that people are all freaking out on acid with this album. You're never gonna be able to get those big elephants that are coming through their heads. You can't capture it: Once it gets to be a film, it's always going to be plodding compared to the album. Those days it was a fantasy thing; it all took place in your mind, and it would really be harder than anything to capture that feeling. And from what I've heard of the Stigwood thing, it doesn't seem to have captured it."[49]

"I just feel sorry for Robert Stigwood, the Bee Gees and Pete Frampton for doing it," George Harrison later said, "because they had established themselves in their own right as decent artists and suddenly . . . it's like the classic thing of greed. The more you make the more you want to make, until you become so greedy that ultimately you put a foot wrong. And even though *Sgt. Pepper* is no doubt a financial success, I think it's damaged their images, their careers, and they didn't need to do that."[50]

"I hated doing the film, recording the music," Robin said after it tanked. "We didn't have a chance to act because we didn't talk. We were just mouthing Beatles' lyrics. And I am not happy singing other people's songs."[51]

"I spoke to George about a year after it was out," Maurice said, years later. "He told me he loved it—he thought that we sang the songs marvelously." In response, Barry said: "But no one ever wrote us and said, 'Great work, lads.'"[52]

"It should have had more excitement," Robin said. "As we were making it, I was thinking, 'I hope they are going to put some visual effects in here.' When I saw it, it was exactly how we shot it, nothing was improved. On the set the camera is pointed at you and you're thinking to yourself, 'It's gotta be more than just me sitting here in this room, 'cause nothing's happening.' Then you see the film and that's all there is." When asked how he would have preferred the film to be done, he added: "Well, *Saturday Night Fever* had fucking in the back seat, you know. I mean *that* is the kind of film people are seeing these days. *Sgt. Pepper* comes out and people sort of expect to see fucking every now and then, but there were no fucks, you know? It was too goody-goody. I knew the film wasn't going to be a big hit. Well, better luck next time."[53]

"You don't watch it," Barry said. "You *tolerate* it."

Robin answered. "Our *Sgt. Pepper*? With hand on heart, that was the biggest load of shit ever."[54]

spirits having
flown

The Bee Gees came away from *Sgt. Pepper's* with plenty of plausible deniability. It wasn't their project; it was Stigwood's. It wasn't their record; it was Martin's. No one told them how crude the film would be; no one explained anything about acting; they had no input into the story; they had to share screen and music space with Frampton. Happily for them, no one cared. *Sgt. Pepper's* collected its share of condemnation and sank, never to be seen again, beneath the juggernaut sales of *SNF*. Ben Fong-Torres wrote in *Rolling Stone* that RSO expected to "do about $250 million in the US alone in 1978."[1]

Despite his poor-mouthing over *Pepper's* failure, Stigwood took home 45 percent[2] of the gross of *Saturday Night Fever*, the movie, which did $285 million worldwide. He was in fine shape and, as ever, wanted more. So did the Bee Gees. With a discipline that few bands could have matched, they headed back to their beloved home base, Criteria Studios in Miami. By March of 1978, they were in their usual groove, working from 3:00 P.M. to midnight on a new record. "In this position," Barry said, referring to the pressure caused by the success of *SNF*, "we are constantly up against the wall with people saying, 'Please us!' It's an invisible thing, but you can feel that wall behind you, and you can hear the whole industry saying, 'Give us a surprise, we *expect* you to outdo yourselves.'"[3]

The pressure was unrelenting in part because they were growing ever more famous, and attention from their fans rose accordingly. Tour boats drove by Barry's waterfront home in Miami Beach several times a day. "It's like living in a bloody goldfish bowl," Barry said. "We've asked them if they could please keep the boat at least 200 yards out, but they don't. The boats come past every hour on a nice day, and the people all have cameras and binoculars. They have a Universal Tours-type bus that comes down our road every hour with loudspeakers. The *Miami Herald* did us a real nice favor last year: they printed our address, with a picture of the front gates. You can't stop the press from doing these things. They can say, 'Oh, who do they think they are? They've got everything they want. So let's play a little game.' But they oughta try playing that game for a while. Imagine all these people coming past. I'm fortunate to live well, but on the other hand, if you've got a family, there's got to be a little bit of privacy."[4]

"[Fans] are out here all the time," said Peter Wagner, one of the Bee Gees' drivers. "They sit there waiting for them to come out." "These kids are consumers," Barry said. "You've got to give them equal time. You can't go through life saying 'No autographs'—y'know, the Paul Newman syndrome. It's what you wanted, what you worked for. The other day there were four or five kids standing outside the studio and they had each bought a copy of our new album. The only thing I could think of saying was, 'Would you play it as much as you can and come back and tell me which songs you liked best?' It's important, and it's nice to get input from people."[5]

Part of their relentless drive to outdo themselves with the SNF follow-up—and part of the replenishing of the perpetual chip on Barry's shoulder—came courtesy of the Motion Picture Academy of Arts & Sciences' shocking refusal to recognize any of the songs from *SNF*. Not one track received a 1977 Oscar nomination. The movie got zilch as well—a total shutout. Stigwood was outraged. He filed a formal complaint with the Academy and milked the publicity for all it was worth.

The competition was tough. John Williams was a lock for Best Score for *Star Wars*. The Best Song Oscar went to "You Light Up My Life," as rendered by Pat Boone's ultra-vanilla, one-hit daughter Debbie. Except for "Nobody Does It Better," from the James Bond film *The Spy Who Loved Me*, the other nominees were all middle of the road whitebread. No matter how many weeks *SNF* and its singles spent at #1, losing out to "You Light Up My Life" would have irked a saint, never mind someone as competitive and ready to perceive a snub as Barry.

John Rockwell, writing in the *New York Times*, damned the band with faint praise while acknowledging that the Academy had screwed them: "Conservative professional organizations such as those that award the Oscars have generally picked the safe and old-fashioned over the contemporary, so the slighting of the Bee Gees by the Oscars is no surprise. But it's ironic, for ultimately the group represents the spirit the Oscars prize. The Gibb brothers are basically pop craftsmen, cranking out entertainment in response to the fashions of the day. When the disco trend sputters out, the Bee Gees will probably rally and reappear a few years later purveying the next hot style."[6]

No wonder Barry was so driven and resentful. His band—his blood kin—could not catch a break. The Bee Gees invented a new recording technology, defined the zeitgeist, converted a nation to their sound, broke every sales record there ever was and filled the charts with original material. Then the *New York Times*, hardly a cultural trend spotter, derides them as herd followers.

Barry told David Leaf: "[The success of *SNF*] made us work harder. We haven't been able to sit down and say, 'Jesus, last year was amazing.'" Barry was thrilled to be away from Hérouville and back in his own, familiar universe. "The studio is my spaceship. I lose all sense of the outside world. I turn into the music. I have the studio personality, the patience and the perfectionism. The moment when the song is realized is my payoff."[7]

As the band settled into its work routine, Maurice's usual breakfast consisted of Coca-Cola and scotch. If he was awake, he drank. Maurice claimed that he had hurt his back and couldn't play, so Alan Kendall and studio ace Harold Cowart took over the bass parts. "I had to sit there," Maurice told the press, "and tell the bass player what to play. It was a bitch."[8] Maurice hid booze around Criteria; a worker renovating the bathroom had sixteen liquor bottles fall onto him through the ceiling. Maurice said: "My brothers could never understand how, when I was in the studio, I would have only two beers and get sloshed as a newt. I had backup everywhere—in the glove box, under the seat, wherever."[9] It was around this time that Maurice first began to admit to his drinking problem. He blamed his drinking on the stress of balancing his professional and personal lives. "I was burning the candle at both ends," he said later. "My body couldn't take it."[10]

There are many unsubstantiated and unattributed tales of Maurice's drunken antics and nonstop drinking from this era; they have to be taken as gossip. But the sheer volume of those tales—including the ones that Maurice supposedly told on himself—suggest that Maurice's alcoholism was beyond control. To paraphrase AC/DC guitarist, songwriter and singer Angus Young describing his brother Malcolm's habits: "Playing interfered with his drinking." Barry and Robin came to see that Maurice would not heed their advice or accept their care. Maurice did not contribute a bass part to any *Spirits* tracks. Blue, Dennis, Alan and Cowart alternated his bass parts. Additionally, Joe Lala added percussion, George Terry played guitar and Herbie Mann blew flute on "Spirits." Chicago was cutting their *Hot Streets* album in the studio next door; the Chicago horns—James Pankow, Walter Parazaider and Lee Loughnane—sat in on "Stop (Think Again)."

On May 27, 1978, as the band labored away, the Stigwood co-produced movie *Grease*, starring John Travolta, hit the theaters. An adaptation of the stage play, the film needed, in Stigwood's opinion, a hit single. A title song was added, sang by Four Seasons songwriter and lead singer Frankie Valli. It slowly climbed to #1, hitting the top on August 26, 1978, where it stayed for two weeks. Before it hit #1, the Rolling Stones briefly displaced *SNF* at the top. RSO, in the person of Al Coury, went batshit.

Al Coury went to the *Billboard* offices: "I screamed and yelled. I really thought *Grease* was gonna replace *Saturday Night Fever* at Number One. I honestly believed and I tried to convince the trades that at the time they made the Stones Number One, my *Grease* album was outselling the Stones. Their argument to me was, 'Well, what do you care? You're gonna be Number One next week, anyway. What are you hassling over a lousy fucking week for?' But goddamnit, my fucking plan was to be Number One all year!"[11]

Barry wrote "Grease," of course. In an hour or two.

"Robert Stigwood called up," Barry said. "And said he and [film co-producer] Allan Carr had everything they wanted for the film *Grease*, but the strangest thing is that they didn't have a song called 'Grease.' They asked me if I would write a song for the movie. I went and sat back in the lounge and basically sketched the song out while I was watching television. I didn't think that much of it. The word was that Allan Carr didn't really like it, but Robert Stigwood did. [Frankie Valli] was real smart casting, because they found someone to sing it that reflected that era."[12]

"To write songs with Barry," Albhy Galuten said, "I referred to the process as the Barry Society, because he would sit down at the piano, and the song would spew out of him. You could tell by the way he was singing what the next chord was that he wanted. Then he would write all the lyrics. Sometimes he would write a song in ten minutes. He would give you half writers on it. He didn't like the process of saying well, you know, you wrote 10% of this song. You were either in for 50% or not in at all. For Bee Gees songs, you were kind of never in. For songs for other people you were in.

"One of the financial repercussions is that when we were working at Barry's house, Robert Stigwood called up and said, 'I need a song called "Grease."' And Barry said, 'What do you mean a song called "Grease"?' Stigwood said; 'You know, like "Grease," like "ba da ba da ba da ba da GREASE!"' And Barry was like, 'Sure.'

"So, I think I had to go somewhere. Barry said, 'Well, I think we should sit down and write this song "Grease."' I said: 'You know, you hear this stuff, you hear the chords in your head. You know what chords you're looking for. Sometimes when I play a chord, you go "No, no not that one, *that* one!" So you know what chords you're hearing. You know the melody. You know the words. I think you could write the whole song in your mind. Just write down the words, remember the melody, and we'll find out what chords you were imagining later.' And he said, 'Okay, I'll try that.' I left. And he did just that, except he wrote all of 'Grease.' Had I stayed there and written the song with him, I would've made a lot of money."[13]

A tossed-off #1 single was the least of what went on at Criteria. The boys had comedy routines, most revolving around sixth-grade-level dirty jokes that they'd honed over the years. It's hard to believe, given their trials and success, and hard to remember, that as they recorded the music that would become *Spirits Having Flown*, Barry was only thirty-two and the twins newly twenty-nine.

The Gibbs wrote, directed, videotaped and starred in videos of their comedy skits. They made a lot of them and watched them over and over. Maurice showed a journalist a Betamax video tape titled "Collected Items." The tape held roughly an hour of blackout comedy skits that were intended as parodies of TV news and shows. Among the skits were "a cinema verite minidocumentary about an inept band cutting its debut record, entitled 'Wankers by the Moonlight'; a Don Kirshner-style conversation-at-the-piano with an effeminate pop-schlock songwriter; a current events talk show called The Eugene Shitass [pronounced *sheit-arse*] Report and 80 Minutes, a TV news-magazine featuring an interview with Robin playing a noted surgeon after the first successful penis transplant."[14]

That tape apparently showcased the apex of the Bee Gees' comedy stylings—the others were nowhere near as funny. Producing the skits was a regular hobby for the band during recording. The penis surgery is the strangest of the lot and the most aligned to Robin's sense of humor. "Robin's into blue humor," Karl Richardson told *Circus Weekly*. "I don't know if you'd be able to print his jokes. He also draws caricatures of everybody and hangs them up in the studio. If a group gets too serious and stops bantering when they record, you stagnate and lose your creativity."[15]

This was the first time the band recorded using multiple twenty-four-track machines. "It was so stimulating to be able to take 18 tracks of Barry singing," Albhy said. "No one had been able to do that before. Barry wanted things a certain way. He had a vision. Those years we were together I tuned into his vision. Feel, pitch, meter were incredibly important to him.

"We started doing the multi-track overdubs on the song 'Too Much Heaven,' and there were 18 tracks of Barry singing. Eighteen tracks, all done live and with no guide vocal track. Not one. Michael Jackson, for instance, when he doubled a vocal in the studio, he would want the vocal he was doubling"—a vocal track he had already recorded to his satisfaction—"playing back in his headphones as he sang the new doubling vocal. The recorded vocal would be in one ear of his headphones, and he took the other ear off to hear himself sing along with it. That's what everybody did.

"Barry didn't do that. Barry knew exactly what he wanted to sing, and he would sing exactly that. He had unbelievable control. So when you listen to those 18 vocals in 'Too Much Heaven,' it was three-part harmony, each part tripled in two octaves. There were three parts on each of the three bottom voices and three parts on each of the three top octaves. Barry would sing each track without listening to any other. Every breath, every meter, every pitch and every vibrato was exactly in tune and in time. He would take these 18 tracks, literally one after the other. I'd push the faders up and all 18 would be exactly together in tune, in time and breathing at the same moment. I don't believe there's ever been a craftsman like that in the world."[16]

As rightfully in awe as Albhy was of Barry's virtuosity, he saw something being lost among the Bee Gees in the deus ex machina. "They say that technology is magic until you understand it," Albhy said. "Stimulus is important. Some bands are stimulated with drugs and manage the drug intake so they're at the right high for the job at hand. You stimulate people by not allowing them to get too excited if its not the final take, so you can, in a coitus interruptus sort of way, keep people's vibe right. Having a new technology, being able to do things that you have never done before, is a stimulus as well, a creative stimulus. And so having multiple 24 tracks was stimulating, being able to make the multiple tracks of 'Too Much Heaven' or 'Tragedy.'"

"The point is, we're talking about—for the first time—an essentially unlimited number of tracks. You can keep what you have and then go on and try something else. And this was new, before we'd all gotten spoiled. Do something new, do extra double tracks, have your cake and eat it too. So that was the beginning of not playing live as a band."[17]

Every available track encouraged breaking the music down into increasingly smaller component parts. Each musician plays only a portion of a song until it's perfect, then plays the rest, portion by portion. Something of the collective sound and feel is lost in the process.

"Is there a specific, graphable connection between the increase of control and the lack of spontaneity in the studio?" Albhy said.

"Do they weave back and forth? Are they absolutely in opposition, do you just have to figure out how to make them harmonize?"[18]

These philosophical questions were being played out daily in the studio. In an NBC television special aired in 1979, Barry spoke with interviewer David Frost about building a song. "When the voice drops out, the instrument that comes in has to be really interesting. And when the instrument drops out and the voice comes back, that has to be even more interesting. So where there's an empty space, it has to be filled." Having 24 tracks available put even more pressure on Barry to find something to fill every moment of every song. And fill them he did.[19]

"Whatever the new album is, I can tell you the pressure was mountainous to follow up *Saturday Night Fever*," Barry said. "And we felt that there was great pressure to follow up *Children of the World* with *Saturday Night Fever*. And *Children of the World* followed *Main Course*, which everyone was talking about! It always goes on that way. I mean if *Spirits* is a monster—pray that it is—then once again we'll be against the wall."[20] With every confidence that the record would be a monster, the band shifted its workaday life from recording to preparing for what would be their grandest, most ornate tour.

The Bee Gees rented a warehouse from TK Records—KC and the Sunshine Band's label—not far from South Beach in Miami. They wanted their own, private rehearsal space and built a full-size stage with a lighting rig and sound system to hone their live show. The band commissioned Karl and Albhy to build a studio in the warehouse and to have it ready when they came back from their tour. They christened the studio Middle Ear.

Karl and Albhy created an enormous one-room space—twenty-eight by thirty-eight feet, with twelve-foot ceilings and a six-by-six-foot isolation booth for vocals—using only part of the warehouse. The studio featured wood-slatted walls "dotted with indentations into which amplifiers and microphones can be positioned to create a wide diversity of niche space ambiences." The slatted walls were, as explained by Albhy "to break up the sound so that there would not be even reflections. If all sound reflects in the same way, it creates bumps in certain frequencies and if the walls are smooth it creates extra ambience." Every piece of gear was to the moment and state of the art. Middle Ear was for the Bee Gees only. They recorded at Middle Ear from its completion in 1980 until 1993. Once it opened, fans stood in front of its doors all day, rather than at Criteria.[21] After 1993, the Bee Gees rented Middle Ear out to other bands. "The studio has been broken-in in the best way a studio can be," said one tenant. "The boys developed it into a warm, personal and creative space. There's nothing cold or impersonal about it. It's a single-room facility, so when an artist rents it out, it's all theirs. And everything comes with it; there are no additional rental charges."[22]

As the release of the first single neared, Barry was already defensive. "We spent ten months doing this new album," he said. "You've gotta believe that a lot of times we cut a track, then said, 'No! No good!' A lot of tracks we cut a dozen times. We did not want to go wrong with this album. And a few critics will say that we did. Our father always said, 'Look, no one ever criticizes you when you're down; you only get the criticism when you're up, so shut up.' We try to live like that, or at least live with it. But I've never gotten over harsh criticism. I can never pick up a review and finish it if the guy doesn't like the album, 'cause the rest of my day is screwed up. It's so painful."[23] Before the first single came out, Stigwood, never one to lag when it was time to hype, said: "Not only do I think it's the best album [the Bee Gees have] ever done, I think it's the best album I've ever heard."[24]

November 18, 1978, saw the release of the first single, "Too Much Heaven." The single charted for twenty-one weeks, hit #1 on January 6, 1979, and held the top spot for two weeks. "Heaven" gave the Bee Gees their seventh #1 of the 1970s, which made them

the band with the most top singles in the decade. The Gibbs donated all proceeds of "Heaven"—$7 million—to the United Na-
tions children's charity UNICEF, once called the United Nations
International Children's Emergency Fund.

The English television host and celebrity interviewer David
Frost promoted a benefit concert, *Music for UNICEF*. Knowing of
their connection to the charity, Frost reached out to the Bee Gees
in March 1978. "People have come to us and said, 'Do you realize
how much power you have now? You could change the world with
some of the things you say.'" Barry said. "And I say to them, 'Leave
me alone.' Power is fleeting; so is ego. When you start putting religion or whatever into it and tell the world how it can be saved, it
rubs up against people. Politicians have no idea how to save the
world, so why should pop stars? Instead you can do things like the
UNICEF thing, which is a positive move to help children."[25] The
Bee Gees sent letters to schools and children's organizations, suggesting they hold fund-raising disco dances to raise money for
UNICEF. The *Music for UNICEF* broadcast featured a wide range
of top stars who agreed to donate their performances.

George Harrison's *Concert for Bangladesh* in 1971 was the first
of the rock-celebrity, all-star charity blockbuster concerts, and perhaps the subject of Barry's jab at pop stars who "tell the world how
it can be saved." But if the idea of marshaling pop music for charity was hardly new, the breadth of the talent and the worldwide
broadcast was. The Bee Gees were ahead of the curve, prefiguring
shows like Live AID, Farm AID and the multi-celebrity charity
shows that have become regular features of the concert landscape.
Music For UNICEF was recorded live and broadcast the next day,
January 9, 1979, on NBC, after two weeks of setup. The timing was
perfect as promotion for the release of *Spirits Having Flown*.

Someone in the live audience said: "If you look at the yearly
record sales of the people here, it is equal to the gross national
product of some of the member states of the UN. Throw a bomb

in here and you have knocked out half the music industry." Frank Rocco, the talent coordinator on the project said, "They do not normally allow liquor to be brought into the UN, but we told them, 'Hey, some of the guys here do their jobs a little bit differently than you may be used to.' They were cool about it and let us bring it in."[26]

Among the performers were Donna Summer, Kris Kristofferson, John Denver, Olivia Newton-John, Rod Stewart, Rita Coolidge and, fresh off their one-song appearance in *Sgt. Pepper's*, Earth, Wind and Fire. Ken Ehrlich, one of the show's producers, said: "A lot of massive egos were sublimated for the cause."[27] Rod Stewart sang "Do Ya Think I'm Sexy," and got treated like Elvis Presley on *The Ed Sullivan Show*. Because the program was broadcast worldwide, which meant a large non-Western audience, Stewart was shown only from the waist up.

Spirits Having Flown was released on January 26, 1979. Punk rock had gone from pure rage to slowly inching into the mainstream. Commercial funk music was both glossy and raw. *Spirits*, owing to the depth of its twenty-four-track production, had a rich, shiny, but artificial and overproduced sound. It's slickness worked against it as far as the critics were concerned. Bee Gees' fans loved it even while disco was starting to fade.

Because disco songs are long and disco listeners expected extended sets, disco radio shows could not offer the conventional number of commercial breaks per hour. This made disco a tough format to sell in syndication. Large, disco-crazy markets, like New York and Miami, had entrenched disco radio shows. Smaller Midwestern cities seldom offered disco on the airwaves. Jim Kefford, who led a company that produced taped radio shows for syndication, said: "I remember calling one station owner in the Midwest and asking, 'How's disco doing in your town?' He said, 'Well, we had one. But it closed.'" Leo Bortel, a former radio DJ and owner of a Cleveland discotheque, said about the difficulty of establishing disco as a radio format: "If you present this music differently than it is heard in the clubs, it stands out like a sore thumb."[28]

Billboard reported that by the end of 1979, radio in New York was shifting from music identified as disco. Frankie Crocker, a New York DJ who in the beginning of 1979 said disco had "replaced rock and become a whole new culture," opened a show in December 1979 by saying he would play music that made listeners "think a little more"—and less disco. In December, a station that had called itself "Disco And More" embraced "the Sounds of the 80s."[29]

Looking back years later, Barry said: "There seems to be an inclination to reject certain artists at the end of each decade in favor of the new decade and what that might bring. We were always a target for that."[30] Barry has a point. The first single, "Too Much Heaven," has nothing to do with disco. It's a glossy funk love ballad in the style—especially in the solo vocal—of the Delfonics' "La La Means I Love You." The lead vocals and arrangement reflect the influence of the later, softer work of Maurice White of Earth, Wind and Fire. The harmony on the chorus shifts out of soul mode, though, and becomes pure Bee Gees. As Barry and Robin argued to anyone who would listen, "Heaven" is modern—at that time, current—R&B, not disco. Despite the cornball opening, somewhat juvenile lyrics and an excess of falsetto, "Heaven" remains one of the great high school slow-dancing songs of all time.

On January 12, the Bee Gees were awarded a star on the Hollywood Walk of Fame. They went to LA for the ceremony and thousands of fans jammed the streets. On February 15, *SNF* won four Grammy Awards. The record won Album of the Year; "Stayin' Alive" was nominated for Song of the Year but did not win. The Bee Gees won Producer of the Year, Best Arrangement of Voices and Best Pop Vocal Performance.

"Tragedy," the second single from *Spirits*, was released February 17, 1979, debuting at #4. By March 24, it was #1, stayed at the top for two weeks and in the charts for twenty weeks total. By March, it was #1 in the UK and Canada. If the critics were tired of the Bee Gees, the record-buying public was not.

"Tragedy," with its amazing stacked Barry self-harmonies, ain't exactly disco either. The rhythm section features the classic disco hit-hat shuffle, but the guitar licks and synthesizer accents evoke Electric Light Orchestra. The song's bombastic layered sound and pushier, grander-than-disco dance beat suggest that Barry was listening to a lot of Giorgio Moroder, the groundbreaking producer behind Donna Summer's breakout hits, and of Blondie, David Bowie and Irene Cara. "Tragedy," like much of Moroder's post-disco work, draws on disco elements, but reaches beyond for a richer, self-consciously epic aural landscape.

Rock critic Stephen Holden recognized an international sound. He wrote that the Bee Gees had melded American R&B with "Europop production." Holden argued that the Beatles did something similar, but in all the world, he's the only person who ever thought so. Holden astutely recognized what today is known as Esperanto Pop; music that shares certain pop—as opposed to rock—values can originate anywhere on the globe and find an audience anywhere else. Esperanto Pop, like the Bee Gees, is not limited to the culture or language of its origin. ABBA and Korea's K-Pop are two of the most cited examples. Much of *Spirits* fits that model. "Tragedy" features several ABBA motifs and "Spirits (Having Flown)," for all the emptiness and insincerity of its lyrics, is Brazilian bossa nova filtered through Miami's Funky Nassau sound. Holden, having accurately parsed what the Bee Gees were doing, and even praised them, proved that he had only raised the Beatles as a straw man with which to batter *Spirits*. "The global consciousness that the Gibbs conjure," he wrote, "is far different from that of the Beatles, who embodied a nonbureaucratic world community of hippie individualists. The Bee Gees' global village would be a junior high of androgynous, conformist goody-goodies:

a world with no violence or sex, only puppy love, and every toy in creation. That's why *Spirits Having Flown* is a Sunday-school heaven of eternal childhood, stringently regulated by angels."

Holden's perceptions only went so far. He also wrote: "From the beginning, the Bee Gees' mating of pop and R&B was shaky."[31] That is patently, absurdly untrue: ass backward to the highest degree. The essence of—the predominant aspect of, the best-selling and most widely imitated aesthetic of—the second half of the Bee Gees' career is their genius merging of pop and R&B.

"We're trying to avoid disco," Barry said. "We're keeping solid rhythms but we're not saying, 'Hey, you have to dance to this song.' We have to convince everybody that we write all kinds of songs. Some call it selling out, but the most critical thing today is adaptability. If you're adaptable, you stay; if you're not, you go when the crowd changes its mind."[32]

Holden went on to say: "This album's weaknesses are synonymous with the Gibbs' pseudodeific, megastar self-conception. Most of the songs are sung with perfect pitch, but the trio's piercing collective falsetto (built around Barry's lead vocals) is so relentless that the few moments in which the voices drop to their natural register come as a relief. The Four Seasons, alas, and not Smokey Robinson are the prototype for such an unearthly style: shrill, stiff, mechanical yowls that generate tension yet aren't expressive enough to carry an entire LP."[33]

There, though overstating his case, Holden has a point.

To the accusations of too much falsetto, Barry said: "*Spirits* is really a listener's album—if you can stand the falsettos long enough. You have to listen to it four or five times, if you like it enough to listen to it that many times."[34]

"Though most people consider *Saturday Night Fever* a Bee Gees record," Mark Kernis wrote in the *Washington Post*: "The band contributed only six tracks—and two of those, 'Jive Talkin'' and 'You Should Be Dancing,' were previously issued. The fact that the four new songs were the four strongest pieces that the Bee Gees have ever done should not obscure the fact that the band rocketed to fame on the strength of less than one full side of one record. It's astounding that the critical demolition of *Sgt. Pepper's Lonely Hearts Club Band* didn't demolish their standing the way it seems to have derailed the career of Peter Frampton, who hasn't done a thing since. So, besides providing a pleasant diversion, *Spirits Having Flown* shows the Bee Gees' resilience."[35]

That resilience seemed to irk critics. They were done with the band, apparently, so what was up with all these millions and millions of people buying Bee Gees records?

The Bee Gees official biography, *Bee Gees: The Authorized Biography*, as told by the band to David Leaf, came out in March. The Bee Gees wrote the photo captions for the large-scale trade paperback themselves, and many—reflecting their juvenile, inside-the-band humor—border on the bizarre. Robin proves plenty willing to tell bad tales about himself. It's a curious artifact. The content lies somewhere between blind adoring hype and genuine confession. The Bees Gees come off as both remarkably unguarded and fiercely paranoid about protecting their image. There are a number of wonderful photos, especially those from the early days.

Robin had a deadly near miss that March. "A couple of weeks ago," he told Stan Soocher of *Circus Weekly*, "I was out in my 31-foot boat off the coast of Florida. At night, a storm started. I lost my two engines and control of the steering, and was heading for a bridge. I was half a mile from land, the wind was dreadful and the current was intolerable. I hadn't been swimming for ten years, but I had to jump into the water. The boat was demolished."[36]

"Love You Inside Out," the third single, debuted on April 21. It hit #1 on June 9 and the Bee Gees became the first band since the Beatles with six consecutive #1s. Maurice, citing the band's first version of the song, said: "'Inside and out, backwards and forwards with my cock hanging out!' That's the version we sent to Robert."[37]

The consecutive #1s meant a lot to the band. When asked how the Bee Gees reacted to the unbelievable sales of *SNF*, Albhy said: "They never cared about numbers. They care about hits—Number Ones. Chart position. That's their benchmark. They always assumed that if they got the Number Ones, sales would follow. So they were happy, of course, about the sales, but what they tracked was their hits."

Robert Christgau wrote perceptively about *Sprits*, shedding new light on its limitations and presenting what would become the canonical critics' take on the LP. "I admire the perverse riskiness of this music, which neglects disco bounce in favor of demented falsetto abstraction, less love-man than newborn-kitten. And I'm genuinely fond of many small moments of madness here, like the way the three separate multitracked voices echo the phrase 'living together.' But obsessive ornamentation can't transform a curiosity into inhabitable music, and there's not one song here that equals any on the first side of *Saturday Night Fever*."[38]

The songs do suffer from a rococo ornamentation, as if Barry recognized their slightness and tried to compensate by adding more voices, more falsetto, filling every space. It suggests music that was no longer instinctual—however quickly the songs were written—and more engineered. Everyone seems to be playing as hard as they can, reaching for a grand statement with every note. *Sprits* holds to the usual Bee Gees pattern of three hit singles, one or two interesting non-hits and six tracks of filler. Christgau recognized some of the nuttiness of the filler, but remained unconvinced.

By May, *Sprits Having Flown* was certified platinum, the Bee Gees made the cover of *Rolling Stone* yet again and Hugh and Barbara appeared on *The Dinah Shore Show*, a popular daytime talk show.

The Bee Gees and the band rehearsed for their upcoming tour five to six hours a day throughout May and June. With the album finished, they put their musical energy into rehearsing. They were so devoted to rehearsals that they skipped that year's *Billboard* Music Awards; they won eleven awards in absentia. The band conceived a mega-tour, their first in years. Doing *Sgt. Pepper's* had prevented them from touring to capitalize on *SNF*. They were itching to play live and travel properly. In planning their first-class private travel accommodations, Barry said: "The only way to stay straight is to stay above it." "This is the tour we have dreamed of all our lives," Maurice said. "And never expected to do."[39]

The brothers regarded this as their farewell tour. They recognized that disco was fading, and wanted to close out this phase of their career absolutely on top. With any other band, financial motives might have been the driving consideration, but the income from their record sales meant that this tour was as much for fun and posterity as lucre. The Bee Gees wanted the tour to be majestic and memorable. The brothers and the band knew they would not be performing together again any time soon. Barry and Robin had been writing songs for a planned Barbra Streisand album that Barry would produce. Barry also wrote with Albhy for that record and Barry, Robin and Maurice wrote one song together. Additionally, Barry was writing for Andy Gibbs's next record, which Barry would also produce. Robin and Blue Weaver were going to work on a record for Jimmy Ruffin. Maurice, seemingly, was going to drink.

The band rented a custom fifty-five-seat Boeing 707 for $1 million and had it painted glossy black with the *Spirits* logo on the tail. During the tour, the jet flew to and from one of five base cities to each show and returned nightly to a base city at each show's end. Family and friends traveled on the jet, along with Maurice's wife, Yvonne, and Barry's wife, Lynda, and their children. Robin was estranged from Molly—who remained in England—and toured without her. A film crew accompanied the tour, taking footage for an upcoming Bee Gees NBC special to be hosted by David Frost.

The Bee Gees traveled with their own stage, sound and lighting rig, carried on seven semi-trucks and followed by two custom buses bearing the crew and those not lucky enough to be on the jet. The stage was a huge disco floor, lit from beneath. At climactic moments in various songs, the floor would light up in patterns of red and yellow squares.

Barry wanted the tour to be as stress free as possible and planned every detail. Security was tight, and the tour was designed so that no one ever needed to leave its protected cocoon. "For all intents and purposes," Robin said, "this tour is like being in prison. To go out and buy a shirt would require two hours' planning for logistics and security."[40] Stigwood had to get a movie theater manager to agree to "cordon" off a balcony so the band could see *Alien*.

The touring band was Alan Kendall on guitar, Dennis Byron on drums, Blue Weaver on keyboards, Joey Murcia on rhythm guitar and Joe Lala on percussion. "This band was more than just a group of musicians," Maurice said. "Having a band that knows how we play and sing and write has really been one of the keys to our sound."[41]

Everyone knew Maurice was not up to playing bass live on stage. He told the press that playing guitar was more exciting. Harold Cowart joined the touring band as the bass player. With Joey Murcia—behind Maurice—covering the rhythm parts and Barry—next to Maurice—working his acoustic, there was little need for another guitar. On videos of the shows, Maurice's guitar is not easily heard, and the bass is turned way up in the mix.

The six-piece Miami brass session group, the Boonero Horns, came along, as did the RSO vocal trio, the Sweet Inspirations. The Inspirations were accomplished backup singers and had worked with Elvis and Ray Charles.

Barry discussed not taking along an orchestra, as they had routinely done in their earlier years. "Before, we played it safe and strict," he said. "We used the orchestra as a cushion. It was beautiful, but we weren't taxing our abilities.

"When I look back at the days when we toured with 30 pieces, I know we were on display and opposed to communicating with the audience. Going to a bigger band and leaving the orchestra at home was a logical extension. We didn't want to cling to something that didn't make us feel comfortable. I think our stage act improved 100 per cent. The orchestra was lovely, but restrictive at times.

"The kids and younger people want to open up at concerts. We're now more self-contained on stage and I really dig working with our band. Blue Weaver is playing string synthesizer and it fuses the Sixties to the Seventies. If you want to extend the concert experience you have to be visible to your audience. Looking back, the orchestra did colour many of our songs. But at times we might have overused the strings and some of our work became mushy."[42]

On the road the families would hang out, sightsee and head for the venue in the late afternoon. The backing band and the crew, traveling by bus, got to the gigs around 5:00 p.m. The Bee Gees and their entourage arrived by limousine. The doors opened at seven. The Sweet Inspirations opened for the Bee Gees at eight and usually did around forty-five minutes. When the house went dark again at nine, people started shrieking. The Gibb brothers burst onstage under white lights in their white outfits and the crowd went berserk. Every show opened with "Tragedy," as fireworks exploded above.

The tour opened in Fort Worth, Texas, on June 28 and closed—where else?—in Miami on October 6. It spanned forty-one shows, including Montreal, Toronto and three sold-out nights in a row at New York's Madison Square Garden. The tour hit massive arenas—sports stadiums—like Dodger Stadium in Los Angeles, the Summit in Houston and the Silverdome in Detroit. "I've never seen them as nervous as they were before the tour started," Dick Ashby said. "They're at the pinnacle of their careers, and people will try to tear them down." Tickets were going for $700 for scalpers, and in LA at least, Bee Gees merchandise sold at the rate of $3,000 a minute.[43]

The Bee Gees wore their iconic outfits of white satin flared pants and white spangled jackets and scarves. Most nights those jackets were open down to their beltlines. The lights, the clothes, the stage, the postures—Barry with his legs akimbo, braced to send the sound outward and receive the applause coming in; Maurice goofy and self-conscious, always moving around the stage; Robin quite loose, hands on his hips, graceful and dreamily responsive to the rhythm of the music—turned every show into what the Bee Gees intended: a spectacle. A bigger than life, aggressively perfect, show-biz spectacle, half pop-music, half Las Vegas and determined to be the best at both.

The younger fans squealed like they were seeing the Beatles at Shea Stadium. An eighteen-year-old Maryland girl said: "I can't help it, it just comes out. I want them to know I'm their fan. Nothing can top them—not the Beatles, not nobody."[44] "I couldn't take it," Dick Ashby said. "I had to break off two cigarette filters and stick them in my ears."[45] Which is just what the cops at Shea Stadium had done.

"Tragedy" was one of only two songs from *Spirits* on the set list. The middle of the show was a medley of "NY Mining Disaster," "Run To Me," "Too Much Heaven," "Holiday," "I Can't See Nobody," "Lonely Days," "I Started a Joke," "Massachusetts" and "How Can You Mend a Broken Heart." The show-stopping climax—when the mirrored disco balls and gigantic Bee Gees logo descended—was "Nights on Broadway." The show closed with "Jive Talkin'." The band came back out for one encore, "You Should Be Dancin'." "Dancin'" had an extended percussion break and ended with a bang. Within a minute of that bang, Barry, Maurice and Robin were in their limos, rolling either toward their hotel or the 707.

"Nineteen fifty-five was when we first stepped on stage," Barry said later. "So we've been doing it longer than people think. After we toured America in '79, the exhaustion of being the Bee Gees set in and we couldn't see what tomorrow was going to bring." And yet, despite the length of the tour, the logistics and security and the nightly pressure to be unforgettable, there is not one moment in videos of their performance when anyone on stage appears bored, disengaged or even tired. Some nights some folks might appear totally wasted, but that's different. What the Bee Gees appear to be, night after night, is present, attentive, fulfilled and happy. They did not regard this tour as a chore. They had a tremendously good time. The sales, the Grammys, the #1s from the new record, the sold-out forty-thousand-seat arenas; this wasn't validation, this was victory. And it was valedictory—the Bee Gees were graduating, on stage, in front of the world, to whatever was next.

John Travolta showed up in Houston and danced with the band. There were sixty thousand paying fans at Dodger Stadium in LA. Celebrity guests included Harry Wayne Casey of KC and the Sunshine Band, Barbra Streisand, Cary Grant, Karen Carpenter and the Jackson family. At Madison Square Garden the guests included Billy Joel, Diana Ross, Gene Simmons and Paul Stanley from KISS—who were always interested in spectacle—and Al Pacino. President Jimmy Carter invited the band to the White House prior to the September 24 gig in Washington, DC, to honor the Bee Gees for their work with UNICEF.

Touring is unspeakably dull for those touring, especially those who don't get onstage. Naturally, there must be distractions. But the security on this tour not only kept outsiders out, it kept inside information in. Few backstage stories of outrageous behavior ever emerged. One good way to quantify drug use on a tour with tight security is to consider the level of denial of drug use. On this tour, that denial was absolute. A tour security guy, an ex-FBI agent, claims there were no drugs at all anywhere at any time: "I checked my sources on these guys. I wasn't going to risk my rep on three rock stars who are into hard drugs." Robin said: "There is no Happy Hour on this tour, where everybody throws a TV set out the window."[46] Indeed, it is hard to throw a TV out of a moving 707.

The band protested mightily about their straightness to *People* magazine. Barry said that he had tried cocaine on an earlier tour, but "my nose was like a block of concrete for a week." Robin proclaimed: "If you can't face reality and be happy with it, what's the point of living?" Always ready to be on both sides of an argument, Robin added: "But we're not choirboys, either." Maurice insisted he was not drinking, and *People* wrote: "If there is a silver spoon near his face pre-concert, it's full of honey."[47]

In October, RSO released *Bee Gees Greatest*, a double-album compilation of hits from the *SNF* era forward. Side three offered B-sides and cover versions, including Yvonne Elliman and inexplicably, Vegas crooner Wayne Newton.

Greatest hit #1 on the album charts on January 12, 1980.

The tour ended with two triumphal concerts at the Miami Stadium. The final show took place on October 6.

The Bee Gees aired on NBC during prime time on Wednesday, November 21, 1979, the night before Thanksgiving, one of the most sought-after time slots on network TV.

David Frost wore the interviewer's uniform, a blue shirt with epaulettes. The Bee Gees sat on what appears to be Barry's couch—with Barry leaning toward Frost in the middle—and told bits of their life's story. Their chat is intercut with footage from the tour, and even more interesting footage of the band in their studio, recreating working through a song.

"It's almost as if the songs are in the air and we hear them," Barry said, describing their songwriting process. Robin said: "They're already written, but they're only written for us and they're out there." "We go into the studio," Maurice said, "and most of the lyrics are written during the laying down of the backtracks." Every single time Robin or Maurice speak, Barry interrupts. "We have a band of such strong musicians," Barry said. "It's hard to remember that they can't hear the song like we do. They can't always hear what you're talking about. That's the most difficult part."

During the recreation, the band plays standing near to one another in a cramped room with no separation for the drums and no separation for the singers. Barry runs the session—which is, after all, only a restaging—with an iron hand. That makes the recreation seem all too real. Standing at the mic wearing his guitar, Barry raises a hand and says: "Solo." He hums the part with perfect pitch as everyone watches, waiting for the next order. The show depicts how the band cut the backing tracks for "Tragedy" before Barry had written any lyrics beyond the one word of the title. Once the tracks were done to his satisfaction, Barry hummed the melody of the vocal. The brief clip showcases their attention to detail and familiarity with Barry's process. It was a fitting portrait with which to close an era.

"Success like we have now was a distant dream in 1971," Barry said. "We thought it was all over for us then. Now we can't really accept what we've done and where we are when we read magazines saying, 'The Bee Gees are hot.' I would like for the Bee Gees to stop before we wane. I don't know if it's easy or accurate to say that in the next two years the Bee Gees will decline or continue at this pace. None of us can say. But all bubbles have a way of bursting or being deflated in the end."[48]

The Bee Gees would not tour together again for ten years.

andy gibb

March 5, 1958–March 10, 1988

*A*ndy was not a genius like his eldest brother. He was a talented, sweet soul and his young death was a great waste. Andy's sweetness proved no defense against his melancholy and his melancholy was no defense against drink or drugs. Drugs and melancholy consumed Andy and—despite three #1 singles, two platinum albums and all the riches and fans they brought—swept him away. Still, Andy never possessed the gravitas for tragedy. His curse was being a good-looking lightweight.

Even Andy's obituary in the grave *London Times* praised his handsomeness: "His immense success could hardly have been founded on vocal qualities alone. What sent the young fans wild was his pretty face, flowing blond locks and his lithe figure, which radiated the healthy, tanned sex-appeal of a male Farah Fawcett-Majors."[1]

The passing decades have proven the *Times* obit author to be the only person who ever claimed that Andy evoked Farah Fawcett-Majors, the *echt*-University of Texas cheerleader turned pinup girl turned Charlie's Angel (the first go-around, on TV), turned quote serious actress close quote who walked around beneath a single unchanging hairstyle for forty years. The obit writer's surprising reference speaks more to his own obsessions than it does to Andy Gibb. It does underscore one of Andy's several small tragedies: grown men found it difficult to take him seriously. Including, apparently, his three older brothers.

Andy did have a great head of hair. For most of his career he wore it shaped away from his boyishly handsome face, shoulder length and feathered, more of a Peter Frampton cut, without the bangs or bottom flips of, say, a Greg Allman. Unlike his siblings, Andy—the only conventionally attractive Gibb brother—possessed truly stellar teeth: a perfectly scaled movie-star blaze of white. And then there were his piercing, sparkling blue eyes

On various television shows during his drug addiction, rehab, drinking, drug relapse and more rehab days, Andy would aim those eyes at whichever professional blonde was interviewing him about his heartache over his goddess former girlfriend, actress Victoria Principal. Under Andy's gaze, that professional blonde would melt, right there on camera. Armored, overcoiffed morning network stars went all empathetic and motherly lustful when Andy spoke wistfully about how Victoria turned her back on his sweet innocent love. It speaks to a more naïve age to see a TV reporter manifest a genuine emotion, and these reporters and hostesses were genuinely moved. They, like so many of Andy's fans, were moved to a primal emotion: desire. Desire fueled by the need to nurture. Ladies loved Andy Gibb. They all wanted to mother him before, during and after they took off his clothes. While he sang.

The one lady who didn't quite love or mother Andy sufficiently, according to Andy, was Ms. Principal. When she spoke about their time together, which she did reluctantly, she offered a brief, unsentimental version: "Our breakup was preceded and precipitated by Andy's use of drugs," she said. "I did everything I could to help him. But then I told him he would have to choose between me and his problem."[2] Andy, in her view, chose his problem.

Andy chose his problem, mostly cocaine, sometimes Quaa-ludes, sometimes alcohol, in many situations. His problems in-cluded drug use or drunkenness or the depression of staying clean or the stress of appearing in public when his cripplingly low self-esteem or his paralyzing, incongruous shyness took him over. Hangovers or ennui or lack of self-discipline or sheer laziness got him fired from what had to be the easiest gig in show business at the time, or perhaps of all time: co-hosting the unintentionally hi-larious variety music and dance show, the 1980s incarnate, *Solid Gold*.

Solid Gold aired on Saturday nights, mostly, and featured paired hit makers from widely disparate demographics, for exam-ple, Irene Cara (*Fame*) and Dionne Warwick, lip-synching either their latest or best known material. Even for the 1980s, the sets, lighting and artist presentation were cheesy and cheap. The real viewer-lure was the *Solid Gold* dancers, mega-buff men and women who writhed suggestively to the week's top 10, usually clad in shoulderless leotards and lamé leggings over their golden ankle boots. Their elaborate camp routines combined Las Vegas show-girl review moves with ersatz Bob Fosse hip jerks and knee-up toe points. Both genders wore lots of hair gel. This is not to downplay *Solid Gold*'s audience share or its influence. Its raw tackiness and graphically sexual dance numbers brought in tweeners by the mil-lions. *Solid Gold* was Andy's demographic. He was perfect for it.

It's hard to find Andy on TV with his shirt buttoned or singing live. His golden chest hair seems as much a part of his wardrobe as his pressed jeans. It was an era of open shirts and gold medal-lions, and Andy was a man of his era.

Andy provided a unthreatening whitebread sweetness and co-host Marilyn McCoo, of the Mamas and the Papas–lite black har-mony act, the 5th Dimension, the equally unthreatening black showbiz polish. Andy came across as sincere and without artifice,

chatting as if the god-awful showbiz banter between him and Mc-
Coo were his natural tongue. Andy could make his eyes glow
while lip-synching with the most detached uninterest in the whole
proceeding. He always seemed most natural in the most artificial
situations, whether lip-synching with Olivia Newton-John or
meeting, for the first time, Victoria Principal live on the set of *The
John Davidson Show.*

Which is another of his tragedies. If Andy were thirty today, instead of in 1988, his star would be on the ascent in a way he could
never have imagined. Because Andy was the perfect 2000s and
2010s celebrity—the adorable, world-famous walking train wreck
with yet unrealized potential. He lived out his emotional life on
talk shows and sought publicity for his addiction and sojourns in
rehab, as damn few did in 1985. He dated or crushed out on other
celebrities. There was a brief public infatuation with Marie
Osmond, with whom he actually sang live on a south Florida
telethon.

Andy went public with his love, but soon learned that Marie did
not fool around and would never marry outside her Mormon faith.
Andy had an undefined relationship with Olivia Newton-John,
which lasted little longer than Andy's stint as the leading man in
Broadway's *Joseph and the Amazing Technicolor Dreamcoat.* The
Dreamcoat producers fired Andy barely a week's run into the show.
Broadway was hard work, harder than Andy could bear.

On the day that Andy met Victoria on *The John Davidson
Show*—the day, Andy insisted, that all his troubles began—he was,
naturally, exposing his chest to his navel. Andy wore sharply
creased light blue jeans, an unzipped blue Fila athletic jersey and
what appear to be golden boots. Victoria Principal walked onto the
set supposedly unannounced, and Andy's surprise seems genuine.

Andy tells Davidson that he told *People* magazine that he
watched the hit nighttime soap *Dallas* only for Victoria Principal,
and that he'd sent her a note. Davidson says: "So if there's one per-

son you'd like to meet, it's Victoria Principal?" And behind Davidson, already onstage in advance of her cue, appears the woman
herself.

Victoria Principal became a household name as Pamela Barnes
Ewing in *Dallas*, a role she played from 1978 to 1987. *Dallas* dominated television and all the concomitant industries—gossip, fashion, fitness, talk shows—as few shows ever did and none could
today. During Principal's reign on *Dallas*, it was impossible to turn
on prime-time television and not see her face.

Davidson—a genial third-tier daytime talk-show host—
becomes a spectator to history on his own show. Victoria moves
slowly, approaching Andy from behind, and he turns on the couch
to follow her entrance. Her helmet of Jheri-curled black hair
gleaming under the lights, Principal glides onto the set in an an-
kle-length embroidered white lace dress that evokes satanic wed-
dings in heavy metal videos. In front of her left ear she wears a
gargantuan white flower that obscures a quarter of her face.

Victoria Principal is really something, a force of nature. She
has had a singular, cross-media career that overturns numerous
firmly held Los Angeles showbiz truisms. Foremost among them
was that starlets who strip for *Playboy* never amount to anything.
As, indeed, most of them don't. Ms. Principal posed for the magazine in 1973. Her career was launched by a small role in John Hus-
ton's farce of a western, 1972's *The Life and Times of Judge Roy
Bean*, starring Paul Newman; for that she earned a Most Promis-
ing Newcomer Golden Globe. In 1975 she quit acting to become
an agent.

That shift speaks volumes. Ms. Principal was an Air Force brat,
and manifested the hard shell and adaptive social dexterity associated with a rootless upbringing. Her sideways move into agenting
demonstrates a cold-blooded insight into where the power lay in
Hollywood and into her own chances at viable stardom. She was
an agent from 1975 to 1977. Her agenting career stood her in good

stead when she later moved into producing TV movies, all of which did well.

When Victoria met Andy on air in 1981 she was, despite his worldwide #1s, a far bigger star, less naïve and more adept at living the star's life. When she sits down on that couch beside him and hands Andy a sealed letter, he's gobsmacked. Andy's shyness and lack of worldliness was no act. At times he seemed to forget his status and what it meant. All Andy had to do was ask his agent for an introduction and Victoria would have had lunch that day; instead, he wrote a letter to a TV star like an eighth grader. And like an eighth-grader's fantasy, she answered. Andy reads Victoria's letter on air and tells the world, happily, that Victoria signed it with a happy face. Andy and Davidson recount—with Victoria on the couch next to Andy—that Andy had a crush on Victoria from the first moment he saw her. Andy blushes like a schoolboy and Victoria seems self-conscious. It's a touching, human moment.

Victoria sits as she always did, with her back ramrod straight, posing like a good girl with her ankles crossed. When Davidson presses him to say what he likes about Victoria, Andy says: "I'm a very shy person basically," turning red from his forehead to the top of his chest hair. He's tongue-tied and she's charmed.

That charm and what it camouflaged was the core of Victoria Principal's appeal. With her dancer's carriage, feral-innocent face and unshakeable goody two-shoes vocal style, Principal incarnated the dirty/sweet southern sorority girl, the girl from across the tracks determined to be above reproach, to act so "nicely" that none of the more highborn homecoming queens could ever censor her behavior. But no matter how civilized she pretends to be, it's clear that if you ever got Victoria into the backseat after a game, she would learn you a thing or two. Victoria Principal was formidable; a self-contained, self-motivated handful to say the least, and yet there she was, appearing on live daytime TV to hand a sweet note to a man she'd never met.

When she gave Andy her letter, Victoria Principal was thirty-one and Andy Gibb, twenty-three.

Andy Gibb was the first solo artist ever to have his or her first three singles hit #1 on the *Billboard* top 100 charts. Andy's debut album—*Flowing Rivers*—released when he was nineteen, sold over a million copies in 1977, and cracked the *Billboard* top 20. Andy's "I Just Want to Be Your Everything" is touted as "the most played song of 1977" and peaked at #7 on the UK charts. Along with his albums and singles, Andy's fans bought myriad Andy posters and other merchandise. He was a money-making machine, a household name before he achieved his majority, an idolized tween idol in the footsteps of David Cassidy of *The Partridge Family* or Leif Garrett.

That niche, and the sort of fame associated with it, did little for Andy's self-esteem, which was always low. "Andy never saw anything in the mirror," a family friend said. "He saw an empty vision."

Andy, like many before him in other fields, joined the family business. His mentor, co-songwriter and producer—Barry—happened to be the greatest pop hit maker in the world at the absolute top of his game. In an inversion of the usual formula, Andy's hits and worldwide fame came first, then he paid his dues.

Andy Roy Gibb was born at the Stretford Memorial Hospital in Manchester on the cusp of his family leaving England for Australia, on March 5, 1958. Andy was five months old when his family took ship for Oz. When Andy was four, he loved to sing along with his brothers. He and Barry shared a special bond; Barry said of Andy: "My parents had two sets of twins, one [set] separated by 12 years."

When the Gibbs moved back to England, Andy claimed to have taken the Bee Gees' success in stride. He'd stroll through the five or six hundred kids who routinely crowded outside the family house waiting for a glimpse of the famous brothers and hang with his kin, who were inside watching themselves on TV. Andy told *Co-Ed* magazine: "When you're ten years old, you don't really think about show business, with the glitter and stardom . . . I just accepted it."[3] When the older brothers went through their acrimonious spilt, Andy was eleven. He could hardly choose a side, but his natural connection to Barry made the feud all the more uncomfortable for him.

In April of 1969, when Andy was nine, he told an interviewer from *Fabulous 208* magazine: "I think [Barry's] my favorite brother, he's so kind and generous, and when he comes to visit us he plays with me. I've only got to ask for something and he'll buy it for me. I think he's too softhearted, people can talk him into things and he hates hurting anyone. For my eleventh birthday he bought me a horse, which I've called Gala. He has just bought the saddle for it and he also paid for the delivery from Sussex. I hope when I grow up I'm like him."[4]

When Andy was twelve, Barry gave him his first guitar. At the time, Andy was obsessed with show jumping. According to Hugh, Andy was a champion rider who liked to sleep in the stalls with his horses. Andy also liked to rent limousines and take his friends for joyrides to London.

In 1971, Hugh and Barbara moved with Andy to the Spanish resort island of Ibiza. The Bee Gees were gone touring most of the year and Manchester had grown too small for the little brother of superstars. In a 1978 interview with enduring Los Angeles radio personality Robert W. Morgan, Andy said: "I have never had a good day at school in my life. That's why I left school on my 13th birthday. There were kids there that I would do anything to get along with them, [but] any game of sport was 'you think you're great, don'cha, cause you're the Bee Gees' brother, you think you can do that fabulously.' To have that for quite a few years thrown at you, it got to me so bad in the end I just couldn't handle it any more. I had to leave it."[5]

It speaks to the bottomless provincialism and complacency of Hugh and Barbara that they could have lived anywhere in the UK and chose to return to Manchester. Maybe they wanted to lord success over their old neighbors, maybe they thought London was above them. Maybe they liked it there.

Andy didn't care for school any more than his brothers, though he stayed all the way to eighth grade. One story that pops up regularly is that Andy caught shit from his classmates because his mum and dad dropped him off and picked him up from school in their Rolls-Royce. This story gets applied to Andy in both Manchester, where it makes sense, and in Ibiza, where it makes none. Being picked up in a Rolls might drive other Manchester twelve-year-olds to want to murder Andy, but in Ibiza a Rolls would be no big deal.

Andy didn't suffer any greater a yoke of parental supervision than had his brothers. He had plenty of the hellion genes that had seen his brothers run out of the UK a decade earlier. In a 1978 conversation with the *Philadelphia Daily News*, Andy claimed to have been "a skinhead in a skinhead gang. With the skinheads, the main thing was football matches. You take a hammer into the stadium and throw it as high as you can into a capacity crowd of thirty thousand. And wherever it lands, it lands. We were really very nasty."[6]

Any photograph of Andy makes it difficult to picture him in the skinhead mufti of suspenders and steel-toed combat boots. The skinhead ranks were filled with the picked upon, but Andy's tales of hammer throwing sound like wistful thinking; being bullied by classmates seems more his speed. Andy was a child of privilege already working hard to present himself as somehow a victim. Or perhaps tales of youthful skinheaddom were Andy's grabbing after gravitas, making himself into someone who took a journey, who overcame something to become a star, rather than a scion of the most successful family in music.

Ibiza suited Andy and his new guitar. When *Circus* magazine interviewed him in 1978, Andy discussed his first gig. "I started singing in a tavern on Ibiza called Debbie's Bar on St. Patrick's Day when I was thirteen. I sang Paul Simon's 'The Only Living Boy In New York' and 'Feelin' Groovy' and the Bee Gees' 'Words.'" Andy played a round of clubs on the island and, smitten with a tourist girl, wrote his first song. He played it for Barry, and Barry encouraged him to keep writing.[7]

Andy told *Co-Ed* magazine: "When my mother and father and I moved to Ibiza, and I got work in nightclubs playing to Swedish tourists." Andy smiled at the memory of those Swedish tourists— 90 percent female and between the ages of 18 and 24. "That was really fun," said Andy. "But it was then that I got a feeling for what I was suited to do—sing and play music! That was it!"[8]

No fourteen-year-old ever had it better than Andy Gibb. He spent his eighth and ninth grade years singing covers to clubs packed with Swedish, Dutch and German tourist girls, a new crop every week. At that age his big brothers had been touring the shit-holes of Australia in ill-fitting tuxedos singing lounge material that was twenty years out of date. Adolescent Andy's musical appren-ticeship consisted of a sea of blond, sunburned, drunken faces falling in love with him. "We'd start playing at about 8 at a piano bar," Andy said. "There'd be about 300 to 400 people sitting around the bar. I'd finish at midnight and start at another club at 1 AM and work pretty late. We'd occasionally have a week off and I'd go to England." Andy slept late, lay on the beach, water-skied and sang for free—because English citizens were not allowed to work for pay in Spain.[9]

Andy began to write songs: "I was 13. And there was this Swedish girl who was 16. I was head over heels in love, but she seemed like an adult. I wrote this song. I told Barry about it one night when just the two of us were together. He asked me to play it for him, but I said, 'No, no, not for you of all people. You've written good songs, you know what good songs are.' He insisted—and when I finished, he said that he was amazed, that I'd proven to him I could write. Then he told me the important thing was to keep writing"[10]

At times, his brothers took the stage at his gigs. In 1977, Andy told the *Lakeland Ledger*: "My brothers Barry, Robin, and Maurice would come down to the club and get up and sing with me. We'd have a four-part harmony going that sounded absolutely amazing."[11] Barry was Andy's idol. He copied Barry's singing style; he tried to hold and play his acoustic guitar like Barry.

Andy told Robert W. Morgan: "I didn't have permanent friends. I've always been surrounded by people in the business . . . all my friends were older than me. And it was always 'tipsy' (moving) in my family as far back as I can remember. We never stayed in a house more than 8 or 9 months. We never lasted a year at any one house, I don't know what it was, we would have to get up and move somewhere else."[12]

By 1973, Hugh and Barbara, tired of Ibiza, moved to the Isle of Man. Andy hated it and Barbara stepped into the breach. She bought Andy the equipment to start a band. Hugh found him a gig at a hotel. Andy put together a group of locals barely older than himself. To the band's displeasure, Barbara, as bankroller and mom, insisted on naming the band. Andy let her; he was sixteen. His letting her unknowingly set the pattern for the rest of his music career: older family members would always make the decisions for Andy.

Barbara chose Melody Fair. Or maybe Melody Fayre. Or even Melodye Fair; confusion exists over the spelling. However it was spelled, the other guys in the band hated it, but what could they do? Andy told *Circus* magazine: "In 1973 we moved to the British Isle of Man, and I put my first band together for one year, named Melody Fayre [*sic*] after a song from my brothers' *Odessa* album."[13] "Melody Fair" concerns a girl who needs to comb her hair in order to be beautiful. It's a mighty twee name for an all-guy rock band.

As they put together a set list, Andy's taste came to the fore. He liked Neil Sedaka, Neil Diamond and "The Long and Winding Road." Before Melody Fair's first gig, Barry came back to the Isle of Man and helped finalize the list, which included Elton John's "Rocket Man" and "I Gotta Get a Message to You." When the band played their first show, Barry was front and center. The show was a success, and the band members remember Andy as being shy and ill at ease around the girls in the audience.

In 1981 Andy told Robert W. Morgan: "It was a different life I've had from most kids. I left school young and I think my whole youth was kind of a risk in a way, a big gamble. I didn't have any education to fall back on if things didn't work out. If I didn't make it in singing or didn't make it in show business, I didn't think there was anything else I could do."[14]

Melody Fair played a series of barely paid gigs at venues like the Peveril Hotel on Loch Promenade. The boys made a couple of pounds for each show. Andy's name was prominent on the posters. When Barry was in town, he came to every performance. Barry made the other Melody Fairs self-conscious. The band quickly depleted all the local possibilities, but was not ready for London and lacked original material. An interim step was needed. Andy told Morgan in 1978: "At the end of that year, Barry and my dad said: 'Australia.' [They] suggested I go out there and try to become a big name there like they originally did. So they controlled [my career] even from that point. Before I [had] any single at all, they were guiding [me] and planning for the future. They were planning for me to eventually come back to America, for Barry to produce me at the right age and to sign with RSO. Even when I was young they told me basically how they had it all worked out and I let them do it . . . it went pretty nice."[15]

Barry told *Circus*: "We talked Andy into going to Australia for his performing apprenticeship like we did ten years before. He needed to get his legwork in without the rest of the world knowing what he was doing."[16]

Andy's bandmates were not all willing to move six thousand miles from home; only two agreed to go. They timed their arrival to coincide with the Bee Gees' 1974 tour. The boys shared the Bee Gees' hotel, rode in the band's limos to their shows and jammed in hotel rooms with the brothers. The luxury, normal for Andy, blew his bandmates' minds.

Australian Col Joye handled their Australian career. He wanted to record the band, and that meant song writing. The group wrote together, later claiming that Andy composed lyrics but lacked discipline and never wrote anything down. They also maintain that they supplied most of the musical backing. They cut "To a Girl" at Joye's studio, along with some demos, but the track was never released. Andy later recorded three of their demos — "Westfield Mansions," "Flowing Rivers" and "Words and Music" — on his solo albums.

When the Bee Gees left Sydney for their tour, Andy and his band moved to less prestigious lodgings. The other boys complained that while Barbara claimed to be hustling gigs, she was more concerned with keeping a tight rein on Andy. She got the band excited over upcoming shows that never worked out. Tours backing bigger Australian bands were discussed, but never materialized. The boys' savings dwindled. Barbara refused to put them on salary, insisting that upcoming performances would pay them all they needed. The boys found crap part-time jobs. They were not happy. Andy went to the beach.

Andy performed "To a Girl" on Australian TV. He left the band behind in Sydney to go to Melbourne for regular TV and game show appearances. He had time and energy for his solo performances, but little for the Fair. His bandmates took the hint and went back to the Isle of Man, embittered and broke.

Col Joye announced auditions and a local three-piece, Zenta, were hired to back Andy. Andy's management released "Words and Music" as a single and it got some airplay. Andy was to record "Can't Stop Dancing," written by Ray Stevens—the American singer-composer of the immortal "Ahab the Arab," which hit #5 in the US in 1962. Andy cut part of an album and another single, but nothing from those sessions was released.

Andy said: "I had one single out in Australia and it never did anything. [Australia's] a great training ground, because you can be the biggest name in Australia and without outside help you will not get heard outside of Australia. You can make a lot of mistakes there and there are also very tough audiences."[17] He spoke of driving five hundred miles one way to the state capital city of Adelaide, only to discover that no gig awaited. Andy's biggest show in Australia came when he and Zenta opened for the Sweet ("Ballroom Blitz") in Sydney on August of 1975. Andy might not be the first guy you'd pick to open for a blistering glam-rock guitar band, but he told of being assaulted by groupies after the show, so he must have made an impression. Andy and Zenta went on to support the Bay City Rollers on a short tour. It's ironic that Andy complained about shrieking teenage girls who drowned out the band they'd come to see. Soon, the same girls would be shrieking for him, and louder.

Andy met Kim Reeder, sixteen. A sweet girl from around the way, Kim lived near Andy in Sydney. As was the habit of the Gibb boys when they met the women who would become their first wives, Andy fell instantly for Kim. Kim told Susan Duncan of the *Australian Women's Weekly*: "When we were together, we did really simple things—we'd go to dog shows, the movies, we'd go fishing at four o'clock in the morning. When he was living in Australia, he never seemed to want or to need drugs. And he was so loving. He latched onto our family in those early days like a lifeline. None of us was impressed with his brothers or his background. My dad is a bricklayer and my mum was a machinist. It's hard to impress people like us, so we loved Andy for what he was—a bright, enthusiastic and considerate person."[18]

Kim and Andy were inseparable. According to Kim, they had an "understanding" that they would wait to marry until they were older. But Barry reached out to Andy in June 1976. It was time for Andy to come to America. Robert Stigwood would become his manager and Barry would produce his records. "I want to produce you," Barry told Andy, calling after a show in Alaska.

Andy gave Kim the news and proposed. He pressured Kim as her family and his sought to delay the nuptials. Nobody thought it was a good idea except Andy, including Kim. She told Susan Duncan: "I never thought about marriage except to think that one day we would probably do it, but Andy got a call from his brother, Barry. It was time for Andy's career to be launched in a big way. The Gibb family mapped their careers with precision and great professionalism. When Andy told me he'd been summoned, he said we'd have to get married before he left so I could go with him."

Despite the warnings and reservations of both families, Andy refused to go to America without Kim. They married in Sydney on July 11, 1976, at the Wayside Chapel in Sydney. Kim: "[Andy] gave me money from his Christmas club account to buy a wedding dress. I'd shown him how to work those accounts the year before and taught him to save money for the first time in his life."[19] Andy and Kim flew to Robert Stigwood's estate in Bermuda for their honeymoon.

Awaiting the newlyweds were Barry and Stigwood. Andy and Kim may have thought they going to have a romantic idyll in the sun, but Barry forced Andy's attention toward his career. Stigwood told Andy what his future would be and Andy signed with RSO. While Kim sat on the beach, Andy tried to write, but mostly he watched Barry.

Andy told Robert W. Morgan in 1981: "Robert Stigwood and my brother Barry asked me to fly out to Bermuda as kind of a honeymoon-*cum*-working set-up to meet with Barry and to sign up with Robert for RSO Records. This was all at Robert's home in Bermuda. And me and Barry locked ourselves in a bedroom and Barry just started writing, and when Barry writes it is hard to collaborate with him, because he is so quick. And before I knew it he was starting to do the chorus (sings) 'I just want to be your everything,' and I thought 'wow, what a hook,' it was right in there."[20]

Perhaps Andy felt the oncoming steamroller looming. He'd sung in bars for blondes and tips and toured Australia singing mostly other people's material, waiting for his call to the big time. When the call came, Andy learned on the first day what the big time entailed: his seventeen-year-old bride ignored as his beloved older brother, writing before his eyes and in minutes, created the song that would define him. What Andy got to do was sit and watch; Barry didn't need his help. Whatever collaboration Andy envisioned was reduced to its essence: the pro shows the new guy how it's done. The dynamic between the brothers was set. Did Andy feel grateful for the gift he was about to receive? Or was his shaky self-worth diminished further when he—a talented, charismatic amateur—came face to face with genius and the methods genius demands?

Some reports have Andy and Kim going back to Australia before recording began at Criteria Studios. Others have them moving straight from Bermuda to Miami, where Karl Richardson, Albhy Galuten and Barry ran the sessions. Galuten assembled a band: a veteran of the Funky Nassau sound and a collection of southern-soul session musicians with a number of Atlantic tracks to their credit, including guitarist Cornell Dupree. When asked how he chose the eccentric ensemble, and what the guys assembled had to do with Andy's sound, Galuten said only: "I chose from among the local musicians I knew could play."[21]

Guitarist Joe Walsh of the Eagles visited the sessions and guested on "I Just Want to Be Your Everything." Walsh's sitting in led to claims from Andy about the "country-rock" sensibility that he says pervades the record. There is an attempt at 1976 Los Angeles soft rock semi-country that seems as forced and ersatz as the Bee Gees/disco-lite that dominates the record. The jaunty track "Come Home for the Winter" features fingerpicking, pedal-steel guitar, Eagles-like flourishes at the end of each verse and multi-track vocals on the choruses that evoke the horror that is Dan Fogelberg.

"Let It Be Me" runs with an almost–shuffle beat, more pedal-steel accents and Tony Joe ("Polk Salad Annie") White–style wah-wah solos. Andy tries to sing in a bouncy country rhythm, but sounds like he's reciting a nursery rhyme. The problem is the dissonance between Andy's obvious sincerity and the equally obvious synthetic quality of his material. The two hits — and what astonishing hits they proved to be — "Everything," and "(Love Is) Thicker Than Water" were Barry's. The rest are Andy's, mostly written during his time in Australia. The album, though produced with a glossy sheen, proves shockingly inconsequential, even with all the soulful playing the Criteria pros provide. What Barry, Maurice and Robin could all do at eighteen, Andy could not; write and sing something profound, unique, memorable and moving. Despite Andy's inexperience, the same mystery attaches to his songs as to his brothers': Are they attempts at commercial pop or do they contain at least some self-expression? Andy often accused himself of lacking interior substance. His first record proves his case.

Of "(Love Is) Thicker Than Water," Andy told Robert W. Morgan: "Even though it says on the credits 'B & A Gibb,' it is really Barry's song. It is hard to write with Barry, but he said: 'Help me think of a great title.' That was a period where Barry was thinking of titles first and seeing how they would inspire him to write a song. We were thinking of good titles and I said: 'How about thicker than water?' I did not say: 'Love is . . .' just 'thicker than water.' He said: 'That's great!' Then [Barry] came up with [Andy sings]: 'Love is higher than a mountain, love is thicker than water.' He just went on from there."[22]

Barry split the songwriter credit and royalty with Andy. In the understatement of his career, Andy said: "I like to do most of my own material, but I don't mind having Barry involved in one or two."[23]

Billboard reported that during this Bermuda writing session, Barry and Andy also wrote "(Love Is) Thicker Than Water," which Stigwood wanted to issue as the first single. Three days before the scheduled release date he changed his mind and put out "I Just Want to Be Your Everything."

Of his own abilities, Andy said: "I don't arrange. I read chord sheets in bars and count in timing but I can't read notes. I can't read intricate parts of the music. I'd love to be able to do that, but not one member of my family can read the music. A lot of my songs sound distinctly Bee Gees in places, but as far back as I can ever remember that's how I've sung. I don't think there's any way I could change. I would be worse if I had a different voice. This is my voice, and these are mostly my songs."[24]

Andy and Kim headed for Los Angeles and set up housekeeping. Andy's friends and bandmates in Australia never mentioned Andy having any great fondness for or issues with drugs. But as soon as he arrived in LA, Andy vanished—much to his wife's surprise—down the LA cocaine wormhole. In California, Andy discovered three things: he liked cocaine a lot, he could afford a lot of it and there were a lot of people who wanted to hang out with him while he did it. His transformation from sweet kid to sweet kid who did a ton of cocaine was almost instantaneous. As was his transition from sweet kid playing covers in Australia to married man awaiting the release of his first album on a major red-hot label.

"I Just Want to Be Your Everything" entered the *Billboard* charts at #88 on April 23, 1977. It took fourteen weeks to hit #1 and stayed there for three weeks. That is a long grind to the top—reflecting genuine grassroots popularity—and an even longer time to stay in the public pop consciousness. The Emotions knocked "Everything" out of #1 with "Best of My Love," but "Everything" stayed in the top 10 and regained #1 after a month. No song before had ever made the top spot, fallen off and returned. Ever. "Everything" remained in the top 40 for twenty-three weeks—from May to October—and reached #19 on the Black Singles chart, an impressive feat.

In June 1977, while "Everything" was working its way up the charts, Andy appeared on *Top of the Pops*. Bands usually lip-synched on that show, but Andy appears to be singing live, as Barry was known to do. Andy looks impossibly young and a bit shattered. Live TV's famous for terrible makeup. Andy's seems to have been laid on with a trowel. But in close-up, under the pancake, he's pale, haggard and his eyes are swollen. Andy wears a guitar as a prop; it's not plugged into anything. He strums away, awkwardly, gamely, and with weird self-taught mannerisms, bar chording with his left thumb. Most revealing is that throughout the song Andy keeps looking down at his left hand for the chord changes. And the chords in "Everything" are not that hard; maybe Andy didn't know how to play his own song. Of the myriad clips of artists appearing on *Top of the Pops*, Andy's the only one checking his left hand.

From the perspective of thirty years on, learning that Andy had a #1 single at a time of the Bee Gees' dominance of the charts might raise the specter of the RSO public relations machine manipulating the process, or of payola or some other contrivance. The first notion that comes to mind is of the song shooting to #1 on the week of its release, as if RSO employees all over America raced into the record stores that reported sales to *Billboard* and raced out with wheelbarrows full of the single, artificially driving it up the charts. But the song's progress renders those fantasies fantastic. "Everything" entered the charts low and built an audience, an army of listeners and buyers, that got bigger and bigger and bigger. It was a legitimate, monster hit.

Circus magazine interviewed Hugh. "I'm not all that surprised," Hugh says. "I taught Andy and the Bee Gees their stage techniques: how to walk on, smile, bow, dress. And I arrange Andy's stage program and lighting. Once he walks out there he almost never stops moving. The sweat pours out, he shakes his head and sprays the first four rows."[25]

Of that era, Kim Reeder told Susan Duncan: "The hangers-on in the rock industry are like piranhas. They hang around stars and offer drugs as a way of making friendships. I suppose they think the stars will become dependent on them for drugs. I kept finding buckets of bleach around the flat. I finally understood that's how cocaine was tested for purity. If a substance floated to the top, then talcum powder had been added. If the drug sank, it was pure. So we argued. But he was trapped so quickly. Some people have addictive personalities and he was one of them. He wasn't a bad person, he was a wonderful person. I don't think he could handle the fame, the pace—everything—so quickly. It all happened so fast. He seemed to have it all, but really, he had nothing."[26]

If Andy suffered from feeling a fraud, much in his success fueled it. His brother wrote both hits on his record. The world pretty much ignored Andy's originals. Of his first record, Andy said: "I always thought that people were buying my records as an extension to the Bee Gees. I was automatically getting the Bee Gee fans who liked that sound and I never thought there was any individual thing in there that they liked."[27]

He told *Teen Beat* magazine: "I have evolved totally from what the Bee Gees have done. I have no 'roots' of any kind and I'm the first to admit I've not paid my dues musically speaking. My brothers handed it down to me on a silver platter. I know that people try for years to break into even the lowest level of the music business, and I just stepped into the top level. I never even had to audition. So it doesn't bother me when people connect my break with my brothers, because I realize that, without them, I would not be where I am. But it also makes me feel that I haven't paid my dues."[28] No other star with a platinum album and three #1 singles ever described himself as so bereft.

His mother remembered a telling moment: "We were in Dallas once, driving from the airport, and he saw the Arena had 'Andy Gibb' and [below] 'Younger brother of The Bee Gees.' He went crazy. His personal assistant had to go get it taken down. Things like that would upset him."[29]

By the time Andy left LA to tour opening for Neil Sedaka in August, Kim was in Australia, pregnant and ignored. Kim said: "I told him I had been to the doctor and I was having a baby. It wasn't planned or anything, it just happened. He was a bit two-ways about it at first. I think he thought I had come at a bad point in his career—his songs were just starting to catch on."[30]

Andy did not listen to Kim's entreaties about drugs, or anything else. She fled back to her family. Andy claimed that "my wife said I'm a slave to fame but it's just not true. She left me before my first record was a hit. Her mother came and took her away from me. It's all very sad—she's a lovely girl. But she came from a working class family in Sydney and she couldn't cope with show business. If I had to go out in the afternoon and do an interview she'd blow her top. We were together 98 per cent of the time and I worshipped her. I would never look at anyone else. I used to think, 'Oh God it's such a shame—we have so much more to come but she's not going to be able to handle it.'"[31] Kim said: "I was so lonely and wasn't feeling well because of the baby. I left him to make him see sense. If I couldn't get him off the drugs, no one could. I couldn't sit by and watch him do it to himself. He was self-destructing."[32]

His performances were not being well received. John Rockwell wrote in the *New York Times*: "He has a plaintive, whispery, throbbing tenor that recalls the Bee Gees, yet his musical style naturally doesn't rely on that group's harmonies, nor does it emulate its current mode of balladic disco. His style is set firmly into the kind of up-tempo middle-of-the-road that will surely dominate Las Vegas and the suburban theatres for years to come—a kind of grudging admission on the part of the adult schlockmeisters that once upon a time, in some distant realm, rock and roll did exist. Mr. Gibb is handsome in a carefully coiffed way but [his] set wasn't very interesting. This looked like an obvious talent that has sold itself out to the packagers and merchandisers a bit too soon. Not too soon for commercial success, of course, but too soon for any real individuality to have developed. Mr. Gibb, for all his good looks, sounded like an old man's idea of what a young man's music should be about."[33]

Obviously, Rockwell set himself up as a defender of rock and roll and Andy as one of its besiegers. With American punk rock raging—though never on the radio—and the airwaves full of disco, many felt rock needed defending. A new Gibb brother with a #1 record seemed the manifestation of all that was banal and conformist in commercial music. Andy proved an easy target, and his material, aside from the Barry-penned hits, was baby food. As a young man overwhelmed by a sense of a lack of identity, Andy's show was not exactly self-expression. It was a performance, entertainment, and almost too earnest, given the superficiality of Andy's material. Critical opinion would later vary little from Rockwell's. Rockwell, blaming handlers and shadowy image-consultants, found it hard to conceive that Andy's show might be precisely what Andy thought it should be and enjoyed doing.

Andy played the decadent, infamous Sunset Strip bacchanal and hangout, the Roxy. Stigwood coroneted Andy onstage by handing him his gold record for "I Just Want to Be Your Everything." Andy returned to Miami Beach and, living his self-parody to the hilt, moved into an eighty-foot houseboat that had belonged to a recently deceased Miami drug lord. It featured a round bed with a mirrored ceiling overhead. The former owner had been shot to death in that mirrored room, and there was a grand piano in the main lounge. *People* magazine reported that "Andy's only home is his boat, berthed in Miami. He chats incessantly about compass calibrations, autopilots and radar, and carries two semi-automatic machine guns, a .357 magnum and a riot gun, to protect the three-stateroom, three-head (bathroom) cruiser from modern-day Caribbean pirates."[34] By the time Andy spoke to *People*, he no longer kept his pet lion cub, Samantha, on the houseboat. She shared the space with Andy for a while after he bought her at auction, but Andy "donated her" to the Miami Zoo. Speaking from Australia, Kim's response to Andy's new digs was: "I think the houseboat sounds unpleasant and kinky."[35]

On August 27, Andy's album *Flowing Rivers* climbed into the *Billboard* top 40. It charted eighteen weeks, peaking at #18.

Kim told the *Australian Weekly*: "There I was, sitting at home with Mum and Dad, pregnant, believing Andy would be with me for the baby's birth because he'd promised, no matter what, he would be there, and suddenly the Sydney press were calling, telling me a press release had gone out saying that Andy and I were getting a divorce. The divorce papers arrived two weeks before Peta was due. I don't think I stopped crying until her birth."[36]

People reported that Kim was "dependent on $51.70 weekly Australian welfare, and has retained a lawyer." "We're discussing a separation agreement," contends Andy. "Funds have been and are still available for her use."[37]

Andy never went to Australia. He filed for divorce from the States, and by filing in advance of their baby's birth, sought to keep their child from being his legitimate heir. On January 25, 1978, Kim gave birth to their daughter, Peta Jaye Reeder Gibb. The Reeder family sought counsel to fight for Peta's future.

The UK's *Daily Mirror* gave Kim's separation from Andy the full tabloid treatment. Under the headline PLEASE TELL HIM, KIM ASKS MIRROR, the article began: "Kim Gibb, the estranged wife of pop star Andy Gibb, wonders if her husband is even aware he has a six-week-old daughter. Kim has not heard from him since she gave birth to Peta in January. And she has been unable to penetrate the protective screen around her husband to tell him of the birth." The *Mirror* further claimed: "In a midnight telephone call from Sydney, Kim asked if the *Daily Mirror*'s New York bureau had heard if Andy was aware of the birth. 'Does Andy know he's got a daughter? That's all I want to know,' Kim said. 'I can't get in contact with him and his associates have made sure I can't get his number. If you are speaking with him would you tell him she looks very much like him. She has his nose and his mouth and his eyes. And she has his brown hair. Actually, Andy has blond hair now, but it is brown underneath. I know, because I dyed it.' Meanwhile, Andy left the Bee Gees' family compound in Miami yesterday—after a lavish party to celebrate his 20th birthday—for a European concert tour."[38]

A month later the *Mirror* reported: "Kim Gibb, estranged wife of millionaire pop star Andy Gibb, had a joyful reunion with her daughter, Peta, at Sydney Airport yesterday. Mrs. Gibb had returned from New York where her lawyer, Mr. L. Gruzman, worked out a settlement believed to be almost $250,000. Smiling happily and smothering Peta with kisses, she said she was looking forward to 'some peace and quiet.' Mrs. Gibb would not give any details of the settlement. She said she had not seen her husband during her three weeks in America. 'All the discussions were handled by lawyers, we had about 15 between us,' Mrs. Gibb said. 'All I want to do now is settle down with Peta.'"[39]

By most estimates, Andy had already made between one and two million dollars, with more pouring in. A quarter-of-a-million-dollar settlement for his child was nothing compared to what she and her mother might have been entitled to in a divorce in a community property state like California. Given how close-knit the Gibb family had always been, and how his other brothers remained committed to their children, Andy's behavior toward Peta could be explained by that old reliable—denial—or perhaps by a combination of youthful selfishness, drugs or simple terror at the idea of responsibility.

It was time for a new album, *Shadow Dancing*. Journalist, screenwriter and producer Mitch Glazer reported on the sessions for *Playboy*. As he drove to Criteria with Maurice, Andy's "Thicker Than Water" came on the car radio. Maurice told Glazer: "It's funny; years ago, we'd been furious if Andy bumped us from number one. Jesus, the three of us were fighting amongst ourselves to be the biggest star. Now, like Barry says, it's all in the family. Barry wrote and produced the bloody song, anyhow."[40]

The co-producers were Karl Richardson, Albhy and Barry. When Andy goes into the booth, he wants it darker. Barry tells him: "Now, Andy, come closer to the mike and get a little sexy with these lyrics." Andy answers: "It's hard to get horny in a hospital." Barry guides Andy, asking for one more take. And another. Barry's relaxed, and by his demeanor communicates to Andy that the evening is no big deal, no stress. Andy seems to nail the song, and behind the glass the producers all smile. Barry still asks his younger brother, "Can you beat it, mate?" Andy tries again. Glazer wrote: "To watch this process is to watch success." Barry later told Glazer: "We overdubbed a breath once. The song was right, but there was a breath missing, so I went in there and put it in."[41]

Shadow Dancing, despite or because of Barry's level of control, proved a retrenchment. The songs Barry wrote for Andy, like the hit "Shadow Dancing," seem even more like pallid, second-rate Bee Gees songs than Barry's songs on Andy's first record. "Shadow Dancing" has a decent hook, but runs out of steam even on the Bee Gees version. Gone are the country rock attempts of Andy's first album. The disco-derived dance and soul music is generic and contentless, save the consistently soulful guitar and whimsical Barry White–style strings. Andy's voice sounds weaker, reedier, with less punch and more breathiness. His breathiness or Barry's, who can say?

The question of why Barry couldn't or didn't create first-rate material for his beloved little brother raises potential issues of sibling rivalry. Maybe Barry didn't want to be overshadowed, maybe Andy couldn't tell the difference between bad material and good, maybe he couldn't stand up to his big brother. Albhy Galuten maintains that Barry only wanted the best for Andy and never sabotaged him consciously or otherwise.

Galuten wanted to set up collaborations for Andy with other songwriters, foremost among them John Oates of Hall and Oates. Andy was psyched, but Stigwood lowered the boom. He absolutely forbade Andy—as communicated via Galuten—to write with anyone other than his brothers. Andy certainly couldn't stand up to Stigwood. Neither did Galuten, but he could reasonably claim to be a hireling, and forced to obey. Barry, the one Gibb who could brace Stigwood, remained silent.

A Gibb insider believes that Stigwood wanted control over Andy as a pop product, which meant controlling what Andy wrote and sang. Stigwood did not want Andy discovering a world outside his brothers and RSO. The insider offers a simple reason for Stigwood's rigidity: If a Gibb writes a song, Stigwood owns a piece. If an outside collaborator comes in, Stigwood owns a smaller piece.

Andy set out to tour Europe behind *Shadow Dancing*. On the first day, he fell asleep during a live radio interview. Unable to finish a photo shoot a few days later, Andy flew home and the tour was cancelled. Andy told Robert W. Morgan: "For three weeks we would be going from 6 in the morning until 2 in the morning. I was getting called away to all these meetings, not being able to finish my meals. I broke down, it certainly wasn't mental, it was a sort of physical collapse and we had to cut the tour a few weeks short and bring me home to Miami. I get tired very quickly."[42]

Barry said: "First fame is a dangerous thing. You read about yourself, believe what people say about you, you believe that you have something special to say, and God speaks through you and the public need to know, you know. This happens to you when you become famous for the first time, and especially on an international level. So I think it was a little crazy for him for a while."[43]

"(Love Is) Thicker Than Water" was another slow builder. Barry's composition bumped Barry's composition "Stayin' Alive" from #1, held the top for two weeks and was then bumped by Barry's composition "Night Fever." "Shadow Dancing" followed, and that Barry composition stayed at #1 for seven weeks. Andy's first three singles—Barry compositions all—hit #1. No artist—not Elvis, not the Beatles, not the Bee Gees—had done that before. If Andy had feared success, now he had good reason to fear failure. Because anything less than a #1 would be seen as exactly that.

Andy launched a US tour and played the sex symbol in satin trousers. Stan Soocher wrote up the tour for *Circus* magazine and stayed on message, pinning Andy's collapse in Europe on the long hours and grueling schedule of promotional events. He titled his piece "Andy Gibb Is More Than Just a Clone of His Successful Siblings," which states the problem and the supposed solution. Andy *wasn't* a Bee Gees clone—that was news. Andy walked into the interview and "he picks up a copy of Mark Twain's *The Adventures of*

Huckleberry Finn. 'I ought to read this,' he decides, tilting his freshly combed golden mane. A gold medallion with a diamond in the center hangs around his neck. 'Robert Stigwood, my manager, gave me this. It says, "Happy Gold Christmas." My brothers all have platinum ones. I'll be getting a new one soon.'"[44]

"Everlasting Love" went to #5 in the US in July. *Shadow Dancing* went platinum. Andy's singles brought *Flowing Rivers* along in their wake, and it went platinum as well. As the tour ended, RSO released "Our Love (Don't Throw It All Away)," written by Barry and Blue Weaver. The single made #9 in America and no impression on the UK charts.

It's a weak ballad in Andy's hands, with soaring MFSB strings and a glistening Fender Rhodes as the lead instrument. The song's designed as a voice showcaser, and Andy showcases some range, reaching high and coming close to hitting the notes he's aiming for. But Andy leaves the impression of a poor Barry Gibb impression. Barry seems to have written the song for his range, not Andy's.

The later Bee Gees version of the song sounds richer, more detailed in production, and though the arrangements are almost identical, far more professional, accomplished and polished. The Bee Gees version can be listened to repeatedly; Andy's sounds like a low-fi knockoff. The difference between the two versions is shocking, and in that gap lies Andy's dilemma. He wasn't Barry, but Barry kept giving him Barry material and producing that material at lower-than-Barry standards.

But with three #1s, a #9, two platinum records and girls going ape on two continents over Andy's satin trousers, who was going to slow the gravy train? Conversely, who wouldn't stand on such a pinnacle and realize there was only one direction to go—besides Barry, of course? Andy had risen further faster younger than anyone in the history of pop music. He showed little inclination toward moderation.

Barry said: "With the sudden success he's had, his head has been turned around. We're concerned for the boy. There's a lot of heavy drugs around, a lot of shady characters, and he's not always within the realms of the family."[45]

His mom said: "He never grew up. He was like Peter Pan. He was just like a little boy all of his life. He was a baby all his life."[46]

Andy, with his usual optimism, told Robert W. Morgan: "They're going to bury me tomorrow . . . 20 years old and three #1s is a lot; and I'm just worried about 10 years or all those years until I'm 30."[47]

Andy went back to the studio without Barry. Maurice said: "I think he thinks that he still had to prove himself to be as good as we were in many ways, or to gain the same success. I think that there's always that brotherly, sibling type of rivalry."[48] The sessions came to naught as Andy's drug use accelerated and he embraced the incarnation of late 1970s and early '80s Miami: Quaaludes.

'Ludes—the long-since outlawed and discontinued synthetic barbiturate-like methaqualone—were super-downers that gave the user's perceptions a thick, sensual glow and a sense of moving through the world in slow motion. Folks liked to combine them with cocaine to go up and down at once; 'ludes cut the edginess of coke and coke cut the syrupiness of 'ludes. It was a popular and debilitating combination, best undertaken by those who spent their evenings being driven around, and not driving. Add a little alcohol and the most likely event was a period of horny agitation followed by a deep restful snooze. Unless you were twenty years old, and had even more coke to wake back up with.

In mid-1978, the brothers joined Andy at Miami's Jai-Alai Fronton onstage for the last show of Andy's US tour. Hugh said: "This was the proudest moment of my life." Andy began "Words" and Barry Gibb walked onstage already singing. Maurice sat down at the piano. When Robin hit the stage they burned through a fifteen-minute version of "Shadow Dancing." Barbara said: "I never thought I'd be around to see it. I haven't seen Andy perform since last year when he opened for Neil Sedaka. I told him (then) to move around a little more. Tonight my boy moved around, wouldn't you say?"[49] The show was a harbinger of what would become Andy's most profound ambition: to become a Bee Gee.

On July 10 or 11, 1979, the Bee Gees poured onstage at the Oakland Coliseum on the Spirits Having Flown tour, resplendent in glittering white satin pants and open silver jackets with no shirts. Robin leans into the mike to say: "Ladies and gentlemen, our brother Andy!" as the band tears into "You Should Be Dancing." Andy shares a mike with Maurice singing backup, and it's hard to pick out his voice over the three falsettos and the shrieking crowd. But the few close-ups of his face tell a clear story. While Andy at moments seems self-conscious, mostly what he looks is overjoyed.

In the staged documentary *It Might Get Loud*, Jimmy Page of Led Zeppelin, the Edge of U2 and Jack White of the White Stripes get together to play and talk guitars. White and the Edge visit Page's mansion, and Page slings his famous starburst Les Paul low on his hips and, right there in the amp-filled living room, tears into the signature riff from "Whole Lotta Love." The Edge and White undergo an instant, shared transformation—they appear for a moment stunned and then ecstatic. These two stars—two virtuosi—who, it can be reasonably argued, have seen a million faces and rocked the vast majority, morph into eighth graders. Both are obviously thinking: "Holy shit! I'm in Jimmy Page's living room and he's playing 'Whole Lotta Love!'" That's how Andy looks on stage with his brothers.

In November of 1979, Andy appeared with his brothers on *The Bee Gees Special* on NBC. Willie Nelson and Glenn Campbell also guested. Andy's performance did not go well. One critic wrote: "Andy Gibb has to fight for space at the microphone. When he gets there, it is hardly worth the effort. The poor boy is obviously out of his league attempting to compete with the big sound, and that's not taking into account the adoring, screaming masses."[50]

Attempts to record Andy's third LP, *After Dark*, proved a shambles. Andy wouldn't show up, and he only had to show up to sing. Barry and Albhy wrote the songs, created the arrangements and rehearsed the band, and Barry even sang vocal guide tracks.

The guide tracks are nothing unusual for pop music and much more common today. Today's pop star's have producers and hit makers to write lyrics, find beats and riffs, and teach them how to sing word by word. Pop stars sing a bar, or a verse, at a time and their producers construct songs from myriad five-syllable vocal takes. But today's pop stars live armored within concentric rings of salaried best friends and bodyguards and image protectors and managers who understand how valuable the pop star is and work to preserve the golden goose. Andy had his family nearby, but his brothers were accustomed to functioning addicts. They expected Andy to pull it together when the time came to be a pro, as had they all.

Top studio musicians came in to play their parts. Barry and Albhy grew increasingly excited about the tracks and the record became a Barry album in all but name. They only needed Andy to come in and sing along, with Barry's guide vocals in his headphones. But the drugs took a toll on Andy's voice as well as his will. Complicating the process was that Barry wrote songs that worked for his falsetto, but Andy couldn't hit the high notes. When Barry and Albhy coaxed Andy into the studio, Andy fought his way through the recording a line at a time. His pitiful performances made him more reluctant to come back and try again.

Kim Gibb flew to Los Angeles in January of 1980. There had been no contact between her and Andy since she went to Australia; Kim blamed Andy's parents. Regardless, she brought two-year-old Peta to see her father for the first time. When Kim called

RSO to find a way to contact Andy, his lawyers stonewalled her; when she convinced them she didn't want money, they said Andy would call. She waited in her hotel room, staring at the phone. Andy's first words were: "Hello, Kim, how much money do you want?" Andy told Kim he didn't think he could "cope" with seeing his daughter, but Kim persisted. They met at a Beverly Hills Hilton. Of Andy's appearance, Kim said: "He was clearly not well."[51] Andy spent a day with his daughter and had a bracelet engraved for Peta with the inscription ALL MY LOVE, A. G. And that was that. Andy later told *People* of the visit: "It went real well."

Kim never saw Andy again. Neither did Peta.

After Dark was released in February of 1980. It reached #67 in the US and did not chart in the UK. Seven years later, Andy said of that time: "I am sure you heard of my drug problem. I checked myself into a place for it. The kind of drug that I was doing that was big in Florida about that time . . . cocaine. I started not turning up for recording sessions, leaving Barry to cover for me. On a couple of my albums you will hear Barry singing a line and you think it's me, but it was really him. Me and Barry have an uncanny similarity vocally. We are the closest mentally too, and writing style, everything. He is the first boy born and I am the last boy born and it's funny. The other two, there is no resemblance."[52]

On *After Dark* it can be hard to tell if the vocalist is Andy or Barry. The weaker performances, like "Warm Ride," are clearly Andy. "One Love" sounds like Barry attempting an Andy imitation, with dropped-in Andy lines here and there that showcase the vocal problems Andy suffered. The backing tracks are overworked, even for that era, played with machinelike precision and little soul. The most sadly credible track is "Man on Fire," a Barry version of a Bruce Springsteen–style love anthem with—for *After Dark*—a spare, dramatic arrangement. Andy describes himself, with conviction, as self-immolating. The brothers—it sure sounds like all the brothers—come together in a moving, almost gospel, chorus. For all the pain in Andy's voice, moments remain that might be Barry on the vocals.

Rock critic Bill Holden gave with one hand and took away with the other: "Though the songs here are literally sweet nothings filled with images of teardrops and angels, *After Dark* surpasses even the Bee Gees' *Spirits Having Flown* for consistency of aural beauty. *After Dark* may have scant appeal to rock fans, but on its own pop terms, it's a production triumph. There's no cheap filler. As ice-cream parlor music for Romeo and Juliet, it's first class."[53]

After Dark is a production triumph. But it contains little except pop filler and is not remotely in the same league as *Spirits Having Flown*. Holden demonstrates that even the most thoughtful critics of the time couldn't hear what the Bee Gees, or Andy for that matter, were doing.

Andy performed at an Olympic tribute at the Kennedy Center in Washington, DC, on July 20, 1980. He told an interviewer: "People forget too quickly. They don't talk about you much. I see how quiet things can become." When asked about the wages of fame, he said: "It gets a little chaotic. I carry a pistol and put it next to my bed at night. I carry it in a holster, and I never keep it loaded. I keep the bullets nearby. I've left it in motels before, and I have to call back and say, 'Could you send me my gun, please?'"[54]

Al Coury, who worked with Gibb at RSO Records in 1977, said of Andy: "He was treated like a superstar from Day 1, paid very well, lived like a king, travel[ing] in private planes. That can be dangerous to even the most mature person. And here was someone still in his teens. You had to worry about him, because you knew some day the hits were going to stop."[55]

With *After Dark*, the hits stopped. And since they stopped, the next logical step, in record company logic, was to release *Andy Gibb's Greatest Hits*, in September of 1980. "Time Is Time," the first single, was written by Andy and, as he tells it, produced with minimal input from Barry. The vocals sound like Andy. They sound like they were recorded on various days when Andy was in various states of mind and voice. The bridge features an over-worked, overproduced pure '80s guitar break that must have sounded as laughable then as it does now. It's hard to imagine Barry or Albhy countenancing such a solo. The track hit #15 in the US—which, as the Bee Gees' disco-grip on the radio faded a bit, remains an admirable charting and testimony to the loyalty of Andy's fans. As per pattern, it did nothing in the UK. "Me Without You," also an Andy composition, made it to #40 in the US. The record contained three previously unreleased tracks, and even though two of them charted, titling an artist's fourth record *Greatest* tells fans, other labels and the artist himself that his recording career is over.

Andy told *People:* "There's a lot to do yet, and I can't imagine retiring at 23. I'd hate to think that everything that's happened so far is the high point of my life." In a nice piece of cross-promotion, as if to prove the truth of his words, on September 27, 1980, Andy co-hosted *Solid Gold* for the first time.

As demonstrated by that hosting, Andy had moved to Los Angeles to pursue show business opportunities and to do drugs in peace, away from his nagging family. His new record didn't sell, but Andy's popularity remained weirdly undiminished. He was still handsome, boyish, charming, famous, rich and mediagenic. By escaping Miami, and leaving recording for entertainment, Andy shifted his career responsibilities from Barry's and Stigwood's shoulders to his own.

There are many delicious, unsubstantiated, uncorroborated rumors and slanders attached to Victoria Principal and her time with Andy. For many Andy fans, she's still the source of his ruination. To those fans, the most heinous crime seems to be not so much that she left Andy, but that she got over him. For more or less thirteen months, though, each was the love of the other's life.

People wrote of Andy in 1980: "He had two dream girls, he told friends. One was Bo Derek [star of the movie 10], 'the most beautiful thing on two legs.' The other was Pam Ewing—'that girl on Dallas. Every time I see her I kind of tingle all over,' he said. 'She's so beautiful, there's a kind of haunted look about her that really turns me on.'"[56]

After *The John Davidson Show* on January 6, 1981, John Davidson spokesman Paul Nichols said of Andy: "He was acting like a 16-year-old."[57] Andy said: "It was a great day for me. I'd always wanted to meet her. And two or three days later, I called her up. We had dinner at home." Victoria said: "He offered to cook, and I ended up doing it. I made BLTs. We didn't want to go out anywhere, especially since it was our first date. I didn't want anything written about us."[58]

Victoria fell ill and Andy brought her flowers and chicken soup. A few days after that, he moved in.[59]

Victoria and Andy kept their affair as secret as they could for as long as they could, sneaking in and out of each other's houses. For their first public outing, they chose the American Music Awards. Principal said: "When we emerged from the limo, photographers were so startled, they forgot to take pictures and we ran right through them. Not one photograph of us going in. But they were waiting for us when we came out."[60] The couple was tabloid heaven.

US Magazine interviewed Andy and, like everyone else, got catty about it: "'I'm tired of being a teen love object,' Gibb said. 'I'm twenty-three going on forty-five.' (Principal, who gives her age as 'somewhere between Tatum O'Neal and death,' can certainly meet him on that level, being no spring 'poulet' herself). 'I've had a lot of adventures and I've already traveled to most countries of the world,' Gibb says matter-of-factly. 'I've always been around older people and been accepted as an adult equal. My feelings and my outlook on life are adult experiences.'"[61]

Principal said: "People think I have been cradle-snatching since puberty. That's not true. I have dated men my own age and men older than me, but these relationships never made headlines. Some people seem to find it immoral that Andy and I should be together, with our age gap. So what?"[62] She told *People*: "It's not that I'm attracted to younger men, but to a certain kind of spirit. I love spontaneity, enthusiasm, courage and a positive, unjaded attitude."[63]

Maurice, who always seemed to take the most benign view, said: "I think the relationship with Victoria Principal was absolutely beautiful. It was everything he had dreamed of and that's the important thing, not what I think or everybody else thinks."[64]

After teasing the New York producers of the smash revival of the Gilbert and Sullivan operetta *The Pirates of Penzance* that he might take over one of the two male leads, Andy bailed and flew back to LA. He hated to be away from Victoria, who had to stay in California to shoot *Dallas*. Andy opened in the LA production, instead, in June of 1981, co-starring with Pam Dawber from *Mork & Mindy*.

People pretty much codified the public perception of Andy as over, but tried to be encouraging: "*The Pirates of Penzance* is a lifeboat for a pair of youthful stars who thought their careers were lost at sea. As *Mork*'s Mindy, Pam Dawber has watched her once top-rated series nose-dive this season; likewise, teen throb Andy Gibb has languished of late in the professional doldrums. 'My career's been going nowhere,' the 23-year-old kid brother of the Bee Gees admitted before the operetta premiered. 'Let's face it, I haven't had a hit for quite a while.'"[65]

People quoted *Los Angeles Times* critic Dan Sullivan as saying that Andy's and Dawber's version "'blows you out of the water.' Compared to Dawber and Gibb, he sniped, their Broadway counterparts, Linda Ronstadt and Rex Smith, 'put you in mind of the high school play.'" Andy credits Victoria, saying: "She's brought a whole new confidence into my life." *People* adds: "*Pirates* was no picnic for Andy. With no formal voice training, he quickly went hoarse tackling Arthur Sullivan's arias. 'My voice was so worn out that when I went to blast, it came out like a croak. It scared the life out of me,' he says. . . . 'He's going through all the agonies of "Oh, I can't act, I can't dance," a sympathetic Dawber explains. 'In fact, he can.'"[66]

By July 7, Andy couldn't any longer. Victoria had to take Andy to the emergency room with crippling abdominal pain. After four days of testing he was released. No cause for his pain was found. Andy did not return to the show. A syndicated gossip column said: "Pop singer Gibb didn't much care for the discipline of the theatre and wanted out almost from the beginning."[67]

In August, Victoria and Andy released one of the most embarrassing vanity projects in the history of the music business: their duet of Felice and Boudleaux Bryant's hit for the Everly Brothers' "All I Have to Do Is Dream." Andy speak-sings a single verse repeatedly and in videos of their lip-synching, Victoria does appear to open her mouth and exhale during the choruses, but all that can be heard is a faint feminine whisper. The gooey, shimmering mediocrity of the production, the blatant studio techniques used to enhance Principal's voice and the conviction with which they perform face to face, noses inches apart, speaks to the depth of their love and to the inescapable *Spinal Tap* dynamic of what happens when the singer's girlfriend wants to sing. If the girlfriend is Victoria Principal, then her boyfriend makes a simpering ass of himself and their song hits #52. The upside is that Victoria got Andy into a studio, and made him sing when no one else could. The irony is that while Andy appears more than capable of dreaming his life away, Victoria, even while singing into Andy's eyes, seems to be calculating her next move.

Andy and Victoria appeared on the *Donahue* show, and Phil couldn't stop kissing their asses. Andy did manage to say: "I was curious, or a little wary at first, what my fans would think of me having a serious relationship, which I haven't had before. And my fans seem to be very much for our relationship and seem to like us very much."

Or at least as much as #52.

Phil gushed over and over on one topic: Andy and Victoria were one damn attractive couple, wrapped in an almost visible cocoon of infatuation and mutually replenishing sexual energy. They were a pair of happy stars, in love and in lust. Donahue asked his audience: "Is there a better looking couple in America?" The short answer was no.[68] Their hair was beautiful, their eyes were beautiful, their skin was beautiful, they had such animal attraction—a pair of Narcissi gazing avidly into their own reflections. Their desire encircled them like halos. In other words, they had glamour.

But not top of the line glamour, not Cary Grant–Grace Kelly glamour. Their glamour had a taste of kids from working-class circumstances who, through work and luck and grabbing the main chance when it appeared, had ended up together showcasing their love on national TV. Despite their beauty, both retained the common touch and their fans adored them. Again, Andy proved sadly far ahead of his time. If their romance began tomorrow—instead of in 1981—the reality show leading up to their televised bogus wedding would have made them both millions. And their nuclear breakup, millions more.

Andy commenced what should have been the gig of his life on September 12, 1981, when he became an official co-host of *Solid Gold*. The job had no downside. There was only one episode a week and the show kept Andy in front of America on network TV. Between his blazing love affair and his perfect job, on his early appearances on *Solid Gold*, Andy actually looks content. He was still doing copious amounts of cocaine.

Hugh confronted Andy about his coke use, saying: "What are you taking this rubbish for?" Andy replied: "It's the only way I can handle her."[69] Hugh demonstrated his usual helplessness and passivity in the face of his sons' self-destructive habits as Andy gave him the classic addict's cop-out: "It's not my fault."

Describing the slowly escalating Andy-Victoria dynamic, Barbara said: "They have been splitting up every other week since the middle of last year. Whenever they have a falling-out, it's always a big fight and Andy moves back to his Malibu beach house. But this time, he was really rundown and at a low ebb."[70]

"It became apparent to me that his behavior was becoming erratic and that he was very, very thin," Victoria said. "Andy was a kind person, and a gentle person and some of his behavior seemed so the antithesis of what he used to be and I finally realized that it had to be drugs."[71]

After a series of increasingly physical rows in February of 1982, Victoria threw Andy out and ended things. "Victoria and I went to pick up some Indian curry and went back to her house," Andy said. "We were fighting in the car and when we got back to the house we started ranting and screaming and pushing and shoving. In the end it got a little physical. I stormed out and drove back to my house at Malibu Beach. That was the last time I saw Victoria."[72]

He called and called, begging to be taken back, but she was adamant. "Watching someone you care about to be destroyed because of drugs is a horrifying experience," Victoria said. "I did everything I humanly could to stop him."[73]

"I just fell apart and didn't care about anything," Andy recounted. "I started to take cocaine around the clock—about $1,000 a day. I stayed awake for two weeks locked in my bedroom. The producers kept calling up, sending cars for me, but I refused to go. . . . the major reason I fell from stardom was my affair with Victoria."[74] Victoria's position was simple: "Our breakup was preceded and precipitated by Andy's use of drugs. I did everything I could to help him. But I told him he would have to choose between me and his problem."[75]

Victoria had been suppressing her doubts, and when the dam burst she was ready to be over Andy. His immaturity and addiction left her feeling emotionally vulnerable and concerned about her image and career. If Andy got busted, or if his cocaine habit became public knowledge, she feared she would never escape the scandal. Between being the older woman and her *Playboy* past, Victoria knew she would catch the blame.

"I have been to hell and back," Andy said. "I had a bad nervous breakdown. There was a lot of pressure on me and Victoria. There was a sweet dream of a relationship and also a nightmare at some point. She's an ambitious girl and I think it was mutual. We both pressured each other. We couldn't spend five minutes apart. We split up several times before the final split. It was inevitable. I turned to drugs for a month and did quite an awful lot of cocaine. I gave up everything. I started missing taping of *Solid Gold* and I was a very bad boy. I didn't care. I didn't care about people. I didn't care about life."[76]

The *Solid Gold* producers did their best to lure Andy back. Andy refused to leave his house and they gave up. "He really meant well," said Lachman, the producer of *Solid Gold*. "He wasn't being difficult. He was going through problems he couldn't deal with. He wanted everyone to love him. He had so much going for him. After repeated warnings, he was fired."

Shortly afterward, Andy got the not unexpected news that Stigwood would not renew his expiring contract with RSO. Nineteen eighty-two was a time of heightened tension between the Bee Gees and Stigwood, and Andy's older brothers did not or could not prevent Stigwood from dropping Andy. Perhaps, they thought the additional shock of being cast off the label might help Andy see how serious his situation was. By his own hand, Andy had become a singer without a label and a personality without a platform.

"For about twelve months," Barbara said, "he was devastated."[77]

Andy later told reporter Robin Leach: "I had lots of money. Lotta hit records. I think [Victoria] took me in and calmed me down. She was good for me and in a lot of ways she was bad for me. I looked to her as a motherly figure. She looked to me as a son figure. She had my life totally organized and when we outgrew each other, or she outgrew me even though she was older, there was no one there."[78]

Andy's parents moved in with him, and, as Andy tells it, one night after weeping all day from the moment he awoke, Andy remembered that his nearby neighbor was a psychiatrist. Andy called him, and he guided Andy to St. Francis Hospital in Santa Barbara; Andy checked in under the name Roy Lipton.[79] He stayed for three days.

Rumors spread that Andy had attempted suicide. To quell them, Dick Ashby released a statement: "We heard rumors about Andy's suicide attempt, and the family called to make sure he was okay. Barry Gibb's wife spoke to him last night, and he sounded calm."[80]

"I felt like a black-widow spider," Victoria said later. "I know how it looks from the outside, especially as I didn't come forward. Everybody assumed I split with Andy. But I didn't want to go into it at the time and that is something I will have to live with. There is no point in defending or explaining what actually happened, but it would be unfair to say it was my choice to end the relationship."[81]

"It put me on an incredible position, a terrible dilemma: To speak out on my own behalf, to reveal the fact that the problem had been ongoing and that was the reason for the break-up would have been to add to the tremendous burden Andy was carrying, and so I chose to remain silent."[82]

When Andy went back home, Barbara came to stay and looked after him. Andy grew ready for the next phase of his career:

confessing on national television. On July 23, 1982, he went on *Good Morning America* and told Joan Lunden about his coke habit. He wore a white sweatshirt and gold chains. He talked about checking into therapy, about missing the taping of a Bob Hope special and how he feared that might have gotten him black-balled from television.

Andy had attended the People's Choice Awards in March 1982, and there promised Bob Hope he would appear on Hope's special. As the day of taping drew nigh, Andy hid in his house and wouldn't answer his phone, even when Hope made a personal call. Pat Boone replaced Andy. To spurn Bob Hope, for any reason, was pure self-undermining. Hope's specials were, even then, pathetically retrograde. They were tailor made for Andy as he sought to leave teenybopper audiences behind and build a name in the mainstream. His failure to appear sent a powerful message to the television networks.[83]

Andy admitted selling off possessions to pay for cocaine. Speaking of his fans, Andy said: "They've never really quite known the truth of what I've been through or the things that I've done. I'm no longer a teenybopper idol." Here, again, Andy was ahead of his time, using his addiction as a springboard for his hoped-for come-back. "I had everything I wanted and I blew it all apart," Andy said. "I've been lucky. I've kept my fans. It's rare and I'm grateful." Joan Lunden appears genuinely moved. She wishes him good luck and Andy says: "I need it."[84]

On December 1 of 1982, after working in preview performances out of town, Andy hit Broadway to star in the Andrew Lloyd Weber and Tim Price musical, *Joseph and the Amazing Technicolor Dreamcoat*. Andy appeared on *Entertainment Tonight* to promote the show, which presented him in costume wearing a midriff T-shirt, a pink feather boa and a white sweatband. Maurice said: "He always said that one day he was going to make it on Broadway."[85]

Andy's early performances were auspicious and the sold-out houses cheered him madly. Within a month, Andy was skipping shows.

"When he started rehearsals his brothers were jumping up and down with excitement,' said Zev Buffman, the show's producer. "His mom and dad came from England. He was always talking about it as a new start. But we'd lose him over long weekends. He'd come back on Tuesday and he'd look beat. He was like a little puppy—so ashamed of something he did wrong. He was all heart, but he didn't have the muscle to carry through."[86]

"When he missed the entire week between Christmas and New Year's, he heard that I was in the process of replacing him and came in to see me."[87] "I told [Andy] 'You may be a sick boy, with throat problems and chest problems and so on, but you may also be staying up too late and running around. I tried to stress the fact he had to stay in training and protect his voice. He promised me he wouldn't miss another one. He said: 'If I do, you won't even have to call me, I'll be gone.'"[88] When Andy missed two shows on February 12, 1983, Buffman replaced him.

In August, Andy worked the Resorts International Casino Hotel in Atlantic City followed by a brief stand at the MGM Grand in Las Vegas. Andy might have had a fulfilling career in an earlier time, kicking a microphone cord across the stage, driving ladies crazy singing standards in a tux at high-line clubs, casinos and hotels and becoming a junior, hard-partying member of the Rat Pack: Peter Lawford, Joey Bishop and Andy Gibb . . . that life, with its lower standards of originality and more lax ideas about what comprised entertainment, might have suited him well.

In August 1984, Andy was found unconscious in his New York hotel room; he cancelled his tour dates and went back to Malibu. The week before, Andy had done shows in New Jersey, New Hampshire and Ohio. An aide said: "His schedule has been so difficult. Many of the places are not reachable by direct traveling.

He's doing a lot of one-nighters and he simply collapsed out of exhaustion." Andy cancelled upcoming shows in Louisiana; he had been drinking heavily.[89]

People magazine recounted Andy's troubles. "He knew how to spend, both on drugs and in countless other ways. He blew millions," Stigwood said. "He got paranoid. He couldn't fly on a public plane. He had to hire private planes." "It was hard for him not having the royal treatment anymore," says Marc Gurvits, who managed Andy from 1983 to 1985, after Stigwood left the music business. "Whenever he was depressed on tour, he wanted to cancel the engagement."[90]

In April 1985, Andy checked into the Betty Ford Clinic at Rancho Mirage, California. His publicist, Michael Sterling, said: "He checked into the centre and is doing well. Andy is making extraordinary progress at the centre, has become ardently involved in its program and will continue an additional maintenance program after completing his treatment next month."[91] Andy later told Lifetime TV, while sitting poolside in an open shirt and a choker chain of enormous, square gold links: "I checked myself into Betty Ford and did six weeks, which is the longest you can do." Other sources said Andy fought to get out of the clinic, and that pressure from his family kept him in.

Andy closed the year touring in Asia and thought he might be on the verge of realizing his greatest aspiration: "I got a feeling that deep down in the pit of my stomach that '86 is going to be good for me. Because I am clean now and I know what I'm doing and [that is] to work with my brothers—and joining my brothers at the end of the year as a Bee Gee. We're going to be one group and we will start my new album in May with Barry again, now [that] we have confidence in me."[92] Andy kept busy playing a relentless schedule of smaller venues in America. He went back into the studio in May of 1986 to record demos for a new album.

In the spring of 1987, Andy checked into rehab again. When he got out, he moved back to Miami. He worked with his brothers on demos for a new record. Andy seemed to have blown his fortune on drugs, private planes and other extravagances. He lived in a penthouse at the Venetia apartment complex rent free in exchange for the apartment using his name in their promotions. His brothers loaned him furniture and musical instruments and put him on a $200 a week cash allowance. Nobody was talking about him joining the Bee Gees anymore.

And why would they want him? That was Andy's fantasy, with a small push from Barry, who later said, unconvincingly: "Six months before his death I campaigned to get him included. It was put to the vote and I'm afraid I was out-voted two to one."[93] It seems unlikely that Maurice or Robin would want a younger, handsomer, more energetic, more out of control version of themselves joining them onstage. Barry had demonstrated for years how few lead vocals there were to be shared, and his brothers knew Barry favored Andy. Their harmony parts had always been for three and those parts created instinctively. Moreover, they had busted their asses to be the Bee Gees; why should they let their wasted little brother step in?

In early September 1987, Andy filed for Chapter 7 bankruptcy in Miami. He claimed to have earned only $24,727 in 1985, and $7,755 in 1986. Andy owed $187,041 and had assets of only $1,432.79. One of his largest debts, $23,353.59, was owed to an aviation company, Business Jet Airlines.[94] Andy had grown frightened of flying commercial, or too shy to be seen in public. He developed the habit of hiring private jets on a whim. The *Miami Herald* reported: "Other creditors included a New York accounting firm, a Los Angeles limousine service, a Los Angeles public relations firm, an instrument rental company in Hollywood, Calif., the Sun City Resort in South Africa, two medical doctors and a dentist.

Unspecified amounts are owed the Internal Revenue Service and the Dade County Property Appraiser."[95]

Andy took flying lessons, got his longed-for pilot's license and played ferocious rounds of tennis with Barry. The two talked about an Andy comeback record. Barry brought Andy to London to meet with Island Records. After hearing his four demos, Island signed Andy in February of 1988. He stayed in England, moving into an outbuilding, the Chancery, on Robin's medieval estate, Prebendal. Andy's stated intention was to work on songs. He called Kim in Australia to make plans to see Peta. Kim did not want to come to LA, so they worked on the logistics of Kim flying to England with their daughter.

After the deal was signed and Andy had to sing, his old patterns resurfaced. He holed up in the Chancery for days, drinking and refusing to leave. According to Robin, the new recording deal terrified Andy. He would sit inside a window at the Chancery; from that perch he could spot anyone coming to see him, and hide. Barry said: "He didn't need to be away from his family and we didn't want him away from us and I think he went into a decline because of that." Maurice called. Robin told him Andy was too drunk to talk to him. Maurice later said: "I said, 'Oh, sod him, then,' and I put the phone down. I never forgave myself for that for a long time."[96]

Barbara, concerned that Andy would not come to the phone, asked Robin how her youngest boy was doing. Robin told her: "Don't come, Mum. You're babying him too much. He's fine." Barbara got on a plane the next day.[97]

On March 5, 1988, Andy spent a quiet, isolated birthday with his mother at the Chancery. On the seventh, he suffered "stabbing pains in his chest and abdomen" and was rushed to the local hospital. The doctors there did not delve into Andy's history and so learned little of his cocaine and alcohol abuse. They did not contact his American doctors. If they'd known Andy's history, and what sustained cocaine use does to the heart, they would have handled Andy differently. Barbara said: "When he died it had nothing to with drugs at all, but the damage that had been done by the drugs in the first place."[98] Andy went back to Robin's.

On the ninth Andy returned to the John Radcliffe Hospital in Oxford. Barbara wanted to stay the night, but "they wouldn't let me. In England you can't stay in the ward. I had to go."[99] Andy's last words to his mother were: "You can't die from this, can you?"

In the morning, his doctor said: "Do you mind if we draw blood from you one more time?" According to Barbara, Andy said no, "turned around, gave one big sigh, and was gone."[100]

Andy was pronounced dead at 8:45 A.M. on March 10, 1988.

Barry said later: "The last time I spoke to him it was an argument, which is devastating to me. I have to live with that all my life. I was saying: 'you've got to get your act together and this is no good.' Because someone had said to me at some point: 'tough love is the answer.' For me, it wasn't, because that was the last conversation we had."[101] Victoria Principal said: "I had to live with the awareness for many years that it would not be if Andy would die, it would be when Andy would die."[102] Robin said: "I don't think he liked the world out there, so he constructed his own."[103]

The tabloid reporters surrounded Robin's estate and wrote one unfounded story after another about Andy's purported "cocaine overdose." The family issued a statement: "His passing was completely unexpected and occurred just as he was looking forward to resuming his career and working on a new recording contract."[104] Hugh flew to London, met with Robin and delivered the sad news to Kim. She and Peta immediately flew to London. On March 13, she joined the Gibbs at Prebendal and they dined together. Peta had at last met her father's family. The older brothers, finally showing concern for Andy's child, later worked out financial arrangements for Peta's education and gained significantly higher royalty rates on Andy's album sales for her benefit. Peta was Andy's sole heir to what remained of his estate and posthumous income.

Andy's body was flown to LA and buried in Forest Lawn Cemetery on March 21. As part of the service, Barry read a poem Andy had written in 1985.

"That was the saddest, most desperate moment of my life, when I heard he had gone," Barry told the *Sunday Mail*. "Since then I've asked myself a thousand times, could I have done more or said more to help him? He always seemed to have a zest for life. But beneath all the fun was an incredible sadness that only a few of us could see. He was the most insecure man in the world and even when he had hit records, he felt it was still not good enough. Whatever I'd say to reassure him, he would still go away and hide in the depths of depression."[105]

Victoria Principal, demonstrating a certain level of self-regard, said: "Several years ago I had a dream and in that dream Andy came to me knowing I was haunted by this. He sat down and we had the talk that I certainly always wanted to have. And I thought it was so like Andy to find a way, even after his death, to bring me solace."[106] She said this with a straight face and apparent heartfelt sincerity.

People reported: "When the final call came announcing Andy's death, [Kim] Reeder wasn't surprised. 'I always knew that one day I'd get a call with news like this,' she said. 'It was only a matter of time. I think,' she says of herself and her daughter, 'that we were the only touch with reality he ever had.'"[107]

Kim always thought Andy might come back to her. "He never remarried, did he?" she said. "Neither did I. I wish that he'd never had anything to do with the music industry. He wanted to be a pilot. He was bright. He could have done anything. But his career was decided for him. I believe it killed him."[108]

No matter how the magazines and tabloids screamed about drug overdoses, the postmortem on Andy Gibb was definitive: he was clean when he died. There were no drugs or alcohol in his system. Barbara said: "They showed me at the hospital that there wasn't anything in his bloodstream at all."[109] The medical examiner's report confirms what Barbara was told.

Myocarditis killed Andy—an infection of the heart that inflames and damages heart muscles, but does not generate the arterial blocking that leads to heart attacks and is thus harder to diagnose. Numerous studies suggest a strong causal link between habitual cocaine use and fatal cardiac inflammation. Andy's years of abuse wrecked his system beyond repair. He died of a broken heart.

"the enigma with
the stigma"

---

*T*he Spirits *tour was the high point* of the Bee Gee's career. Like most dramas, the Bee Gees' story lost its narrative thread after the climax. The Gibbs entered a phase of writing and producing for others. They were preposterously good at it and successful, but their own work suffered.

After the tour, the brothers gazed into their enormous vats of money and decided that those vats were not quite as full as they should be.

In the summer of 1980, the Bee Gees commissioned an independent audit of RSO. The audit turned up $16 million of unpaid royalties owed to the band.[1] On October 2, 1980, the Bee Gees filed suit against Stigwood and Polygram, seeking $75 million from each, plus $50 million in punitive damages. Among their claims were that Stigwood "treated the group as his own Ft. Knox,"[2] "failed to offer the Gibbs' services to bona fide third-party record companies or publishing firms and did not solicit offers from such firms" and "fraudulently failed and refused to account properly to the Gibbs for royalties and other income payable to them and concealed the fact that substantial sums were owing to the Gibbs."[3]

Al Coury had a predictably swift and combative response: they asked for "so much money for four songs on the 'Saturday Night Fever' album . . . [that] the record company would have lost approximately 15¢ per album. The Bee Gees still wound up with an excessively high royalty, and I believe that Robert Stigwood even gave them a percentage of the film."

No evidence suggests that Stigwood offered anything of the kind.

"It seems," Al Coury said, "That they have forgotten the costs involved in selling records and are asking for even more than what has already been given. It is impossible for us to be more generous [without] putting ourselves out of business."[4] It's telling that Coury, in the manner of record label presidents since record labels began, used the words "given" and "generous" instead of "earned' and "paid out."

Never one to mess around, Stigwood filed a countersuit on October 27. He asked for $310 million for libel, extortion, corporate defamation and breach of contract. Responding to the Bee Gees' claims of RSO withholding royalties, the countersuit argued: "These accounting claims are not asserted in good faith. Their purpose is to provide a cover for the Gibbs' demand that Robert Stigwood and the corporate defendants make even more concessions to them."[5]

Referring to "Grease," Stigwood's suit alleged: "Barry Gibb has earned more than $3 million for writing and producing the recording of that one song. That is, to defendant's belief, the most money ever paid anybody to write one song and produce a single record."[6] Once again, Stigwood didn't address whether he owed the band unpaid royalties; instead he cited monies Barry earned straight up. For the kicker, Stigwood claimed: "Plaintiffs' publication of the false allegations in the unverified complaint is a flagrant abuse of the judicial process" and that the Bee Gees were trying to "bludgeon" him "into extra-contractual concessions by disseminating false accusations to the world wide press."[7]

It's amusing to see Stigwood accusing someone else of hype. Author Gore Vidal wrote that as he aged, litigation replaced sex. Stigwood's obvious glee at the chance for a good legal fight brings Vidal's words to mind.

Freddie Gershon said: "What you're dealing with is a bunch of guys who are trying to renegotiate their contracts through the press. The Bee Gees have reached a certain point in their careers, and they're trying to capitalize on it, and they're frustrated because, for the last year and a half, Robert has refused to renegotiate. I don't believe that the Bee Gees believe in this lawsuit. Barry Gibb looked me in the eye and said, 'We have to start with a high number, Freddie, so we can negotiate down to a new deal.' I know that Robin and Maurice told Robert Stigwood that they'd never read or seen these papers. Robert has a Victorian sense of morality. He will see to it that this goes on and on until it's proven publicly and clearly that he has done no wrong."[8]

On May 19, 1981, the Bee Gees withdrew their suit and it first appeared that they had to grovel a bit. An RSO press release ran: "The Bee Gees deeply regret the distress caused by allegations made ostensibly in their name. The Bee Gees and Robert Stigwood . . . are delighted to continue their immensely successful long-term association." Gershon said: "If you've been in the business long enough, you know that all artists go through periods of temporary insanity. The Bee Gees started investigating the facts, and they realized it wasn't worth it to go through several years of litigation only to have a judge or jury tell them the same thing they found out themselves: that Robert Stigwood has always treated them fairly and correctly. I believe they were embarrassed to find that out, and they dropped the suit and went away with their tails between their legs."[9]

On August 6, 1981, the band ran full-page ads in *Rolling Stone* and *Variety* asserting that they never apologized to Stigwood and never would. They detailed the terms of their settlement, which suggests that the Bee Gees' tails were hardly between their legs. Their ad suggests they kicked Stigwood's ass and settled for most of what they wanted rather than dragging out the lawsuit. To complete their victory, the Bee Gees took out the ads to make sure the world knew they had won. The brothers had learned a thing or two about public relations from their decades with Stigwood and were not feeling repentant.

According to their ad, the Bee Gees won increased advances and increased royalties for the two albums they still owed RSO. After that, they could sign with whomever they chose. Stigwood was out as the Bee Gees' manager and RSO would have no say over or participation in any future projects. That meant they could write and produce for third parties as much as they liked and Stigwood could not take a percentage of their earnings as his management fee. The Bee Gees also achieved the nirvana of all pop songwriters—they took back their publishing rights. Their publishing deal with RSO had been prohibitive; it stated that all songs by the Bee Gees in perpetuity would be published by RSO. That deal was terminated. The Bee Gees would create their own publishing "entity" and all songs dating back to 1967 would be vested in that entity. Stigwood would get a modest sum for those works, but nothing like what he had been taking. "Substantial arrears" in royalties, totaling millions, had been paid to the Bee Gees, and further audits were taking place. Stigwood's $310 million suit had been dropped and the Bee Gees hadn't paid him a dime.[10]

RSO issued a statement: "The press release issued by the Bee Gees is inconsistent with the terms of the settlement. Indeed, as was clearly understood, any settlement with the Bee Gees was conditional on a worldwide apology and without it no settlement would have been concluded."[11] Stigwood said later: "They had some mad, bad attorney who ended up costing them a fortune. If they have some crook bending their ear and the whole world is at their feet, it's hard for them. So there are no recriminations; it happened, and we're the best of friends."[12]

The lawsuit undid Stigwood. He wound down RSO and retreated to his manse in Bermuda. RSO employees could not get him to make decisions. His health was not perfect. One friend said he "had never seen anyone dole out such a staggering degree of punishment to their body in the pursuit of such an astonishing degree of fun."[13] Later, Stigwood would buy a castle in England, which he spent years refurbishing.

In 1980, Barry produced Barbra Streisand's *Guilty*. Barry wrote the title track and co-wrote all the other tracks with his brothers and Albhy Galuten in various combinations. The album sold 12 million copies, won a Grammy for Best Pop Performance by Duo or Group with Vocal (for "Guilty"), the single hit #3 on the charts and the album went to #1, stayed there for three weeks and spent forty-nine weeks total on the charts. "Woman in Love," written by Barry and Robin, went to #1 and held it for three weeks. *Guilty* was Streisand's biggest-selling record and introduced her to a vast new audience. Before this album she had had difficulty embracing contemporary forms. She had recorded show tunes, standards and Vegas and Broadway showstoppers that suited her operatic range and meticulous singing.

As is often the case, the deal making that led to the album proves a more compelling story than the recording of it. Streisand read a profile of Barry in which he said he'd love to work with her. Negotiations commenced and Stigwood wanted three-quarters of all royalties, because three Gibbs were involved but only one Streisand. "They all sound alike," Streisand snapped. "How much for one?" Streisand was known for being a prima donna and a pain to work with. But she and Barry established a professional relationship and responded well to one another. Later, Barry complained about her method of making tea, which was to throw a teabag into a cup of hot water. He regarded her tea-making as barbaric.

Barry recalled, "Barbra said: 'Do you think I'm the most famous woman in the world? Do you think I'm really as big as I say they am?' I'd say: 'You should relax Barbra, because I don't think there's anyone ever going to surpass what you've done.' 'Are you sure? Are you sure?'"[14]

Guilty's sales—and Barry eliciting such a commercial performance from someone as famously difficult as Streisand—put him and his brothers in demand as a hit-making writing-producing team. The experience was a watershed for Barry; he was in control and he loved it. Working on Andy's albums had given him a glimmer of what studio musicians could do. His experience on *Guilty*, with the top session players of the day, changed his modus operandi forever. First-rate session musicians could manifest whatever Barry wanted, almost instantly. Barry was not the first genius they'd dealt with who couldn't read music. The real pros needed less explanation. Barry swore off having a band and intended to work only with session players on all upcoming projects.

The Bee Gees next record, *Living Eyes*, came out in October of 1981. It was their first LP since *Spirits*, which had sold upward of 30 million copies. *Living Eyes* sold fewer than 800,000. It hit #41 in the UK and the US. Despite using a band of session wizards, they created not one memorable song. The Bee Gees' sound was trapped in post-disco.

"We've always perceived ourselves as a songwriting group," Barry said later. "We're a vocal group second. If there hadn't been some kind of a backlash after *Saturday Night Fever* there wouldn't have been 'Islands in the Stream.' There wouldn't have been 'Chain Reaction.' They were the kinds of things we did because we were diverted."[15]

"From 1980–87," Maurice said, "all we did was record and produce other people. We had a lot of artists out there doing our music. If we had put all that music out as Bee Gees, no one would have touched it because the *Fever* period was such a saturation that people got bored with us. People said, 'Hey, enough's enough!'"[16] "Everything we've written for other people, we said, 'Gosh, we wish we were doing this.' But we're professional, so we'd give it to them even though I might cry a little on the way home."[17]

In 1982, Barry, along with Karl and Albhy, produced Dionne Warwick's *Heartbreaker*. Barry, Maurice and Robin wrote six songs for the record. Barry and Albhy wrote another three. The single "Heartbreaker," written by the Bee Gees, went to #2 in both the US and UK. Warwick was skeptical of the song and surprised by its success. The album sold 3 million copies worldwide and made it to #2 on the UK charts. The Bee Gees, Karl and Albhy were proving their adaptability and the stars came calling.

Barry, Albhy and Karl produced Kenny Rogers's 1983 *Eyes That See in the Dark*. The Bee Gees wrote five songs; Barry and Maurice wrote three; Barry and Albhy wrote two more. The monster from that record was "Islands in the Stream" by Barry, Maurice and Robin. The single went #1 in the US on the pop and country charts and was the best-selling single of 1983. "Buried Treasure," also by the Gibbs, hit #3 on the country charts; "This Woman," by Barry and Albhy, made the top 20 in pop and country. "Islands in the Stream" was the Bee Gees' first #1 on the country charts. (Olivia Newton-John had taken their "Come on Over" to a country #5 in 1976.)

"They wrote ['Islands in the Stream'] and they gave it to me," Kenny Rogers said. "I sang it for four days and I finally turned to Barry and I said, 'I don't even like this song anymore.' And like an epiphany, that quickly, he says, 'We need Dolly Parton.' And I said, 'I don't know Dolly,' but my manager had run into her. So he said, 'Let me call her.' Forty-five minutes later she walked in the studio and she marched—you know, Dolly marches. She doesn't walk. She came in the studio and that song was never the same and I give her full credit for it."[18]

It seemed to studio insiders that Rogers was disengaged, especially in contrast to the obsessive Streisand. He seemed to do little preparation for the sessions, they said, and had difficultly learning his lyrics. He had to record his parts singing one line at a time. Barry was frustrated by Rogers's lack of effort.[19]

RCA had acquired Rogers and Diana Ross. The industry at large regarded both as albatrosses who would never justify their outsized signing fees. Paul Atkinson, an executive at RCA said: "Those are artists that RCA took some heat for signing, but I think the sales figures have borne out the wisdom of the deals."[20] The Gibbs had been called in as miracle workers on Rogers and had worked a miracle. They were hired to work another with Ross. Maurice said, "We thought, 'Wouldn't it be great to make a great Supremes record—we've got the lead singer!'"[21]

Barry, Karl and Albhy produced Diana Ross's *Eaten Alive* in 1985. Michael Jackson came into the sessions to co-produce the title track; he and Barry sang background vocals on it. The Bee Gees wrote six songs on the LP; Andy joined them for one more; another is by Barry and George Bitzer; Barry, Albhy and Andy wrote one; and Barry and Maurice wrote "Eaten Alive," later sharing songwriter credit with Michael Jackson. The LP reached #45 on the US charts. "Eaten Alive" reached #77 on the pop charts and #10 on the R&B charts. The production mimics *Thriller* and Ross imitates Jackson, singing in a breathy staccato. Jackson is listed as a background vocalist, but the voice on the verses sounds a lot more like him than Ross. The music is derivative, behind the times, as if the Bee Gees were recreating yesterday's R&B tropes. Or, possibly, as if Ross had demanded that they make a clone of Michael Jackson's hit sound.

"'Chain Reaction,' that's my favourite," Barry said. "We were so into Motown as kids. Diana Ross came to us and was quite surprised when we hit her with something retrospective of her own career, a respectable parody, as it were. She's on the phone all the time asking us to do it again."[22]

The Bee Gees released *E.S.P.* in September of 1987. Given their successful work for other artists, *E.S.P.* is shockingly weak, another collection of indistinguishable songs. But the single "You Win Again" went to #1 in the UK and elsewhere in Europe; it barely charted—hitting #75—in the US. The album, the Bee Gees' first under a new long-term deal with Warner Brothers, went only to #76 in America.

One, written in the months after Andy's death, was produced by the Bee Gees and Brian Tench and released in April of 1989. In May, the band launched their first tour in almost ten years, playing twenty dates in Europe. Barry was battling severe arthritis in his lower back and the shows were agony for him. He had to find the smallest, lightest guitar made; he could not bear the weight of his usual guitar. His back pain affected his vocal performance. Barry feared he might never tour again. "I'm 43 years old," he said. "If I was a lawyer, I would be considered to be in the prime of my career. Why shouldn't I be considered in the prime of my singing career? I have greater strength and control, my performances are better. Image shouldn't determine what a good record is; it has to be the performance. That's something I intend to prove."[23]

The album reached #68 in the US and #29 in the UK. The title track hit #7 on the US singles charts and was their best-selling single of the 1980s, logging ten weeks in the top 40. The rhythm tracks feature a combination of overproduced drum sounds associated with Michael Jackson and a "Jive Talkin'" melody.

Memories of Andy dominate the songwriting. Maurice, speaking of "Wish You Were Here," said, "We were halfway through writing that song when we realised we were writing about Andy. Originally we planned to do this album with Andy, who had never been part of the Bee Gees. It was supposed to be four of us on the album cover. He was only 30, you think, 'well, what happened?' After Andy died, I found about 50 bottles of vodka under his bed. I mean, the guy was supposed to have been sober for two years! I guess he couldn't take the pressure of being in England trying to do a solo album. He had a lot going on in his head that I don't even know about."[24]

Speaking to the lukewarm US sales, Barry said: "I'm not about to accept that the Bee Gees' popularity died with the disco craze in 1980, because that music only represented two albums in our long career. It never revealed the whole picture of what we do."[25]

High Civilization came out in April of 1991, reached #24 in the UK and went platinum worldwide but did not chart in the US. The Bee Gees had reached the end of their album commitment to Warner Brothers. The Gibb camp thought that Warners did not promote the record worth a damn. *High Civilization* is, by any reasonable standard, terrible.

In November of 1990, Warner Brothers released *Tales from the Brothers Gibb: A History in Song*. Organized into four chapters, it covers the Bees Gees from *Bee Gees 1st* to *One*, and totals seventy-one songs. The chapters, split into four CDs, cover 1967–70, 1971–74, 1975–79 and the 1980s. Given the Bee Gees' mediocre output in the '80s, it's little wonder that one disc covers ten years of material.

On March 6, 1992, one day after what would have been Andy Gibb's thirty-fourth birthday, Hugh Gibb died at seventy-six. The cause of death was listed as internal bleeding. After Andy died, Hugh lost interest in his life, and his interest in drink, always substantial, increased. Hugh lies buried next to Andy in Los Angeles.

"I believe all this was meant to happen," Barry said. "I miss my father of course, but he stopped living when Andy died and I'm sure he's happier now."

Robin was feeling on the outs of popular music. Or, in other words, he felt old. Anyone who begins a sentence with "kids today" feels old. "Kids today," he said, "are being starved of a certain standard of music. Pop music has lost its colour, its vitality, its excitement, its means of being different—there are so many guidelines imposed on it these days. The great new songwriters of the Nineties are not being developed. This is sound bite time. There's also the feeling around that pop music may have peaked. It stormed forward with the Beatles, who took it to a new level, suddenly it was credible. The Sixties barnstormed the avenues of creativity. In the Nineties, it's a question of where do we go from here? It's not a question of what the next trend is, it's a question of what else is there?"[26]

Speaking of *Saturday Night Fever*, Robin said: "This was the peak of record sales in all of history. Since 1967, there have only been three albums that have truly affected the culture, and that's *Sgt. Pepper* [Robin refers to the Beatles record, not the Bee Gees film soundtrack], *Fever* and *Thriller*. There's not many people who know what that feels like. We're like the guys who have been to the moon."[27]

When the band was down, Robin complained. When they were up, he gloated. Regardless, like his brothers, he always went back to work. By the 1990s, none of the brothers ever needed to work again, even were they to start buying small countries. It's said of Hemingway that he killed himself because he knew he could not write like he used to, but he could not stop writing. Neither could Barry. And if he couldn't stop, neither could his brothers.

On April 22, 1997, the Bee Gees released *Still Waters*. Their record label had rejected an earlier version, a collection of ballads. *Still Waters* is glossy Bee Gees generica. Only "Alone," with its doo-wop influenced choruses and driving beat, stands out. Even so, *Still Waters* reached #28 in the US and #5 in the UK. The album was an unqualified success, their best-selling since *Spirits*. Worldwide, it went quadruple platinum. "I Could Not Love You More" and "Still Waters (Run Deep)" both made UK's top 20. Arif

Mardin returned to produce, along with four other producers. Barry sings most leads. There's a pronounced 1980s drum sound and Van Halen guitar-solo aesthetic. *Still Waters'* commercial reception made it clear that the Bee Gees' audience was aging along with the band and was present and loyal in huge numbers.

"What you are getting is an honest album from us," Barry said. "For a few years, people were saying, 'Oh, it is a Bee Gees record, don't even listen to it.' That is what hurt us the most—the idea that you shouldn't even play it, that radio stations might have 'Bee Gees-free weekends.' The heart and soul you hear on our songs in this new album is our hunger. In each track, there's the idea that no matter who surrounds us, we are really alone anyway, individually, deep inside, so we may as well concentrate on living up to things we should demand and expect of ourselves. What came out of the last decade for us, spiritually, was maybe a new level of humility, compassion. We call ourselves the enigma with the stigma. The thought within the first single, 'Alone,' is that nobody really wants to be alone, and when you're in pain, nobody else feels it. But these actually can be good reasons to reach out."[28]

On October 20, 1997, the Bee Gees committed the public relations error of appearing on Clive Anderson's BBC talk show. Anderson behaved famously like an asshole on-air—Anderson was renowned for obnoxiousness and for asking offensive questions in a rat-a-tat style.[29] The interview starts innocuously. Anderson hammers away about their history, giving the band enough rope to hang themselves. Robin stays calm and self-possessed; Maurice tosses in a laconic one-liner now and then. When Clive shifts the tone of his questions, which he does constantly, Barry reacts each time. Barry waits to dominate the conversation in his usual control-freak fashion, leaning forward and interrupting his brothers, but Anderson proves too slippery. When Anderson raises the issue of the band splitting, the show grows tense. Anderson and Barry spar over calling the band "tossers" [masturbators], but Barry defends his family with ease. What he cannot handle is when Anderson singles out the other brothers for praise. The anger in Barry's face kicks up a notch when Clive mentions Robin's hit "Saved by the Bell." Barry instantly reminds him that at the same time, he and Maurice put out "Don't Forget to Remember." Clive says: "I forgot that one." Though there's been an undercurrent to Clive's remarks, Barry takes that mild, punning comeback as putting his song down in favor of Robin's and as a final straw. He stands up and stalks out. Robin follows. Maurice hangs a bit and says: "Well, I guess I should leave." Clive says; "You could speak for the other two." Maurice answers: "I don't do impressions," and ambles off.

Barry had said at the onset of the 1990s: "I want to see the Bee Gees where they are not made fun of. That's my cause. And I'll go on until that happens. It may never happen, but I don't care. I'm prepared for the fight."[30]

In November of 1997, the Bees Gees filmed *One Night Only*—a live performance before ten thousand fans in Las Vegas—for broadcast on February 14, 1998, on HBO. Their band of anonymous backing pros is tight, and the brothers are in good voice. Robin looks remarkably healthy. His appearance here is the benchmark against which his later deterioration would be measured. The band preferred doing large-scale one-off shows to touring. "We're not going to go and slog our guts out and not have fun," Maurice said. "You do two shows in a row, we need a night off, especially when you're doing falsettos—that's a killer, you need three days' rest after a show!"[31] *One Night Only* yielded both a live CD and a DVD. Barry's bad back had worsened, and the band regarded this gig as a possible final show. They did twenty-four songs; a demonstration of their stamina and drive.

On May 5, 1998, Stigwood's *Saturday Night Fever* stage production opened at the London Palladium. Stigwood had said many times how *SNF* the movie succeeded because he never took out the "fucks" and "shits" that the studio demanded he remove. Promo material for the stage play, however, emphasized that "the stage musical has been adapted and is suitable for all the family. There will be no foul language, drug use or violence against women."[32]

There were two new Bee Gees songs in the play. Neither had been written expressly for the show. "It's My Neighborhood" was later covered by Celine Dion and "Immorality" appeared on the Bee Gees album *One*. The play ran for almost two years in the West End and garnered three Laurence Olivier nominations.

The success of the stage play was read as proof that the Bee Gees had returned. David Adelson, the managing editor of *Hits* magazine, said: "The Bee Gees are once again a combination of cool and kitsch. They evoke favorable memories and seem to have won a renewed respect, proving that longevity enables certain artists to become hip again. If you survive long enough, you can thrive again."[33]

Nik Cohn, the originator of the *Fever* story, had a different take: "The consensus seems to be that the '70s are a laugh—a camp fad no more profound than pet rocks and hula hoops. 'It's all so uncool, it's cool,' one young vision in paisley polyester informed me. The recent debut of *Saturday Night Fever—The Musical* in London stirred more wariness in me than glee. Nor was my confidence level helped by my next-door neighbour. When I told him I was flying to England to catch the opening night, he gave me a pitying look and muttered, 'I'd fly to England to miss it.'"[34]

"We're not a nostalgia act," Robin insisted. "We're still making contemporary music." "A segment of the industry wanted to shed the whole disco movement," Barry said, accurately. "We were the heads they put on a stick." "A lot of bad records were made in that era," Robin said, hitting the nail on the head, "but the Bee Gees' songs hold up and will still be in clubs in 2050. It was exciting, progressive R&B, and the world went mad. The backlash was led by dinosaur critics who thought rock and heavy metal were the only music people should hear." Barry described their 1990s comeback as "the greatest shock." "People are liking songs," he said, "that weren't supposed to be liked anymore." "We're persistent little buggers," Maurice said.[35]

One Night Only, the album, was released on November 3, 1998. It stayed in the charts for thirty-six weeks, until July 1999, and sold 2 million copies. The DVD sold 1,700,000 copies in the US alone, making it one of the most successful music DVDs.[36]

The TV broadcasts once again bore out Stigwood's belief in cross-promotion, a practice the boys adopted as their own. When *One Night Only* aired in the UK, sales of the album went up by 546 percent the next week. Sam Wright, the head of TV promotions at Polydor, said: "It was amazingly valuable. It was a real talking point. People kept ringing us up, asking us for a copy. It really re-positioned [the Bee Gees]."[37]

One Night Only hit Australia on March 17, 1999. Forty-four thousand tickets sold the first day and the one-off show sold a total of 61,000. "It's the biggest top show undertaking," the local promoter said, "that I've been involved in."[38]

On October 21, 1999, *SNF* opened on Broadway. "The film affected people in two ways," the director, Arlene Phillips said. "They either remember John Travolta in his white suit, and the music and the discos, and they forget about the story. Or they remember the quite-shocking story. And it seems that nobody really ever remembers the combination of the two. There's a lot that one can hardly bear to watch or look at. And somehow in musical theater, the question arises . . . how far do you go into the depths of the story with all the ugliness and still enjoy this disco music? It was very hard to get the balance right."[39] "The music sounds distant and tinny, as if it were being played on some souped up 8-track tape system," wrote *New York Times* theater critic Ben Brantley, letting his response to the overture stand in for this take on the entire play. "Against the odds, there is nothing at all infectious about it; your tappable feet and snappable fingers stay alarmingly still. And there arises an ominous feeling that any nostalgia on offer here is not of the wet warm embracing kind but more of the freeze-dried variety."[40] Despite lukewarm reviews, by opening night the show had sold $20 million of advance tickets and it ran for 501 performances.

In April of 2001, the Bee Gees released *This Is Where I Came In*. The album hit #6 in the UK and #16 in the US, demonstrating the strength of the Bee Gees' audience. The album suggests that the success of *One Night Only* rejuvenated the band. The title track is their most intelligent, fully realized, sing-alongable, compelling song in years.

In the sparse intro, Robin sings over Maurice picking guitar. Barry comes in for a verse, and all three soar together. Robin sings a solo verse in strong, full voice. The hook of the song sounds half stolen from Toto's *Africa*, but after their previous anemic efforts, the single presents the Bee Gees as a band reborn, confident and willing to attempt new forms. They've clearly been listening to 1990s dance music. "Walking on Air" evokes ABC; "Voice in the Wilderness" features a Nine Inch Nails–influenced rave-up with severe '90s dance-music production. "Embrace" and "Walking on Air" would sound at home on a Pet Shop Boys album—not surprising, since the album's co-producer, Peter-John Vettese, also produced the Pet Shop Boys. The Bee Gees' voices merge with the instrumentation as they had not in years. Even the video is witty and well executed, with the band looking remarkably unselfconscious. Robin appears well fed and healthy.

"We didn't want one of those big production things," Barry said. "This album for us is variety. It stands on its own—it's not like another *Fever* or *Main Course* or anything before. We thought, 'How many different kinds of songs can we do?' And we gave each other the space to go away individually and come up with things ourselves—which we used to do without any feelings of malice. So we did four songs together, and three or four each, and chose from them. It's our definitive album of our collaborations and their diversity."[41]

The Bees Gees seemed poised for a great leap forward.

"walkin' by the
railroad"

Maurice, a longtime, hard-drinking alcoholic, always said that John Lennon gave him his first taste of real liquor. Maurice was a mythomaniac, and Lulu recalls him making up stories about time spent with John and Yoko, but this has the ring of truth.

Of his early drinking days Maurice said: "I was into beer and stuff. Then, at the Speakeasy club, Lennon said: 'Scotch and Coke, innit?' Cream were playing that night. It was a star-studded evening. You must remember, these guys [the Beatles] are our gods! John was my guru. He said 'Scotch and Coke'—yes! And I'd never drunk Scotch and Coke in my life. I was 17. All of a sudden I'm hanging out with him. And there's Keith Moon. There's Pete Townshend. There's Otis Redding. To be thrust into the middle of it, sitting having drinks with your idols . . . So if he'd said cyanide, I'd have drunk it. One moment I was looking at a Beatles fan club book and five months later we were in a club with them. We felt part of something although we were 16 or 17 years old.[1] I can still feel the nervousness in my stomach. I was with John many times when he was tripping, and I didn't know he was tripping. Oh, he was funny [on LSD]. He was so funny. When he got drunk, he was real arrogant, a pain in the ass. But when he was tripping, the drink would counter it. So he was always in between. He'd become sarcastically funny, not sarcastically arrogant, and he became tremendously lovable. We had many late nights doing that shit. Throwing up in the back of his white Roller. At that time, it was multi-colored.[2]

"Ringo was my neighbour and we were going to Tramp every night, parking our Mini Coopers outside the Speakeasy and driving home totally blitzed. It was good fun. No one had minders then—we used to get drunk with Prince Charles at Tramp, and Michael Caine and Peter Sellers'd be in the corner. When I was married to Lu, the doorbell would go at three in the morning and it would be Rod Stewart or David Bowie. We'd go down in our dressing gowns and get the bar open."[3]

With the success of *Saturday Night Fever*, Maurice's drinking, and its effects, took a turn. "Every day," he said, "I didn't want to get up. I had all these beautiful things around me and I didn't appreciate a damn thing. Had my own Falcon 20 jet, you know. Hardly ever used it. I sold all that shit. Sold my boat. 'Cos I wasn't happy with me, and it was the boozing, of course. I was totally unhappy, even though we were having hit records and getting on great."[4]

Before Andy died, Maurice had achieved a functional level of sobriety. After Andy's death, Maurice's drinking increased. Whether he had too much time on his hands, the relative hard times the band was facing, or as he said, guilt he felt for not being able to communicate with Andy before he died, Maurice blamed Andy. Alcoholics need someone to blame. "I liked drinking because it was sociable," he said. "It was going to the pub and having a pint. It was a way of life. I became a Jekyll and Hyde figure. I was never physically abusive but I was vicious with my tongue. After Andy's death it got worse. I drank and drank to numb my mind."[5]

On October 4, 1991, Maurice pulled a gun on his family in their house in Miami. He had been on a monthlong brandy binge, drinking every day from the moment of awakening to the moment of passing out. He ran upstairs, grabbed his handgun and came back down. "I was waving a gun around and stuff like that," he said. "And normally I don't even like guns."[6] "He came out with a gun," Maurice's son Adam, who was sixteen at the time, said. "I couldn't believe it and then my mum said: 'Go upstairs and get some clothes' and I thought 'Oh my God, he's going to shoot us.'" "The kids were scared to death," Yvonne said. "He said he had to do something about this problem and he cried and cried."[7] "I didn't have a blackout," Maurice said. "I remembered all of it. That scared the hell out of me. I asked my daughter to throw the gun in the bay, which she did. I said: 'I've just got to do something about this.' I'd reached the bottom and I couldn't take any more. I didn't like being that person. I became that monster."[8]

Yvonne took the children and ran to Barry's house. She called Maurice and told him she would not come home until he straightened out. Maurice says he drove himself to rehab the next day. "If I was her I'd run out," he said. "If I could run away from me I'd run away from me."[9]

Maurice broke down during a group session in rehab after citing how much Yvonne had supported him. He called her; the next day was their sixteenth wedding anniversary. "She sent me a card saying, 'We've gone this far together, it can only get better.'"[10] When Maurice got out of rehab, he was down with the program. "AA," he said. "Regular meetings. Staying in contact with people in the program. See, all my friends now are on the program. They're not the people I used to booze with or go to pubs with.

They say 'people, places, and things.' I don't hang out with the same people I used to hang out with, I don't go to the same places. And the things that used to make me drink—I don't let them bother me any more."[11]

On February 23, 1992, Maurice and Yvonne renewed their wedding vows. "We thought it would be a good time to celebrate," Maurice said. "Not only our marriage but also my life as a non-drinker and non-drug abuser. It's a funny thing, but it also marks our starting a new life—new journey—together. Yvonne supported me through the bad times; it's hard to find a lady like that."[12] In July, Maurice appeared on *Fighting Back*, a BBC show hosted by actress Lynn Redgrave. Stars from various fields came on to talk candidly about their illnesses and how they had dealt with them. "This is a wonderful form of giving back in return for all the help I was given when I was in trouble," Maurice said. "I felt that the main point of this programme was to get across to other alcoholics and their families that something can be done and that they are not struggling alone."[13]

In 1994, there were rumors of Maurice having a relapse and being arrested for drunk driving. He denied them, saying: "I did what every recovering person should do—go back [to rehab] before you relapse."[14]

In 2002, Maurice sang with Lulu on her television special. In September, he participated in the World Paintball Championships with his team, the Royal Rat Rangers. Maurice had become a freak for paintball. The team's emblem was a rat holding a paintball gun, surmounted by a crown. Maurice competed constantly, sponsored the Rangers and opened his own paintball store, Commander Mo's Paintball Shop, in North Miami Beach. The "Commander" referred to Maurice's royally granted CBE (Commander of the British Empire). Maurice called paintball "the most rock and roll thing." In October, Maurice sold his house on Biscayne Bay. He bought a new home for $7.1 million near Barry's house, on the same residential island between Miami and Miami Beach. Maurice said that he moved to be closer to his brother.

In January of 2003, Maurice collapsed at home and was rushed to the hospital. The doctors feared he had had a heart attack, and performed surgery for an intestinal blockage. Barry was with Maurice at the hospital; Robin was in England. A hospital spokesman said: "Maurice has undergone surgery for an intestinal blockage. He is in critical condition in intensive care. We are awaiting a full medical prognosis later today but everyone is very, very worried."[15] "It was completely out of the blue," Maurice's manager, Carol Peters, said. "No pains or anything beforehand, just all of a sudden, boom. After the operation, he opened his eyes, wiggled toes and feet, so it's good."[16]

"It was all quick and sudden," Robin said. "The last 24 hours have been the most crucial. The latest update is that all his vital organs are A1 and recovering, which is good. Obviously, it's been bad, but every hour is a bonus." Robin, as had Maurice the day of Robin's train wreck in 1967, knew something was wrong. "The morning Maurice was taken ill," he said, "I had stomach pains for an hour to two hours at the very time. It was a discomforting feeling that something wasn't right and I hadn't had any pains like that before. It was at exactly the same time as he fell ill."[17]

Few outside the family understood the gravity of Maurice's condition. The *Daily News* did not take it seriously. They ran a headline reading BEE GEE HIT BY MORE THAN NIGHT FEVER. The *News* reported that Maurice "was reunited with his Bee Gee brothers at a Miami hospital last night as he recuperated from a severe stomach ailment that nearly turned their famous three-part harmonies into a duet."[18]

On January 11, Robin and Barbara flew to Miami. Maurice was deteriorating. "Maurice's doctors initially diagnosed a mild heart attack and an intestinal blockage," a family friend said. "What they found wasn't good. They had to remove part of his intestine, which was gangrenous, and also some of his stomach. They believe he has had an undiagnosed twisted intestine from birth. I don't want to be too downbeat but it is pretty devastating news."[19] Maurice remained unconscious and the doctors feared brain damage. There were unconfirmed reports that he opened his eyes and squeezed his daughter's hand. The *Sunday Mail* reported that Michael Jackson had visited.

Maurice Gibb died on January 12, 2003. He was fifty-three.

The family issued a statement: "It is with great sadness and sorrow that we regretfully announce the passing of Maurice Gibb this morning. His love and enthusiasm and energy for life remain an inspiration to all of us. We will all deeply miss him."[20]

"We are both devastated," Robin said. "We've actually been in shock for the last few days since Maurice was taken ill. I still can't come to terms with it now. It's like a nightmare that you wake up to every day. It's going to take a long time for it to sink in."[21]

The brothers called for an investigation of Maurice's treatment and the procedures utilized. "The fact that they had to operate on Maurice during the shock of cardiac arrest is questionable," Barry said. "We will pursue every factor, every element, every second of the timeline, of the final hours of Maurice's life. We will pursue that relentlessly. That will be our quest from now on."[22]

"They knew by late Saturday that Maurice wasn't going to make it," said a friend of the family. "Barry is absolutely devastated, he's beside himself . . . . inconsolable. Robin is obviously deeply upset, but he is relieved he was at least able to share a few hours with Maurice."[23]

"His drinking did upset his system," friend of the family Christopher Hutchins said. "He was greatly weakened by what he put himself through, in terribly destructive years. His marriage to Lulu was torn apart by the fact that he did indulge in all of these things to try to take the pain away, and stop what was going on in his mind. He was a much tormented soul. He was not the star, and he knew it, he felt it. He would often go back to the dressing room after a show and drink so heavily, and during the time of his marriage to Lulu, it was crockery smashing time every night."[24]

"Not as handsome as his taller brother Barry," one rock writer wrote, "nor as intense as his bucktoothed twin Robin, Maurice was the group's engine room; the bass and keyboard player, the rock-steady one who kept the others together. In private, he was the easygoing, amiable one of the group, the one who would talk to critics like me."[25]

Maurice was cursed to be described as what he wasn't or by his absence. Maurice made himself into a middle brother—the bridge between Robin and Barry. By doing so, Maurice placed himself third in the hierarchy; he liked it there. He always felt less talented than his brothers. Maurice's drinking rendered him more or less a spectator to the best-selling records and most successful tour of his career. That certainly must have increased his self-loathing, and led to even more drinking. Unlike his brothers, Maurice was naturally good natured. The good-natured brother is always the unappreciated brother.

Maurice was the Bee Gees' glue. For as long as he was capable, Maurice was the crucial instrumentalist in the studio. His un-selfish harmonies—his compliant surrender of the lead vocal role—made Robin's and Barry's voices mesh seamlessly, which they never could without Maurice's uncompetitive collaboration. His willingness to always be third meant one less ego in a band of ego clashes. Maurice had rich timbre and a beautiful voice, effort-less, sincere and unaffected; he didn't need Robin's melodrama and, unlike Barry, was at home with the emotions he sang. Mau-rice was a patient singer; he let the material come to him. His solo record vocals evoke the relaxed pacing and soulful ease of country greats like Charlie Pride or Merle Haggard.

Days after Maurice's death, Robin and Barry regretted going public with their suspicions about Maurice's medical treatment.

They tried to get the BBC not to air their complaints. "It was a case of wrong place, wrong time," a family friend said. "They withdrew their comments. We are all completely grief-stricken and things get said that are not necessarily intended. Barry and Robin have lost a dear brother and they are obviously emotional and have questions, but the family has had a good respectful relationship with the hospital for something like 25 years. They are upset that those comments went out."[26]

Maurice's funeral, held on January 16, 2003, in Miami, at the Riverside Gordon Memorial Chapels, was private. *Billboard* reported that two hundred people attended. Maurice's paintball teammates were there, as were Lulu and Harry Wayne Casey of KC and the Sunshine Band. Barry was too distraught to be part of the ceremony, and stayed behind until it was over, as did Michael Jackson. They paid their respects to Maurice together. On January 22, Robin announced that the name Bee Gees would be retired.

Maurice was cremated. Four purple gems were made from his ashes. They were given to Yvonne, Barbara, Robin and Barry.

"down came
the sun"

he toxic level of Robin's amphetamine addiction in the late 1970s and early '80s turned him threatening, rageful, and paranoid during his divorce from Molly Hullis. One late night, wired up on speed and accompanied by a private detective, Robin broke into his former house—where Molly lived with their children—while Molly and the kids were elsewhere. Robin still held the deed to the house and had keys to the locks. He did not have to force his way in, but he did. Robin found innocuous documents in the house that—in his deluded state—he thought suggested a plot by Molly and her lawyers to extort him for £5 million.

Robin believed that Molly was having an affair with her divorce attorney. He sought documents that would prove that the attorney and Molly were baiting him, and trying to get Robin to publicly accuse Molly of infidelity. If he did, Robin's fantasy went, Molly would then sue him for £5 million.

That delusion led to a harrowing series of letters, phone calls and threatening telegrams, which were eventually forwarded to the FBI. Part of one telegram read: "What you have done is just about the limit. I warned and warned you. The situation is now very serious. Know [*sic*] one walks all over me . . . I have had enough. I have taken out a contract . . . It is now a question of time."[1]

The FBI looked for Robin, but couldn't find him. "Miami office unable to determine present location of the rock group Bee Gees at this time," an internal memorandum went. "Any direct inquiries would alert Mr. Gibb to inquiries being made by the Miami office of the FBI, so no further attempt to verify present location of the group being made by the Miami office."[2] Robin came to New York and the FBI wanted to interview him. Robin sent his attorney, who said that "his client would not be foolish enough to carry out any threat especially in view of his singing career," and that his Molly and her lawyers were "attempting to use the FBI to embarrass Gibb and to bring pressure on him in the divorce proceedings."[3]

Robin was running wild. Speed is poison and damages almost every processing system in the body. In a public service announcement from the early 1970s Speed Kills campaign, Frank Zappa speak-sings: "Speed! Rot your brain! Rot your teeth! Rot your Liver! Rot cha cha!" He wasn't kidding. Robin's intake had produced all the classic speed-freak symptoms: frightening weight loss, paranoid delusions, irrationality, hypersexuality and becoming an unbearable pain in the ass to anyone who cared for him.

"I remember being asleep and getting a call from Robin at 1 a.m.," said Christopher Hutchins, Robin's former manager. "He was saying, 'It's an emergency!' and asking me to drive to his house in Knightsbridge." When Hutchins got to Robin's house, he found Robin in bed with a woman. "We have to go out and get a woman," Robin told him. "[Robin's] thing was to watch two women together," Hutchins said. "In his drugged-up state he thought I would help him. His house at the time was a beautiful Georgian place near Harrods. One time, I noticed handprints on the walls, about 8 ft up. Obviously, some strange sexual adventures had been going on. He was always seeking a treatment for his drug addiction. He'd work through the night, never going to bed. Night and day meant nothing to him. He took uppers to keep him awake and downers to put him to sleep."[4]

Around this time, Robin met his future wife, Dwina Murphy. Nobody in the Bee Gees' saga was ever on the receiving end of so much rage and scorn, not only from the Gibb family, but from Bee Gees fans as well. It's hard to see why Dwina was selected as the arch-villain. She and Robin talked about their sex lives with a candor so explicit it could be traumatizing to the listener, but they appear to have been genuinely in love. Dwina helped Robin with his drug addiction, and they stayed together until his death. Dwina's been labeled a gold digger and sorceress; things written about her imply that she somehow had Robin under a spell. The logical truth seems to be that for all their eccentricities, they liked each other and, in their way, got along.

"My marriage had broken up and I needed a minder," Robin said. "Someone to drive me around. I got Ken Graydon through a recruiting firm. He told me he was meeting his cousin and would I mind if he took time off. I said: 'Maybe I'll come with you.' I saw Dwina's drawings, liked them and commissioned some from her. Two weeks later she came house-hunting and it all accelerated." "Robin asked Ken to bring me round so he could commission some drawings for his new home," Dwina said. "I dressed up in big zigzagging black and white lines, very artsy, just the sort of thing Robin doesn't like. I recognised him immediately and wished I wasn't wearing the artsy outfit. I decided to do the story of Persephone for him, and I made the drawings detailed so they took a long time and I could go on seeing him. I wouldn't finish them, because I'm superstitious—I'm afraid that if I did, that would be it." "We had a couple of one-night stands towards the end of 1980," Robin said. "I was attracted to her, but it didn't get really serious until the following year, when she moved into my house in Barnes. She kept her house in Plumstead in case she had a change of heart, but it did work out, it worked very well, and she became pregnant with Robin-John."[5]

Robin's divorce was finalized near the end of 1980. There was endless litigation; custody battles over their children raged until 1983. Robin narrowly avoided jail after a judge ordered him not to discuss the custody proceedings and Robin told the press all about them.

On October 28, 1983, Robin announced to the world that he had a new son, Robin-John, who had been born the previous February. "We wanted little Robin and he's wonderful," Robin said, "but neither Molly, my former wife, nor my other two children know about him yet. I will be introducing the children to their little brother, but it's still too early and the situation is too fragile." Robin explained his curious behavior about the baby and his divorce by saying: "I developed a terrible mistrust of women. It's taken a while for me to get over it. But having the baby with Dwina sealed our happiness."[6]

Robin and Dwina were married on July 31, 1985.

"I'd always fought against the idea of marriage, living with one person," Dwina said. "But I liked the idea of having a child with Robin. I recognised his creative spirit, his gentleness, the poet in him, and I thought ours would be good genes to put together. We tried to have a child, off and on, but it didn't happen until I moved in with him. We got closer and closer; I felt he was my brother, my lover, my son, my father. We got married in 1985, on the eve of Lughnasadh, the turning point of the year."[7] Citing Lughnasadh, a Gaelic harvest festival, in one of her first public pronouncements, set the tone for Dwina's image; she was henceforth regarded as a New Age nutcase.

Dwina, conversely, regarded herself as a Druid priestess, an artist and an author. She wrote historical novels concerning a third-century Celtic king who trained his warriors to be poets and thus brought peace to Ireland. Perhaps her historical research gave her insight into Druidism. Little is known about ancient Druids, what they believed and how that belief functioned. They are thought to be have been pagans in Ireland, Britain and Gaul. Perhaps they committed human sacrifice, perhaps not. The ideology of modern Druidism is hard to pin down; they wear white robes and like Stonehenge a lot. In June of 1992, Dwina was elected a patroness of the Druids. "My job is basically to spread the word," Dwina said. "To tell people about Druidry not only as a religion but a way of life. People are becoming more interested in the environment and part of my job will be to show how that fits in with our beliefs."[8] As part of her belief system, Dwina made plans to have the tennis court in the estate she shared with Robin converted to a smaller version of Stonehenge. "When it is completed," she said, "I will be able to tell what time of the year it is by looking at which stone the sun is shining on . . . It will be of far more use than a tennis court."[9]

The tennis-court-henge sits in Prebendal, near Thames, Oxfordshire. Prebendal was built in the thirteenth century as a training college for monks. Robin acquired it in 1984. Covering twenty acres, the estate has its own chapel, and was visited by Henry VIII and Anne Boleyn. Mick Jagger sought to buy Prebendal but the owners feared wild parties and the like. Robin convinced them to sell by doing copious research on Prebendal. They trusted in his sincere love of the place, which was no act. Robin had a genuine preservationist and curatorial interest in the place. "I've always loved history," he said. "Which might surprise some people, as Bee Gees songs don't have many historical references—it's hard to slip them into pop songs."[10] He and Dwina put in medieval-style furniture, restored a dragon-decorated fireplace and ordered a suit of armor for Robin-John and a gypsy wagon for Dwina. "The house has a resident ghost," Robin said, "who seems to mysteriously fill up the water font in the chapel, part of which has now been converted into a dining room."[11] Dwina and Robin would visit the

Gibbs in Florida, but Dwina preferred Prebendal. "I can completely relax and wear long flowing gowns instead of beach gear," she said. "It's wonderfully cool here. I actually hate the sun in Florida and spend a lot of my time inside. Given the choice, both Robin and I would rather live in our Oxfordshire home permanently, it makes me feel part of history."[12]

On November 24, 1993, Barry, Maurice and Robin went on Howard Stern's radio show. Stern opened up the conversation by asking Barry if he'd "nailed" Barbara Streisand when they worked together. Robin volunteered: "My wife cheats on me now. But not with men. She has a steady girlfriend at the moment. My wife looks at other women like guys look at women." Stern asked how their mother felt about Dwina bringing her girlfriends to family gatherings. Barry said: "This is the nineties and I think our mother is about as hip . . . as anybody else is."[13] "His comments did upset me," Dwina said. "But only because I was worried about how my mother and our son, Robin-John, would take it. I don't have shame about what Robin said and I still don't. I've always been liberated. No one can hurt me in anything they do or say. I just carry on living my life."[14] Robin and Barry went on Stern to promote their new album, but once Stern heard about Dwina, he hardly mentioned it.

Of their arrangement, Dwina said: "Robin doesn't tie me down. He says, 'Go ahead, do what you want to do, go where you want to go.'" "It turns me on to see her in bed with other girls," Robin said. "I'm allowed to watch and join in as well. I was thinking as I lay in bed last night with my wife and her lover either side of me, that I'm getting thoroughly spoiled."[15]

Time passes differently when one is married to a Druid priestess, and by all accounts, Robin spent much of the 1980s, 1990s and 2000s enjoying the comfort of his family, the comfort of others, and learning that some things are better left unsaid. He appeared in the papers again in 1997, when the British government, at the conclusion of an investigation of music stars who weren't paying taxes on their royalties, forced the Bee Gees to pay £3 million in a settlement. Robin had to pay the most—£1.8 million. Regardless of the size of the settlement, Robin's quality of life did not seem to suffer.

The year 2009 marked the fiftieth anniversary of the formation of the Bee Gees. To celebrate the occasion, Barry and Robin began performing under the Bee Gees' moniker, despite retiring the name upon Maurice's death. Among other events, they appeared on *Dancing with the Stars* and *American Idol*. Robin hinted at a reconciliation tour with his brother, but no concerts were ever booked.

On November 4, 2009, Dwina and Robin's housekeeper, Claire Yang, thirty-three, gave birth to her and Robin's daughter, Snow Robin. "At first Dwina was happy for Robin to sow his oats because it allowed her to stay committed to her Brahman beliefs," said a family friend (Dwina had converted to the Brahman religion, which called for sexual abstinence), "but she never expected him to actually plant his seed, as it were. When the truth came out, Dwina was furious. To say she hit the roof is an understatement. She felt betrayed."[16] Snow Robin's birth certificate listed Robin, "professional musician," as the father. Robin installed Claire and Snow Robin in a nearby farm, hired Claire a nanny and was a frequent visitor.[17]

On March 19, 2012, Robin released *The Titanic Requiem*, which he composed and executed with his son. "It has been an incredible experience working with my son RJ," Robin said. "There is a creative freedom and uninhibited state that comes from working with a family member. Working on this album and with RJ has been a driving force, and one that has helped me on the road to recovery."[18] Robin had been looking increasingly skeletal, and rumors abounded about his ill health.

"I get annoyed with false stories about me," he said, "because I feel great and I look forward to the future. Recent months have been a testing time. I've had a scare. But now I'm happy to say I'm nearly better. For more than 18 months, I lived with an inflammation of the colon. Then I was diagnosed with colon cancer, which spread to the liver. It's taken a toll, naturally. I have undergone chemotherapy, however, and the results, to quote my doctor, have been 'spectacular.'"[19]

"The prognosis is that it's almost gone and I feel fantastic and really from now on it's just what they could describe as a mopping up operation," he told the *New Musical Express*. "I feel better than I did 10 years ago. I'm active, my appetite's fantastic, the plumbing is all in perfect working order. If I had a choice about how I'd like to feel for the rest of my life, this would be it. If I wanted to tick all the right boxes about my sense of well being, it would be now. This is the way I'd like to feel. I don't know how I could feel any better."[20]

Robin spoke of Maurice's last days: "Maurice was in hospital for just three days. I flew to Miami to see him and he was in a coma. They told Barry and I that, if Maurice didn't have any brain activity within ten minutes, he would die then and there. To our horror, we found out there was none. And Maurice died. How did I get over Maurice's death? I didn't. And I never will. I just don't accept it. I tell myself he's away on a long holiday and that we'll be seeing each other again soon. I sometimes wonder if all the tragedies my family has suffered, like Andy and Maurice dying so young and everything that's happened to me recently, is a kind of karmic price we are paying for all the fame and fortune we've had. However, I'm truly grateful that working on *The Titanic Requiem* distracted me from my illness to such a degree that I truly believe it might have saved my life."[21]

Despite his protestations, Robin's condition was worsening. In March he had surgery to remove a blood clot. After his surgery, Robin spoke of wanting to get back together with Barry. "My next main priority is to work with Barry," he said. "I'd love to make an album with him. He has expressed an interest and I want to hold him to that." Robin discussed his terror over his physical condition. "I can't deny there was a point when I was scared it was the end," Robin said.[22] "I found the whole experience had a much more profound effect on me emotionally than it did physically. I went into a deep depression, and there were many times I was reduced to tears. But I'm over that now and my sense of well-being has returned."[23] He told Robin-John that he was in remission. "It's gone," he said. "They can't see it no more. I've done it."[24]

But a week later, news reports had his family and friends gathering at Prebendal, concerned that Robin had come down with pneumonia. "They fear it may be the last time they'll see Robin," said a family friend. "His recovery and determination has been remarkable, but there's been a turn for the worse. His body's taken a hell of a beating. The doctors fear for him but he's determined to battle on."[25]

"The past two weeks have been devastating," said another friend. "The one aim Robin had was to be at the *Requiem* premiere. It was his motivation, passion and goal throughout the battle against cancer. His spirit has been shattered since the pneumonia and he has gone visibly downhill. Before he slipped into a coma he was struggling to get out of bed without a wheelchair."[26]

On April 10, 2012, *The Titanic Requiem* debuted live, performed by the Royal Philharmonic Orchestra. Robin was too ill to attend. "The day before the concert it suddenly struck me that, instead of singing the beautiful song 'Don't Cry Alone' that evening," Dwina said, "Robin was in a coma and might die. I suddenly thought, 'If he never comes out of the coma, I will never hear his voice again.' Many nights we've been together as a couple, I've woken to hear him composing on the keyboards in the next room, singing like an angel. I couldn't bear it if his beautiful voice was silenced forever. We all had to accept that Robin couldn't go to the premiere.

We all realised that the show had to go on without him. I stayed with him in the hospital until the last minute, because I really didn't want to leave him. The audience at the concert stood and cheered, but I couldn't help breaking down. I pulled myself together and told myself that Robin would survive. I am forever grateful that RJ has been at my side throughout this ordeal. RJ had made sure the premiere was filmed—we all passionately believed that one day Robin would watch it."[27]

On April 8, Robin went into a coma. The cause was pneumonia, but his doctors feared the presence of another tumor. "His family are taking it hour by hour," said a family friend, "and praying for a miracle. But with Robin they know never to give up."[28] "Barry sang a song he had composed for Robin," Dwina said. "We played him Bee Gees music—and each time we did, tears began trickling down his cheeks. As we played him 'I Started a Joke,' he opened his mouth on cue to sing. The doctors know relatives of coma patients are always looking for hopeful signs. They told me it could be an automatic response. But it seemed too much of a coincidence that Robin opened his mouth at the exact point in the song when he would have started singing. We persuaded them to let us test my theory by attaching electrodes to Robin's brain and monitoring his reactions to the music."[29]

After being unconscious for two weeks, Robin emerged from his coma on April 21. The first thing he said upon awakening was: "Hello, RJ." "The doctors asked Robin," Dwina said, "if he wanted them to do everything in their power to save his life—or if he felt the time would come when enough was enough. He told them, 'There will never be a time when enough is enough. I want to live no matter what.'"[30] Robin told those gathered around him: "I wish Mo was here. I can't believe he's gone."[31]

Robin's doctor, Andrew Thillainayagam, said: "It is testament to Robin's extraordinary courage, iron will and deep reserves of physical strength that he has overcome quite incredible odds to get where he is now. Only three days ago, I warned Robin's wife, Dwina, son, Robin and brother, Barry that I feared the worst. We felt it was likely that Robin would succumb to what seemed to be insurmountable obstacles to any form of meaningful recovery. As a team, we were all concerned that we might be approaching the realms of futility. But now Robin is fully conscious, lucid and able to speak to his loved ones. He is breathing on his own, with an oxygen mask. He is on intravenous feeding and antibiotics. He is exhausted, extremely weak and malnourished. Our immediate goals are to ensure that Robin's swallowing mechanism is safe enough to allow him to eat and drink, and that he recovers enough strength to breath effectively, without needing high levels of oxygen by mask. When this happens, we will be able to begin the process of nutritional and physical rehabilitation and may be able to move him from the intensive care unit to the ward. The road ahead for Robin remains uncertain but it is a privilege to look after such an extraordinary human being."[32]

In late April a family friend told the press: "Robin is still weak but getting better by the day. His recovery is nothing short of a miracle. Weeks ago Dwina and the family were prepared for the worst, now they are hoping he will be home very soon."[33]

But Robin never left the hospital. "He can't speak at the moment because he has a tracheotomy," Robin's friend Jim Dooley told the press. "He has to communicate by blinking his eyes. Dwina said that because he spent so long in a coma there are a lot of things he will have to learn to do again if he comes through it. He will have to re-learn how to walk. It's 50/50 whether he comes through this but Dwina is a wonderful woman and she is giving him all the love and TLC you can give. He is receiving prayers and blessings from every religion all over the world and I'm told there is a special blessing on the way from the Pope. The plan is to get his strength up so he can resume chemotherapy treatment for his cancer."[34]

Robin died on May 20, 2012. He was sixty-two. Dwina, Robin-John and Robin's children Spencer and Melissa were at Robin's bedside. The cause of death was kidney failure.

In October, the press reported that Robin's fortune was estimated at £93 million. Robin's children from both marriages and Dwina would share his estate. Shortly before Robin died, he had arranged a one-time payment to Claire Yang of £5 million.

Robin was buried in Thames, Oxfordshire. A single bagpiper led his funeral cortege. Robin's casket was borne in a white carriage pulled by four plumed, black horses. Robin's Irish wolfhounds, Ollie and Missy, followed the cortege. Claire Yang did not attend the funeral. Dwina had said earlier that she would be "devastated" if Yang came, but would not bar her presence. Among the pallbearers were Robin's sons, RJ and Spencer, Barry's son Steve, and Dwina's son, Steven Murphy. The family brought the precious gems made from Maurice's ashes to the church to symbolically reunite the twins in the afterlife. "I Started a Joke" and "Don't Cry Alone" were played in the church.

Barry gave a eulogy at Robin's funeral. Speaking of their various disagreements, Barry said: "Even right up to the end we found conflict with each other, which now means nothing. It just means nothing. If there's conflict in your lives—get rid of it. I think the greatest pain for Robin in the past ten years was losing [Maurice]. And now they're together."[35]

barry gibb's
first ever
solo concert

*F*ebruary 21, 2012: Barry Gibb is about to perform *Barry Gibb's First Ever Solo Concert.*

He's sixty-five.

The Hollywood, Florida, Seminole Hard Rock Hotel's Hard Rock Live—part of a casino complex with a labyrinthine mall built like a Martian's idea of an old-fashioned village—is sold out. It's a medium-size, anonymous, multi-purpose arena, with a stratospheric ceiling, an endless flat floor filled with folding chairs, a broad stage overhung with enormous video screens, and bleachers rising high and steep on either side the length of the room. The sound system, as you'd expect in a concrete-floored, athletic arena, is soggy. But the speakers are many and gigantic; there will be volume . . .

There are over five thousand people in the hall. The tickets were not cheap. There are no empty seats. Most of the crowd is younger than Barry Gibb. The majority seem to be between forty and fifty-five. They're all glad to be there and everyone looks excited. There are no visible ironists or hipsters. Out of the over five thousand members of the paying public, approximately seven are African American. It's a white crowd, dressed like middle management on a night out. They're not a great-looking bunch; there's little glamour. These are Barry's mainstream peeps.

The band comes onstage: two keyboard players, a conga-percussionist, a drummer behind a clear sound barrier, two guitarists, a bass player and three babe backup singers in 1980s babe backup singer outfits. The band lines the rear of the stage. To the left of the main microphone, on a tall stool, right up front, sits a lean guitar player in his late thirties, with movie star–pirate good looks, tats all up and down his arms, a tight T-shirt and a Les Paul; that's Barry's son Steve.

The hall goes dark, the lights go all blue, the clavinet riff from "Jive Talkin'" starts up and Barry ambles nervously into the lights in a shimmering dark green shirt and wearing a thin, red guitar. He doesn't look bad: silvery hair to his shoulders, bit of a gut, slightly puffy face, but he moves like the back pain that tormented him in the later years of Bee Gees touring is gone. His teeth, as ever, are perfect and blindingly white.

It's not that the place goes berserk—it does. But these are not the normal berserker whoops and screams and whistles and cheers. This is the vocal incarnation of pure love, adoration, worship. The crowd is entirely willing to go on whatever ride Barry has to offer.

Barry seems nonplussed, even shy, in the face of this heartfelt, deafening ovation. He points and waves to a few people up front and breaks into a whisper-falsetto to sing. Everyone shuts up—they want to hear what he's got left. As the song goes on, Barry's energy increases visibly. If he had nerves, they're gone. Halfway through the song, he's moving his hips and swaying side to side. This is his home; he's been onstage since he was nine.

His band proves competent; they're unexcitable, studio pros reading music from charts. A band for radio, as one audience member put it: a collation of not attractive, squat, middle-aged men at home with their machines and blank faced as can be. But they are tight. They rehearsed a lot. The look of the band, their cold precision and the unremarkable arrangements underscore the Las Vegas presentation.

Barry's voice proves more than workable. He has no range or power on the falsetto; he mostly whispers. When he tries to belt on "You Should Be Dancing" his voice cracks. But Barry's midrange is potent; he sings in full voice on the non-falsetto numbers, like "Lonely Days." His energy never flags. Performing is invigorating him. Toward the end of the evening he's sweating heavily and downing a small bottle of water between every song.

Barry dedicates "First of May" to his wife, Lynda. Maurice's daughter Samantha, dressed like any other college student, strolls onstage to duet on "End of the World." She's unfazed by the situation and sings competently, on the level of a good wedding singer. Steve Gibb sings Maurice's little known "On Time" in a rich baritone, and takes an extended show-offy guitar solo. He has a skilled, buzzing tone; he could be the lead player in a band opening up for country-rock arena headliners. "On Time" wasn't the only obscurity. Barry pulls out "Every Christian Lionhearted Man Will Show You" from 1967's *Bee Gees 1st*. It has a building, spellbinding psychedelic feel and clocks in at 2:59. Even Barry's psych excursions are structured as hit singles.

Barry brings up one of his backups to sing "Islands in the Stream" and "Guilty." She's passable, and Barry is gracious, if a little condescending, toward the end of their collaboration. How must that have felt, harmonizing in public with a stranger? What courage it must have taken to attempt those songs alone, in front of thousands who knew every word and note. How could he not have expected Robin and Maurice—and maybe even Andy—to lend their voices?

But, true to Barry's nature, and his career of never saying what he felt or singing with genuine emotion, internal barriers remain. Even when introducing his niece or his son or urging everyone to pray for Robin, who was still alive but mortally ill, Barry never sounds quite sincere. At the most intimate moments, whether expressing thanks or saying how proud he was to have Steve onstage, Barry reverts to showbiz patter, often with one hand in his pocket, as if declaiming at the dinner table like some dull paterfamilias.

Even so, Barry's gratification is plain from the back row—never mind on the immense close-ups filling the video screens. As the show goes on, he becomes increasingly joyous to discover that he can still do it, overjoyed that doing it gives him pleasure and overjoyed at the unalloyed love of the crowd. He is still Barry and the world is thrilled that he is.

After a "Night Fever–More Than a Woman" medley, Barry introduces "Immortality" by mentioning prayer: "I know there are people in the audience with an inclination for prayer," he says quietly. "I know that I'm one as well." As he speaks, images of Robin appear on the screens. Barry loses himself in singing for his brothers. He especially emphasizes the lyric "We never say goodbye."

Barry leaves the stage, clearly moved, and a sea of fifty-year-olds dancing on their chairs with reckless ecstasy take their love to a whole new level. It wasn't only that Barry, by any standard, had done a stellar show for a sixty-five-year-old. He'd cut no corners; he gave it up with total commitment. After a few minutes of cheering and screaming that grow louder and louder, Barry returns.

He introduces the band, says that a couple of them, including the musical director, had come over from England for six weeks of rehearsal, and squeaks out a credible, whispered-falsetto show-stopper of "Stayin' Alive.'" Even more grandparents climb onto their chairs to dance, film with their phones, shriek with delight and wave their hands in the air.

Afterward, there was a shocking lack of souvenirs or T-shirts or glossy programs or merchandising of any kind. Had Barry failed to anticipate how beloved he really is? Everyone filing out looked happy, satisfied and a little starry-eyed.

A twenty-five-year veteran of rock and roll, whose band had two platinum albums, made a couple of key points after the show. "He did this," the veteran said, "to see if he has the stamina to tour. He was auditioning for himself." The veteran, who had blown count-less wads renting buses to haul Marshall stacks, reckoned the costs to Barry—of bringing musicians from England, housing and feed-ing them, paying them and local studio players to rehearse daily, booking the hall, renting equipment, bringing in lighting and sound crews, buying ads and promotion—at $250,000 minimum. Given the size of the crowd—despite the expensive tickets—there's no way Barry broke even. He lost $150,000 or more.

It's beside the point to say that to Barry Gibb $150,000 is cab fare. What matters is that Barry invested in himself, and got the most out of his investment.

In July, Barry appeared, for the first time ever, on the *Grand Ole Opry*. Ricky Skaggs introduced him. Barry seemed relaxed, and happy to be there. He sang "When the Roses Bloom Again," by A. P. Carter of country's Carter Family, as a gesture of outreach to the *Opry* crowd. He was in fine voice and harmonized beautifully with Skaggs and multiple backup players. Barry followed that with "To Love Somebody." Singing in his midrange without reaching for falsetto, Barry performed with uncharacteristically true and ex-posed emotion. On the next song, "How Can You Mend a Broken Heart" Barry sang as if a door had slammed. The feeling left Barry's eyes, and his performance was automatic, disconnected, as if the previous show of genuine feelings had undone him.

But for that one song, there stood Barry Gibb, revealed.

In October of 2012, Barry was interviewed for Australian television. He was remarkably open. "My greatest regret," he said, "is that every brother I've lost was in a moment when we were not getting on and so, I have to live with that. I'm the last man standing." Of his father, Barry said: "Dad was undemonstrative. He couldn't show his emotions. You're probably looking for acceptance all the time and if you get that too easily you don't work for it." When speaking of his brothers, Barry wiped tears from his eyes. He claimed that Australia was "his country." He seemed, in this small sample, like a different man, ready to reveal new aspects of himself. In an interview with Australia's *OneNews*, Barry revealed that he had not spoken to Robin for a year before Robin's death.[1]

It's shocking to see—after all these decades of such impenetrable armor—Barry embrace his own mortality, show emotion and admit vulnerability and regret. Being Barry, he can't quite embrace or admit it fully, but a change has come. Given that he needn't ever play again, and that his vanity or ego certainly needs no more appeasing, Barry's new openness seems a sincere attempt at healing his wounds.

In February 2013, Barry played for two and a half hours before a crowd of twenty-five thousand delirious fans in Melbourne.

notes

"Lollipop"

1. Beth Neil, "We Were Young Tearaways," *Mirror*, November 4, 2009.
2. Oliver Bennett, "Fever Pitch," *Times*, February 15, 1997.
3. Judith Whelan, "Still Staying Alive," *Sydney Morning Herald*, February 18, 1997.
4. Chris Buckland, "Oh Boys! How Mr. and Mrs. Bee Gee Helped to Make Their Sons Shine," *Daily Mirror*, April 17, 1979.
5. Neil, "We Were Young Tearaways."
6. Paul Baratta, "The Bee Gees Straight Talkin'," *Songwriter*, February 1978.
7. Paul Dacre, "Off to the Sun—The Family Gibb," *Daily Express*, April 19, 1979.
8. Nick Logan, "Meet a Bee Gee: Robin Gibb," *New Musical Express*, December 2, 1967.
9. Ibid.
10. Ibid.
11. Ibid.
12. Neil, "We Were Young Tearaways."
13. Dacre, "Off to the Sun."
14. Kerry McGlynn and Liane Maxfield, "No Looking Back for the Bee Gees," *Australian Women's Weekly*, June 14, 1967.
15. "Early TV Start for Three Boys," *Australian Women's Weekly*, June 29, 1960.
16. Frank Rose, "How Can You Mend a Broken Group? The Bee Gees Did It with Disco," *Rolling Stone*, July 14, 1977.
17. "Early TV Start for Three Boys," *Australian Women's Weekly*.

18. Logan, "Meet a Bee Gee: Robin Gibb."

19. "Early TV Start for Three Boys," *Australian Women's Weekly*.

20. Ibid.

21. Barry, Robin, and Maurice Gibb, *Bee Gees: The Authorized Biography*, as told to David Leaf (New York: Pinnacle Books, 1980), 25.

22. Rose, "How Can You Mend a Broken Group?"

23. Greg Mitchell, "The Act You've Known for All These Years," *Crawdaddy*, August 1978.

24. Timothy White, "This Is Where We Came In," *Billboard*, March 24, 2001.

25. "*Billboard* Salutes the Bee Gees," *Billboard*, September 2, 1978.

26. White, "This Is Where We Came In."

27. "Stayin' Alive and Coming Back for Some More," *Sunday Times*, December 30, 2001.

28. Robin Eggar, "Bee Gees," *Courier-Mail*, October 3, 1987.

29. Bruce Elder, "Stayin' Alive," *Sydney Morning Herald*, March 20, 1999.

30. Logan, "Meet a Bee Gee: Robin Gibb."

31. Joseph Brennan, Gibb Songs, http://www.columbia.edu/~brennan/beegees/63.html.

32. Baratta, "The Bee Gees Straight Talkin'."

33. Campbell Reid, "They Said We'd Never Make It," *Advertiser*, November 9, 1989.

Bee Gees' 1st

1. Michael Pye, *Moguls: Inside the Business of Show Business* (New York: Holt, Rinehart and Winston, 1990), 234–35.

2. David Ansen, Janet Huck, Kartine Ames, and Susan Agrest, "Rock Tycoon," *Newsweek*, July 31, 1978.

3. Pye, *Moguls*, 239.

4. Ibid.

5. Peter Brown and Steven Gaines, *The Love You Make: An Insider's Story of the Beatles* (New York: New American Library, 1983), 217–18.

6. The Beatles, *The Beatles Anthology* (San Francisco: Chronicle Books, 2000), 268.

7. Rose, "How Do You Mend a Broken Group?"

8. Ibid.

9. Buckland, "Oh Boys!"

10. Baratta, "The Bee Gees Straight Talkin'."

11. Alan Smith, "Meet a Bee Gee: Barry Gibb," *New Musical Express*, November 25, 1967.

12. Logan, "Meet a Bee Gee: Robin Gibb."

13. Baratta, "The Bee Gees Straight Talkin'."

14. White, "This Is Where We Came In."

15. Johnny Black, "The Rogue Gene," *Mojo*, April 2001.

16. White, "This Is Where We Came In."

17. Norrie Drummond, "The Bee Gees May Give You 'World' Next!" *New Musical Express*, October 14, 1967.

18. Baratta, "The Bee Gees Straight Talkin'."

19. Brennan, Gibb Songs, http://www.columbia.edu/~brennan/beegees/63.html.

20. Paul Gambaccini, "A Conversation with Paul McCartney," *Rolling Stone*, July 12, 1979.

21. Dick Tatham, *The Incredible Bee Gees: Barry, Robin and Maurice—The Full Inside Story of Their Golden Success* (London: Futura, 1979), 21.

22. Black, "The Rogue Gene."

23. Alan Smith, "Meet a Bee Gee: Maurice Gibb," *New Musical Express*, December 16, 1967.

24. Black, "The Rogue Gene."

25. Brennan, Gibb Songs, http://www.columbia.edu/~brennan/beegees/63.html.

26. Black, "The Rogue Gene."

27. Brown, *The Love You Make*, 222.

28. Nick Logan, "Meet a Bee Gee: Vince Melouney," *New Musical Express*, December 9, 1967.

29. White, "This Is Where We Came In."

30. "The Bee Gees Have No Time to Be Frustrated," *Melody Maker*, September 23, 1967.

31. Richard Goldstein, "The Children of Rock Belt the Blues," *New York Times*, July 30, 1967.

32. Norrie Drummond, "Bee Gees Happened Everywhere—But Here!" *New Musical Express*, September 30, 1967.

33. "Bee Gees—Five Australians with a Bright Future," *Melody Maker*, May 27, 1967.

34. Review of "New York Mining Disaster 1941," *New Musical Express*, April 15, 1967.

35. Review of "New York Mining Disaster."

36. "The Bee Gees Have No Time to Be Frustrated."

37. Ibid.

38. Lulu, *I Don't Want to Fight* (New York: Time Warner, 2002), 112–13.

39. Brown *The Love You Make*, 240–41.

40. "Bee Gees Banned from Britain," *Melody Maker*, October 14, 1967.

41. Drummond, "The Bee Gees Happened Everywhere."

42. Ibid.

43. "Stigwood and NEMS Enterprises Split," *Melody Maker*, November 4, 1967.

44. "Bee Gees No. 1 Hit Started as a Send-Up," *Melody Maker*, November 4, 1967.

45. Drummond, "The Bee Gees Happened Everywhere."

46. Black, "The Rogue Gene."

47. Ibid.

48. Brown *The Love You Make*, 251–52.

49. Beatles, *The Beatles Anthology*, 268.

50. "Stigwood and NEMS Enterprises Split."

51. Ibid.

52. Drummond, "Bee Gees May Give You 'World' Next!"

53. Ibid.

54. Logan, "Meet a Bee Gee: Robin Gibb."

55. Alan Walsh, "Time to Bring Glamour Back to Pop," *Melody Maker*, October 21, 1967.

56. "Bee Gees No. 1 Hit Started as a Send-Up."

57. Drummond, "Bee Gees May Give You 'World' Next!"

58. Logan, "Meet a Bee Gee: Robin Gibb."

59. Walsh, "Time to Bring Glamour Back to Pop."

60. Ritchie York, "Keith Richard on Mick, Beatles, Led, Faith, Tull, Gees," *New Musical Express*, December 6, 1969.

61. Timothy White, "Earthy Angels: How the Bee Gees Talk Dirty and Influence People," *Rolling Stone*, May 17, 1979.

62. Corrina Honan,"I Never Get Up Until Midday; Bee Gee Robin Gibb, 42, Currently Recording a New Album, Talks to Corrina Honan," *Daily Mail*, February 2, 1992.

63. Ibid.

64. Ibid.

65. Nick Logan, "All About the Ghostly Gibbs," *New Musical Express*, January 13, 1968.

66. Drummond, "Bee Gees May Give You 'World' Next!"

67. Walsh, "Time to Bring Glamour Back to Pop."

68. "Bee Gees Banned from Britain."

69. Walsh, "Time to Bring Glamour Back to Pop."

70. Smith, "Meet a Bee Gee: Maurice Gibb."

71. Review of "World," *New Musical Express*, November 18, 1967.

72. Nick Jones, "Bee Gees: Who Needs Drugs to Make Music?" *Melody Maker*, December 16, 1967.

73. "It's the Song That Matters Now . . . Says Bee Gee Barry," *Melody Maker*, January 13, 1968.

74. Jones, "Bee Gees: Who Needs Drugs to Make Music?"

75. "Bee Gees Have No Time to Be Frustrated."

76. Jim Miller, "Bee Gees *Horizontal*," *Rolling Stone*, December 21, 1968.

77. Nick Logan, "Bee Gees 'Words' Mystery," *New Musical Express*, February 24, 1968.

78. Logan, "All About the Ghostly Gibbs."

79. Richard Green, "Bee Gee Maurice Plays Up-Tempo Raver," *New Musical Express*, June 21, 1969.

80. Ibid.

81. Logan, "Bee Gees 'Words' Mystery."

82. Jim Miller, "Bee Gees *Horizontal*" *Rolling Stone*, December 21, 1968.

83. Lulu, *I Don't Want to Fight*, 115.

84. "It's the Song That Matters Now."

85. Black, "The Rogue Gene."

86. Keith Altham, "Bee Gees Sitting Targets for the Cynics," *New Musical Express*, May 4, 1968.

87. Nick Logan, "Barry: 'Important We Have Respect,'" *New Musical Express*, August 10, 1968.

88. Keith Altham, "Big Night for the Bee Gees," *New Musical Express*, April 6, 1968.

89. Ibid.

90. Altham, "The Bee Gees Sitting Targets for the Cynics."

91. "'Offensive' Bee Gees TV Play?" *New Musical Express*, April 6, 1968.

92. Altham, "The Bee Gees Sitting Targets for the Cynics."

93. "Illness Wrecks Bee Gees Tour," *Melody Maker*, August 3, 1968.

Odessa

1. Honan, "I Never Get Up Til Midday."

2. *The Atlantic Recordings: Percy Sledge*, Rhino Records, 2001.

3. Andrew Sandoval, *Bee Gees: The Day-By-Day Story, 1945–1972*, (RetroFuture Day-By-Day Series, 2012), 110.

4. Alexis Petridis, "The Bee Gee's Odessa File," *Guardian*, January 30, 2009.

5. Altham, "The Bee Gees Sitting Targets for the Cynics."

6. Nick Logan, "I've Never Been 100 Per Cent a Bee Gee: Vince," *New Musical Express*, November 2, 1968.

7. Jan Nesbit, "I Want More Respect—Barry," *New Musical Express*, December 7, 1968.

8. Mark Paytress, "Stayin' Alive," *Mojo*. December 2010.

9. Nick Logan, "Bee Gee Colin Happy to Be the Outsider," *New Musical Express*, March 15, 1969.

10. Nick Logan, "Barry Reveals Bee Gees' Plans and Takes You Round His Penthouse Pad," *New Musical Express*, October 12, 1968.

11. Bob Dawbarn, "I'm Not Leaving—Yet," *Melody Maker*, September 28, 1968.

12. Ibid.

13. "Bee Gee Barry Wants to Quit—But Commitments Until 1970," *New Musical Express*, September 14, 1968.

14. Logan, "Barry Reveals Bee Gees' Plans."

15. Ibid.

16. Paytress, "Stayin' Alive."

17. Nesbit, "I Want More Respect."

18. Paytress, "Stayin' Alive."

19. Logan, "Bee Gee Colin Happy to Be the Outsider."

20. Logan, "Barry Reveals Bee Gees' Plans."

21. Ibid.

22. Lulu, *I Don't Want to Fight*, 122.

23. Ibid.

24. Ibid.

25. Pye, *Moguls*, 260.

26. Ibid., 246.

27. Black, "The Rogue Gene."

28. Alan Smith, "My Wife Comes Second to Me," *New Musical Express*, August 30, 1969.

29. White, "This Is Where We Came In."

30. Paytress, "Stayin' Alive."

31. Tatham, *The Incredible Bee Gees*, 49.

32. Ben Sisario, "Robin Gibb, a Bee Gee with a Taciturn Manner, Dies at 62," *New York Times*, May 20, 2012.

33. Dawbarn, "I'm Not Leaving—Yet."

34. Smith, "My Wife Comes Second to Me."

35. Nick Logan, "Marriage Might End Bee Gees Feuding," *New Musical Express*, March 1, 1969.

36. Nick Logan, "The New Man Who Is Bee Gee Barry," *New Musical Express*, February 15, 1969.

37. Lulu, *I Don't Want to Fight*, 12.

38. Ibid, 133.

39. Bruce Harris, "Please Read Me: A Definitive Analysis of the Bee Gees' Lyrics," *Jazz & Pop*, May 1971.

40. Petridis, "The Bee Gee's Odessa File."

41. Author interview, November 10, 2012.

42. Don Short, "Barry Gibb Backs Out of Bee Gees' First Film," *Daily Mirror*, March 13, 1969.

"Nervous Wrecks"

1. Don Short, "Robin Breaks the Silence with a No. 1 Sound," *Daily Mirror*, May 3, 1969.

2. Johnny Black, "The Bee Gees Discover Disco," *Q*, April 2000.

3. "Robin Gibb Unveils His Plans," *New Musical Express*, May 10, 1969.

4. Alan Walsh, "The Strange Saga of the Bee Gees," *Melody Maker*, March 29, 1969.

5. Nick Logan, "Barry Says Robin 'Extremely Rude,'" *New Musical Express*, May 3, 1969.

6. Ibid.

7. Smith, "My Wife Comes Second to Me."

8. Geoffrey Wansell, "Tragedy for the Bee Gees," *Daily Mail*, January 13, 2003.

9. "Robin: Plans Not Settled," *Daily Express*, April 24, 1969.

10. Short, "Robin Breaks the Silence."

11. Richard Green, "Barry Plans Thank You Tour for Loyal Fans," *New Musical Express*, October 4, 1969.

12. "Robin Gibb Unveils His Plans," *New Musical Express*, May 10, 1969.

13. Logan, "Barry Says Robin 'Extremely Rude.'"

14. Green, "Bee Gee Maurice Plays Up-Tempo Raver."

15. Ibid.

16. Nick Logan, "Happy Robin Not Gloating Over the Bee Gees Miss," *New Musical Express*, July 19, 1969.

17. Review of "Saved by the Bell," *New Musical Express*, June 28, 1968.

18. Ibid.

19. Ibid.

20. Author interview, October 2012.

21. "Blind Date with Robin Gibb," *Melody Maker*, August 16, 1969.

22. Laurie Henshaw, "The Saga of the Bee Gees Continues," *Melody Maker*, August 16, 1969.

23. Laurie Henshaw, "Strange Case of the Sacked Drummer," *Melody Maker*, September 6, 1969.

24. "Colin Quits the Bee Gees," *New Musical Express*, August 30, 1969.

25. Richard Green, "Bee Gee Barry Censored Colin in an Effort to Stop Any More Bee Gees Feuding," *New Musical Express*, September 13, 1969.

26. Ibid.

27. Green, "Barry Plans Thank You Tour."

28. Ibid.

29. Nick Logan, "It's My Duty to Appear Unreal, Says Robin Gibb," *New Musical Express*, August 2, 1969.

30. Dacre, "Off to the Sun."

31. David Wigg, "Ex–Bee Gees Answers 'Ward of Court' Threat," *Daily Express*, September 5, 1969.

32. Green, "Bee Gee Barry Censored Colin."

33. Ibid.

34. "The 'Pride' of a Sacked Bee Gee," *Daily Mirror*, September 25, 1969.

35. Royston Eldridge, "Out of the Whole Mess Comes the New True Bee Gees Says Barry," *Melody Maker*, October 4, 1969.

36. Green, "Barry Plans Thank You Tour."

37. Smith, "My Wife Comes Second to Me."

38. Nick Logan, "Bee Gees Laugh Off Those Split Rumours," *New Musical Express*, August 24, 1968.

39. David Wigg, "Bee Gee Barry Quits," *Daily Express*, December 2, 1969.

40. Judith Simons, "The Millionaire Proud to Be Living in Lulu's Shadow," *Daily Express*, February 19, 1970.

41. David Wigg, "Ex-Bee Gee Barry Says: I'm Quitting Britain," *Daily Express*, January 21, 1970.

42. Jeremy Gilbert, "Robin at Christmas," *Melody Maker*, December 29, 1969.

43. "Robin Forgets Quality," *New Musical Express*, January 17, 1970.

44. Don Short, "Bee Gee Booster!" *Daily Mirror*, September 5, 1970.

45. Ibid.

46. "The Bee Gees Back Together," *New Musical Express*, November 14, 1970.

47. "Bee Gees Re-form," *Melody Maker*, August 29, 1970.

48. Short, "Bee Gee Booster!"

49. Chris Charlesworth, "The Bee Gees' Lonely Days," *Melody Maker*, November 14, 1970.

50. Ibid.

51. White, "Earthy Angels."

52. Robin Eggar, "The Bee Gees Keep on Bouncing Back," *Advertiser*, October 17, 1987.

53. Mitchell Glazer, "The Rise and Fall of the Brothers Gibb," *Playboy*, August 1978.

54. William Leith, "Saturday Night, Sunday Morning," *Independent*, July 18, 1993.

55. Dacre, "Off to the Sun."

56. Leith, "Saturday Night, Sunday Morning."

57. Dacre, "Off to the Sun."

58. Harvey Kubernik, "How The Bee Gees Captured America," *Melody Maker*, January 21, 1978.

59. Eggar, "The Bee Gees Keep on Bouncing Back."

60. Glazer, "The Rise and Fall of the Brothers Gibb."

61. Kubernik, "How the Bee Gees Captured America."

"Please Pretend It's Not Them"

1. Pye, *Moguls*, 246.

2. Brennan, Gibb Songs, http://www.columbia.edu/~brennan/beegees/63.html.

3. Lulu, *I Don't Want to Fight*, 157.

4. Ibid, 160.

5. Ibid, 162.

6. Fred Bronson, *The Billboard Book of Number One Hits* (New York: Billboard Books, 1997).

7. Black, "The Bee Gees Discover Disco."

8. Richard Harrington, "Grammy Granddaddy: Arif Mardin, Norah

Jones's Hall-of-Fame Producer, Was Winning Them Before She Was Born," *Washington Post*, February 23, 2003.

9. Ibid.

10. Ibid.

11. Kubrnik, "How the Bee Gees Captured America."

12. Ibid.

13. White, "Earthy Angels."

14. "Right Hook Was a Lulu," *Daily Mirror*, February 13, 1979.

15. Glazer, "The Rise and Fall of the Brothers Gibb."

16. Black, "The Bee Gees Discover Disco."

17. Glazer, "The Rise and Fall of the Brothers Gibb."

18. Black, "The Bee Gees Discover Disco."

19. Rose, "How Do You Mend a Broken Group?"

20. Black, "The Bee Gees Discover Disco."

21. White, "Earthy Angels."

22. Kubernik, "How the Bee Gees Captured America."

23. Black, "The Bee Gees Discover Disco."

24. Ibid.

25. White, "Earthy Angels."

26. Adam Bernstein, "Record Producer Arif Mardin: Won 11 Grammy Awards," *Washington Post*, June 27, 2006.

27. White, "Earthy Angels."

28. Bill Altman, "Bee Gees Banquet: Some Funk in the Syrup," *Rolling Stone*, September 11, 1975.

29. Tom Doyle, "Arif Mardin: Producer," *Sound on Sound*, July 2004.

30. Glazer, "The Rise and Fall of the Brothers Gibb."

31. Ibid.

32. Bruce Elder, "Stayin' Alive," *Sydney Morning Herald*, March 20, 1999.

33. Black, "The Bee Gees Discover Disco."

34. Rose, "How Do You Mend a Broken Group?"

35. Black, "The Bee Gees Discover Disco."

36. Ibid.

37. Ibid.

38. Altman, "Bee Gees Banquet."

39. Tatham, *The Incredible Bee Gees*, 84–85.

40. Stephen Holden, Review of *Main Course*, *Rolling Stone*, July 17, 1975.

41. Baratta, "The Bee Gees Straight Talkin'."

42. Anonymous author interview.

43. Author interview, May 2012.

44. Anonymous author interview.

45. Kubernik, "How the Bee Gees Captured America."

46. Joe McEwen, review of *Children of the World*, *Rolling Stone*, November 4, 1976.

47. Chris Charlesworth, "Nights on Broadway," *Melody Maker*, December 4, 1976.

48. Rose, "How Do You Mend a Broken Group?"

49. White, "This Is Where We Came In."

50. Altman, "Bee Gees Banquet."

51. Glazer, "The Rise and Fall of the Brothers Gibb," *Playboy*.

52. Charlesworth, "Nights on Broadway," *Melody Maker*.

Saturday Night Fever

1. Glazer, "The Rise and Fall of the Brothers Gibb."

2. Ben Fong-Torres, "'Saturday Night' Bumps 'Rumours,'" *Rolling Stone*, March 9, 1978.

3. Paul Grein, "'Fever Sells at White Hot Pace Setting New Record," *Billboard*, April 22, 1978.

4. Sam Kashner, "Fever Pitch: How Travolta and the Bee Gees Shook the Night," W, December 2007.

5. Brother Cleve to author, July 2012.

6. Jack Egan, "Cashing in on the Boogie to the Tune of $5 Billion; Disco" *Washington Post*, June 26, 1978.

7. Sara Stosic, "Marketing the Illusion of Inclusive Exclusivity: How Communications/Public Relations Play a Key Role in Creating and Sustaining Vibrant Venues in the New York Nightlife Industry," thesis, New York University, 14.

8. Dave Marsh, "American Grandstand: Saturday Night Fever," *Rolling Stone*, June 1, 1978.

9. Lisa Robinson, "Boogie Nights: An Oral History of Disco," *Vanity Fair*, February 2010.

10. Leslie Bennetts, "An 'In' Crowd and Outside Mob Show Up for Studio 54's Birthday," *New York Times*, April 28, 1978.

11. Stosic, "Marketing the Illusion of Inclusive Exclusivity," 13.

12. Ibid.

13. Nik Cohn, "Fever Pitch," *Guardian*, September 17, 1994.

14. Ibid.

15. Craig Rosen, *The Billboard Book of Number One Albums* (New York: Billboard Books, 1996).

16. Anthony Haden-Guest, *The Last Party: Studio 54, Disco, and the Culture of the Night* (New York: William Morrow, 1997), xxv–xxvi.

17. Haden-Guest, *The Last Party*; White, "Earthy Angels."

18. Richard Buskin, "Classic Tracks; The Bee Gees Stayin' Alive," *Sound on Sound*, August 2005.

19. Ibid.

20. White, "Earthy Angels."

21. Ibid.

22. Albhy Galuten to author, May 2012.

23. John Swenson, "The Bee Gees' Record Setters," *Rolling Stone*, September 21, 1978.

24. Matt Blackett, "Alan Kendall on Playing with the Bee Gees," *Guitar Player*, July 2009.

25. Ken Sharp, "In One of His Last Extensive Interviews, Bee Gees' Maurice Gibb on the Group's Long Career," *Goldmine*, September 3, 2004.

26. Buskin, "Classic Tracks."

27. Glazer, "The Rise and Fall of the Brothers Gibb."

28. Stan Soocher, "Can the Bee Gees Stay on Top?" *Circus*, March 13, 1979.

29. Buskin, "Classic Tracks."

30. Ibid.

31. Ibid.

32. Larry Pryce, *The Bee Gees* (London: Granada, 1979), 54.

33. Ibid.

34. Buskin, "Classic Tracks."

35. Rose, "How Can You Mend a Broken Group?"

36. Anonymous author interview.

37. Soocher, "Can the Bee Gees Stay on Top?"

38. Albhy Galuten to author, May 2012.

39. Ibid.

40. Ibid.

41. Swenson, "The Bee Gees' Record Setters."

42. Pryce, *The Bee Gees*, 87.

43. Buskin, "Classic Tracks."

44. Kashner, "Fever Pitch."

45. Robinson, "Boogie Nights."

46. Ibid.

47. Paul Sexton, "Q&A with Robert Stigwood," *Billboard*, March 24, 2001.

48. Robinson, "Boogie Nights."

49. Fong-Torres, "'Saturday Night' Bumps 'Rumours.'"

50. Gibb, *Bee Gees: The Authorized Biography*, 110.

51. Fong-Torres, "'Saturday Night' Bumps 'Rumours.'"

52. "*Billboard* Salutes the Bee Gees."

53. Fong-Torres, "'Saturday Night' Bumps 'Rumours.'"

54. Rosen, *The Billboard Book of Number One Albums*.

55. Charlesworth, "Nights on Broadway."

56. "*Billboard* Salutes the Bee Gees."

57. Swenson, "The Bee Gees' Record Setters."

58. Ibid.

59. Ibid.

60. Ibid.

61. Ibid.

62. Buskin, "Classic Tracks."

63. Ibid.

64. Ibid.

65. Albhy Galuten to author, May 2012.

66. Buskin, "Classic Tracks."

67. Albhy Galuten to author, May 2012.

68. Mark Small, "Albhy Galuten '68," *On the Watchtower*, Summer 2002.

69. Albhy Galuten to author, May 2012.

70. White, "Earthy Angels."

71. Buskin, "Classic Tracks."

72. Small, "Albhy Galuten."

73. Bronson, *The Billboard Book of Number One Hits*.

74. Buskin, "Classic Tracks."

75. Swenson, "The Bee Gees' Record Setters."

76. "Movies: Kid from 'Kotter' Leaps Out of Pack and Into Disco Film," *New York Times*, February 18, 1977.

77. Grein, "'Fever Sells at White Hot Pace."

78. Merrill Shindler, "The Tavares Family: Up from Doo-Wop," *Rolling Stone*, July 28, 1977.

79. David Wild, "The Bee Gees," *Rolling Stone*, May 29, 1997.

80. Haden-Guest, *The Last Party*, 79–80.

Sgt. Pepper's Lonely Hearts Club Band

1. Simon Yeamon, "Bee Gees' Party of Life and Death," *Advertiser*, April 6, 1998.

2. Jamel Clayton Miller, *Legends: Bee Gees*, VH1 (1999) transcription (2002).

3. Rose, "How Can You Mend a Broken Group?"

4. White, "This Is Where We Came In," *Billboard*.

5. Glazer, "The Rise and Fall of the Brothers Gibb."

6. Goldstein, "The Children of Rock Belt the Blues."

7. Glazer, "The Rise and Fall of the Brothers Gibb."

8. Gibb, *Bee Gees: The Authorized Biography*, 112.

9. Robert Christgau, Dean of American Rock Critics, http://www.robertchristgau.com/xg/music/rocktheater.php.

10. Henry Edwards, "Inventing a Plot for 'Sgt. Pepper,'" *New York Times*, July 16, 1978.

11. Ed Zukerman, "Sgt. Pepper's Taught the Band to Play and Stigwood's Gonna Make It Pay," *Rolling Stone*, April 20, 1978.

12. Ibid.

13. Ibid.

14. Cameron Crowe, "The One and Only Peter Frampton," *Rolling Stone*, February 10, 1977.

15. Edwards, "Inventing a Plot for 'Sgt. Pepper.'"

16. Stephen Demorest, "The Bee Gees Are Back and They're Having a Ball," *New York Times*, November 28, 1976.

17. Crowe, "The One and Only Peter Frampton."

18. Zukerman, "Sgt. Pepper's Taught the Band to Play."

19. "*Billboard* Salutes the Bee Gees."

20. White, "Earthy Angels."

21. Zukerman, "Sgt. Pepper's Taught the Band to Play."

22. White, "Earthy Angels."

23. Ibid.

24. Paul Grein, "A Day in the Life of Dee Anthony," *Billboard*, November 26, 1977.

25. "*Billboard* Salutes the Bee Gees."

26. Ibid.

27. White, "Earthy Angels."

28. Gibb, *Bee Gees: The Authorized Biography*, 113.

29. Ibid.

30. Robert Stigwood, *The Official Sgt. Pepper's Lonely Hearts Club Band Scrapbook: The Making of a Hit Movie Musical* (New York: Pocket Books, 1978).

31. White, "Earthy Angels."

32. Ibid.

33. Ibid.

34. Stigwood, *The Official Sgt. Pepper's Lonely Hearts Club Band Scrapbook*.

35. Martin, George and Jeremy Hornsby, *All You Need Is Ears* (London: Macmillan, 1979), 154–55.

36. Ibid, 217–18.

37. White, "Earthy Angels."

38. Grein, "'Fever' Sells at White Hot Pace."

39. Glazer, "The Rise and Fall of the Brothers Gibb."

40. Ben Fong-Torres, "'Sgt. Pepper' Returns," *Rolling Stone*, November 2, 1978.

41. Ibid.

42. Brennan, Gibb Songs, http://www.columbia.edu/~brennan/beegees/63.html.

43. Anthony Haden-Guest, *The Last Party: Studio 54, Disco, and the Culture of the Night* (New York: William Morrow, 1998), 79.

44. Stanley Mieses, "Celluloid Heroes," *Melody Maker*, December 10, 1977.

45. Janet Maslin, "Screen: Son of 'Sgt. Pepper,'" *New York Times*, July 21, 1978.

46. Marilyn Laverty, "You Can Fool . . ." *Record Mirror*, August 12, 1978.

47. Paul Nelson, "Sgt. Pepper Gets Busted," *Rolling Stone*, October 5, 1978.

48. Fong-Torres, "'Sgt. Pepper' Returns."

49. Paul Gambaccini, "A Conversation with Paul McCartney," *Rolling Stone*, July 12, 1979.

50. Mick Brown, "An Interview with George Harrison," *Rolling Stone*, April 19, 1979.

51. Soocher, "Can the Bee Gees Stay on Top?"

52. Wild, "The Bee Gees."

53. White, "Earthy Angels."

54. Jim White, "The Gift of the Gibbs," *Independent*, February 21, 1991.

Spirits Having Flown

1. Ben Fong-Torres, "Al Coury Owns Number One," *Rolling Stone*, October 5, 1978.

2. Ansen, "Rock Tycoon."

3. White, "Earthy Angels."

4. Ibid.

5. "Even at Miami Studio, the Bee Gees Stay Close to Fans," *Palm Beach Post*, November 27, 1981.

6. John Rockwell, "The Bee Gees Are Getting as Big as the Beatles," *New York Times*, March 19, 1978.

7. Gibb, *Bee Gees: The Authorized Biography*, 132.

8. White, "Earthy Angels."

9. Cutler Durkee and Jonathan Cooper, "The Bee Gees Search for Life after Disco," *People*, August 7, 1989.

10. Eve H. Malakoff, "Personalities," *Washington Post*, August 21, 1960.

11. Fong-Torres, "Al Coury Owns Number One."

12. Rosen, *The Billboard Book of Number One Albums*.

13. Albhy Galuten to author, May 2012.

14. White, "Earthy Angels."

15. Soocher, "Can the Bee Gees Stay on Top?"

16. Ibid.

17. Ibid

18. Ibid.

19. Barry Gibb to David Frost, *The Bee Gees Special*, NBC, November 15, 1979.

20. White, "Earthy Angels."

21. Dan Daley, "Stayin' Power," *Studio Sound*, June 1997.

22. Ruskin, "Classic Tracks."

23. White, "Earthy Angels."

24. Gibb, *Bee Gees: The Authorized Biography*, 135.

25. White, "Earthy Angels."

26. Roman Kozak, "Backstage at a Gift of Song," *Billboard*, February 3, 1979.

27. Ibid.

28. Ray Herbeck Jr., "Radio Syndicators Wary of Disco," *Billboard*, January 13, 1979.

29. "Word 'Disco' Dirty in New York Radio," *Billboard*, December 8, 1979.

30. Richard Harrington, "The Bee Gees, After the Fever; Once Stung by Critics, the Brothers Gibb Return from the Disco Dungeon," *Washington Post*, August 3, 1989.

31. Stephen Holden, "The Bee Gees' Millennial Fever," *Rolling Stone*, April 5, 1979.

32. Mitchell, "The Act You've Known for All These Years."

33. Holden, "The Bee Gees' Millennial Fever."

34. White, "Earthy Angels."

35. Mark Kernis, "The Bee Gees: Still Ready for a New Start," *Washington Post*, March 2, 1979.

36. Soocher, "Can the Bee Gees Stay on Top?"

37. White, "Earthy Angels."

38. Robert Christgau, "Christgau's Consumer Guide," *Village Voice*, April 1979.

39. Jim Jerome, "Bee Gee Mania," *People*, August 6, 1979.

40. Ibid.

41. Maurice Gibb to David Frost, *The Bee Gees Special*, NBC, November 15, 1979.

42. Kubernik, "How the Bee Gees Captured America."

43. Ibid.

44. Geoffrey Himes, "Monday Night Fever; Shrieks and Lasers for the Bee Gees," *Washington Post*, September 25, 1979.

45. Jerome, "Bee Gee Mania,"

46. Ibid.

47. Ibid.

48. White, "Earthy Angels."

Andy Gibb, March 5, 1958–March 10, 1988

1. "Heart Inflammation Killed Andy Gibb," Associated Press, March 11, 1988.

2. Eric Levin, "Death of a Golden Child," *People*, March 28, 1988.

3. Alison Steele, "Andy Gibb Close Up," *Co-Ed Magazine*, November 1978.

4. "'Oh Brother, You're Famous,' Says Andy Gibb," *Fabulous 208*, April 1969.

5. Andy Gibb to Robert W. Morgan, 1978.

6. "Glib Andy Gibb," *Philadelphia Daily News*, June 5, 1978.

7. Stan Soocher, "The Littlest Bee Gee: Andy Gibb Is More Than Just a Clone of His Successful Siblings," *Circus*, August 17, 1978.

8. Alison Steele, "Andy Gibb Close-Up," *Co-Ed*, November 1978.

9. "The Bee Gees Secret Weapon," *Teen Bag Magazine*, August 1977.

10. Connie Berman and Marsha Daly, *Andy Gibb* (Middletown, CT: Xerox, 1979), 15.

11. Soocher, "The Littlest Bee Gee."

12. Andy Gibb to Robert W. Morgan, 1978.

13. Soocher, "The Littlest Bee Gee."

14. Andy Gibb to Robert W. Morgan, 1981.

15. Andy Gibb to Robert W. Morgan, 1978,

16. Soocher, "Littlest Bee Gee: Andy Gibb Is More Than Just a Clone."

17. Andy Gibb to Robert Mogan, 1978.

18. Susan Duncan, "I Want Justice for Our Daughter, Says Andy Gibb's Ex-Wife Kim," *Australian Weekly*, August 1989.

19. Ibid.

20. Andy Gibb to Robert W. Morgan, 1981.

21. Anonymous author interview.

22. Andy Gibb to Robert W. Morgan, 1978,

23. Berman, *Andy Gibb*, 87.

24. Ibid, 86.

25. Soocher, "Littlest Bee Gee."

26. Duncan, "I Want Justice for Our Daughter."

27. Andy Gibb to Robert W. Morgan, 1981.

28. "I've Never Paid My Dues! Why Andy Gibb Is Scared of Success," *Teen Beat*, July 1979.

29. "Final Days of Andy Gibb," *Behind the Music*, VH1, August 1997, http://www.youtube.com/watch?v=6lq6WyysnAI.

30. Brook Bayvel, "My Life with Andy," *Advertiser*, March 15, 1988.

31. Tatham, *The Incredible Bee Gees*, 119.

32. Bayvel, "My Life with Andy."

33. John Rockwell, "The Bee Gees Are Getting as Big as the Beatles," *New York Times*, March 19, 1978.

34. Jim Jerome," It's Singles Time for Bee Gee Baby Andy Gibb: He's Got 1977's No. 1 Hit and a Marital Split," *People*, November 14, 1978.

35. Duncan, "I Want Justice for Our Daughter."

36. Ibid.

37. Jim Jerome, "It's Singles Time for Bee Gee Baby Andy Gibb," *People*, November 14, 1977.

38. "Please Tell Him, Kim Asks Mirror," *Daily Mirror*, January 1978.

39. "$250,000 Smile," *Daily Mirror*, April 23, 1978.

40. Glazer, "Rise and Fall of the Brothers Gibb."

41. Ibid.

42. Andy Gibb to Robert W. Morgan, 1981.

43. "Final Days of Andy Gibb," *Behind the Music*.

44. Soocher, "The Littlest Bee Gee"

45. Mitchell, "The Act You've Known for All These Years."

46. "Final Days of Andy Gibb," *Behind the Music*.

47. Robert W. Morgan interview, 1981.

48. Ibid.

49. Fred Schruers, *Anchorage Daily News* (syndicated from *Rolling Stone*), July 28, 1978.

50. Donn Downey, "Bee Gees Special Steers Clear of the Hokey," *Globe and Mail*, November 21, 1979.

51. Soocher, "Littlest Bee Gee."

52. Andy Gibb to Bob Durant, 1985.

53. Stephen Holden, review of *After Dark*, *Rolling Stone*, April 17, 1980.

54. Carla Hall, "The Fame Game," *Washington Post*, August 21, 1980.

55. Robert Hilburn, "Andy Gibb, 1970s Pop Music Sensation, Dies in England at 30," *Los Angeles Times*, March 11, 1988.

56. "Picks and Pans Review: Andy Gibb," *People*, December 29, 1980.

57. David Gritten, "*Dallas* Darling," *People*, March 30, 1981.

58. Carla Hall, "Stars and Austerity at Ford's Theatre Gala," *Washington Post*, March 23, 1981.

59. "Mum Sees Andy Gibb Died," *Sun*, March 11, 1988.

60. Ibid.

61. Jayne Reed, "Principally, Gibb," *U.S. Magazine*, April 1981.

62. Tony Brenna and Riva Dryan, *Victoria Principal* (Boston: St. Martin's Press, 1989.

63. Gritten, "*Dallas* Darling."

64. "Final Days of Andy Gibb," *Behind the Music*.

65. David Gritten, "Pam Dawber Casts Off from Mork to Crew with Andy Gibb and 'The Pirates of Penzance,'" *People*, June 21, 1981.

66. Ibid.

67. "Tipoff," *Lakeland Ledger*, September 23, 1981.

68. *Donahue*, http://www.youtube.com/watch?v=ADM6ksWPoYk.

69. *Entertainment Tonight*, March 10, 1989, .http://www.youtube.com/watch?v=_3YoGa6FlTw>.

70. Brenna, *Victoria Principal*.

71. "Final Days of Andy Gibb," *Behind the Music*.

72. Brenna, *Victoria Principal*.

73. Ibid.

74. Levin, "Death of a Golden Child."

75. Giolia Diliberto, "Awol from Broadway Once too Often, Andy Gibb Is Ordered to Turn in His Dreamcoat," *People*, January 31, 1983.

76. Bruce Baskett, "Andy Gibb," *Courier-Mail*, August 16, 1986; *Good Morning America*, July 23, 1982, http://www.youtube.com/watch?v=nlPzyKjITMU.

77. "Final Days of Andy Gibb," *Behind the Music*.

78. *Entertainment Tonight*, March 10, 1989.

79. Bayvel, "My Life with Andy."

80. Malcolm Boyles, Joanna Patyn and Richard Motlock, "Lovesick and Suicide Scare," *Globe*, 1982.

81. Brenna, *Victoria Principal*.

82. "Final Days of Andy Gibb," *Behind the Music*.

83. "Break-Up Has Gibb on Edge," *Star-News*, April 27, 1982.

84. *Good Morning America*, Jul 23, 1982.

85. *Entertainment Tonight*, December 1, 1982.

86. Levin, "Death of a Golden Child."

87. Leslie Bennetts, "Absenteeism Said to Be Rising," *New York Times*, March 9, 1983.

88. Diliberto, "Awol from Broadway Once Too Often."

89. Levin, "Death of a Golden Child."

90. "Police Guard Threatened Bee Gee, and Brother Found Unconscious After Tour Leaves Him Exhausted," *Montreal Gazette*, August 20, 1984; Levin, "Death of a Golden Child."

91. "Drug Treatment for Andy Gibb," *Courier-Mail*, April 8, 1985.

92. Andy Gibb to Bob Durant.

93. Guy Phillips, "My Torment over Brother's Death," *Sunday Mail*, April 30, 1989.

94. Jacqueline Lee Lewes, "Fall of a Bankrupt Star," *Sydney Sun Herald*, September 13, 1987.

95. "Singer Andy Gibb Files for Personal Bankruptcy," *Miami Herald*, September 11, 1987.

96. Ibid.

97. "Final Days of Andy Gibb," *Behind the Music*.

98. Ibid.

99. Ibid.

100. "Andy Gibb," *Behind the Music*, VH1, November 30, 1997.

101. Ibid.

102. Levin, "Death of a Golden Child."

103. "Final Days of Andy Gibb," *Behind the Music*.

104. "Doctors Say Heart Inflammation Caused Death of Singer Andy Gibb," Associated Press, March 12, 1988.

105. Phillips, "My Torment over Brother's Death."

106. "Final Days of Andy Gibb," *Behind the Music*.

107. Levin, "Death of a Golden Child."

108. Duncan, "I Want Justice for Our Daughter."

109. *Entertainment Tonight*, March 10, 1989.

"The Enigma with the Stigma"

1. Cynthia Kirk, "Bee Gees Sue Stigwood in N.Y. for Coin & Freedom After Audit," *Variety*, October 15, 1980.

2. Ibid.

3. Marc Kirkeby, "Bee Gees Sue Stigwood, Charge Mismanagement," *Rolling Stone*, November 23, 1980.

4. Kirk, "Bee Gees Sue Stigwood."

5. "Stigwood Files Counterclaim to Bee Gees Suit, Seeks $310-Mil," *Variety*, October 29, 1980.

6. Ibid.

7. Richard M. Nusser, "Stigwood Countersues Bee Gees," *Billboard*, November 8, 1980.

8. Kirkeby, "Bee Gees Sue Stigwood."

9. Steve Pond, "Bee Gees Say They're Sorry," *Rolling Stone*, June 25, 1981.

10. "The Bee Gees Didn't Say They're Sorry . . ." *Rolling Stone*, August 6, 1981.

11. Ibid.

12. Sexton, "Q&A with Robert Stigwood."

13. Simon Fanshawe, "Stigwood," *Provocateur with a Purpose*, December 1, 2006, http://simonfanshawe.com/?p=39.

14. Spencer Bright, "Now the Bee Gees Are Coming Alive Again," *Daily Mail*, August 6, 1993.

15. Elder, "Stayin' Alive."

16. Ken Sharp, "In One of His Last Extensive Interviews, Bee Gees' Maurice Gibb, on the Group's Long Career," *Goldmine*, September 3, 2004.

17. Melinda Newman, "The Beat," *Billboard*, November 17, 2001.

18. "Kenny Rogers: 'Luck or Something Like It: A Memoir,'" *The Diane Rehm Show*, WAMU, October 1, 2012.

19. Anonymous author interview.

20. Paul Grein, "Paul Atkinson Rocks RCA's Roster," *Billboard*, July 20, 1985.

21. White, "This Is Where We Came In."

22. White, "The Gift of the Gibbs."

23. David Sly, "Evergreen Bee Gees Shrug Off Disco," *Advertiser*, September 28, 1989.

24. Amruta Slee, "Just Stayin' Alive," *Sydney Sun Herald*, October 22, 1989.

25. Sly, "Evergeeen Bee Gees."

26. Pete Clark, "It Has Never Been Cool to Admit Liking the Sobbing Sound of the Bee Gees, But After 30 Years They Deserve Their Place in the Pop Pantheon," *Evening Standard*, August 5, 1993.

27. Claire Noland, "Robin Gibb, 1949–2012, *Los Angeles Times*, May 21, 2012.

28. Timothy White, "Bee Gees: 'Still' Taking Chances," *Billboard*, February 15, 1997.

29. The Bee Gees Walk Out of Clive Anderson, http://www.youtube.com/watch?v=VHa6vYq6Nyk.

30. Durkee, "The Bee Gees Search for Life After Disco."

31. "Stayin' Alive," *Evening Post* (Wellington), October 19, 1998.

32. Anjie Blardony Ureta, "Fever Pitch at the Palladium," *BusinessWorld*, May 7, 1999.

33. Edna Gundersen, "The Bee Gees Are Back in the Groove; 'Fever' Trio Is Earning a Healthy Respect Again," *USA Today*, May 6, 1997.

34. Elder, "Stayin' Alive."

35. Gundersen, "The Bee Gees Are Back in the Groove."

36. We Are One, www.brothersgibb.org/chart-info.html.

37. Tracey Snell, "Bee Gees TV Special Shows Value of Peak Viewing Slots," *Music Week*, August 14, 1999.

38. Dino Scatena, "Rockin' Retro Is Really on a Roll," *Daily Telegraph*, October 28, 1998.

39. Ward Morehouse III, "Stayin' Alive on Broadway," *Christian Science Monitor*, October 15, 1999.

40. Ben Brantely, "Singed by a Disco Inferno," *New York Times*, Oct 22, 1999.

41. White, "This is Where We Came In," *Billboard*.

"Walkin' by the Railroad"

1. Phil Gould, "Off the Record: They Win Again," *Birmingham Post*, April 7, 2001.

2. Leith, "Saturday Night, Sunday Morning."

3. Julia Llewellyn Smith, "From Superstars to Pop Pariahs—And Back Again—The Bee Gees Have Seen It All," *Express*, March 29, 2001.

4. Leith, "Saturday Night, Sunday Morning."

5. Smith, "From Superstars to Pop Pariahs."

6. "The Day I Nearly Killed My Family; Bee Gee Waved a Gun and Scared Himself Off Drink," *Daily Mail*, July 29, 1992.

7. Allan Ramsay, "The Day Bee Gee Maurice Drew a Gun on His Family," *Evening Standard*, July 28, 1992.

8. "The Day I Nearly Killed My Family."

9. Ibid.

10. Ibid.

11. Leith, "Saturday Night, Sunday Morning."

12. Nigel Dempster, "Stayin' Alive . . . and in Love," *Daily Mail*, February 24, 1992.

13. Alasdair Buchan, "Primed and Timed for Healing," *Times*, June 26, 1992.

14. "Bee Gee Denies He's Back on Booze," *Sunday Mail*, January 30, 1994.

15. Tim Cooper, "Bee Gee Maurice Critically Ill After Mystery Collapse," *Evening Standard*, January 10, 2003.

16. Hugh Davies, "Bee Gee Maurice Critically Ill After Surgery," *Daily Telegraph*, January 11, 2003.

17. Ibid.

18. Corky Siemaszko, "Bee Gee Hit by More Than Night Fever," *Daily News*, January 11, 2003.

19. "Bee Gee Flies Out to Be with Sick Twin," *Mail on Sunday*, January 12, 2003.

20. Tony Jones, "Bee Gees Lose a Brother and the Harmony Is Gone," *Advertiser*, January 13, 2003.

21. "Bee Gees' Anger at Maurice's Op," *Bath Chronicle*, January 13, 2003.

22. "Probe Call in Bee Gee Death," *Birmingham Evening Mail*, January 13, 2003.

23. Helen Rumbelow and Jacqui Goddard, "Shocked Bee Gees Thought Maurice Was Recovering," *Times*, January 13, 2003.

24. Emma Pearson, "Obituaries: Tormented Soul Brought Magic to Band of Brothers," *Birmingham Post*, January 13, 2003.

25. Geoffrey Wansell, "Tragedy for the Bee Gees," *Daily Mail*, January 13, 2003.

26. Jacqui Goddard, "Hospital to Probe Death of Bee Gee," *Australian*, January 15, 2003.

"Down Came the Sun"

1. Federal Bureau of Investigation, Robin Gibb file, December 23, 1980.

2. Ibid.

3. Ibid.

4. Paul Scott, "The Bee Gee Who Hired a Hitman to Bump Off His Wife; FBI Files Reveal the Raging Jealousy and Drug-Fuelled Paranoia of Robin Gibb's Astonishingly Toxic Divorce," *Daily Mail*, September 21, 2012.

5. Shirley Lowe, "How We Met," *Independent*, March 15, 1992.

6. Monica Porter, "15 Years Ago . . . Oct. 28," *Daily Mail*, October 28, 1998.

7. Lowe, "How We Met."

8. "After Saturday Night Fever, Sunday Afternoon Ceremony," *Daily Mail*, June 22, 1992.

9. Lynn Barber, "As Someone Said, the Rich Are Different," *Independent*, June 28, 1992.

10. York Membery, "My Passion," *Daily Mail*, February 25, 2006.

11. Ibid.

12. Jane Bidder, "Spirits Having Flown In," *Times*, April 18, 1992.

13. *The Howard Stern Show*, November 24, 1993.

14. Wendy Leigh, "House of Decadence," *Daily Mail*, December 28, 2006.

15. Anna Pukas, "The Sleazy Bee Gee," *Express*, February 10, 2009.

16. Grant Hodgson and Victoria Murphy, "Ah, ha, ha, ha, Straying Alive," *Sunday Mirror*, February 8, 2009.

17. Ibid.

18. Elise Roche and John Ingham, "Brave Robin 'Is Feeling Good,'" *Express*, January 21, 2012.

19. "Gravely Ill? I'm at Home Writing Music and Feeling Great, Says Robin Gibb," *Mail on Sunday*, January 22, 2012.

20. "Bee Gees' Robin Gibb 'Feels Fantastic' After Cancer Recovery," *New Musical Express*, February 5, 2012.

21. Wendy Leigh, "I've Been at Death's Door," *Sun*, March 10, 2012.

22. Marc Baker, "I'll Get Bee Gees Back Together," *The People*, April 1, 2012.

23. Dominic Herbert, "Bee Gees Mum Flies in to See Sick Robin," *Sunday Mirror*, April 1, 2012.

24. Simon Boyle, "Son, It's Gone . . . I've Done It," *Mirror*, April 3, 2012.

25. "The Bee Gees' Barry Gibb Flies to the UK to Be by Ill Brother Robin's Side," *New Musical Express*, April 9, 2012.

26. Herbert, "Bee Gees Mum Flies in to See Sick Robin."

27. Wendy Leigh, "Robin Told Docs: There Will Never Be a Time When Enough Is Enough . . . I Want to Live," *Sun*, April 26, 2012.

28. Herbert, "Bee Gees Mum Flies in to See Sick Robin."

29. Leigh, "There Will Never Be a Time When Enough Is Enough."

30. Ibid.

31. Simon Boyle, "'I Wish Maurice Was Here,' Robin Gibb's Touching Deathbed Tribute to his Late Twin," *Daily Mirror*, May 22, 2012.

32. Anita Singh, "Robin Gibb Confounds Doctors by Waking from Coma," *Telegraph*, April 22, 2012.

33. Dominic Herbert, "Miracle Robin Out of the Hospital This Week," *Sunday Mirror*, April 29, 2012.

34. Gordon Rayner, "Bee Gee Robin Gibb Has 50/50 Chance of Recovering after Coming out of Coma, Wife Tells Friends," *Telegraph*, May 9, 2012.

35. Chris York, "Robin Gibb Death, Barry Gibb Tells of Conflict with Brother Before His Death," *Huffington Post UK*, July 6, 2012.

Barry Gibb's First Ever Solo Concert

1. Barry Gibb to Rahni Sadler, *Sunday Night*, Channel 7, September 23, 2012.

selected bibliography

"After Saturday Night Fever, Sunday Afternoon Ceremony." *Daily Mail*. June 22, 1992.

Altham, Keith. "Big Night for the Bee Gees." *New Musical Express*. April 6, 1968.

_____. "Bee Gees Sitting Targets for the Cynics." *New Musical Express*. May 4, 1968.

Altman, Bill. "Bee Gees Banquet: Some Funk in the Syrup." *Rolling Stone*. September 11, 1975.

"Andy Gibb." *Behind the Music*. VH1. November 30, 1997.

Atkinson, Terry. "The Bee Gees in Heaven." *Rolling Stone*. September 6, 1979.

Baker, Marc. "I'll Get Bee Gees Back Together." *The People*. April 1, 2012.

Baratta, Paul. "The Bee Gees Straight Talkin'." *Songwriter*. February 1978.

Barber, Lynn. "As Someone Said, the Rich Are Different." *Independent*. June 28, 1992.

Baskett, Bruce. "Andy Gibb." *Courier-Mail*. August 16, 1986.

Bayvel, Brooke. "My Life with Andy." *Advertiser*. March 15, 1988.

The Beatles. *The Beatles Anthology*. San Francisco: Chronicle Books, 2000.

"Bee Gees," *Legends*. VH1. July 21, 2000.

"Bee Gee Barry Wants to Quit—But Commitments Until 1970." *New Musical Express*. September 14, 1968.

"Bee Gee Denies He's Back on Booze." *Sunday Mail*. January 30, 1994.

"Bee Gee Flies Out to Be with Sick Twin." *Mail on Sunday*. January 12, 2003.

"Bee Gee Sounds Off on U.K. High Taxes." *Billboard*. October 18, 1975.

"Bee Gees' Anger at Maurice's Op." *Bath Chronicle*. January 13, 2003.

"Bee Gees Banned from Britain." *Melody Maker*. October 14, 1967.

"Bee Gees—Five Australians with a Bright Future." *Melody Maker*. May 27, 1967.

"Bee Gees Have No Time to Be Frustrated." *Melody Maker*. September 23, 1967.

"Bee Gees No. 1 Hit Started as a Send-Up." *Melody Maker*. November 4, 1967.

"Bee Gees Re-form." *Melody Maker*. August 29, 1970.

"Bee Gees' Robin Gibb 'Feels Fantastic' After Cancer Recovery." *New Musical Express*. February 5, 2012.

"Bee Gees Tour with 60-Piece Orchestra." *Melody Maker*. December 2, 1967.

Bennett, Oliver. "Fever Pitch." *Times*. February 15, 1997.

Bennetts, Leslie. "An 'In' Crowd and Outside Mob Show Up for Studio 54's Birthday." *New York Times*. April 28, 1978.

_____. "Absenteeism Said to Be Rising." *New York Times*. March 9, 1983.

Bernstein, Adam. "Record Producer Arif Mardin: Won 11 Grammy Awards." *Washington Post*. June 27, 2006.

Bidder, Jane. "Spirits Having Flown In." *Times*. April 18, 1992.

"*Billboard* Salutes the Bee Gees," *Billboard*, September 2, 1978.

Black, Johnny. "The Bee Gees Discover Disco." *Q*. April 2000.

_____. "The Rogue Gene." *Mojo*. April 2001.

"Blind Date with Robin Gibb." *Melody Maker*. August 16, 1969.

Boyle, Simon. "Son, It's Gone . . . I've Done It." *Mirror*. April 3, 2012.

_____. "'I Wish Maurice Was Here,' Robin Gibb's Touching Deathbed Tribute to His Late Twin." *Mirror*. May 22, 2012.

Brantely, Ben. "Signed by a Disco Inferno." *New York Times*. October 22, 1999.

"Break-Up Has Gibb on Edge." *Star-News*. April 27, 1982.

Brenna, Tony and Riva Dryan. *Victoria Principal*. Boston: St. Martin's Press, 1989.

Bright, Spencer. "Now the Bee Gees Are Coming Alive Again." *Daily Mail*. August 6, 1993.

Bronson, Fred. *The Billboard Book of Number One Hits*. New York: Billboard Books, 1997.

Brown, Mick. "An Interview with George Harrison." *Rolling Stone*. April 19, 1979.

Brown, Peter and Steven Gaines. *The Love You Make: An Insider's Story of the Beatles*. New York: New American Library, 1983.

Buchan, Alasdair. "Primed and Timed for Healing." *Times*. June 26, 1992.

Buckland, Chris. "Oh Boys! How Mr. and Mrs. Bee Gee Helped to Make Their Sons Shine." *Daily Mirror*. April 17, 1979.

Burke, Tom. "Hey Mom, Look at Me Now." *Record Mirror*. October 7, 1978.

Buskin, Richard. "Classic Tracks; The Bee Gees Stayin' Alive." *Sound on Sound*. August 2005.

Caroli, Daniele. "Robin & Barry Gibb Preparing Own Label." *Billboard*. October 14, 1978.

Charlesworth, Chris. "The Bee Gees' Lonely Days." *Melody Maker*. November 14, 1970.

_____. "Nights on Broadway." *Melody Maker*. December 4, 1976.

Clark, Pete. "It Has Never Been Cool to Admit Liking the Sobbing Sound of the Bee Gees, But After 30 Years They Deserve Their Place in the Pop Pantheon." *Evening Standard*. August 5, 1993.

Cohn, Nik. "Fever Pitch." *Guardian*. September 17, 1994.

"Colin Demands Apology." *Melody Maker*. September 13, 1969.

"Colin Quits the Bee Gees." *New Musical Express*. August 30, 1969.

Cooper, Tim. "Bee Gee Maurice Critically Ill After Mystery Collapse." *Evening Standard*. January 10, 2003.

Crowe, Cameron. "The One and Only Peter Frampton." *Rolling Stone*. February 10, 1977.

Dacre, Paul. "Off to the Sun—The Family Gibb." *Daily Express*. April 19, 1979.

Daley, Dan. "Stayin' Power." *Studio Sound*. June 1997.

Davies, Hugh. "Bee Gee Maurice Critically Ill After Surgery." *Daily Telegraph*. January 11, 2003.

Dawbarn, Bob. "Bee Gee Barry Decides . . . I'm Not Leaving—Yet." *Melody Maker*. September 28, 1968.

"Death Not Unexpected: Ex-Wife." *Advertiser*. March 12, 1988.

Demorest, Stephen. "The Bee Gees Are Back and They're Having a Ball." *New York Times*. November 28, 1976.

Dempster, Nigel. "Stayin Alive . . . and in Love." *Daily Mail*. February 24, 1992.

Diliberto, Giolia. "Awol from Broadway Once Too Often, Andy Gibb Is Ordered to Turn in His Dreamcoat." *People*. January 31, 1983.

"Doctors Say Heart Inflammation Caused Death of Singer Andy Gibb." Associated Press. March 12, 1988.

Downey, Donn. "Bee Gees Special Steers Clear of the Hokey." *Globe and Mail*. November 21, 1979.

Doyle, Tom. "Arif Mardin: Producer." *Sound on Sound*. July 2004.

"Drug Treatment for Andy Gibb." *Courier-Mail*. April 8, 1985.

Drummond, Norrie. "Bee Gees Happened Everywhere—But Here!" *New Musical Express*. September 30, 1967.

————. "Bee Gees May Give You 'World' Next!" *New Musical Express*. October 14, 1967.

Duncan, Robert. "Aerosmith." *Creem*. December 1978.

Duncan, Susan. "I want Justice for Our Daughter, Says Andy Gibb's Ex-Wife Kim." *Australian Weekly*. August 1989.

Durkee, Cutler, and Jonathan Cooper. "The Bee Gees Search for Life After Disco." *People*. August 7, 1989.

"Early TV Start for Three Boys." *Australian Women's Weekly*. June 29, 1960.

Edwards, Henry. "Inventing a Plot For 'Sgt. Pepper.'" *New York Times*. July 16, 1978.

Egan, Jack. "Cashing in on the Boogie to the Tune of $5 Billion; Disco." *Washington Post*. June 26, 1978.

Eggar, Robin. "The Bee Gees Keep on Bouncing Back." *Advertiser*. October 17, 1987.

Elder, Bruce. "Stayin' Alive." *Sydney Morning Herald*. March 20, 1999.

Eldridge, Royston. "Out of the Whole Mess Comes the New True Bee Gees Says Barry." *Melody Maker*. October 4, 1969.

"Even at Miami Studio, the Bee Gees Stay Close to Fans." *Palm Beach Post*. November 27, 1981.

"Ex-Bee Gee Robin Makes Single Debut." *Melody Maker*. June 28, 1969.

"'Fever' Success OK, But Could Affect Tavares' R&B Roots." *Variety*. April 26, 1978.

Fong-Torres, Ben. "'Saturday Night' Bumps 'Rumours.'" *Rolling Stone*. March 9, 1978.

_____. "Al Coury Owns Number One." *Rolling Stone*. October 5, 1978.

_____. "'Sgt. Pepper' Returns." *Rolling Stone*. November 2, 1978.

"For One Night Only—Lesley As a Bee Gee." *Daily Mirror*. April 25, 1969.

Gambaccini, Paul. "A Conversation with Paul McCartney." *Rolling Stone*. July 12, 1979.

Garland, Phyl. "Saturday Night Bee Gees." *Stereo Review*. May 1978.

Gibb, Barry, Robin, and Maurice. *Bee Gees: The Authorized Biography*, as told to David Leaf. New York: Pinnacle Books, 1980.

Gilbert, Jeremy. "Robin at Christmas." *Melody Maker*. December 29, 1969.

Gillard, Michael and David Connett. "Rock Stars in Secret Pounds 25m Tax Deal." *Observer*. March 2, 1997.

Glazer, Mitchell. "Golddiggers of '77!" *Crawdaddy*. September 1977.

_____. "The Rise and Fall of the Brothers Gibb." *Playboy*. August 1978.

"Glib Andy Gibb." *Philadelphia Daily News*. June 5, 1978.

Goddard, Jacqui. "Hospital to Probe Death of Bee Gee." *Australian*. January 15, 2003.

Goldstein, Richard. "The Children of Rock Belt the Blues." *New York Times*. July 30, 1967.

Goldstein, Toby. "Andy Gibb: The Bee Gee's Smarter Brother?" *Creem*. February 1978.

Goodman, Chris. "Why We Still Feel Andy's Presence." *Sunday Express*. November 11, 2001.

Gould, Phil. "Off the Record: They Win Again." *Birmingham Post*. April 7, 2001.

"Gravely Ill? I'm at Home Writing Music and Feeling Great, Says Robin Gibb." *Mail on Sunday*. January 22, 2012.

Green, Richard. "Bee Gee Maurice Plays Up-Tempo Raver." *New Musical Express*. June 21, 1969.

————. "Bee Gee Barry Censored Colin in an Effort to Stop Any More Bee Gees Feuding." *New Musical Express.* September 13, 1969.

————. "Barry Plans Thank You Tour for Loyal Fans." *New Musical Express.* October 4, 1969.

Green, Robin. "What the Bee Gees Mean to Me." *Rolling Stone.* April 15, 1971.

Grein, Paul. "A Day in the Life of Dee Anthony." *Billboard.* November 26, 1977.

————. "'Fever' Sells at White Hot Pace Setting New Record." *Billboard.* April 22, 1978.

————. "KC & the Sunshine Band Coming in from the Cold." *Billboard.* April 14, 1979.

————. "Paul Atkinson Rocks RCA's Roster." *Billboard.* July 20, 1985.

Gritten, David. "*Dallas* Darling." *People.* March 30, 1981.

————. "Pam Dawber Casts Off from Mork to Crew with Andy Gibb and 'The Pirates of Penzance.'" *People.* June 29, 1981.

Gundersen, Edna. "The Bee Gees Are Back in the Groove; 'Fever' Trio Is Earning a Healthy Respect Again." *USA Today.* May 6, 1997.

Haden-Guest, Anthony. *The Last Part: Studio 54, Disco, and the Culture of the Night.* New York: William Morrow, 1997.

Hall, Carla. "The Fame Game." *Washington Post.* July 31, 1980.

————. "Stars and Austerity at Ford's Theatre Gala." *Washington Post.* March 23, 1981.

Harmetz, Aljean. "Annie Hall Wins 4 Academy Awards." *New York Times.* April 4, 1978.

Harrington, Richard. "The Bee Gees, After the Fever; Once Strung by Critics, the Brothers Gibb Return from the Disco Dungeon." *Washington Post.* August 3, 1989.

————. "Grammy Granddaddy: Arif Mardin, Norah Jones's Hall-of-Fame Producer, Was Winning Them Before She Was Born." *Washington Post.* February 23, 2003.

Harris, Bruce. "Please Read Me: A Definitive Analysis of the Bee Gees' Lyrics." *Jazz and Pop,* May 1971.

"Heart Inflammation Killed Pop Singer Andy Gibb." Associated Press. March 11, 1988.

Henshaw, Laurie. "The Saga of the Bee Gees Continues." *Melody Maker*. August 16, 1969.

———. "Strange Case of the Sacked Drummer." *Melody Maker*. September 6, 1969.

Herbeck, Ray Jr. "Radio Syndicators Wary of Disco." *Billboard*. January 13, 1979.

Herbert, Dominic. "Bee Gees Mum Flies in to See Sick Robin." *Sunday Mirror*. April 1, 2012.

———. "Robin's Hospital Bed 'Bucket List.'" *Sunday Mirror*. April 15, 2012.

———. "Miracle Robin Out of the Hospital This Week." *Sunday Mirror*. April 29, 2012.

Hilburn, Robert. "Andy Gibb, 1970s Pop Music Sensation, Dies in England at 30." *Los Angeles Times*, March 11, 1988.

Himes, Geoffrey. "Monday Night Fever; Shrieks and Lasers for the Bee Gees." *Washington Post*. September 25, 1979.

Hodgson, Grant and Victoria Murphy. "Ah, ha, ha, ha, Straying Alive." *Sunday Mirror*. February 8, 2009.

Holden, Stephen. Review of *Main Course*. *Rolling Stone*. July 17, 1975.

———. "The Bee Gees' Millennial Fever." *Rolling Stone*. April 5, 1979.

———. Review of *After Dark*. *Rolling Stone*. April 17, 1980.

Humphrey, David. "Family Keeps Vigil as Singer Recovers from Emergency Op." *Western Daily Press*. January 11, 2003.

"Illness Wrecks Bee Gees Tour." *Melody Maker*. August 3, 1968.

"It's the Song That Matters Now . . . Says Bee Gee Barry." *Melody Maker*. January 13, 1968.

"I've Never Paid My Dues! Why Andy Gibb Is Scared of Success." *Teen Beat*. July 1979.

Jerome, Jim. "It's Singles Time for Bee Gee Baby Andy Gibb: He's Got 1977's No. 1 Hit and a Marital Split." *People*. November 14, 1978.

———. "Bee Gee Mania." *People*. August 6, 1979.

Johnson, Jane. "Life with Robin's Cupboard Loves." *Daily Mirror*. August 24, 1995.

Johnson, Rebecca. "Family Vigil as Bee Gee Robin 'Slips into Coma.'" *Express*. April 14, 2012.

Jones, Nick. "Bee Gees: Who Needs Drugs to Make Music?" *Melody Maker*. December 16, 1967.

Jones, Tony. "Bee Gees Lose a Brother and the Harmony Is Gone." *Advertiser*. January 13, 2003.

Katz, Robin. "In the Family Way." *Record Mirror*. July 16, 1977.

Kernis, Mark. "The Bee Gees: Still Ready for a New Start." *Washington Post*. March 2, 1979.

Kirk, Cynthia. "The Bee Gees Sue Stigwood in N.Y. for Coin & Freedom After Audit." *Variety*. October 15, 1980.

Kirkeby, Marc. "Bee Gees Sue Stigwood, Charge Mismanagement." *Rolling Stone*. November 23, 1980.

Kozak, Roman. "Backstage at a Gift of Song." *Billboard*. February 3, 1979.

Kubernik, Harvey. "How the Bee Gees Captured America." *Melody Maker*. January 21, 1978.

Laverty, Marilyn. "You Can Fool . . ." *Record Mirror*. August 12, 1978.

Leigh, Wendy. "House of Decadence." *Daily Mail*. December 28, 2006.

_____. "I've Never Been at Death's Door." *Sun*. March 10, 2012.

_____. "Writing Titanic Music Helped Me to Battle Cancer." *Sun*. March 25, 2012.

_____. "Robin Told Docs: There Will Never Be a Time When Enough Is Enough . . . I Want to Live." *Sun*. April 26, 2012.

Leith, William. "Saturday Night, Sunday Morning." *Independent*. July 18, 1993.

Levin, Eric. "Death of a Golden Child." *People*. March 28, 1988.

Lewes, Jacqueline Lee. "Fall of a Bankrupt Star." *Sydney Sun Herald*. September 13, 1987.

Logan, Nick. "The Bee Gees Here to Stay." *New Musical Express*. November 25, 1967.

_____. "Meet a Bee Gee: Robin Gibb." *New Musical Express*. December 2, 1967.

_____. "Meet a Bee Gee: Vince Melouney." *New Musical Express*. December 9, 1967.

_____. "All About the Ghostly Gibbs." *New Musical Express*. January 13, 1968.

_____. "Bee Gees 'Words' Mystery." *New Musical Express*. February 24, 1968.

_____. "'People Don't Listen to the Words' Says Bee Gee Barry." *Melody Maker*. March 2, 1968.

_____. "Barry: 'Important We Have Respect.'" *New Musical Express*. August 10, 1968.

_____. "Bee Gees Laugh Off Those Split Rumours." *New Musical Express*. August 24, 1968.

_____. "Barry Reveals Bee Gees Plans and Takes You Round His Penthouse Pad." *New Musical Express*. October 12, 1968.

_____. "I've Never Been 100 Per Cent a Bee Gee: Vince." *New Musical Express*. November 2, 1968.

_____. "The New Man Who Is Bee Gee Barry." *New Musical Express*. February 15, 1969.

_____. "Marriage Might End Bee Gees Feuding." *New Musical Express*. March 1, 1969.

_____. "Bee Gee Colin Happy to Be the Outsider." *New Musical Express*. March 15, 1969.

_____. "Barry says Robin 'Extremely Rude.'" *New Musical Express*. May 3, 1969.

_____. "Happy Robin Not Gloating over the Bee Gees Miss." *New Musical Express*. July 19, 1969.

_____. "It's My Duty to Appear Unreal, Says Robin Gibb." *New Musical Express*. August 2, 1969.

Lowe, Shirley. "How We Met." *Independent*. March 15, 1992.

Lulu. *I Don't Want to Fight*. New York: Time Warner, 2002.

Manila, Ronald. "What's Next for the Bee Gees?" *BusinessWorld*. April 30, 1999.

Marsh, Dave. "American Grandstand: Saturday Night Fever." *Rolling Stone*. June 1, 1978.

Martin, George with Jeremy Hornsby, *All You Need Is Ears*. London: Macmillan, 1979.

Maslin, Janet. "Screen: Son of 'Sgt. Pepper.'" *New York Times*. July 21, 1978.

Mayer, Ira. "The Bee Gees Touch." *Crawdaddy*, August 1978.

McEwen, Joe. Review of *Children of the World. Rolling Stone.* November 4, 1976.

McGlynn, Kerry and Liane Maxfield. "No Looking Back for the Bee Gees." *Australian Women's Weekly.* June 14, 1967.

Membery, York. "My Passion." *Daily Mail.* February 25, 2006.

Mendelsohn, John. Review of *Two Years On. Rolling Stone.* March 4, 1971.

Mieses, Stanley. "Celluloid Heroes." *Melody Maker.* December 10, 1977.

Miller, Jim. Review of *Bee Gees 1st. Rolling Stone.* December 21, 1968.

Mitchell, Greg. "The Act You've Known for All These Years." *Crawdaddy.* August 1978.

Morehouse, Ward III. "'Stayin' Alive' on Broadway." *Christian Science Monitor.* October 15, 1999.

"Movies: Kid from 'Kotter' Leaps Out of Pack and Into Disco Film." *New York Times.* February 18, 1977.

"Mum Sees Andy Died—Cocaine Horror." *Sun.* March 11, 1988.

Neil, Beth. "We Were Young Tearaways." *Mirror.* November 4, 2009.

Nelson, Paul. "Sgt. Pepper Gets Busted." *Rolling Stone.* October 5, 1978.

Nesbit, Jan. "I Want More Respect—Barry." *New Musical Express.* December 7, 1968.

Newman, Melinda. "The Beat." *Billboard.* November 17, 2001.

Noland, Claire. "Robin Gibb, 1949–2012." *Los Angeles Times.* May 21, 2012.

Nusser, Richard M. "Stigwood Countersues Bee Gees." *Billboard.* November 8, 1980.

"'Offensive' Bee Gees TV Play?" *New Musical Express.* April 6, 1968.

"'Oh Brother, You're Famous,' Says Andy Gibb." *Fabulous 208.* April 1969.

Paytress, Mark. "Stayin' Alive." *Mojo.* December 2010.

Pearson, Emma. "Obituaries: Tormented Soul Brought Magic to Band of Brothers." *Birmingham Post.* January 13, 2003.

Phillips, Guy. "My Torment over Brother's Death." *Sunday Mail.* April 30, 1989.

"Picks and Pans Review: Andy Gibb." *People.* December 29, 1980.

"Police Guard Threatened Bee Gee, and Brother Found Unconscious After Tour Leaves Him Exhausted." *Montreal Gazette*. August 20, 1984.

Pond, Steve. "Bee Gees Say They're Sorry." *Rolling Stone*. June 25, 1981.

Porter, Monica. "15 Years Ago . . . Oct. 28." *Daily Mail*. October 28, 1998.

"Probe Call in Bee Gee Death." *Birmingham Evening Mail*. January 13, 2003.

Pryce, Larry. *The Bee Gees*. London: Granada, 1979.

Pukas, Anna. "The Sleazy Bee Gee." *Express*. February 10, 2009.

Pye, Michael. *Moguls: Inside the Business of Show Business*. New York: Holt, Rinehart, and Winston, 1990.

Ramsay, Allan. "The Day Bee Gee Maurice Drew a Gun on His Family." *Evening Standard*. July 28, 1992.

Rayner, Gordon. "Bee Gee Robin Gibb Has 50/50 Chance of Recovering after Coming Out of Coma, Wife Tells Friends." *Telegraph*. May 9, 2012.

Reid, Campbell. "They Said We'd Never Make It." *Advertiser*. November 9, 1989.

Review of "New York Mining Disaster 1941." *New Musical Express*. April 15, 1967.

Review of "World." *New Musical Express*. November 18, 1967.

"Right Hook Was a Lulu." *Daily Mirror*. February 13, 1979.

Rockwell, John. "The Bee Gees Are Getting as Big as the Beatles." *New York Times*. March 19, 1978.

"Robin Forgets Quality." *New Musical Express*. January 17, 1970.

"Robin Gibb Unveils His Plans." *New Musical Express*. May 10, 1969.

"Robin: Plans Not Settled." *Daily Express*. April 24, 1969.

Robinson, Lisa. "Boogie Nights: An Oral History of Disco." *Vanity Fair*. February 2010.

Roche, Elise and John Ingham. "Brave Robin 'Is Feeling Good.'" *Express*. January 21, 2012.

Rose, Frank. "How Can You Mend a Broken Group? The Bee Gees Did It with Disco." *Rolling Stone*. July 14, 1977.

Rumbelow, Helen and Jacqui Goddard. "Shocked Bee Gees Thought Maurice Was Recovering." *Times*. January 13, 2003.

Sandoval, Andrew. *Bee Gees: The Day-By-Day Story, 1945–1972*. Retro-Future Day-By-Day Series, 2012.

Scatena, Dino. "Rockin' Retro Is Really on a Roll." *Daily Telegraph*. October 28, 1998.

Scott, Paul. "The Bee Gee Who Hired a Hitman to Bump Off His Wife: FBI Files Reveal the Raging Jealousy and Drug-Fuelled Paranoia Behind Robin Gibb's Astonishingly Toxic Divorce." *Daily Mail*. September 21, 2012.

Sexton, Paul. "Q&A with Robert Stigwood." *Billboard*. March 24, 2001.

Shapiro, Susan. Review of *Saturday Night Fever: The Official Movie Sound Track*. *Rolling Stone*. March 23, 1978.

Sharp, Ken. "In One of His Last Extensive Interviews, Bee Gees' Maurice Gibb on the Group's Long Career." *Goldmine*. September 3, 2004.

Sheldrick, Giles. "Bee Gee Star Robin Leaves £93m Fortune." *Express*. October 24, 2012.

Short, Don. "Barry Gibb Backs Out of Bee Gees' First Film." *Daily Mirror*. March 13, 1969.

———. "Robin Breaks the Silence with a No. 1 Sound." *Daily Mirror*. May 3, 1969.

———. "Bee Gees Booster!" *Daily Mirror*. September 5, 1970.

Shwartz, Tony and Martin Kasindorf. "Stigwood's Midas Touch." *Newsweek*. January 23, 1978.

Shindler, Merrill. "The Tavares Family: Up from Doo-Wop." *Rolling Stone*. July 28, 1977.

Siemaszko, Corky. "Bee Gee Hit by More Than Night Fever." *Daily News*. January 11, 2003.

Simons, Judith. "The Millionaire Proud to be Living in Lulu's Shadow." *Daily Express*. February 19, 1970.

Singh, Anita. "Robin Gibb Confounds Doctors by Waking from Coma." *Telegraph*. April 22, 2012.

Sisario, Ben. "Robin Gibb, A Bee Gee with a Taciturn Manner, Dies at 62." *New York Times*. May 20, 2012.

Slee, Amruta. "Just Stayin' Alive." *Sydney Sun Herald*. October 22, 1989.

Sly, David. "Evergeen Bee Gees Shrug Off Disco." *Advertiser*. September 28, 1989.

Small, Mark. "Albhy Galuten '68." *On the Watchtower*, Summer 2002.

Smith, Alan. "Meet a Bee Gee: Barry Gibb." *New Musical Express*. November 25, 1967.

_____. "Meet a Bee Gee: Maurice Gibb." *New Musical Express*. December 16, 1967.

_____. "My Wife Comes Second to Me." *The New Musical Express*. August 30, 1969.

Smith, Julia Llewellyn. "From Superstars to Pop Pariahs—And Back Again—The Bee Gees Have Seen It All." *Express*. March 29, 2001.

Snell, Tracey. "Bee Gees TV Special Shows Value of Peak Viewing Slots." *Music Week*. August 14, 1999.

Soocher, Stan. "Littlest Bee Gee: Andy Gibb Is More Than Just a Clone of His Successful Siblings." *Circus*. August 17, 1978.

_____. "Can the Bee Gees Stay on Top?" *Circus*. March 13, 1979.

"Stayin' Alive." *Evening Post* [Wellington], October 19, 1998.

"Stayin' Alive and Coming Back for Some More." *Sunday Times*. December 30, 2001.

Stead, Geoff. "The Bees Knees." *Daily Telegraph*. May 10, 1997.

Steele, Alison. "Andy Gibb Close-Up." *Co-Ed Magazine*. November 1978.

"Stigwood and NEMS Enterprises Split." *Melody Maker*. November 4, 1967.

"Stigwood Files Counterclaim to Bee Gees Suit, Seeks $310-Mil." *Variety*. October 29, 1980.

"Stigwood-Gees Plans After Nems Split." *New Musical Express*. November 4, 1967.

Stigwood, Robert. *The Official Sgt. Pepper's Lonely Hearts Club Band Scrapbook: The Making of a Hit Movie Musical*. New York: Pocket Books, 1978.

Stosic, Sara. "Marketing the Illusion of Inclusive Exclusivity: How Communications/Public Relations Play a Key Role in Creating and Sustaining Vibrant Venues in the New York Nightlife Industry." Thesis, New York University, 2011.

Swenson, John. "The Bee Gees' Record Setters." *Rolling Stone*. September 21, 1978.

Tatham, Dick. *The Incredible Bee Gees: Barry, Robin and Maurice—The Full Inside Story of Their Golden Success*. London: Futura, 1979.

"The Bee Gees Back Together." *New Musical Express*. November 14, 1970.

"The Bee Gees' Barry Gibb Flies to the UK to Be by Ill Brother Robin's Side." *New Musical Express*. April 9, 2012.

"The Bee Gees Didn't Say They're Sorry . . ." *Rolling Stone*. August 6, 1981.

"The Bee Gees Secret Weapon." *Teen Bag Magazine*. August 1977.

The Bee Gees Special. NBC. November 15, 1979.

"The Day I Nearly Killed My Family; Bee Gee Waved a Gun and Scared Himself Off Drink."

Daily Mail. July 29, 1992.

"The 'Pride' of a Sacked Bee Gee." *Daily Mirror*. September 25, 1969.

"Tipoff." *The Lakeland Ledger*. September 23, 1981.

Uhelszki, Jaan. Review of *Main Course*. *Creem*. October 1975.

Ureta, Anjie Blardony. "Fever Pitch at the Palladium." *BusinessWorld*. May 7, 1999.

"U.S. Tour Unlikely for Bee Gees." *Melody Maker*. September 13, 1969.

Walsh, Alan. "Time to Bring Glamour Back to Pop." *Melody Maker*. October 21, 1967.

———. "The Strange Saga of the Bee Gees." *Melody Maker*. March 29, 1969.

Wansell, Geoffrey. "Tragedy for the Bee Gees." *Daily Mail*. January 13, 2003.

Watts, Michael. "The Man with the Midas Touch." *Melody Maker*. December 16, 1972.

Whelan, Judith. "Still Staying Alive." *Sydney Morning Herald*. February 18, 1997.

"When the Curtain Falls, It Is Time to Get Off the Stage." *Newsweek*. May 12, 1997.

White, Jim. "The Gift of the Gibbs." *Independent*. February 21, 1991.

White, Timothy. "Earthy Angels: How the Bee Gees Talk Dirty and Influence People." *Rolling Stone*. May 17, 1979.

———. "Bee Gees: 'Still' Taking Chances." *Billboard*. February 15, 1997.

———. "This Is Where We Came In." *Billboard*. March 24, 2001.

Wigg, David. "Ex-Bee Gee Answers 'Ward of Court' Threat." *Daily Express*. September 5, 1969.

_____. "Bee Gee Barry Quits." *Daily express*. December 2, 1969.

_____. "Ex-Bee Gee Barry Says: I'm Quitting Britain." *Daily Express*. January 21, 1970.

Wild, David. "The Bee Gees." *Rolling Stone*. May 29, 1997.

Windeler, Robert. "Screams, Squeals Welcome Bee Gees." *New York Times*. January 29, 1968.

"Word 'Disco' Dirty in New York Radio." *Billboard*. December 8, 1979.

Yeaman, Simon. "Bee Gees' Party of Life and Death." *Advertiser*. April 6, 1998.

York, Chris. "Robin Gibb Death; Barry Gibb Tells of Conflict with Brother Before Death." *Huffington Post UK*. July 6, 2012.

York, Ritchie. "Keith Richards on Mick, Beatles, Led, Faith, Tull, Gees." *New Musical Express*. December 6, 1969.

Zuckerman, Ed. "Sgt. Pepper Taught the Band to Play." *Rolling Stone*. April 20, 1978.

acknowledgments

My gratitude to my patient and astute editor, Ben Schaffer.

My agent—the all-knowing, stalwart, hilarious Marc Gerald of the Agency Group—is an insightful and devoted Bee Gees connoisseur. I'm honored and terrified that he suggested I write their biography. My enduring thankfulness to Marc, who has never been wrong when he suggested I listen again, more carefully.

Bee-Gees-world is like *Fight Club*; we all know you don't talk about *Fight Club*. More than one person said to me, graciously: "But if I talk to you, Barry will never speak to me again." My thanks to all those who were brave enough to share so many backstage stories, and who trust me to keep their identities secret.

Devin McGinley and I thank these invaluable resources: the New York Public Library for the Performing Arts, the New School research resources, the Institute of Jazz Studies at Rutgers University, the Library of Congress and the Michelle Smith Performing Arts Library at the University of Maryland.

Thanks to Jené LeBlanc for her superb photo research and editing.

Thanks to Justin Lovell and everyone at Perseus Books.

Thanks to Joe Brennan for his indispensable online archive, Gibb Songs: www.columbia.edu/~brennan/beegees. Everyone who listens to the Bee Gees owes Joe for his accuracy, completeness, ceaseless effort and generosity.

I am indebted to the Facebook and Internet Bee Gees community for their passion, helpful information and wonderful videos. Thanks to everyone at Everything Gibb.

Thanks to Sasha Raskin and everyone at the Agency Group.

Thanks to Kendra Kabasele at BEI/REXUSA.

Thanks to Christine Marra, Jane Raese, Gray Cutler, Jeff Georgeson and Donna Riggs at *Marra*thon Production Services.

Thanks to Random House Australia.

My gratitude to John Schaefer, Joel Meyer and everyone at WNYC's *Soundcheck*.

Thanks to Brother Cleve—mixmaster, toastmaster, keyboardist, bossa nova avatar, DJ and SubGenius—for his treatise on the history of disco and for his musical tour through that history.

Thanks to Bruce Bennett for his illegal shout-out on WFMU; you still owe me "The King Is Gone."

Thanks to Beppe Manca of Manhattan, Creativity Activation Coach extraordinaire, who once again helped me break through my self-made obstacles.

Thanks to my friends for their sometimes bewildered but always steadfast encouragement: Steve Fishman, Debra Drooz, Greg Burke, David Wilentz, Marcos Liberski, Rob Kahn, Jesi Khadivi, Martha Kehoe, Cristina Seckinger, Myk Gordon, Federica Gianni, Jan Cox, Adam Elias, Eben and Jennifer Denton-Walker, Caroline Greeven, Colter and Katy Keller-Rule, Catherine Higham, Oren Shai, Robert (Bob-O) Chapman, Sarah Bass, Dean Rispler, Cullen Gallagher, Jeffrey L. Sapir and Dr. Jeffrey Gross. In the United Kingdom, thanks to Johnny Rogan and Andy Martin.

Thanks to all my Facebook friends who supported me so.

Thanks to my students and colleagues at The New School.

Thanks to my co-workers worldwide at getAbstract.com.

In Los Angeles, two families took me in and looked after me, much to their own inconvenience. In Los Feliz, my gratitude for their wonderful meals, conversation, affection, hospitality and tolerance to the Burk-Drooz family: Greg, Deb and Lily. In Sherman Oaks, inexpressible appreciation for their patience, kindness and generosity to the Reff-Holiday family: Jonathan, Lisa, Annika and Charlotte. I didn't mean to overstay my welcome.

Thanks to Sarahjane and Dan Murphy for the great concert tickets and insights.

Thanks to Joy Rothke for her research, videos, access to information and perceptive assistance.

Thanks to Darren Paltrowitz for his perseverance, hard work and invaluable research.

Thanks to Kate McCoy.

Thanks to Daniel Baird of Toronto, Canada, and Bishkek, Kyrgyzstan, for our brilliant, startling conversations and his unmatched perceptions of music and its social gestalt.

Thanks to Tessa DeCarlo and Julie Ardery for their friendship, inspiration, grammatical perfection and the merciless asperity and loving good humor of their advice, which I strive to follow.

Shalom, love and gratitude to Erica Rauzin of Miami Beach for all her care and encouragement.

Thanks and love to Sarahjane Blum of Minneapolis, Minnesota, for her guidance, editing, hard work and much needed support.

No Devin McGinley; no book. Devin worked with fervor, dedication and discipline; haunted libraries up and down the east coast, read miles of microfiche, mined the Web and brought his perceptions as a musician to bear on all he learned. Devin's good humor and drive never flagged. My heartfelt thanks to Devin.

Mad love to Jené LeBlanc of Chappaqua, New York, for everything. And I mean everything.

source
acknowledgments

David N. Meyer and Devin McGinley thank these publications, networks, authors, journalists, critics and cultural commentators. To correct any inadvertent omissions or incorrectly attributed quotes, please contact the author at beegeesbiography.com.

Keith Altham, Bill Altman, Paul Baratta, Bruce Baskett, Johnny Black, Matt Blackette, Fred Bronson, Peter Brown, Richard Buskin, Chris Charlesworth, Robert Christgau, Nik Cohn, Bob Dawbarn, Tom Doyle, Norrie Drummond, Alice Echols, Henry Edwards, Robin Eggar, Bruce Elder, Ben Fong-Torres, David Frost, Mitchell Glazer, Richard Goldstein, Richard Green, Robin Green, Paul Grein, Edna Gundersen, Anthony Haden-Guest, Richard Harrington, Bruce Harris, Laurie Henshaw, Geoffrey Himes, Stephen Holden, Jim Jerome, Nick Jones, Mark Kernis, Harvey Kubernik, Wendy Leigh, William Leith, Nick Logan, Lulu, Auggie McGowan, Dave Marsh, George Martin, Ira Mayer, Stanley Mieses, Jim Miller, Greg Mitchell, Robert W. Morgan, Beth Neil, Paul Nelson, Jan Nesbit, Mark Paytress, Guy Phillips, Michael Pye, Lisa Robinson, Frank Rose, Andrew Sandoval, Paul Sexton, Peter Shapiro, Ken Sharp, Alan Smith, Julia Llewellyn Smith, Stan Soocher, Sara Stosic, John Swenson, Dick Tatham,

Alan Walsh, Judith Whelan, Jim White, Timothy White, David Wild, Ed Zuckerman.

Rolling Stone, The New Musical Express, Melody Maker, Billboard, Record Mirror, Creem, Crawdaddy, Fabulous 208, Playboy, Circus, Mojo, Q, People, Vanity Fair, Entertainment Weekly, Spin, Songwriter, Co-Ed, VH1, Daily Mail, Daily Mirror, The New York Times, The Washington Post, Variety.

index

about the author

David N. Meyer is the author of *Twenty Thousand Roads: The Ballad of Gram Parsons and His Cosmic American Music,* which was chosen by the *Los Angeles Times* as one of the Twenty Best Nonfiction Books of the Year; *Rolling Stone* selected it as one of the Five Best Books of the Year, and the United Kingdom's *Uncut* magazine honored it as Book of the Year. Mr. Meyer also wrote *The 100 Best Films to Rent You've Never Heard Of* and *A Girl and a Gun: The Complete Guide to Film Noir on Video.* He is proud to have contributed, in a small way, to *The Book of the SubGenius.* He can be reached at beegeesbiography.com.

CPSIA information can be obtained
at www.ICGtesting.com
Printed in the USA
LVHW031513081020
668323LV00021B/453/J